SUMMON UP REMEMBRANCE

SUMMON UP REMEMBRANCE

by

Marzieh Gail

GEORGE RONALD
OXFORD

George Ronald, *Publisher*
Oxford
www.grbooks.com

© Marzieh Gail 1987
All Rights Reserved

ISBN 978-0-85398-259-3

British Library Cataloguing in Publication Data

Gail, Marzieh
    Summon up remembrance.
    1. Khan, Ali-Kuli 2. Diplomats—Iran—
    Biography 3. Bahais—United States—
    Biography
    I. Title
    327.2'092'4   DS 316.9.K5

Contents

IN PERSIA

1	Safe from the Evil Eye	1
2	Born with a Tooth	5
3	A Son Meets His Father	9
4	A Sense of Station	15
5	Trials and Tantrums	20
6	Your Best, Not Your Smallest	24
7	House of Oblivion	35
8	Death Owns All Seasons	42
9	The Mad Mírzá	49
10	Wine and Roses	55
11	With Hashish through the Keyhole	59
12	Bottle in Hand to the Bahá'í Faith	62
13	Journey to the Muslim Shrines	67
14	A Bridge of Boats	75
15	A Prince Accepts the Faith	79
16	Khan Becomes a Dervish	85
17	Escape from Sanandaj	90
18	The Point of No Return	97
19	In Sight of the Goal	104

IN THE HOLY LAND

20	The Arrival	107
21	Working for the Master	109
22	Red Ink for Martyrs' Blood	116
23	The Covenant-Breakers Attack	122

24 A Crisis of Faith	127
25 The Goal of the Living Martyrs	134
26 Prayer is not Enough	139
27 The Frightening Change	143

IN THE WEST

28 Paris and Natalie	149
29 No One at the Dock	155
30 Visions, or Vision?	161
31 Mírzá and Khan Stop Smoking	167
32 When the Lights Went Out	173
33 The Trials of Mrs Cole	178
34 The Prime Minister Cometh	182
35 Khan Meets His Fate	189
36 Florence	192
37 Attractions of Boston	196
38 A Victorian Love	200
39 *Vinculum Matrimonii*	213
40 Khan – Come – Abbas	220

ON PILGRIMAGE

41 To the Land of All Desiring	222
42 The Welcome	225
43 The Uses of Adversity	228
44 Questions and Answers	231
45 Consider the Candle	235
46 Munavvar's Dream	239
47 The Lure of Leadership	247
48 Bibliomancy	250
49 Always the Cause Goes Forward	253
50 Give Her Her Money	258
51 The Splendoring Dawn	261
52 The Food of Love	267

53	No Fear Can Come upon Me	270
54	Episodes	274
55	The Path of Jewels	278
56	The Leave-Taking	282
	Appendix	285
	Bibliography	287
	Notes	290

List of Illustrations

A Persian cradle
House in a Persian garden
Husband and wife traveling in their 'hanging-crooked' (kajávih)
A travel-litter and howdah
Khan's grandfather, Mírzá Ibráhím Zarrábí of Káshán
Khan's father, Mírzá 'Abdu'r-Rahím Khán Zarrábí, Kalántar of Tehran
Khan in his dervish days, with book and water-pipe
'Abdu'l-Bahá
Bahá'íyyih Khánum, the Greatest Holy Leaf
Munírih Khánum, wife of 'Abdu'l-Bahá
Shoghi Effendi, at about the time Khan was living in Haifa
Haifa, in the early part of the century
The Shrine of the Báb under construction in the time of 'Abdu'l-Bahá
Laura and Natalie Barney, painted by Alice Pike Barney
Florence, about the time she met Khan
Florence, before her marriage to Khan
Mírzá Abu'l-Faḍl with Khan in America
Khan as Persian Consul, Washington, 1908

This book is based on a memoir left by Ali-Kuli Khan, writings of his wife Florence, and other family papers and memories. The 'Akká accounts have only the same status as all pilgrims' reports. But Khan was a pilgrim who lived in 'Abdu'l-Bahá's house as His amanuensis for over a year, and spoke His tongue.

For a better perspective, my father is referred to in the third person throughout. He is called Khan because he was widely known by that name, rather than by his state title, Nabílu'd-Dawlih. 'Khan' began as a title, but is now an honorific, like Sir. It must not be thought that every Persian whose name ends with Khan was his relative. All Occidentals addressed as Sir are not necessarily related.

For Harold, as ever,
and
for Dr Richard Ferguson,
who saved my life in San Francisco
when I was halfway through the book

ONE
Safe from the Evil Eye

The small hammock was of hand-woven, wine-colored velvet, embroidered with seed pearls, and threads of silver and gold.

Ten babies would come, one after the other, to sleep in the hammock. Six of the babies would die. It is the ninth one that concerns us here. They guarded him with turquoise-blue beads to ward off the evil eye. The evil eye is the eye of perfection and perfection is always in danger. Never say, 'Oh what a fine baby! Fine horse! Fine sheep!' unless you say 'Máshá'lláh' – whatever God wills – along with it, and for good measure, an admired object ought to have on blue beads.

Around 1879 the ninth baby lay in his wine velvet, hammock-like cradle, the slender black forefinger of his young wet-nurse giving it a gentle push now and then, the flickering moth-like shadows of the poplar tree in the courtyard, moving in a slight breeze, passing over him, under the turquoise sky. All was safe. All was well.

This baby was born in Káshán. His family was of the Zarrábís, keepers of the Mint, and the infant rejoiced in an African nurse who was part of his mother's dowry, when she had come to his future father as a bride. The house where he lived had a large pool with a fountain in the center. A walled courtyard, blind to the street, enclosed flower gardens, fruit and nut trees, herbs, and small beds of vegetables for the family table. Table is the wrong word, for they sat around a cloth, spread on the floor.

Like many Persian houses, this one had separate buildings, one for the men, one for the veiled, secluded life of the women. Such houses were made of sun-baked brick, the same kind of building that passed down the ages from the East to Spain to California, with the rooms usually at ground level, great mansions being the exception. An important feature was the cool cellar, a living-place during the hottest part of the day.

The flat roofs of the house were supported on horizontal poles – the straight trunks of trees, such as poplars. Over the poles there was straw matting and over that a mix of clay and straw to seal out the leaks. The roofs were then rolled, much like a clay tennis court in the West. In winter, in case of a thick snowfall, the roofs would be shoveled off, quite possibly onto the chance pedestrian walking along the lane outside the wall.

Many would sleep on these roofs in summer, under the bright stars. Or an even cooler place might be arranged, over a blue-tiled pool in the courtyard: here a low-fenced, wooden platform could be built, with stairs leading up. Room-sized mosquito nets, with a cloth entry, could be set up on the platform, mattresses serving for beds. The summer nights were thus cool, and near each mattress stood a clay jar, filled with cool water, the same sort of jar that 'Umar Khayyám wrote about eight hundred years before.

Fleeing the midday sun, they would go down and sleep in deep cellars, cool and dry.

Breezes from over the many-colored rose fields brought in the rose scent – attar of Káshán, world-famous.

One day when Khan was not much more than two, his African nurse – dadih is the word in Persian – took the baby to see his grandfather, Pokhteh Khan. A slave before, the dadih was now free and had stayed on with the Zarrábí family as her very own. She had taught herself a Persian which nobody but they understood. They called her Rose of Sheba (Gul-Ṣabá), and she married a Persian attendant in the household, and produced a daughter named Tamáshá (delightful to look at). This daughter, a beauty, died at twenty-two, perhaps of appendicitis, a killer of that day.

Holding Khan in her arms she took him to the high-walled garden of the patriarch. There was a wide courtyard in front of the house, and Khan's grandfather, dressed in flowing robes, and with a long, full beard, came out and patted the baby and kissed him. Pokhteh Khan had many such gardens, walled and with pools, and with rooms and apartments of sun-baked brick, always crowded with family and guests. He was a man of awesome dignity, so that people did not raise their voices in his presence.

Here, too, the scent of roses came in on the wind. Rose water was for washing the right hand after food, to flavor sherbets and sweets, for ablutions. To make it they pressed the petals from thousands of roses into a great iron pot, poured water over the mass, and piled red-hot charcoal around the pot. A tube carried the fragrant steam through a jar of cold water, turning it into a warm, richly-scented liquid that dripped slowly into a bottle. It is well known, at least to Persian poets, that only the roses will bring out the singing from a nightingale's throat, only the nightingale's song will bring out the roses from their buds.

But even the fruits smelled unusually sweet. People would place rows of apples and quinces on their shelves and their rooms would stay fragrant for weeks. Sweet scents and birdsong and long stretches of rich quiet were the people's heritage.

The plains around Káshán border on the Great Salt Desert, and about them are bare mountains sharp against the sky. For an overview of the city, Henry Savage Landor tells of blue mosque domes rising out of the brown plains.[1] He and others write of terrible summer heat, and scorpions that willy-nilly sting themselves to death if you circle them with fire. Of silk factories – maybe three hundred of them at the turn of the century, and maybe seventy thousand inhabitants. Landor saw where precious blue tiles, named Káshí because they are manufactured here, and often left at the mercy of export-minded mullás, were missing from the dome of a great shrine. He noted the hundred-foot-high swaying minaret, like a factory chimney, he said.

He tells of how, to ease the summer heat, there was ice from the ice houses: deep pits under a cone-shaped roof of sun-baked brick, supplied during winter months from the near-by mountains. He visited the copper bazaar, its 'sound waves clashing' under vaulted roofs, where you could not hear yourself think.

There were eighteen mosques and five times that many shrines, and a docile, hard-working population, easy for the mullás to control. Khan's own family were of that same mild temperament. The Zarrábí men were said to come out of the women's quarters only at the age of eighteen – they were mothers' boys. Khan was morally brave himself, but came from a people known for, let us say, extreme prudence in the face of danger. The story goes that when the Shah sent for a hundred men of Káshán to join the army, they replied that they would come if they could have an armed guard.

When the inhabitants traveled it was mostly by horse power. Landor tells how he obtained 'fresh' horses here. It turned out they had already gone forty-eight miles over rough ground and without rest or food. Now they were sent out for twenty-eight more miles. Their knees constantly giving way, they kept collapsing under their loads. The leader and his attendant had to go forward on foot and drag the animals behind them. 'It was no easy job', Landor says, 'to get them to stand up again. One of them never did. He died, and naturally, we had to abandon him.' This meant the dead animal's load had to be heaped onto the remaining exhausted horses. They went ahead at the rate of about one mile an hour. Around three-thirty in the morning they came to a mountain caravanserai – and at its door all the horses, acting as one, threw themselves down and refused to rise again.[2]

If you had come through Káshán in the old days they would have told you that the city was built by Zubayda, the wife of Hárúnu'r-Rashíd, ninth-century Caliph. She did rebuild it, perhaps. Actually it goes back at least eight hundred years before Christ, thus Firdawsí and the city fought 'Umar at the time of the Muslim Conquest, but all in vain.

A mid-fourteenth century visitor describes its torrid summer months and pleasant winters. He tells of the garden of Fín, and how its reservoir, fed by the Kúh-Rúd river, plus rainwater cisterns, supplied the city. He said the inhabitants were Shiahs, surrounded by eighteen villages of Sunnites. He praised the Káshán melons and figs.

In the next century, the Italian Josefa Barbaro who settled there a while around 1474, wrote of 'Cassan, where . . . they make sylkes and fustian . . .' He says it was walled, with beautiful suburbs.[3]

But the main thing to remember must be that from this city, so legend or tradition has it, the Three Kings, Magi forewarned by Zoroaster the Prophet, set out for Jerusalem to worship the new-born Christ. Jackson says most of the Christian Fathers agree that the Three Wise Men came from Persia and he cites Marco Polo (1272) and Odoric of Pordenone (c. 1320) and their assigning the three to particular cities of Iran. Odoric places them in 'Cassan', and says they got to Jerusalem by divine aid, non-human, in only thirteen days. A royal city, he calls Káshán, but much ravaged by the Tartars. It was rich, Odoric says, in bread, wine, and all else. Marco Polo relates one of the Wise Men to 'the Castle of the Fire-Worshippers' (Cala Ataperistan – Qal'iy-i-Átishparastán) which, says Jackson, may well be in or about Káshán.[4]

On the mountainside, about five miles out of Káshán, is the one-time park and pleasure dome of Fín. Here is a place, now ruined. Here are gardens where Persian kings once took their ease, and avenues of cypresses, and water sparkling over channels of blue and green tiles. This is the place where the Grand Vazír who martyred the Báb was called to account. You can see a portrait of the murderer in the chronicle of Nabíl.[5]

The Shah's armies had finally triumphed and the early believers had been mowed down and destroyed, but nothing stopped the survivors. They loved the imprisoned Báb even more than they had before, if such a thing were possible. And so the Grand Vazír decided the Báb must die.

Gobineau says that first, however, the Grand Vazír wanted to humiliate the Báb – bring Him down out of His mountain prison of Chihríq where He shone out like a sunburst, where He was crowned with a nimbus of holiness and suffering and knowledge – let the populace see Him as the Vazír imagined Him now to be – much, says Gobineau, as you would lead forth a lion who has been beaten down, his teeth and claws pulled out, to expose him to the dog pack, so all could see how easy he is to destroy.[6]

So they brought the Báb to Tabríz and three days after His arrival the Grand Vazír's command arrived to put Him to death. The contemporary Nabíl tells how, with ten thousand people looking on, when the first seven hundred and fifty bullets took no effect, the stunned officer in charge marched his men away and resigned his post. Then another officer marched in his regiment and this time the Báb instantly died. At the end of his book, Nabíl says that the believers had no idea where the Báb's remains were hidden or where they would eventually be transferred.[7] Today, as the whole world knows, the sacred body of the Báb (and of the youth who was shot with Him) lies under the golden dome of the Shrine on Mount Carmel, visited by pilgrims from around the globe.

The public did not fail to note that those who carried out the execution suffered agonies in the years to come. An earthquake killed two hundred and fifty of the officers and men who had done the killing, that same year, 1850, and three years later the remaining five hundred mutinied, and were shot just as they had shot the Báb.

TWO

Born with a Tooth

Some of the people of Tabríz could not help but wonder aloud about these strange events, and they asked themselves whether they were not, perhaps, the vengeance of God. The mullás of the city imposed heavy fines on or beat anyone repeating such sentiments. They knew that the Bábís had prophesied the early end of the Grand Vazír, and that certain martyrs had even announced the way he would die.

The Vazír was the brother-in-law of the Shah and seemed secure, and his princess wife hovered over him with her royal protection. Still, in less than two years after the Báb's execution, the prime mover of it all fell from favor at the Court, and was banished to Fín. When he knew the Shah's men were coming for him, he removed to the hot bath and there severed his veins. People who visited there were shown his blood across the wall for a long time to come.

This took place about twenty-seven years before Khan was born.

At the turn of the century, as 'Abdu'l-Bahá's secretary in the Holy Land, Khan would be working night and day in the vicinity of the Báb's holy remains, not dreaming that the Master had hidden them, safe from all foes, near the place where Khan was at work.

Khan was the last child but one of ten, and four of them lived. This was how it was. A household was a place of continual birthings and dyings. Of the midwife draped in black, reciting her invocation. Of the dreaded Ál – an evil dwarf that swallows down the newborn.

Anyone you saw walking about, you knew was a survivor, for by rights he or she ought to have been dead. The Ál should have gotten him, or smallpox or typhoid. Khan would have the cholera three times, and live.

He came into the world with a tooth, which meant he was a prodigy. Because of this, his eldest sister, sixteen when he was born, taught him the alphabet as soon as she could – how to form the letters from right to left, how to add four extra letters to the Arabic alphabet, thus making thirty-two, for the Persian.

He could read and write when barely four, and could also recite poems from the Persian classics.

It was, after all, a literary household. The baby's father, Mírzá 'Abdu'r-Rahím Khan Zarrábí, was a poet with a mystic turn of mind, and also a painter. Friends of his youth would say that he was very handsome and that many leading families wanted him for a son-in-law. He finally selected his cousin Khadíja, eldest daughter of Abu'l-Qásim Khán. In later years the half-American posterity of this great-grandfather, always looking for laughs, were amused at his title, Pokhteh Khan. The word means 'one of mature judgment', but it also means well-cooked. Khan's father was the eldest of five brothers, all the others richer than he, and two of them married to princesses of the ruling house. Khan brought his children up to take pride in their Káshán forebears, who had given many a great man to the Empire: prime ministers and diplomats, authors, historians, poets. They were particularly proud to know, on those occasions when they did lend an ear to parental accounts, that their grandfather, who, after being Lieutenant-Governor of Káshán, became the Mayor (Kalántar) of Tehran, and was a follower of the Báb and Bahá'u'lláh.

Khan's father had learned of the new Faith from the Báb Himself during the three days in 1847 when the Manifestation of God was in Káshán on His way to being imprisoned in a lonely, four-towered mountain castle of stone. The convert's fervor was so great that he publicly preached the new message, whereupon, inevitably, the mullás arose to silence him; and his fellow-believers, considering him too valuable to be left to the mob, prevailed on him to leave for the capital. He left, but in Tehran again, where enemies of the Faith had aroused the Shah, they kept him in their sights.

His uncle, Farrukh Khán, who was Chief Court Minister at the time, saved his nephew's life by promising the Shah that his kinsman would sever all relations with the new religion. Later on, through this uncle's influence, the nephew became Mayor of Tehran, and held the post till his death.

Outwardly, Khan's father kept his distance from the believers. Still, through returning pilgrims, he received communications from Bahá'u'lláh, and time and again saved Bahá'ís from prison, torture and death. One of those he rescued was the great philosopher and scholar, Mírzá Abu'l-Faḍl of Gulpáygán. This erudite man had committed an act forbidden to Bahá'ís, but for what he considered a good reason: there was an Armenian who had been converted by Protestant missionaries, and one day when Mírzá was speaking on the Bahá'í Faith at a public tea house, this individual vilified the name of Bahá'u'lláh. Abu'l-Faḍl could not bear it, and struck him to the ground.

Khan's eldest sister, a strict Shiah, brought the child up according to her version of Islam, replete with what the mullás had added on down the years. Implanting the fear of God in him was salutary, it goes without saying, teaching him that ultimately good is rewarded and evil is punished. Evil is detestable. Hell, the Qur'án says, is foul with purulent matter which the damned lap up the way a thirsty camel drinks. But Paradise is a place of all delights: of shade trees, sweet fruits and cups of refreshing wine; of maids and ever-blooming youths, dwelling in gardens beneath which rivers flow.

However, she frightened the toddler with her accounts of a being's first night in the grave. She told him that on that first night the walls of his grave would come together and stifle him. Two angels would appear, and each would sit himself down on a side of the new corpse. Their names were Nakír and Munkar. One of them would ask him about the principles of Islam, and ask if his deeds had been righteous. Then the companion angel would coach him as to the answers he must make. If his good deeds had exceeded his evil ones, the two would then make him a tunnel from his tomb to Paradise, and there he would stay until the Day of Resurrection. But if his evil deeds had been more numerous than his good, they would open up a tunnel to Hell, and there he would burn on and on, getting a new skin as each was consumed, till the Resurrection Morn.

She would then conjure up undreamable horrors, tortures which would be inflicted on the evil (not remembering that every Súrih of the Qur'án, except one, begins: 'In the Name of God, the Compassionate, the Merciful,' and says that God has 'imposed mercy on Himself as a law').[8]

The child learned, too, how difficult was the way to Paradise, for even after all other tests had been passed he must cross the abyss of Hell on a bridge called the Sirát that was sharp as a sword-edge and narrow as a hair.

So indoctrinated, even after many decades as a liberated Bahá'í, Khan could recall his infant terrors, and one gathered that of all the promised tortures it was probably being squeezed in his grave that frightened him the most. This inevitable post-mortem experience is called the fishár-i-qabr, constriction in the grave. Being mewed up all alone in the grave's encroaching walls seemed of more immediate concern to the little boy than all the other tortures. It hit home.

How relieved he must have been, in after years, to read Bahá'í Teachings about death in *The Hidden Words*: 'I have made death a messenger of joy to thee. Wherefore dost thou grieve?'[9] '. . .Thou art My robe and My robe shall never be outworn.'[10]

Khan came to realize later on that many of the horrifying things his sister taught him were not from Muḥammad. Some had come down from ancient Magian and Zoroastrian lore, misremembered, misinterpreted by the priesthood and later interwoven with misinterpretations of Islam and its true and authentic Scripture, the Qur'án.

Mother and sisters were determined that the new child should grow up a devout Muslim, not an unclean infidel like the followers of other Faiths. They knew the Qur'án teaches that all the Prophets – Moses, Jesus Christ, all, up to and including Muḥammad, to them the last one forever and ever – came from God, and were authentic and true. But they believed that other religionists had been misled by their priests, and were thus really unbelievers, to be shunned by the chosen – i.e. the Shiah Muslims, to whose religion the child's mother and sisters belonged.

Not only his sister but everyone around the child taught him that non-Muslims were unclean. A Muslim beggar in the street would draw his rags across his palm before accepting the European's coin, though he would not reject the money.

That non-Muslims were unclean – in a religious not a physical sense, what Bible scholars might call Levitically unclean – was a universal Shiah belief. It can be traced back to an unwarranted extension of Qur'án 9:28 where the verse states that 'only they who join gods with God are unclean'.[11] Translators take this to mean the pagans, idol worshippers, who were all around the early believers in Muḥammad. Later, in the popular mind, the verse came to include all non-Muslims. When Khan became a man and went off to the country of the infidels and married a Bahá'í of Christian background, his Shiah family were not sure but that the bride was ceremonially unclean (najis).

THREE
A Son Meets His Father

Khan was four when his family left the large house in Káshán to join the Kalántar at the capital. He could always remember that time. They traveled by way of Qum, the shrine city, accompanied by men and women attendants and horsemen while they sat in palanquins balanced on sturdy mules. The journey of 150 miles took them ten days.

The little cavalcade wound its way into a vast city of sun-baked brick. Tehran lay in a wide, saucer-like plain, with the Alburz wall of mountains to the north. These were bare, sharp against the turquoise sky, and thrusting from the northeastern corner of the Alburz stood great, cone-shaped Dimávand under its snows.

The Shah, Náṣiri'd-Dín, back from Western travels, had modernized his throne city. He had torn down its ancient walls; and his new wall, some ten miles long, was pierced by twelve gates, fairy gates that looked like small castles almost, with bright towers and minarets, their shining colored tiles visible from far away.

He had interrupted the old winding lanes with broad avenues, and these were bustling with European carriages, for by now there were more than five hundred carriages in Tehran. (Herodotus had again been proved right. Back in the fifth century BC he wrote that whenever the Persians heard of a luxury, they instantly made it their own.) But since eras interpenetrate, there were also camel caravans swinging by, nobles on prancing Arab horses, street vendors, peasants in sky blue clothes and beehive hats, priests in turbans and 'abás jogging by on donkeys, bony arms of beggars lifting from the ground, and everywhere the women, black phantoms in wide chádurs over baggy pantaloons.

In the 1880s Tehran was mostly built of sun-baked brick. There was stone and marble in the south, and plenty of wood in the Caspian provinces, but here were no thick forests, only groves and walled parks. Hiding from street life, the dwellings presented only blind earth-colored walls to passersby. This because of the jealously guarded women, wrapped in their veils. Perhaps through an opened door a bed of flowers would be glimpsed, perhaps the tip of a tall poplar tree would wave above a wall.

As a capital, Tehran was new; less than a hundred years before, in

1788, the eunuch-founder of Qájár rule, Ághá Muḥammad S͟hah, had given it that rank. Before then S͟hiráz was the capital, and before then Iṣfahán and Qazvín. Tehran had been of small importance. In 1220 a traveler described it merely as 'a stronghold, one farsak͟h distant from Rayy', a farsak͟h being the distance a loaded mule travels in an hour. The inhabitants, he said, dug out places underground to serve as their dwellings, were against all authority, and fought with everybody. However, modern Tehran covers the area of ancient Rayy which, Jackson says, 'shared with Ecbatana [Hamadán] supremacy over Iran'.[12] According to tradition Rayy was founded four thousand years before the birth of Christ. The Apocrypha's Book of Tobit refers to it as 'Rages of Media'.

But time took a long detour afterward, and power went south in the days of Cyrus (d. 529 BC), founder of the Achaemenian kings. Cyrus built Pasargadae for his capital because it was there that he beat the Medes. Forty miles away is the later capital, Persepolis, both ruined memories under an empty sky. Today, the king's lonely tomb lifts up out of barren desert, and even the inscription he had them carve on it is gone:

> O Man, whoever thou art, whensoever thou comest,
> I am Cyrus. I founded the Empire of the Persians.
> Then begrudge me not this bit of earth that covers my body.

With Tehran's rise to power, Jackson says, 'Media has been able to reclaim once more the supremacy she lost to Persis in the time of Cyrus . . .'[13]

In Qájár days any building fronting on the main avenues must by law be windowless, because the ladies of the Shah's household, as they were driven past, might otherwise be glimpsed, shut in carriages and thickly veiled though they were.

These main avenues were cleared by heralds when the ladies were to leave the royal palace. All shops had to close – and anyone staying in the vicinity of the line of carriages would be killed on the spot. 'Depart! Be blind! (Kúr s͟híd! Rad s͟híd!)' the heralds would shout, and the inhabitants would understandably hasten to comply. As the century wore on, and some gentler ways prevailed, a severe beating of the inadvertent voyeur might replace his execution. But even contemporary with the move of Khan's family to Tehran, should a man dare to raise a woman's veil in public he would be liable to instant death. Many a woman was thus free to go anywhere she pleased, fully disguised in her c͟hádur. Criminals, too, well aware of the veil's protection, when need be dressed as women, leaving the policemen helpless.

A SON MEETS HIS FATHER

The four-year-old now met his father for the first time, and the occasion was etched into his mind. It happened on the day when they arrived in Tehran. He and his elder brother were escorted to the Police Administration headquarters, the Mayor's (Kalántar) office, by their lálih, a kind of bodyguard-tutor-servant. Awestruck, bowing low, the two little boys from Káshán found their father dressed in a dazzling European military uniform of summer white, wearing epaulettes and carrying a sword. The uniform was copied, Khan recalled in later years, from the Austrian military uniform of that day. The Chief of Police was an Italian-Austrian, a Count Monteforte, and the Shah, when on a visit to Europe, had engaged him to reorganize (perhaps organize would be a better word) the Persian police.

Khan's father maintained his household in Tehran with his salary as Mayor, plus whatever benefits went with the office. There was other income as well, some from property in Káshán inherited from Khan's grandparents, some from a certain annual stipend called 'Perpetual' (mustamarrí) that came down to them from long-ago ancestors. In later times such income was discontinued.

The Kalántar's family was thus adequately provided for, but as the years passed the fortunes of his brothers grew far greater than his own. The ones in Tehran were politically ambitious and held lucrative posts, while the Kalántar, a poet and mystic, cared little for material advancement. All he wanted was peace and quiet in which to meditate on spiritual values, and to share his thoughts with his Bábí, later Bahá'í, friends.

Khan's mother, however, a rigid Muslim, and respected as the lady of the family, the daughter of Pokhteh Khan, had other ideals. When the uncles' families would invite her to a lavish party, she, Persian-fashion, was never satisfied until she had outdone them with a party of her own. This kind of rivalry was typical of the time and place. It is epitomized by a tale, which may not be apocryphal, of the hostess who received her guests in a gown of sumptuous Paris materials, and at the return party the following week found that her hostess had dressed all her maids in gowns identical to the one she had worn.

The Kalántar's lady, who had supervised her father's opulent household when her own mother had died, thus placed a heavy burden on the Mayor's finances with her ever-increasing extravagance.

As for her husband, he retained considerable affection for her, going back to days when she was his bride and he had written love poems in praise of her beauty. In appearance she was dark, having an Arab strain inherited from the Prophet, for those with her degree of kinship to the Siyyids – the Prophet's descendants – were called Siyyids-on-Friday-nights. She had *salt* (a kind of sweetness or charm), but also a terrible temper.

Her preoccupation with what the Persians call sha'n involved a good deal of sacrifice on the family's part, otherwise their funds would have been adequate for their needs. Now, however, she set about accumulating the money that to her way of thinking was necessary in order to provide dowries for her two daughters that would assure them of marrying men of importance.

Sha'n is rank, dignity, ancestral prestige, personal talent, intellectual attainment, family honor, social prominence – always combined with ancient blood. Every member of such a family was taught to uphold this unwritten but pervasive principle of sha'n. It was not unlike noblesse oblige – or the Chinese concept of face. It is the most treasured possession of ancient races and can be a great asset, but often, too, a curse. The nobility and gentry of Persia could not part with their sha'n. For example, whether he was on foot or on horseback, it was beneath a gentleman's sha'n to be seen in public without a number of attendants. His relatives of lesser rank could not be permitted to remain seated in his presence, or to approach him on terms of equality. A man of sha'n could not be seen carrying a package in public – that was unthinkable; and he could not possibly consort with tradesmen – even merchant-princes – as equals or friends. Tradesmen considered it an honor to extend credit to such nobles and gentry. If, as normally happened, the latter did not pay up, the merchant, entering the reception hall of the grandee, would have to bend down, a hand on each knee, then stand with folded arms and bowed head, and no courage left to ask for his money. One, returning to the bazaar empty-handed, might boast that the distinguished creditor himself had personally spoken to him and asked him to come back at a later, unspecified, date.

Many of these customs began to be rebelled against and to disappear with the coming of Persia's Revolution (1906), but they still, even today, form a part of the national consciousness.

'I'll tell you how you can measure a family's sha'n,' said a Persian girl, laughing. 'When you go past their stables, observe the height of their manure pile. The more horse manure, the more sha'n.'

The two sisters of Khan would also have been caught up in the matter of sha'n as it related to their dowries. Through their childhood they had heard their mother insisting on the need to do this or that, or to avoid something or other, because the sha'n of her family and of the Kalántar's demanded it. From an early age, as befitted girls of good family, they had learned how to sew and embroider. They could do the difficult zar-dúzí – embroideries of gold and silver wire on bands of velvet or satin, also gold bangles and seed pearls. These bands were then appliquéd on chosen sections of a dress. Now the girls set about making their wedding outfits, a process in those days of endless time which could go on for years.

Other elements of the dowry could include vessels of silver, copper or gold, and while slavery still obtained, slaves of both sexes to accompany the bride, whose parents also provided horses and donkeys, mules, even camels in some parts of the country. At the appointed time, all the dowry would be packed in cases and carried on pack animals to the house of the groom, each load being covered with a large, embroidered cloth. As part of the procession, slaves or other attendants accompanying the bride would sit atop the loads. Alternatively, the dowry might be spread on trays and carried on human heads.

Like all other Persian procedures, they knew their weddings would go forward according to the rasm, or body of ancient customs, that dictated the course of Persian life. Rasm was far deadlier than sha'n. After all, sha'n affected only the gentry – but the entire population lay in the grip of rasm (rite, formality, rule). When 'Abdu'l-Bahá told the Persians that they lay in a strange sleep,[14] the statement applied in no small measure to this rasm. It was rasm that made the puppet masses so easy to control by the clergy – who in the nineteenth century (as in every age when a Messenger of God appears) blocked off the people from accepting the new way, which threatened the clerics' power and their livelihood. When Bahá'u'lláh appeared and said, '. . . know of thine own knowledge and not through the knowledge of thy neighbor',[15] and 'look into all things with a searching eye',[16] He shattered the age-old rasm or custom. Bahá'u'lláh tells in the *Íqán* how one day, in the midst of leading the congregational prayer, Muḥammad suddenly turned Himself about and changed the Point of Adoration (the Qiblih or point toward which the faithful direct themselves in formal prayer) from Jerusalem to the Ka'bih at Mecca — with the result that many who had begun to believe in Him apostasized their Faith.[17] For rasm is in part the dictates of the Faith gone before, rules that have crystallized and become automatic so that anyone daring to break these rules must be attacked and driven out.

The clergy, controlling both the leaders and the mass, will react instantly to the threat posed by the new Messenger from God (be this Moses, Christ, Muḥammad or, today, the Báb and Bahá'u'lláh) because He changes the mind-set, the custom.

There is that episode of the young Qájár prince, walking in the garden where the day was cool, conversing with a great foe of the Báb's brief Dispensation, Áqásí – the clown-Rasputin-like Prime Minister who prevented the Báb from meeting the Shah. Why, the Prince wanted to know, had the Prime Minister sent the Báb away to the distant mountain prison of Máh-Kú?

'You are young yet,' the Prime Minister answered, 'and there are certain things that you do not understand – but be sure that if the Báb had reached Tehran and met the Shah, you and I would not be walking here now, taking our ease, and free, in the cool shadow of these trees.'[18]

The wearing of the veil, the c̲h̲ádur (tent), is a further example of rasm carried into the twentieth century. One day, long afterward, when Khan's half-American daughters had entertained their girl cousins for tea, and the time came for them to leave, the cousins, tooling up as it were, drew their black satin madonna-veil c̲h̲ádurs over their heads, and looked about for their píc̲h̲ihs, these being a black flexible oblong woven of horsehair, and attached to a band that fit over the head. The píc̲h̲ih could be pulled straight down so that no one could see the wearer's face though she herself could look through, or it could be twisted a little to show off a girl's best feature, giving a glimpse of her mouth, perhaps, or her eyes, and allowing a small curl to poke out on her temple. It was much more fetching than the Khomeini woman's look so prevalent in after years. It was coquetry, a mask, intrigue, and went (by the first quarter of the twentieth century) with her high heeled shoes, the rest of her being mystery as she passed along, grasping the edges of the c̲h̲ádur under her chin with the hidden right hand.

Khan's older daughter, fresh from the West, was startled to find her cousins, young modern women, Bahá'ís, and already indignant about the low state of women in Persia, veiled of themselves, wrapped up from head to foot, hunting around for their horsehair shutters.

'Why do you veil?' she asked.

'Because it is the rasm. It is the custom.'

'Why is it the custom?'

They burst out laughing. Nobody ever questioned the custom. Nobody ever said why is it the rasm – automatic behavior passed on down the ages.

Khan's mother would have had no use for feminism. She was supreme in her home, and immersed in rasm. Even her contemporary, Queen Victoria, would write: 'The Queen is most anxious to enliste [sic] everyone to join in checking this mad, wicked folly of Women's Rights, with all its attendant horrors . . .'[19]

Following the demands of custom, Khan's mother accumulated elaborate dowries for her daughters. She did this by careful management, which meant that she used money for this project that should have been spent on other family matters, making everyone suffer in the cause of s̲h̲a'n. The Kalántar had to endure constant complaints that there was not enough money. Patient and dignified, some nights, rather than come home to unpleasantness, he slept in his official quarters. He still had a tender respect for his wife, and she, in her heart, reciprocated; but driven by the concept of sha'n, she could not cease reminding him that although superior to his younger brothers he was doing less well in the world.

She came, after all, from an opulent home, daughter of a rich and hospitable man whose door, as the Persian phrase had it, always stood open. She too wished to rule such a house. She could not understand that the Kalántar was a poet, given to spiritual values, culture, the contemplative life, and was thus enjoying a position which, although not the highest, gave him leisure for what to him were greater concerns than ambition and the encumbrance of wealth – of which, the Persian proverb says, 'Whoever has more roof, has more snow.' (A rich man, that is, has a heavier burden to bear.)

Many and many a mystic had written of this question, and his own Faith also taught in the words of Bahá'u'lláh, 'Busy not thyself with this world, for with fire We test the gold, and with gold We test Our servants.'[20] Although wealth well dispensed was not condemned for Bahá'ís, still it was a test, a hindrance, a responsibility.

Rúmí's thirteenth-century tale of the ragged dervish embodied the ancient concept. The dervish crept into a perfumer's shop where there were shelves and shelves of flowery scents, costly unguents and fragrant, precious oils.

'Begone!' the owner cried.

As the ragged one turned to go, he called back, 'Yes, it is easy for me, unencumbered, to walk out of your shop, but for you, with all these things that you have, how hard it will be when the day comes for you to walk out of the door of the world!'

FOUR

A Sense of Station

The Kalántar's wife attributed her husband's views and his failure to make a fortune to the fact that he had become a Bábí, and later a follower of Bahá'u'lláh, embracing doctrine that to her way of thinking was nothing but a false religion. She forbade him to speak about his Faith to their two boys, and she brought up the two daughters to be rigid Shiahs like herself. The boys learned the rudiments of Islam at school, and at home their mother preached daily on the Muslim Purgatory and Hell for punishments, and the delights of its Paradise for rewards. The Kalántar did not worry as to the religious future of his sons, and from time to time would prophesy to his wife that both boys, either before or after his death, would become Bahá'ís.

As Khan's mother grew ever more rigid in her beliefs, more impatient with her husband, more determined to provide sumptuous weddings for each of her girls, the Kalántar came home less and less often. Besides the obvious reasons for this, his duties at the office had increased. But these absences only made the scoldings worse when he did appear. Khan used to think, looking back when he was older, that no one but an outstanding Bahá'í could have endured it.

Still, Khan's parents must have loved each other. The Kalántar's replies to his wife were invariably kind and gentle, and Khan never heard him address her except as 'Your Ladyship', customary among well-placed Persian families of that time. Only once, after hours of harassment, the Kalántar answered when Khan was by, 'I know, <u>Kh</u>ánum, I do not please you, but it is not my fault. The reason I regret your behavior toward me is this: I fear that I shall die and you will survive me by twenty years, and because of the workings of the divine law, you will then have to bear terrible hardships and trials.' This prophecy was fulfilled, word for word.

No matter how bitterly she attacked her husband, if anyone dared speak in her presence of his 'lack of ambition', she would leap to his defense.

Khan's mother was not entirely to blame for her carryings-on. She had suffered all her life from a stomach ailment which would have turned a less determined woman into an invalid. A leading doctor, a cousin of Khan's parents, begged her to take a glass of old wine with her meals, but the Qur'án forbade this, saying of wine and games of chance, 'In both is great sin, and advantage also . . . but their sin is greater than their advantage.'[21] The Kalántar, however, went to great lengths in that Islamic country to obtain a little fine old wine for her, though at first she refused it. Being persuaded finally to drink some, and finding it did bring relief, she reluctantly began to take a small glass from time to time. On occasions when she did accept the forbidden wine, 'an abomination of Satan's work!'[22] the Book also says, she would first beg God's forgiveness. Then she would curse the infidels – that is, the Sunni Muslims – who had usurped the rightful position of Muḥammad's successor, 'Alí, the first Imám, and put every Imám except the twelfth to death. Then, draining the small cup of wine and making a face, she would call for a woman servant to bring in a ewer and basin and would perform the ritual ablutions of hand and mouth, necessary to cancel out the wine, canonically unclean as well as forbidden.

The Kalántar's home-coming hour was five in the afternoon, and he would arrive in his white military uniform as spotless as he had set out in the morning. He had in early youth formed the habit, later reinforced by the Bahá'í Faith, of being immaculate at all times, and of the four children it was Khan in particular who inherited this trait.

Khan's father loved flowers and ornamental shrubs, and he learned much about their cultivation from the Europeans who were now in the service of the Persian government. Reaching home, he would change into plain, white clothing, take up his gardening tools and go out to the flowers and shrubs he had planted in the four sections of his garden courtyard. This ḥayáṭ had a round pool at the center and about it were fruit trees, flowers, herbs such as mint, patches of kitchen vegetables. The rooms of the house, on all four sides, opened onto this court. One side of the building was a single, large room called the 'orange house', and here were stored, toward autumn's end, orange and lemon trees and other vegetation which would die in the cold Tehran winter. Khan's father loved the return of spring, more fresh and delicate in those days than anywhere else in this world or the next (at least judging by the poets), when hundreds of pots, large and small would be carried out into the garden court and he could plant new flowers as well.

Khan bore in memory the look of his father, gardening in his white clothes, till darkness fell.

Persians still dine late, often around ten in the evening. They wonder why Westerners dine early and then need pills to put them to sleep: when you dine late, the food itself is soporific.

The boys would get home from school fairly late, and their father chose this hour to give them advice as to how they should live.

'Look at yourself as if you were someone else,' he would tell them, teaching cleanliness and good grooming (matters now ably taken care of by the advertisements, but which had to be carefully taught at that time). 'How do you feel when you see someone with bleary eyes, a runny nose, unwashed face, mouth, ears, neck – and spots all over his clothes?' Years afterward – even when Khan was living as a dervish out in the wilderness, walking long miles over the desert, climbing up one side of mountains, down the other, living with tribesmen and peasants on farms, even in a sheepfold – he remembered and kept clean and tidy, though he had only two shirts, each of coarsely-woven cotton: one to wear, a freshly-washed one folded in his pack.

Give good advice, the Qur'án says, and this, to Khan, was the function of a parent: 'Enjoin what is right, and forbid what is evil.'[23]

The Persian father maintained his rank in the household; he kept a certain distance. He did not become a 'pal' to his children; he remained their superior, their kindly teacher and helper, and they respected his station, and listened. One cannot help contrasting this with the behavior of modern American fathers, frantically running about, playing ball with their sons, pretending to a false equality. Perhaps what children need is not another playmate but a superior to whom they can turn. True, the Persian families were often ruled by a tyrannical father (as were Occidental families in those days as well).

The Persians have a great sense of station, of where you belong in the scheme of life, and each rank must receive its due, and none be slighted. In the Kalántar family, despite recriminations about his unworldliness and failure to earn a lot more money, the father's position was always maintained. So was the mother's. 'Paradise lieth at the feet of mothers,' Muḥammad said.[24]

The Kalántar often taught his children manners through stories. Persian children were very fond of sheep's bone marrow and, in spite of the mess, would work hard to suck it out. To discourage this, the Kalántar told of the djinn who also was partial to bone marrow and would bring nightmares to anyone who touched the bones.

The father also taught his children to share whatever they had, and that whenever a poor man begged for something in the street, to give him at least enough for a meal – this was a time and place where the only hope of the needy was a charitable heart. He told them they should not judge the man when they gave him money, nor withhold it although they knew it would be spent on opium or drink.

Years afterward Khan's brother, Ḥusayn, went out one day to visit his father's grave, somewhere along the wall of a mosque. After praying, he remembered another wish of his father's, that whenever a family member visited the grave, he should give some money to a poor man. Ḥusayn looked about. No one was near except a man of good bearing, prosperously dressed. Khan's brother went up to him, apologized, and said his father's wish had been that the family should give alms when visiting his grave, and there was no one else around. The man, with dignity accepting the gift, replied, 'You don't know how much I needed this.'

Graft was rampant in the Police Department, as it was in every department of the government of those days. Various terms for the Persian word madákhil – described as 'a cherished national institution in Persia' – are taken from Lord Curzon's book on Persia and listed in the introduction to *The Dawn-Breakers*: they range from 'commission', through 'perquisite, douceur, consideration, pickings and stealings' to 'profit'. 'Roughly speaking,' explains Lord Curzon, 'that balance of personal advantage, usually expressed in money form, which can be squeezed out of any and every transaction.'[25]

In the case of the Police Department, higher-ups would appropriate money allotted to pay the lower echelons of the force, and there was no way the Kalántar could stop this, for the perpetrators stood in too well with the Shah. Many an employee would wear his policeman's uniform on days when there were parades, but in order to stay alive would work at other jobs most of the time. The poorest of the police were personally looked after by the Kalántar. He gave them money, food and clothing, and when possible a chance at a job that would bring in some extra tumáns. At his death many of them joined the funeral march and as they marched, shed tears.

Khan himself tried throughout his life to follow his father's example of uprightness in office, even when the British offered him substantial sums (refusing which, of course, brought him hostility from many other highly-placed compatriots who saw things differently).

The Kalántar always had great dignity and presence. The children never dared raise their voices when he was by. He would sit on the floor on a cushion and lean on a bolster placed against the wall in the upper corner of the room, called the seat of honor in Persian houses, it being the seat farthest from the door. Entering, the sons, hands folded, would bow before him and stand until he told them to sit down. This practice was an ancient rule in noble homes.

Khan was never punished – his father had no reason to punish him, for the boy was constantly trying to improve himself, not only in school but by learning Persian literature and mystic teachings from his father's everyday conversation. As the Kalántar lay on his death bed after a long period of sickness, he said of his fourteen-year-old son, 'Ali-Kuli Khan will become the leader of leaders.' Khan used to recall the prophecy in later years, when he reached ambassadorial rank and finally headed the Imperial Court.

Although the Kalántar never upbraided Khan, this was not the case with Khan's brother, who on rare occasions could throw his father into a flaming rage – a storm which would remind Khan of the Arab proverb that says, 'Beware the wrath of the patiently-enduring.'

The future general was always up to something. He would see a European on the street, dressed outrageously, differently from the way any self-respecting Persian dressed, and he would pursue the foreigner, snatch off his hat and toss it away. He never appreciated cause and effect. The effect in this case was that the European lodged a complaint with his legation or consulate, which duly protested to Persia's Foreign Office, which then referred the matter to the Kalántar and his Police Administration. The culprit, traced by his Royal College uniform, would turn out to be none other than the Lord Mayor's eldest son. The Kalántar would duly apologize, come home, and thrash Ḥusayn, a punishment the boy would be sure to remember, until the next time.

One day, hunting through their father's closet, the boys discovered a box containing letters in exquisite Arabic and Persian script. They also found a bag of cotton cloth that was almost full of rock candy. Later, they learned that the letters were Tablets from the Báb and Bahá'u'lláh, while the candy was a gift blessed by Bahá'u'lláh and sent by Him to the Kalántar through returning pilgrims. What interested the two boys was the candy. From time to time, one or the other would quietly return to the box and extract a piece until, inevitably, it was finally gone. Khan used to wonder why his father never inquired as to why his candy had disappeared.

Years later they were sure that the rock candy had somehow prepared them for the Bahá'í Faith. No wonder, they thought, that the Shiahs warned one another to drink no tea with the Bábís and accept no sugar from their hands – for such gifts were magic spells and would lure them into the false belief.

Khan, who in early life survived cholera three times, used to say he was alive only because his father had deliberately hidden so much 'holy candy', rock candy blessed by Bahá'u'lláh Himself and put away by the Kalántar, secure in the knowledge that he and Husayn would ferret it out.

Every morning before leaving home – and this impressed his sons above all – the Kalántar would stand near the door of his room and, reverently facing West (not South, where Mecca, the Muslim point of adoration would be), whisper a long prayer. His wife consistently objected, but he ignored her complaints; and the two sisters, Marzieh and Hamideh, sorrowfully informed their brothers that the Kalántar was facing 'Akká, where Bahá'u'lláh was a captive, and reciting a Bábí prayer. They remained Shiahs till the end, and in after years their children would pun on the word Haifa, the other city where the Holy Household lived, and say that the Bahá'í Religion was all hayf (What a pity! Alas!).

FIVE

Trials and Tantrums

Khan had a temper, and what he remembered doing at one of those lavish parties of his mother's left him miserable whenever he thought of the episode, even later in life.

At such events a special protocol was rigidly observed. This is the ubiquitous Persian ta'áruf which means the long exchange of compliments and ritual courtesies, not necessarily heartfelt, the ceremonial greetings, the social formalities, including sentences like, 'May God never remove your shadow from off my head', which indicates that the speaker is the inferior. One aspect of ta'áruf is, if you admire another's possession, he at once offers it to you as a gift. Your only protection seems to be, if he admires your scarf, admire his horse. 'Písh-kish' (I make you a present of it), he tells you, but ritual courtesy forbids you to take the gift.

One of his royal aunts was guest of honor at a women's party when Khan, five years old, disrupted the Persian pattern of social courtesy. The princesses who married Khan's uncles were exquisite young girls – fair-skinned beauties with the long eyes and curling dark lashes featured in so many Persian paintings. Indeed, all the Qájárs were beautiful, proving that beauty not always is as beauty does. Their grandfather, Fath-'Alí Sháh, can be seen in *The Dawn-Breakers*, slim and stately, loaded down with jewels and a magnificent beard.[26] If you have seen portraits of Napoleon on his splendid white Arab horse, that horse was a gift of this same Fath-'Alí Sháh. Of children too numerous to mention, the Shah produced one final son, Jalál-i-Dín Mírzá, the father of these two princesses.

In addition to her royal background, the guest of honor enjoyed a special title because she had visited the holy Ka'bih at Mecca, and her title meant something like Pride of the Lady Pilgrims to the House of God.

Khan, always loved for his precocity, was much petted by all the guests at the party. Very nice, but he himself kept his eye on the food. There was enough to supply ten times the number of guests – food that had taken weeks to make ready: cooked dishes such as chicken breasts with candied orange peel in saffron rice; delicate hearts of lettuce to be broken with the fingers and dipped in a dressing; young cucumbers; elaborate sweets, one of them a favorite of Khan's called sawhán – brown disks, brittle and crunchy; pistachio nuts and roasted watermelon seeds; cherries encased in sugar, the stems sticking outward for handles; quince preserves; diamond-shaped servings of 'ice in heaven', a sort of blancmange. The drinks included sikanjibín, made with vinegar and honey, and a sort of buttermilk with chopped cucumber, ice and mint on top; there was fragrant tea in glasses with silver filigree holders, small cups of coffee at the end, for goodby. The ladies also passed about a qalyán or hubble-bubble pipe, its tobacco water-cooled to a comfortable chugging sound.

Persian-fashion, the princess herself, as guest of honor, prepared a dish well-filled with party food and gave it to the child. The plate was emptied at once, and handed back; and filled again, then emptied again, and filled again; and glasses of fruit juice followed, to wash it all down.

By then the little boy could scarcely draw breath but he saw that the grown-ups continued to eat away. They obviously had plenty of room for more, while he had not. This seemed very unfair. He suddenly let out a string of loud Shiah curses, directed primarily at the guest of honor but at any and all of the other eaters as well. They noted the problem, roared, and hugged him to their breasts, but still more curses came out.

Even years afterward, when on leave from Washington he met his royal aunt in Tehran, he cringed, remembering.

A year or so after the party Khan still had his tantrums. One such took place at a family supper, spread out on the floor according to custom, with each one seated tailor-fashion around the cloth, the food being eaten with the fingers of the right hand (fingers definitely were made before forks). Khan became angry over something, refused to eat and started off to bed. Unperturbed, his mother filled a dinner plate against the time when the child would wake up hungry. Pausing at the door to see what was being piled on the plate, Khan said, 'I don't know who you're saving that for, but whoever he is, it's not enough.'

Marzieh, Khan's eldest sister and his mentor as a child, was well educated for the time and place – certainly her training compared very well with that given to English girls of good family in Victorian times when the boys were favored, not the girls. She could write poetry, she studied painting under her father's care. She was something of a psychic and insisted that she had seen a djinn, a man one foot high, with triangular eyes. (Western psychics do not see djinns, but ectoplasm, vague as to shape.)

Like other ladies of her day she could embroider with silk and seed pearls, silver and gold. She designed and sewed elegant dresses to wear at the women's parties. Once, when Khan was about three, Marzieh made him a never-forgotten suit, a Prince Albert coat in what some considered the 'European' style, cut from fine black cloth, with gold embroidery on the border. In that miniature Prince Albert, with tiny black trousers to match, he was the best-dressed toddler in Káshán.

By the time he was seven, Marzieh was listening to him recite Sa'dí and Ḥáfiẓ by heart and marveling at the original verse he was beginning to compose, using varied forms such as ghazals (odes), quatrains and so on. Even then he showed a mystical turn of mind.

Khan's father taught him to draw and paint and saw to it that he read history and philosophy at an early age, to supplement what he was learning in the boys' school.

In Tehran, little schools were scattered throughout the city, each the size of a small store. Here a mullá taught the rudiments of Islam and made the children recite from the Qur'án, which being in Arabic, a foreign tongue, none of them understood. Even so recently as the mid-twentieth century, and probably still, the mullás have taught that it was evil to translate the Qur'án – the 'Book to be Read', the Book of God. This reluctance to put Scripture into the vernacular cannot fail to remind one of the same struggle in Christianity. In 1559 Pope Paul IV banned all modern language Bibles, enumerating forty-eight editions of them. In 1536 William Tyndale had been burned at the stake for translating the Bible into English. The translators of the King James Bible (1611) who owe so much to Tyndale say in their preface: 'So much are they [the Church of Rome] afraid of the light of the Scripture . . . that they will not trust the people with it . . . we forced them to translate it into English against their wills.'[27] This fear of the study of Scripture had been well expressed in the Middle Ages with the admonition, 'Press not the breasts of Holy Writ too hard, lest they yield you blood instead of milk.'

The students learned something of their country's history and quite a lot of Persian poetry, especially that embodied in a text called the Niṣáb, defined as an Arabic vocabulary in Persian rhyme. This came about because of the conquest of Persia by the Arabs in the seventh century. Arabic words entered the native language much as French entered English with the Norman Conquest. In the Niṣáb the meaning of these words can be learned from poems by classical Persian scholars which translate the words into Persian.

The mullá was quick to apply the bastinado when a student failed his daily or weekly tests, in this case blows from a leather whip applied over and over to the bare soles of a child's feet.

Khan had formed the habit of constant study and was never whipped – a fact which did not increase his popularity with the other boys, always older than he and disinclined to work.

In after years he felt that his real early education had been what he received at home from his sister and his father, the Kalántar. Oddly enough, though good at writing and memorizing poetry, he was a slow learner in other subjects and the family thought him obtuse. He was apt to be off wool-gathering, and not there – with the result that some of the relatives called him a donkey (khar), Persian for slow and stupid. His sister and father told him to ignore this criticism, that his apparent dullness was due to depth of thought – he was given to examining all the aspects of a subject. He was not what we would call today a quick study. Although he learned many poems by heart, in the beginning he had to work hard to do so. These efforts brought two advantages: he retained what he learned and he developed an extraordinary memory later on. The time came when he could repeat an ode from memory after hearing it recited once.

Khan's brother, four-and-a-half years older than he, was brilliant and quick. This brother, Ḥusayn Qulí Khán (who later took the family name, Kalántar) wasted little time in study and spent his days in sports, gymnastics, and outdoor parties in beautiful walled gardens with his close friends. All these pleasures he forbade to Khan. In non-democratic Persia, each individual seemed to have a tyrant over him. This seemed the case down through every hierarchy. Among servants, for example, the least important had the whole staff over him for tyrants, and no one under him to kick. Meanwhile, the top tyrant, the Shah, had the power of life and death over everyone, and no one above to stay him. In between, almost everyone had someone to kick, and be kicked by.

Khan was, with good reason, terrified of his brother, who was given to beating him. The timorous blood of Káshán ran in this child's veins, not the other's. (The Zarrábís were apt to be mothers' pets and cossetted.) Khan, frequently a captive, thus had not much else to do but remain with his books.

He did escape at times to learn something of gymnastics, and to swim and dive. He could walk on his hands for 'blocks' – an American word that crept into his memoirs – and even climb up and down stairs in that position. Though in later years he said of this period, 'I never thought of any obstacles that could deter me,' he never could come up to his brother's feats. Husayn could leap off a high roof and land unscathed but was more famous for being able to jump over a camel. He had a way with horses, and the wildest of them ambled along gently when he was the rider. The animal seemed to understand, and to yield ahead of time, as if it knew that yielding was inevitable.

SIX

Your Best, Not Your Smallest

Being well connected was a great help in Persian society, even more so than in most countries. In later years, Khan tried to interest his half-American daughter Marzieh in family genealogy, without success. To her, all those births, marriages and deaths, births, marriages and deaths, were as hard to sort out as an anthill, and she steadily avoided eye-contact with every remote forebear, from great-grandfather Ives in Illinois to Pokhteh Khan in Káshán. She was inclined to thank God that her grandfather Breed in Massachusetts was adopted, his provenance being unknown.

She did learn that Khan's grandmother married twice, the second time to Ibráhím Khán Ghaffárí, a marriage that produced four sons. Two of these were among the children of the nobility sent off by the

Shah to be educated abroad.

Náṣiri'd-Dín, who came to the throne in 1848 when he was seventeen, was persuaded by foreign ambassadors during the reign of Napoleon III (1852–70) to introduce European ways into Persia. Accordingly, he selected a number of promising children from noble families and sent them off to France and other Occidental countries to be educated. Two of the children were Khan's half-uncles, Zaynu'l-'Ábidín and Niẓám-i-Dín. They were sent to Paris and remained there eighteen years. The elder studied literature, politics and diplomacy; the younger, Niẓám-i-Dín, attended the Polytechnic and was later 'crowned as a graduate' of the prestigious École des Mines. Both had long and distinguished careers in Persia. Niẓám received the title 'Engineer of the Empire' (Muhandisu'l-Mamálik), and for many years held the post of Minister of Mines, Public Works and Education. He also wrote a number of works on higher mathematics.

While his half-brothers were gone, Khan's father devoted much time to improving their holdings. Thus they grew rich even before receiving high posts.

Another of the four, and next in age to the Kalántar, served at the Court of the Crown Prince, Muẓaffar-i-Dín, who came to the throne in 1896. This half-brother, Muḥammad 'Alí Khán, was one of the brothers who married into the royal house.

The fourth and youngest lived out all his days in Káshán, looking after family properties. Famed as a hunter and horseman, he owned and raised hundreds of Arab and Persian thoroughbreds, as well as greyhounds, costly and trained for the hunt. This particular uncle of Khan's had a reputation for killing leopards with his bare hands. He was tall and exceptionally strong, and his technique was much appreciated by the villagers, whose sheep were being decimated by the marauding beasts.

It was he who taught Khan, a boy of fifteen then, to ride, by tying him to the saddle of a high-mettled horse and slapping the animal off at full gallop. The method worked, and Khan was grateful later on when he had to ride the steep rocky trails of roadless Persia.

Of still more importance was the help his uncle Niẓám-i-Dín provided in getting Khan into the Shah's College at a very early age.

The College had been established as a result of one of Náṣiri'd-Dín Sháh's visits to Europe.

Not only was the Shah impressed by Europe, but so was Europe impressed by the Shah. An Austrian ambassador, von Rosthorn, related that after the Shah left Vienna, portions of slaughtered sheep were found heaped in one of the palace rooms, where his cooks had killed the animals in the proper ritual way.

Invited to the races, His Majesty had declined, saying, 'It is not unknown to us that one horse will run faster than another horse.'

At an opera, it was said that he asked the orchestra to replay what they had begun with. They tried to comply, starting this selection and the other, but no, it was not that, and not that. They gave up finally, and began tuning their instruments. That was it. 'Just like the Persian music,' the delighted Shah said.

He so greatly admired the opera ballet dancers in their tutus that he returned home and put the whole harem into tutus, but of heavy materials, and worn over long tight trousers. This style, widely copied, was still to be seen in Persia, especially on older women, as late as the 1920s.

Although the mullás opposed the Shah – why bring back to Persia the ways of unclean foreigners? – all non-believers are najis, they said, not fit for Muslims even to touch – His Majesty decided to establish a college along European lines. To house it, he assigned one of his great palaces with gardens and a drilling ground, not far from the main Imperial Palace. He brought in professors from various European universities and placed the whole institution under the Ministry of Education.

The Shah then selected the student body – two hundred and fifty sons of the nobility and official families – and educated them at his own expense. They were day students only, but were fed the same food as the royal Court, at least in the beginning, although as time went on the college menu became a proverbial term for awful.

This Polytechnical College was the only Persian institution of any moment that was devoted to European languages and culture. When Khan was about nine, and educated beyond his years, the Kalántar and his brother Niẓám decided to place him in the royal College. Niẓám wrote a letter to the Minister of Education, which the little boy was to present, and his father had him compose an ode, a panegyric dedicated to the same Minister.

Thus equipped, Khan was escorted by his tutor to a garden where the Minister and several officials (no Persian is ever alone) were conducting their business. He approached the Minister and handed him the letter. The Minister read it. He looked at the child, much too little, he thought, to have done all that studying, and asked Khan if he could read it. Khan swiftly complied, his bit of a lisp not stopping him. Surprised, the Minister asked him another question or two. Khan begged leave to recite the ode he had composed in praise of the Minister. He then presented it, in his own excellent calligraphy, to the astonished official. Too young or not, Khan was accepted.

He studied at the College for about six years, always ahead of the others in his classes, though some were twice his age. Terror of his brother had made him a good scholar – so that even the Shah and others of the court began to hear of him. All day long at college, and often half the night at home, he applied himself to his work. This meant he did not grow as tall and heavy as the others with their sports, hunting and horseback riding. He had a head covered with shaggy black hair and large in proportion to his small body. Two flaming, disconcerting deep brown eyes peered from his thin face.

At first he was set to work in the French Department under a Persian who had studied abroad with Khan's uncles. This professor was a thin man, carefully dressed, with long, pointed mustachios. He had lived in France so long that he now spoke only broken Persian, but this remnant was still uttered in the accents of Káshán. Although he spoke good French and had published several textbooks on that language, he was more artist than linguist, and enjoyed the title of Head Court Painter (Naqqásh-Báshí). He was considered able enough to teach beginners' French, but sometimes became the butt of the better-trained students when they discovered he had forgotten some French word. When pressed, he would answer with an evasion. Once, when they learned he did not know the French word for toothbrush, some of them backed him into a corner and demanded that he tell them what the word was. His answer, in Káshí accents, was that the French did not eat the kinds of nasty foods that Persians did, and so they needed no toothbrush and had no word for it.

As Artist-in-Chief he trained many a painter, received a great many honors, and was still frequenting the Royal Court when Khan saw him in the 1920s at the time that he himself headed the Court of the Crown Prince Regent. The old teacher lived to be more than ninety.

The professor who most influenced Khan's future was probably an Englishman named John Taylor (in another MS, Tyler) who had lived in Persia many years, a man considered to be of deep learning, who had compiled an English–Persian dictionary. This man was very tall and wore mutton chop whiskers, his chin being clean-shaven. The first day that Taylor started a class in English, Khan enrolled. That afternoon he asked his tutor to take him to the Kalántar's office, and there announced the news to his father. The Kalántar, noted for his powers of precognition, said to his son, in that day when French was the preferred foreign tongue, 'This is an excellent chance for you. This study of English will open up vistas of future achievements. This will have a lasting effect upon your life. Go, and study English.'

With his usual energy, Khan applied himself to English. Feeling he did not get enough of it in class, when he left for home around four in the afternoon he would run after John Taylor, walking long-leggedly to his house, which was far away from the College, in the northwest quarter where were the foreign legations. All along the way, the small boy, books under his arm, notebook and pencil in hand, would run alongside, asking for English words. There is no record of what Taylor thought of it all, but he would deliver, even pausing in traffic – the passing crowds of men and children, some staring at the improbable couple, the vendors and beggars, the horseback riders – to set forth a word or rule.

In addition to Taylor, the College boasted a Frenchman who was believed to have a thorough knowledge of English. Monsieur Richard dressed half in the Persian fashion and half in the European, with an extra tall Persian hat of black lambskin fitted on his clean-shaven head. Persian fashion, the hat remained on, indoors and out. To the Persians, two Europeans greeting each other by doffing hats was comical. 'They wear these chamber pots,' a Persian told a friend, 'and take them off when they meet, and ask each other, "Do you care to urinate (Shásh dárí)?" Then they tell each other, "No, thank you", and replace their pots.' Western hats were always a source of interest – for instance, a gazebo is still called a European hat, no doubt from the shape of hats worn by early travelers to Persia from the Occident.

This Monsieur Richard, in his half-Eastern, half-Western clothes, his tall hat and long white beard, also attracted crowds by riding a large white donkey. Khan would walk alongside the donkey on many an occasion after school, jotting down lists of English words from Monsieur Richard.

The reason the boy memorized so many words, including thousands from his pocket dictionary by Samuel Johnson, was that he felt that was how to master a language. By the time he was eleven he was at the head of the English class and also taught another class, a large group of boys much older than himself.

Unfortunately, being a good student meant that Khan was persecuted all through his college years. His brother had many friends in the classrooms, always eager to join Husayn for excursions and parties and good times. This left little opportunity for study. When the higher-ups saw the results in their poor grades, some of Husayn's friends were given the bastinado. This enraged him, for he thought Khan might have had something to do with the bad reports. When the boy got home on the bastinado night his brother beat him without mercy, finally extracting a promise that henceforth Khan would do all the English exercises of Husayn's friends as well as his own. From then on Khan had to write many a theme for the others, each different as to matter and style. It helped his English along, though it added to his feelings of guilt.

Another of Khan's ordeals was in a class in higher mathematics. The Persian professor, Sulaymán Khán, had been trained by a famed mathematician-astronomer, Najmu'l-Mulk (the Star of Empire), the man who issued Persia's calendar-almanac every year.

Khan, committing everything to memory, regularly came out a winner in the weekly examinations, while the others regularly failed. They finally went on strike, telling Sulaymán Khán that the work was too hard, the assignments too long. His answer was, 'If this little boy can do the work, surely you good-for-nothings could apply yourselves too, and pass the tests.'

The result of this fateful answer was that the playboy element forbade Khan to answer any questions at the next examination. When the day came and the professor called on them, the boys sat silent, and when he called on Khan, Khan said he could not answer, since the lessons were too hard and too long. The professor, guessing what had happened, immediately threatened him with a severe punishment. Terrorized of both the known and unknown evils, Khan passed the test. That afternoon the whole class was whipped, while the worst trouble-makers got the bastinado.

Khan was afraid to go home afterward, certain that his brother would beat him, so he appealed for sanctuary at his uncle's house; seeking sanctuary (often in a mosque) is a venerable Muslim tradition. But the next day when he showed up at the College, a number of the big boys grabbed hold of him and lifted him up onto a shelf, a built-in niche about two feet below the ceiling and ten feet off the floor. Once they had him trapped up there, they produced thin, flexible switches from a pomegranate tree and spelled each other whipping him black and blue. They brought him down only when he screamed a promise never to outdo them again.

Whenever the Shah or this or that liberal statesman attempted any reform in Persia, the Shiah Muslim clergy rose up to block the plan. The Shah had barely managed to wrest a consent from the mullás to establish his College, where there would be (unclean) foreign teachers and foreign studies. To get this he was forced to include a class for Persian and religious studies, under a mullá in the usual large turban and clerical robes. A department for advanced studies included courses in Platonic philosophy and various branches of Muslim theology and culture. Khan had no time left over to study Arabic and the other higher Muslim courses. Only in later years did he find out that the learned mullá, Mírzá Ḥasan Adíb (Educator) who headed the Department was not only a Bahá'í but enjoyed the special rank of Hand of the Faith.

Khan did study the Persian classics and preliminary subjects in Islamic law; and with the erudite Adíb he learned the principles of Shiah Islam, 'The School of the Twelve Imáms', and read from the Qur'án, which, being in a tongue foreign to him, he could not understand.

The students were also given a certain amount of military drill. The teacher would line the boys up in the courtyard facing him. 'Each one raise your right leg,' he would bark. Inevitably, one day someone raised his left leg. Surveying the line, it was clear to the instructor that something was wrong, and he snarled, 'What son of a father burnt in Hell has raised up both his legs?'

In Persia you did not swear at an individual directly – you got better results swearing at his father as being in Hell or impugning his mother as practicing the oldest profession. A donkey boy, running along heavily burdened beasts in a caravan, would not swear directly at a given recalcitrant animal; he would insult the animal's owner's mother. In this way although the boy did not belong to a union or have any rights, he still managed to get back some of his own. There was of course no Society for the Prevention of Cruelty to Animals, or come to that, no SPCM or SPCW. Nobody much protested anyone's cruelty, be the victim man, woman or beast.

Khan's father was expert in calligraphy, especially in the Nasta'líq style, and it was he who taught Khan, giving him penmanship lessons at home, for the boy was far too busy with his Western studies to learn this art at college. The Kalántar knew that to be chosen for a high position a man must have not only connections and ability, but write a beautiful hand as well.

The calligraphic style he used had been brought into the world through a dream. It seems there was once, in the thirteenth century, a holy man named Mír 'Alí of Tabríz, and this man begged the Almighty to give him a writing more exquisite than any the world had ever beheld. Years passed by and his prayer went unanswered. Then one night the Imám 'Alí appeared to him in a dream.

'O, Mír 'Alí,' the Imám said, 'look thou at the concave and convex curves of the neck and eyes of a dove. By these be thou inspired to create thy script.' And Mír 'Alí, awakening, looked at the doves, and invented Nasta'líq.

Educated members of good family were all trained in this Nasta'líq writing, especially in its 'broken' form, <u>Shi</u>kastih, much more rapid and free.

As a child, Khan had already been set to copying the many scripts for which this or that leader was famous, so the Kalántar had laid a good foundation on which to build.

For contrast to the emphasis on calligraphy at this time, when Reza Shah Pahlavi seized the throne in 1925 he could not write at all. Worse yet for the art, steel pens had already been introduced from Europe, to say nothing of typewriters. Then came the atrocious ballpoints.[28]

To produce their lovely scripts, Persian calligraphers used only the thin brown Japanese reed, cut with a sharp knife and stubbed. The stub could be heard on the paper as one wrote, forming the curved letters, hence Bahá'u'lláh's reference to the shrill sound of His pen.

Ink was made from a black powder (so-called 'India ink'), in its own small container in the lacquered pen box, which was slipped into the owner's wide belt: for an example of this, see the portrait of Bahá'u'lláh's father, the Vazír, in Nabíl's *The Dawn-Breakers*. But then came fluid ink from Europe to replace the ink and water mixture. And with formerly endless time cut short, the production of handmade paper was curtailed, its use confined to official farmáns or elaborately-illuminated certificates of marriage.

One can only sigh and look back on what Sir William Jones, who wrote a Persian grammar first published in 1771, called 'perhaps the most beautiful manuscript in the world', a poem on Joseph and Zulaykha in the Oxford library. He describes the 'fine silky paper' favored by the Persians, 'often powdered with gold or silver dust', and the illumination of the first two leaves, and says 'the whole book is sometimes perfumed with essence of roses or sandal wood.'[29] (This is the source, we assume, of Fitzgerald's reference to 'youth's sweet-scented manuscript'.)

Sir William describes the ink, very black, which never fades out – and the 'Egyptian' reed pens, which can make 'the finest strokes and flourishes', also the extreme rapidity which the script permits.

So important was calligraphy to the mullás that the exercises in it and the grades accorded were as important to them as any studies in Occidental colleges are to us.

Although Khan's brother was his chief persecutor in those early days, there was love between them later on, and Ḥusayn Qulí <u>Khán</u> was proud of his younger sibling's success. In fact Ḥusayn claimed a lot of credit for Khan's later triumphs, ascribing them to hard work derived from the beatings he had kindly administered. Fear, discipline, work. All through Khan's life there was one obstacle after another to surmount, and the result was a stubborn determination to reach his goals.

One thing he was bitter about: the fact that for a century or more his country had been cowed by the threats or enticed by the favors of the two great imperialists, England and Russia, whose policy was to nip any native talent in the bud and impede any patriotic soul who dreamed of freeing his country from the foreign yoke.

Khan's uncle, the Minister of Mines and Public Works, found him capable in higher mathematics and decided to prepare the boy for a career in mining engineering, perhaps the most promising field in Persia at that time. He studied under a distinguished professor imported from France, whose name was Vauveille and who conducted his classes in French. The students were outfitted in the same uniforms worn by those in l'École des Mines back in France: dark blue jackets with light blue collars and cuffs, and light blue trousers, complete with belt and sword. Best of all, the sword was partly gilded.

It was the custom of Náṣiri'd-Dín Sháh to pay visits to the College, accompanied by a large entourage of Cabinet ministers, favored members of the Court, and European physicians. One such visit took place on an afternoon in spring. When he reached John Taylor's class the Shah asked the professor to have his best pupil write a theme on the blackboard. Taylor called on Khan.

'We meant your best pupil, not your smallest one,' remonstrated the Shah.

'That one is both,' Taylor answered.

Khan was about twelve and was decked out in his French École des Mines uniform and sword. Too small to reach to the top of the blackboard, he was given a chair to stand on, and proceeded swiftly to cover the board with an English theme, explaining the grammar as he wrote. One of the Shah's doctors, a distinguished Frenchman who spoke English, asked the boy to explain a certain point, was pleased with the correct reply, and told His Majesty that the youngster had capacity. The Shah, having inquired as to Khan's background, said this was no wonder, since he was the nephew of Niẓám-i-Dín Khán, who was crowned at the college in Paris – and that the family was noted for brains. As was the Shah's custom, he rewarded the boy with some pieces of gold.

About two years before he was assassinated (which means about 1894) this Shah, in spite of steady opposition from the mullás, was again persuaded, this time by his enlightened Prime Minister, Amínu'd-Dawlih, to send a large number of young students to France and other countries in Europe to learn the civilization of the West and introduce it into Persia. The Minister of Education was given the task of selecting which youths would be sent.

One morning, led by the officials of the College, about a hundred of the students were marched into the garden of the Gulistán, the royal residence. They were ordered to stand in a long line against the wall. Khan, being the smallest, was placed at the end of the line, that is, in Persia, the extreme left.

The Shah and his courtiers walked past the line of students, reviewing them several times. Each time when His Majesty reached the end of the line, he pointed Khan out as first choice.

Ultimately, twenty or thirty were chosen to go to Europe, but nothing came of it. Various incidents took place which yet again stirred up the mullás and put paid to the Government's liberal policy.

Still, that evening when Khan went home and told his father he was the Shah's first choice remained in memory, especially the Kalántar's joy.

Later, Khan envied the rich boys whose families sent them to Europe. As time went on, however, he was glad he had been obliged to stay on in Persia, since otherwise he might not have been led to the Bahá'í Faith. Besides, he came to see that those who had been sent away to study, theoretically so that they would return and contribute to the progress of Persia, were for the most part carried away by the freedom and the luxuries of life in Europe, particularly France; and all they brought back was disgust for what they now knew was the backwardness of Persia, but no knowledge of how to turn things around.

The returnees would even pretend to have forgotten how to speak Persian, although few had become letter perfect in a foreign tongue. There were, however, exceptions – a brilliant well-trained vanguard who prepared the way for the New Regime and the Persian Revolution, when they would become members of Parliament and officials of the new Government.

A story was told around the College of one student, sent off to Europe and later appointed a faculty member of the College, who had come back speaking broken Persian. This was when the College had only recently been founded, and the Minister of Education was the Shah's uncle, I'tidád-i-Salṭanih. This Minister, at luncheon with the faculty one day, asked the new returnee to pass the eggplant (bádinján, a word almost sacred to a Persian gourmet). Pretending he did not understand what was meant, having been abroad and forgotten the word, he waited till the Shah's uncle pointed out the dish. 'Oh,' said the returned traveler. 'You mean *aubergine*!' The Minister said nothing.

Afterward, the party adjourned to the college courtyard, a garden with a circular pool that had a fountain in the middle. Addressing the youth returned from foreign parts, the Minister said, 'Well, I see you have forgotten your own language. You no longer know the word bádinján. I am going to teach it to you all over again.'

Clapping his hands, the Minister ordered footmen to bring on the bastinado and the whip. Thrown flat on his back, his ankles bound to the horizontal pole which was held at each end by attendants so the raised feet were always in position to be beaten, the youth took a few heavy blows on his bare soles and then cried out, '*Bádinján! Bádinján!*'

While Khan's brother Ḥusayn was not much given to studying, he had a good mind and was quick at mathematics. He was selected to attend the classes in artillery conducted by a German officer, Herr Felmer, a veteran of the Franco-Prussian War. Another veteran, a colleague of Felmer's, headed the Infantry Department. Ḥusayn, though sinewy rather than heavily muscled, became a top athlete, known as such not only at the College but throughout Tehran. Trained by the two German officers, he later won the rank of General in the Persian Army.

After their father died, the Government bestowed the title he had held, that of Lord Mayor (Kalántar), on Ḥusayn and this became the family name. Khan ceased to use it, however, after the Shah gave him the title of Nabílu'd-Dawlih, so that for quite a time his family name was Nabíl. This haphazard taking of surnames, a headache for genealogists, was somewhat remedied later on by a law that tried to regularize matters. Time and circumstances have dealt with the confusion arising from the different surnames of Khan and Ḥusayn. Today, the Kalántar branch flourishes but there is no descendant left to carry on the other name.

Another faculty name that Khan recalled from college days was the noted French music master, Lemaire. His students studied European music and, thereafter, as performers and composers, contributed much to the development of their own. On religious holidays and festivals such as the Shah's birthday, the celebration included military parades, reviewed by the Shah and his Court ministers and grandees. Khan remembered always the excitement of coming first with the rest of his group, in their brilliant uniforms, leading the military procession, directly behind the college band under Lemaire's baton. Another memory was of the delicious picnics, the clear air and streams and waving trees, enjoyed on surveying trips in the mountains and plains around the throne city.

In after years, filling various posts in Paris and elsewhere, Khan would rediscover classmates from his early youth, most of them ranking high as he did himself, and found the old ties still firm. He learned, however, that friendships formed after those college years, during his long official career, based no doubt on his rank and the influence he could exert, ceased as soon as he returned to private life. There was always a childlike side to his nature, and he actually suffered when supposedly firm friendships proved to have been based on personal interests alone.

The Persians apparently have a story to illustrate everything that can ever happen throughout anyone's life. The story for this matter of friendships is about a philosopher who was invited to a banquet. When he arrived at the door in his usual humble garb, the servants would not let him in. He soon returned in a splendid robe, and was received with honor. As he sat at the banquet he dipped his sleeve in the broth and said, 'Drink your fill. You are the guest here, not I.'

Probably every friendship is based upon personal interests in one way or another: you are friends with the people you feel good with. But you and they and the situation can change. Bahá'u'lláh sums up the matter of true friendship in the Persian *Hidden Words*: 'Worldly friends, seeking their own good, appear to love one the other, whereas the true Friend [God or His Manifestation] hath loved and doth love you for your own sakes . . .'[30]

SEVEN

House of Oblivion

Meanwhile, Khan's mother had carefully amassed the necessary dowries for the two daughters. A colonel 'wooed' the elder one, Marzieh Khanum, for months without ever laying eyes on her – although she, of course, could see him, from a window, or from behind her veil. She was a girl so shy that, once married, she veiled even from her father; but such was the rasm, she had to go to bed with a total stranger.

He was much older, of a good family, and supposedly well-to-do, but soon after the wedding it was discovered that he was addicted to opium. Day and night, he and a male secretary spent their life sitting around a brazier of hot coals. With tongs they would lift a coal close up to a piece of opium, it being stuck to a porcelain ball connected to the mouth by a wooden pipe; and as was customary with opium addicts, they would let the smoke mingle with steam from endless cups of strong tea. In those days, one should add, smoking or eating opium was almost universal in Persia, and especially in the Army. Opium was widely known in the West at that time too. For example, New England's famed author, Louisa May Alcott became a user. Poor, gifted Marzieh, her married life was a hell. The couple did produce one child, a beautiful boy, but he died before he was two. The Colonel himself died a few years later – heavy users did not survive long, and it was probably just as well.

A few years later Marzieh was married to a man of family and property who owned land in the lovely summer villages north of Tehran, and who enjoyed the title of Surgeon General of the Army. Here again, her marriage was unhappy and ended in divorce. Years afterward, looking back at that time, she explained, 'It was blows all day and kindness all night.'

Then came a third suitor, a strikingly handsome one, a high government official from the province of Fárs. He too was much older than she, and also addicted to opium. The marriage ended with his death. The couple had produced one daughter, Gawhar-Malik, which means Royal Jewel. She married a cavalry officer and had three daughters, but he then died a hero's death in the conflicts following Persia's 1906 revolution. His horse came back, its saddle empty.

Khan's sister Marzieh was devoted to Royal Jewel, who was in every respect a poetic paradigm of Persian beauty: the gazelle-like eyes, whose black lashes were lances to pierce the heart; the fair, moon-like skin; the straight nose and small, not full-blown rose of a mouth; the sinuous, cypress-graceful body.

Every letter from Marzieh Khánum in later years described her unending fears and anxieties lest any harm come to Royal Jewel. Chief of her worries was any loss of weight, for healthy people must be at least plump, cháq (which also means sound). But any other worries would do as well. This was much the way of an old-time Persian lady's life: first she was a cossetted baby, then a painted, jeweled, decked-out and envied bride; then she birthed a procession of infants, quick or dead – and then almost in a single breath, presto!, yesterday's bride was a crone, rocking back and forth on the floor, a white kerchief on her head, forever bewailing her own physical complaints and forever detailing the illnesses and griefs of her progeny.

In many cases, besides these things, family feuds, gossip, and carrying out the rasm, she had nothing at all to occupy her mind.

As we saw, Khan himself had been subjected to much Shiah fanaticism while he was growing up. This became even stronger when his sister Hamideh married into the family of Lisánu'l-Mulk, a man whose account of the Bábí, and succeeding Bahá'í, Faith had been condemned by Bahá'u'lláh as a falsification of history, one which even an infidel would not have had the effrontery to produce.

The Shah had given the title of Lisánu'l-Mulk (Tongue of the Empire) to the grandfather of the man who married Hamideh, for his eminence as a historian and his ability as a poet. This Tongue of the Empire suffered from no false modesty, calling his history the *Násikhu't-Tavárikh* (the 'history to abrogate all previous histories') and using the nom de plume of Sipihr (the Lofty Firmament) for his poetry. Following the ingenious Persian custom, he would weave this name into the concluding verses of his poems to identify his work and prevent plagiarism. This weaving in of the takhallus, or pen name, required some poetic skill. Once when a friend of Khan's wrote a poem that, toward the end, featured a donkey, Khan's comment was, 'How well you placed the takhallus!'

Comte de Gobineau, first to bring word of Persia's new religion to the Western world, relied more than heavily on the *Násikhu't-Tavárikh* for his book *Les Religions et Philosophies dans l'Asie Centrale*, if we are to accept the testimony of A. L. M. Nicolas, who called Gobineau a 'savant on the cheap' for borrowing so much from the Persian historian. Indeed, Nicolas, who certainly did not clasp Gobineau to his bosom, says the diplomat's famous book is simply taken from a translation into minimal French of the *Násikhu't-Taváríkh* by a scholar named Lalezar, very brilliant, he says, if not always accurate.[31]

In any case, the *Abrogation of Histories* presented the Bábí, forerunner of the Bahá'í, Faith from the Shiah Muslim point of view and was, as one might well expect, hostile and irrational. Náṣiri'd-Dín Sháh, who butchered thousands of members of the new Faith, found no fault with the history, especially as it praised him and even linked this Qájár Shah of Turkish origins to ancient Iranian kings. He bestowed on the Tongue of the Empire gifts still greater in value than another writer had received from an earlier Shah, who is credited with pulling turquoises off a rosary and tossing them one after the next into a favorite poet's mouth at the conclusion of each line of his recital.

By the time Khan was brought to Tehran, the historian had died. His son, however, also noted as an historian and poet, like him received the title Tongue of the Empire. He too enjoyed a high position in the Court and became a man of great means, thanks to the many gifts lavished on him, and his father before him, by the Shah.

When the second Tongue of the Empire died, the title went to his eldest son, the man who married Khan's sister Hamideh. (An onlooker might think the academic skills were somewhat diluted by the third generation.)

As small boys, Khan and his brother had often visited the palatial homes of the second Tongue of the Empire, Mírzá Hidáyat Khán who (genealogy forever rearing its hydra head) had in fact married Khan's youngest maternal aunt.

Khan remembered the garden courts, each one high-walled, enclosing its trees and rare flower beds and turquoise pool of water at the center. The men's reception halls dated from the eighteenth century, were well kept up, and the best of them, the audience hall, was decorated floor to ceiling with diamond-flashing mosaics of tiny mirrors set in floral and geometric designs, that would come alive when anyone walked past. Above the great hall a second story opened onto an inner courtyard, the home of all the veiled women, the Andarún or the 'Within'. The men's quarters, the Bírúní or the 'Without', where guests came, gave onto a long terrace called the mahtábí (the place where the moon shines), which in turn looked down on large gardens where fruit trees abounded – figs, pomegranates, white mulberry. These fruits were the sweetest and most fragrant in the country, for the trees were transplanted from the Shah's own domains, and Khan and his cousins would climb into the branches and blissfully gorge.

Another courtyard housed the stables and there the children could admire splendid Arab colts and their royal dams and sires. This again brings to mind the question of sha'n, alluded to before. The horse manure was dried outside the stable walls, visible to all who passed the mansions of the rich. Heaps were piled at the entrance to each stall. Larger piles were kept above the private, underground bath house to be used as fuel for heating the water. Horse manure also served to cook lamb stew for the stablemen: it was set afire and the stew, in covered clay pots, was buried in it to cook for hours. The young people found this dish more appetizing than the magnificent dinners served at their parties, and they would trade off part of their sumptuous meal with the stablemen for some of the stew.

This second Tongue of the Empire was a short, bearded man with a towering forehead, gentle in manner and courteous to all, even the children. His conversation was literary and philosophical, and included references to famed men of the Occident. He had a large staff of servants of different races and colors. Whenever he went to the Imperial Court, he rode on a gentle horse with a large retinue walking before and behind, the chief ones at his stirrups. Such processions were often seen on Tehran streets leading to the royal palace, and one evaluated the rank of the personage by the number of his attendants. Younger men were escorted by riders on capering Arab horses. Later on, when the Shah got back from Europe, the royal family rode about in carriages drawn by four to eight horses, while those of lesser rank rode in two-horse carriages with a footman on the box, and outriders, beautifully mounted, leading the way. Never did a man of note walk on the street alone. Not even his children went unattended.

Leading scholars, statesmen and clergy flocked to this Tongue of the Empire's home; and the nation's policy was often discussed here and later presented to the Shah and his Prime Minister for adoption. Many a cabinet was chosen here, and plans made to replace this or that provincial governor with another. There was much talk here of furthering and spreading the Platonic doctrines of Persia's Avicenna – Abú-'Alí Síná – in opposition to orthodox Shiah theology.

When the parties were for politicians, there was plenty of forbidden wine – rich wines from Shíráz. Shíráz, incidentally, has given yet another word to English: sherry. Natives of Shíráz were imported to Spain in the early Middle Ages, to teach the Muslims there how to make wine, and they settled in the Spanish town of 'Xeres' (like the wine's name, a corruption of Shíráz).[32]

Hour after hour, games would be played: chess (shatranj) which goes back at least to before the Arab conquest and was brought from

India, Browne says, in the days of Núshírván the Just.[33] Introduced into Europe before the end of the eleventh century, the game was widely spread. Backgammon (nard), called 'tables' in the England of the twelfth and thirteenth centuries, was another favorite.

They ate endless appetizers – roasted game birds, meats, fish brought in at full gallop from the Caspian or high mountain streams, fruits, confections – all this until midnight when the actual banquet was served on the floor, it being first carpeted with a cloth elaborately embroidered or hand-printed, laid over a large mat of thick leather. Servants in their stockinged feet would walk about the banquet cloth, arranging and serving.

Khan, considered a prodigy, would be brought before the company to recite an ode he had himself composed, or to read them a poem in English or French.

The second Tongue of the Empire, from his years of research, developed cataracts as he aged, and was reduced to being helpless and blind. When guests came no more he would spend his evenings with the ladies in the 'Within', dictating history to his two eldest sons, hour after hour. His memory was phenomenal. In the course of the day he could compose a poem of a hundred verses in praise of the Shah or whatever, and dictate it perfectly that night. Another strange faculty he developed in his blindness was that he always knew the time.

Ultimately, the Shah's European surgeon operated on the historian-poet and restored his sight. However, he died at fifty-five, and 'Abdu'l-Husayn Khán, who was by then Khan's brother-in-law, inherited his father's titles and prerogatives. Then came the Revolution of 1906. The Shah was diminished; he became a constitutional ruler, no longer all-powerful as in the old time – and many of the authors, artists and poets about the Court were ousted and reduced to poverty.

Khan's mother and aunt, matchmakers like most Persian ladies, had always wanted to see a marriage between Khan and one of the historian's daughters – betrothals in the Persia of that day could begin with a child's birth. But fate or not, as he grew to marriageable age, say fourteen, Khan managed to evade their schemes, which would have pinned him at home, and the future would see him off to the world of the West.

Who knows what wish as to his future Khan made at a shrine-tree growing in his aunt's beautiful home. During two hundred years this tree had grown to great size on one side of an inner courtyard, with its branches cutting through the roof of the building. It was a strange tree, rather like an elm, but no other of its kind was to be found in the whole region. Because the household attributed miracles to the tree, the base of it had been made into a kind of shrine. There on the eve of Friday –

Friday being the Muslim Sabbath – they would light wax candles, as many candles as they had wishes: healing for a sick child or sick husband, or for one's own self, such were women's wishes. A man might wish for a better future, light a candle, and drive a nail into the trunk of the tree.

A brother of the third Tongue of the Empire had inherited properties nearby, across a large inner courtyard connected by a covered passageway. His given name was 'Abbás-Qulí K͟hán, and since he was also a poet and an historian, the nom de plume of Sipihr (Lofty Firmament) had been handed down to him. However, this man was considered a second class citizen in the family and was the butt of family jokes. He married into the family of a K͟hán of the Qájár dynasty, and outlived his elder brother, the chief heir, by many years. He held the rank of Minister of Authors at the Shah's Court, that is, he headed the department to which all authors belonged.

In the early twenties, when Khan headed the Crown Prince Regent's Court, this Sipihr often called on Khan at the palace. By then an ancient, past eighty, short of stature, with a long white beard, in flowing robes worn by scholars in an age long gone, he came like a symbol of yesteryear to pay homage to the Shah or the Crown Prince, and everyone there showed him great respect.

It is worth noting that the first Lodge of Freemasonry in Persia was established in the home of this family. There was, in one corner of Sipihr's great courtyard, a secret stairway which led through an underground passage to a small, hidden, roofed-over courtyard with a tiled fountain playing at the center. This little court was paved with marble. On all four sides, connecting rooms opened into it, and light came in through a skylight overhead. Here in this carefully hidden place, Persia's first Lodge was established, and two leading members were Tongue of the Empire and his brother Sipihr.

Freemasonry was introduced into Persia from England, where that nation's first Grand Lodge had been founded in 1717. The man responsible was a brilliant young diplomat, a Persian-Armenian named Malcolm Khan. He was considered not only clever, he was also thought to have magical powers – to be one who could, for example, transform one substance into another. Freemasonry, on account of Malcolm Khan's reputation, was thus surrounded with even more mystery than elsewhere – much as it had been in Catholic Europe. Beginning with the Constitution of Clement XII, *In eminenti* (1738), the society was condemned for such matters as secrecy, and for deism independently of any creed. Catholics may not join Freemasonry, since, particularly in Europe, its aim was thought to be (according to Pope Leo XIII) 'the overthrow of the whole religious, political and social order based on Christian institutions' and the establishing, instead, of 'naturalism'.

Small wonder that the Shiah hierarchs condemned Malcolm Khan as a heretic – that is, in their warped understanding of Muslim Scripture, one who must be put an end to, as he did not deserve to live. Accordingly, the Shah banished him – shut the doors of Persia in his face. Still, try as they might, no one was able to discover the secret headquarters of the forbidden heresy, and the name of the surmised place, a corruption of the French franc-maçonnerie, was known among the people as farámúsh-Khánih, house of oblivion. Rumor spread that, in their hideaway, Tongue of the Empire and his brother Sipihr as well as many other members of the Lodge were practicing alchemy.

As a child, Khan found the rumors fascinating, and so too, the term oblivion-house. He did not dream that he himself, as Persia's Chief Diplomatic Representative in the capital city of America, beyond the sea, would one day become a Mason and go through the various degrees to the thirty-second, thus becoming the highest Mason among the Persians. Only later were Bahá'ís asked not to join the Freemasons, primarily because they are a secret society, hence not universal.

Fascinated in her turn by this mysterious order and by her father's Masonic ring and his 'Almas' diamond lapel-pin with its scimitar, Khan's small daughter would leave her chair, go to the end of the table, sit on his lap while the family were finishing luncheon, and beg him to tell her the 'secret' of the Masons.

Malcolm Khan was recalled from exile by Náṣiri'd-Dín Sháh and sent out as ambassador to various countries, among them England. He was given the title of Prince, and because he knew the ins and outs of Europe, his influence at Persia's Court grew until he became a serious rival of the Shah's favored Prime Minister, Amínu's-Sulṭán, 'the great Atábak'.

Malcolm Khan was actually a pioneer when it came to introducing modern liberal and social ideas into Persia – ideas which, opposed by the Court and especially by the clergy, paved the way for the Revolution of 1906, a revolution that really began when the socialist Mírzá Riḍá of Kirmán killed the sixty-five-year-old Náṣiri'd-Dín Sháh on the eve of his Jubilee (1896), when that tyrant had ruled Persia singly and alone for almost fifty years. The revolution reached its peak with the replacement of Persia's absolute monarchy by constitutional rule.

In 1906 Khan, his American wife Florence and their baby Rahim, on their way to 'Abdu'l-Bahá in 'Akká, stopped over in Rome, where Prince Malcolm Khan was the Persian Ambassador. As an old family friend, he entertained them lavishly in the imposing embassy, where he had on display many portraits of European rulers autographed in friendship for him.

EIGHT
Death Owns All Seasons

When Khan was fourteen, the ground gave way. At first it was thought that his father was simply tired out from overwork. He continued to go to his office and to remain in the apartment he had there, but his condition worsened and they brought him home and had several doctors in to treat him. He did not respond, and toward the end his legs swelled up – a form of dropsy, it was thought – and soon he died.

Khan's father had been ill a long time, yet when they got his body ready for burial, it was all beautiful and white. Then they turned his face toward Mecca, and he was readied for burial with camphor and spices, to the thud of hired mourners beating their breasts, and the voices of mullás chanting from the Qur'án.

They were burying him where he wanted to be: with no small difficulty had his grave dug at the shrine of Yaḥyá, posterity of the Holy Imáms. His entire family attended the Kalántar's funeral, following the coffin, many, even passersby, taking turns to shoulder it and thus gain merit. The pace was as rapid as possible. The whole ritual, from the moment of death to burial, was finished within twenty-four hours.

The procession wound from the house to the graveyard, about a mile distant, Khan unseeing as he walked. Beside him his Paris-educated uncle, Muhandisu'l-Mamálik, a close friend of the Prime Minister, tried to comfort him. 'So long as you have me for your uncle, you have nothing to grieve about. As soon as you have finished your studies, you are to live at my house and manage my household. With your languages, too, I can make you an interpreter to the Prime Minister and bring you to the Imperial Court.'

Later on, as a Bahá'í, Khan understood why his father had wished to be buried in this cemetery so crowded with dead that only the family's rank could have persuaded the shrine authorities to let them have a place so precious: at the very threshold of the Holy Saint's tomb. He learned that a number of Bahá'í martyrs lay thereabouts, and not only they, but also (it was believed) for a time the carefully hidden remains of the Báb and the youth who died with Him. When Khan's uncle died, they had a burial room built especially for him, close to the Kalántar's grave.

Now the family's life had to be re-arranged.

It is not easy to explain what the death of the Kalántar meant. Gone would be the immediate family's high place in the world, their all-important sha'n. Gone, unless the young boys could help, adequate funds, maybe at times even adequate food on the table. Their widowed mother could do nothing, nor could her daughters, their own problems not a few, be of much help. Quite apart from searing grief, Khan was laid waste. Why had they lost their mainstay, that gentle, dignified, wise and witty being who, wherever he came, created his own ambience of peace? But Khan remembered from his father's teaching that you do not say 'why' to Almighty God: 'Whoso sayeth "why" or 'wherefore" hath spoken blasphemy!'[34]

The family moved out of their house to another, which happened to be nearer the shrine. The older sister lived with them, with her son, but the baby sickened of a throat infection and died. That same year hundreds of thousands died in Persia of the cholera, which first appeared in Mashhad, a great place of pilgrimage and the capital of Khurásán. It was not even suspected to have reached Tehran when Khan and a few others were stricken. He used to say the violence of the cholera was beyond description. Medical aid proved useless and at the terminal stage Khan's facial bones and his fingers and toes turned black. His devout Shiah sister hurried to Yaḥyá's shrine and knelt and begged the Saint to spare his life; when she reached home his crisis had passed and he was on the way back to life.

The next year Khan finished his college and went to live at his uncle's substantial house, with the usual series of walled courts and gardens and separate buildings to house the men and women.

Khan's uncle, Muhandisu'l-Mamálik, had a daughter from an early marriage which had ended in divorce. By the time Khan came to live with him, this uncle had already taken a young Qájár princess to wife, a grand-daughter of Fatḥ-'Alí Sháh. The bride's father had been only an infant when that fertile Shah died in 1834. The couple produced half a dozen children in almost as many years, the two eldest, at the time Khan joined the household, being about seven and nine. Khan taught them French and a mullá was engaged to teach them their own Persian and the rudiments of Islam. Though so young, Khan was also placed in charge of all household affairs, including the management of a large body of servants, grooms, stablemen and the like.

Khan's uncle always kept a stable of fifteen to thirty Arab horses of various breeds. It was a real joy to Khan to ride these horses and see to it that they were well-groomed and their stables kept in good order.

Every day, attended by a number of grooms, he would gallop through the city gate, over the moat, into the freedom of the countryside.

The year following Khan's arrival it was decided that the Princess, with her mother, children and lady companions and maids, should be sent on a visit to the family's ancestral villages near Káshán, some one hundred and fifty miles from Tehran.

At that time black Percheron horses imported from Russia were favored by the wealthy class to draw their handsome carriages, and Khan's uncle's Percherons were considered the best in town. As the caravan of about thirty persons, with carriage horses and pack mules, started out, Khan rode one of the Percherons, but along the way he found it too powerful to control, and exchanged it for his usual Arab mount. Peasants stared at the carriages, still a novelty outside the capital. Covered litters mounted on shafts hitched to two mules, one ahead, one behind, were still high fashion for ladies to travel in, while their attendants rode on donkey back or in palanquins bound to either side of a mule. Various obstacles slowed Khan's caravan to about ten miles a day: roads – a courtesy title – that wound over rocky terrain, the need to make and break camp each day, the delicately-reared ladies.

Khan was greatly stirred up at leaving the capital after it had been his home for most of his years, and as the days passed, suffered extremely from homesickness for his immediate family. After two weeks of it the caravan reached Burz-Ábád, a few miles from Káshán, and the new arrivals spent the entire summer receiving visits from and paying visits to innumerable uncles, aunts, cousins and other relatives of every degree of kinship. A number of hunting parties were organized and, best of all, there were old-timers who showed Khan certain houses where his parents had spent their honeymoon, long past. They did not set foot in Káshán itself, because of the terrible, dry summer heat, and what its effect might be on the ladies and small children, let alone the others. That autumn they got back to the capital and Khan had the joy of being with his mother, sisters and brother again.

About this time the so-called Tobacco Régie was established, which gave Khan his first opportunity to be out on his own. With Khan's uncle as intermediary, the Prime Minister made certain arrangements with a British tobacco corporation and the Shah then gave that firm a monopoly over the entire tobacco crop of Persia, the Shah and ministers to receive a quarter of the profits each year.

To promote the enterprise, the Régie brought in officials from England, Greece and other countries. All these people needed interpreters, especially to communicate from Persian into English and French, and a few young men, mostly from the nobility, were engaged to form a secretariat. Khan's uncle introduced him to the

General Manager, a tall, striking Briton named Ornstein, and was given what was considered a very high salary, although he was the youngest of the interpreters. This pleased him much, for at his uncle's, while all his needs were seen to, he received only pocket money, which did him no good with his free-spending friends.

Now he could help his mother and also buy clothes in the European style.

The young interpreters were all destined to play important roles in Persia's constitutional government when it came into being about fifteen years later. One of them was Ḥusayn-Qulí Khán Navváb (Nabob), so named because his family had served the British in Persia and India for generations, some as Persian, some as British subjects. They were all educated in England and wore English attire, the only difference being their Persian hats. Ḥusayn-Qulí Khán Navváb kept his Persian citizenship and after the Revolution entered the Persian Foreign Office and later was elected to Parliament, becoming an influential member. Around 1910 he was Minister of Foreign Affairs, and it was he who instructed Khan (who headed the Persian Legation in Washington at that time) to apply to America's President to recommend an American Treasurer-General and other financial advisers for service in Persia. This was the genesis of W. Morgan Shuster's role there, which Shuster later on described in his book, *The Strangling of Persia*.

Still another interpreter – considerably older than Khan – was a man of the same name, Ali-Kuli Khan, but no relation. At first the British called Khan junior and the other senior, but later on they were so impressed by Khan's speed in finishing his work as contrasted to the other's slow pace they took to calling Khan the senior.

That other Ali-Kuli Khan served Persia at St Petersburg for many years, eventually becoming Chargé d'Affaires at that Legation while Khan was serving as Chargé d'Affaires in Washington. The other man was a willing friend of the Russians, who had established a 'sphere of influence' in north Persia, and as a result received an important post as chief of a division in Persia's Foreign Office. He became Minister of Foreign Affairs prior to the end of World War I.

In November 1919, when the Persian Government named Khan as a member of Persia's Peace Delegation to the Versailles Conference, the same other Ali-Kuli was, as Foreign Minister, appointed to head that Delegation. (His title was Musháviru'l-Mamálik.)

The tobacco monopoly had hardly established itself throughout Persia when the mullás rose up and declared that Náṣiri'd-Dín Sháh had sold Persia's sovereign rights to the British. The Chief Mujtahid, or High Priest, came out with his written verdict that this tobacco monopoly was exactly the same as 'waging war on the expected Qá'im' – the Awaited One of Islam. The people rioted and the Shah cancelled his Concession. This was the first step in divesting the Shah of his one-man rule, and it led finally to the Revolution under his successor, Muẓaffari'd-Dín, and the establishment of constitutional government.

The abrupt ending of the Tobacco Régie had a strange effect on Khan's young life. For one thing, no more funds. For another, there would be no more association with colleagues from the Occident. One fact was certain – after so much exhilaration he could no longer return to his humdrum job as manager of his uncle's household. Khan looked about for some European enterprise where he could use his talents, but there were almost none in the country at that time. One, a concession to operate a newly-installed line of horse-drawn tramways on a few of the main thoroughfares of the capital, had been given to a Belgian, but he had already engaged a number of Armenian clerks at low salaries, and offered little to an ambitious young man, fresh from the glories of the Tobacco Régie. In addition to the trams, there was a Belgian company which had recently opened a narrow-gauge railway to join the capital with the shrine of Sháh 'Abdu'l-'Aẓím, four miles to the south under its golden dome. Most Persians had never before seen such modern transportation, and were struck with awe at beholding the toy trains. But here, too, Khan found no opening door.

Nothing for him, anywhere, for the very first time in his whole life. Here he was, trained, qualified, after years of struggle, educated in English and French, familiar with Western culture, and all of it suddenly useless, gone – and he trapped in a blind alley, facing a stone wall. All the past now worse than useless because the old ways were closed off to him and he could not go back again.

He looked about him, and pondered what he had heard of life at the Imperial Court. Theoretically it should have been an example to the nation, actually it was only a succession of scandals. The road to riches and favors was to play clown to the bored Shah. Cringing flattery, and the glorification of the Shah's slightest word or gesture, were indispensable. The Government was simply that agency which administered the continual rivalry for Persia between Russia and England. Whichever of the two powers was in the ascendant would raise its chosen people to the rank of minister, and they would rule, ostensibly under the Shah; then, what with bribery and intrigue, agents of the other side would force a crisis and raise up ministers of their own. Russia's aim in the battle for Persia was to fulfill the testament of Peter the Great, master the Persian Gulf and then conquer India. England's aim was to continue her control of India, and in line with this, to establish 'spheres of influence' in Persia and all the other countries which fell within that grand design. It was geography that made the plateau of Iran the critical battleground. Not even the fine-honed brain of a Machiavelli could have produced the methods which the two powers contrived for the strangling of Persia. The Shiah clergy controlled the masses, and were justly feared by the Shah and the Court. With secret funds, the two opposing imperialists bought up some of the clergy. If any liberal, progressive change were urged by some forward-looking minister upon the Shah, the clergy would instantly mount their pulpits and cry out. European ways, they screamed, European ideas, would undermine the Muslim Faith. Those modern inventions and concepts were Satan's work, and none in the whole land of Iran should learn a foreign tongue.

In spite of it all, Náṣiri'd-Dín had managed in the 1850s to establish his Royal College, and to bring in European professors who were able to reach (out of Persia's perhaps nine million inhabitants) three hundred students. He did this because he had to appease the progressive elements — socialists, radicals — that threatened the ruling class. No women were involved, of course. They were to be taught only rudimentary Islam, and nothing else. 'To whom does Persia belong?' someone asked a Persian woman. 'Why, to the Shah,' she answered.

In these troubled waters, people fished: the Russians, the British, the Shah, the clergy. The masses, in those days of restricted communication, had never heard of democracy. Meanwhile the Bahá'ís had 'Abdu'l-Bahá's rousing words to His countrymen, the book *Secret of Divine Civilization*, written in 1875 but not yet widespread, where among much else he told them they could learn from other nations, and even from animals.

Young as he was, Khan saw that all these forces at work inevitably put paid to national progress. He also saw that, with the usual exceptions, preferment at Court depended neither on education nor ability. It was accorded at whim to those who could best flatter a minister or even to someone favored for no detectable reason, or perhaps for reasons best not examined.

There was an Áqá Ibráhím, in charge of refreshments for the Shah, whose son, 'Alí-Asghar Khán, the Amínu's-Sulṭán, had found favor at the Imperial Court. With no background or particular acquired knowledge he was raised to the rank of Chief Minister of the Court, then to that of Prime Minister, supreme ruler of the Empire, second only to the Shah himself. A man bursting with energy, dynamic, good-looking, he was a favorite with the Czar's representatives, who used him to checkmate the British. To him, an upstart, ministers and statesmen, whose families had enjoyed high office for generations, came to Court and paid homage every day. The few who held out were either deprived of leading positions, exiled as governors to distant provinces, or sent out as envoys to unimportant posts abroad.

In the northern part of the capital, this Amínu's-Sulṭán built himself a magnificent walled park, enclosing a number of European-style palaces, the like of which had never been seen in Iran. These buildings were furnished with rare and costly objects brought in from Asia and Europe, and boasted a large number of cabinets containing the finest examples of lacquer work, of calligraphy, of miniature painting from the time of the first Elizabeth's contemporary, S͟háh 'Abbás the Great.

During the long years when Amínu's-Sulṭán was in power, the grandees of Persia did not fail to present him with other treasures from their own collections, receiving in return titles, governorships, high army posts, offices of State. The great Khans who guarded the nation's frontiers also sent him gifts, for example, mounts bred by them, so that his stables teemed with the finest of Arab and Persian strains.

This remarkable Prime Minister, who ultimately received the high title of Atábak-i-A'ẓam (Father-Lord the Supreme) spent all his evenings in his park, surrounded by the leading ministers of Court and State, the tenure of each of them depending upon his will. Here, during nights given over to wine, music and various other forms of entertainment, the affairs of Persia were discussed and settled.

Those who had been educated abroad would serve as emissaries between the Atábak and the Europeans, and Khan's uncle, Niẓámi'd-Dín K͟hán, was the leader of this group. No matter how much the Atábak needed these men, their weight and their prestige, they could not stay on his good side for long unless they joined his revels. As the night wore on and the wine flowed faster and their jokes became increasingly obscene, the most powerful men in Persia could be seen literally making donkeys of themselves: a high-ranking official loudly braying as his contribution to the party, or another scrambling around on all fours, with a handsome page boy riding on his back.

As the Persian proverb had it, from its very wellspring the water was mud.

A very few of the nation's great would not bend the knee to the Atábak or show themselves at his carousals. One of these was Amínu'd-Dawlih, a true aristocrat, and a champion of reform. He too, early on, had built an extensive and beautiful park to live in. A walled park is Persia's heaven: paradise is an Avestan word – Persian firdaws – and means a park enclosed by walls. And here a handful of men had put up their own heaven on earth. But the people this one gathered around him were persons of dignity and culture, with no mind for the Prime Minister and his unspeakable frolics. For a long period, Amín opposed the Prime Minister and as a result, though he enjoyed the Shah's favor, he held no office at all.

Another like Amínu'd-Dawlih was Khan's eldest paternal uncle, Iqbálu'd-Dawlih, chief officer of the Shah's Court and a devotee of hunting and life in the outdoors. The Shah, a great hunter himself, could not do without this man's companionship, especially summers when His Majesty would visit the game preserves in the Alburz mountains. It was expected that the Shah would make this uncle of Khan's Prime Minister, but Russia and the mullás supported the Atábak and this was an obstacle that the Shah could not surmount. Khan's uncle did, however, finally live to see the day, early in the reign of Muẓaffari'd-Dín Sháh (1896–1907), when he found himself Prime Minister.

Prince Malcolm Khan, clever leader of the underground reform movement, was another rival of the Atábak's, who duly made the Shah send Malcolm Khan away into exile as Ambassador to the Court of St James.

NINE

The Mad Mírzá

Someone less determined might easily have gone the suicide route, for when he found all doors closed to him, Khan took to introspection and found the world desolate. He alternately reached out for bubbles of hope and fell back into despair. Then, all of a sudden, he became the darling of a noble family who valued him for his company alone and whose sons would remain his close friends over a span of many years.

The father was Prince Sulṭán Ibráhím Mírzá, his title being Mishkátu'd-Dawlih. A man of great wealth, he owned property in the bazaars, as well as gardens and villages to the north of the capital and elsewhere in Persia. This prince was a great-grandson of Fatḥ-'Alí Sháh (how monotonously one has to report this provenance when dealing with biographies of the time), and his own father before him, Imám-Qulí Mírzá, had all his life been governor of the city and province of Kirmánsháh. Like many of his kin, Ibráhím Mírzá was often received at the Imperial Court, and he had married a fair Qájár princess, sister to the wife of one of Persia's great liberals, the previously-mentioned Amínu'd-Dawlih, who had introduced a number of European reforms into Persia.

The only trouble with Prince Ibráhím Mírzá was that, although both intelligent and brilliant, he should by rights have been shut up in an insane asylum for the rest of his life. Only his position in society kept him out. Not a day passed when he did not fly into a maniacal rage.

His estate in Tehran was palatial. We can imagine it from other opulent houses described by S. G. W. Benjamin, America's first envoy to Persia, who arrived in Tehran at about the same time as Khan's family. President Chester Arthur had charged Benjamin with the task of establishing America's first legation there. When the administration changed, Benjamin went back to the United States and published his classic *Persia and the Persians*, illustrated, with many carefully observed details of the scene which a born Persian might well have ignored as everyday matters known to all.

The street entrance to the Prince's town house may well have been ornamented with brick and honeycomb work much like that of the Alhambra, and with glazed tiles. Such entrances were formed 'by a recession of the street wall, in a semi-circle furnished with seats and niches, and roofed by an arch'. The arch, Benjamin says, 'was practised in Iran before the Parthenon and the Colosseum'.[35] Some of the Prince's buildings here or up country may well have been similar to one of the royal pavilions that Benjamin also described: this had an arched ceiling covered with bas-relief designs in stucco, gilded, or painted green and scarlet. Colored, spiral columns supported the dome. These columns were made of rough-trimmed branches overlaid with ga<u>ch</u> (a plaster of lime and gypsum mixed with sand and pounded marble) and the plasterers would turn them into spirals or fluted shafts. Commenting on the skills of Persia's architects, Benjamin says that many of them had no idea how closely they were repeating the work of ancestors as far back as the Achaemenians. There were divans in the recesses of the pavilion, and on the floor glowed priceless rugs, perhaps of silk, or perhaps those velvety rugs of Ká<u>sh</u>án which the inhabitants say are woven from the ninth combing of the wool. The pavilion's wide windows of intricate stained glass like a 'Gothic window' could be opened onto the park.[36]

The Prince's central mansion was built in European style and furnished with pieces brought back from Europe when he had attended the great Paris Exposition – one of the few palaces in the capital that was so furnished. But he also had a magnificent estate in <u>Sh</u>imírán, collective name for the cool mountain villages to the north. Here at least one great room may well have been walled to the ceiling with individual, precious glazed portrait tiles, and its flooring slashed through with a wide channel to let in a stream of melted snow from the Alburz.

The Prince's eldest son was fourteen, while the other two were eleven and nine. The fourteen-year-old's name was Qulám-'Alí Mírzá (Prince-Slave of Imám 'Alí) but when a small child he received from the Shah the title of Mu'ín-i-Khalvat.

Such titles were easily come by in those days – through the good offices of a well-placed courtier and a certain amount of gold pieces, some of which found their way into the hands of the Shah. Where the nobility was concerned, however, children of both sexes were given titles. They showed the attachment of the recipient to His Majesty, or to the Court or the Empire, and in other cases they had to do with the recipient's talents, his calling or attainments (for example, King of All Historians, Chief of the Calligraphers, and the like).

The fourteen-year-old had recently come back from attending the Paris Exposition with his father. He was a beautiful boy, and had the fair skin, the long, thickly-lashed eyes, a trifle on the slant, of all the Qájár tribe, most of whom looked like the people in old Persian miniatures. Slight of form, delicate, and of limited education, he was, unlike his father, outgoing and affectionate. His parents worshipped him. He had something wrong with one knee which, later on, turned out to be tuberculosis of the bone, and the doctor who treated him was an American attached to the Presbyterian Mission college in Tehran, a Dr Wishart from Indiana. It was Khan who translated for the doctor during his many visits, and that was how, through his knowledge of English, Khan became friends with the family. The doctor did his best and even performed an operation, saving the patient's life, but the knee joint remained stiff ever after.

The young invalid became attached to Khan, who joked with him and made him forget his ailment, so that the anxious father implored Khan to visit the boy every day. Before long they had installed him in a handsome room at the mansion, and he had become like a member of the family and, as at his uncle's, now gave orders to a large staff. They assigned him two horses and two attendants of his own.

The little prince was a natural-born musician, and, with the nail of his forefinger, plucked expertly on the sitár, the three-stringed Persian guitar. He also played the piano, his father being one of the very few who had, up to this time, imported that instrument.

What marred Khan's happy days and nights was simply the ugly mental condition of the father. Ibráhím Mírzá enjoyed beating up the servants and would contrive one excuse after another to justify his brutalities. (If we want to find like examples of unbridled sadism in the West, we have only to look at the canings in certain English public schools, described in memoirs of that day.) Neither were the maids over in the women's quarters spared. Their cries did not carry to where Khan lived, although inevitably he knew what was going on.

Not content with flogging his servants, the Prince had some of them hauled off to jail, keeping them there sometimes for weeks. This was dreaded more than his whip because of conditions in the prison.

If a servant tried to leave the Prince's service, he, powerful as he was, simply made it impossible for the man to find work elsewhere. In other words, the cruelty was part of the job. In those tyrannical days, when anyone, from the Shah down, could oppress those beneath him, the people endured it all, considering it the way life was.

Because Khan was privileged in the household, some of the servants did come and beg him to intervene. He, despite his youth, and knowing it was not his place to speak up against so important an older man, tried to help them; and in the beginning his overtures on their behalf had some effect. Khan's temerity might well have brought blows on himself, for the Prince was known all over town as the Mad Mírzá, but because of his ailing son's dependence on Khan, and also taking into account Khan's family connections and education, he paid some attention to the diplomatically-worded protest.

However, the Prince began little by little to resent Khan's interference in what he regarded as his own private business. He knew himself to be a generous employer in matters of pay and perquisites, and saw no reason why his servants should resent his outbursts.

All this led to a crisis atmosphere so far as the Prince and Khan were concerned. Khan felt like a brother to the sick boy and did not wish the pleasant relationship to end, but he could not bear to witness the diseased cruelty of the father.

Fortunately, the Prince was invited out several nights a week, and would sleep off the parties till late the next morning. When he was gone the youths would have their own friends in for entertainments. They had plenty of wine, in spite of the Qur'án, and songs and instrumental music, disapproved of by the mullás. Usually this music was provided by the many gifted amateurs who attended, but on some occasions famed professional musicians were invited as well. All male, of course, although sometimes a young professional dancing girl, who might be performing at a simultaneous party over in the women's quarters, would also be called in.

Generally, those present were simply a band of intimates, all under twenty, of leading families, brilliant, poets themselves, esthetes singing their own works, or odes from Sa'dí and Ḥáfiẓ and quatrains from 'Umar Khayyám. Khan's unusual education in French and English, as well as stories he would tell that provoked laughs, placed him at the center of the group.

In this he was following his father, the Kalántar, who, despite his dignity and presence, could send his intimates into hysterics, invented expressions that were much copied, and wrote learned nonsense verses evoking from the unwary great admiration as to their profundity.

It was at these parties that Khan invented the 'language of the dead', the vocabulary of which consisted of corpses, graves and coffins, and bore no relation to the meaning, and all the band had to learn it and use its script. He also bestowed on each member of the band a meaningless name, with no relation to the bearer, but somehow an exact fit. He called the little prince Panjí-Síyáh – síyáh means black – and in the new language the term had taken on many perfections of mind and body not to be conveyed by any known word. The word chicken, or chick, added to elephant, denoted one of delicate and cultivated taste. Khan's own adopted sobriquet was Jújih Shimr-i-Káshí, Chicken Shimr from Káshán, Shimr being the execrated assassin of the Imám Ḥusayn. In this language, the name was a compliment.

As time went on new words, bizarre and almost unpronounceable, were added to the vocabulary; new friends who joined the sacred circle received new names. Khan also invented a title for the imaginary ruler of his infernal regions, to whom all the hellish dead would be consigned. His name was Dog-Tyrant, the Piebald (Sag-Shimr-i-Ablaq), and he would be invoked to curse their gatherings.

Turned cynical by what he had been through, Khan began to develop a philosophy of pessimism, of indifference to the obligations of everyday life, as the highest ideal. Jahannam, Hell, was to be the goal aspired to by all his intimates. The only way to attain that goal was to have perpetual fun, to drink, to stay entirely free from all the duties that the world imposes. Bad people were good; to live far removed from the mystics' Beloved was the ideal state. The real world was the world of the dead. The living were only embryos, to find their maturity by dying. The dead were divided into two groups. First, those who followed the mullás – or whoever their priests might be – and carried out the duties of orthodox religion. They were beings who counted as nothing, were effete and sterile, and would inhabit a Paradise fit only for hibernation. Second, those who, like Khan's small group, championed the cause of Hellfire, lived for their pleasures and drank 'araq (distilled from raisins, stronger than whiskey or gin) and 'blackest' wine. These shunned both mullá and mosque and went happily through the world with a band of like-minded sinful. Their lyric days of dancing and song, and poetry and love, were but a prelude to their future existence in the realms of Hell, where the powerful, the energetic, and the accomplished wielded, through their transgressions and their rebellion, conquering authority over all.

To test how strong the 'araq was, a youth would dip his finger into the cup and then set a match to it. If the drink was pure, the finger would be circled with a halo of fire. To purchase such liquor, Khan had recourse to the Jewish and Armenian inhabitants of the city, for their religions permitted the use of alcohol and some of them had wine vats and stills in their cellars. Their product had to be sold with the utmost secrecy to the Muslims, for these would be rigorously punished if they were found out, or, at best, could only get off by paying an enormous bribe.

A story went the rounds of how, late one night in a dark lane, well after curfew, a constable had held up a passer-by, searched him, and presto! drawn a bottle of liquor out of his robe.

'Off with you to the bastinado and the jail,' the constable exulted.

'But what proof has Your Honor that I drink?' asked the man.

'Why, this bottle that I have seized on your person,' said the officer.

'But that is no proof at all,' said the man.

'No proof!' cried the constable, all indignation.

'None at all,' said the arrested one. 'Your Honor likewise goes about provided with the means for committing adultery, but that is no proof that he commits it.'

There was one dealer whose wine was the purest and his 'araq the strongest of any. He dressed in a wide 'abá and had a streaming white beard. Two or three days a week this man would appear in the Prince's garden, his robe well loaded with bottles of the choicest 'araq for Khan's personal use. His drink was better than any available even in the Prince's household and Khan would share it only with special friends.

Those day-long parties during the blissful hours when the Prince was absent began with small sips of 'araq, followed by many delicacies such as pistachio nuts and roasted watermelon seeds, while skillful Persian conversation would be carried on, interspersed with music, till the main event, a noonday banquet – fruits, game, kabábs, heaps of saffron rice with lamb, or cherry rice, or sweet orange rice with chicken (never the mush that passes for rice in America, but each long grain separate from the rest), ice-in-heaven, recently imported European confections, goblet after goblet of wine – would be brought in by an army of attendants. Following the siesta and tea, the party continued on, till the real banquet around midnight.

Invitations to such festivities would result in more of the same, offered by different members of the band, and so the careless, endless hours glided on.

TEN

Wine and Roses

They say it was the Avestan Jam who decreed that the first day of spring should be New Year's Day (Naw-Rúz). They say this S̲h̲áh Jams̲h̲íd reigned seven hundred years, over fairies and demons, birds and men, and the arts of Persian civilization are unerringly traced back straight to him and his magic bowl, in which the whole universe was mirrored. This Persian festival was suspended when Islam swept over Iran in the seventh century AD, but was reinstated under the 'Abbásíds and their Persianized court of Baghdad, who reigned there roughly from the eighth century till the Mongols destroyed that capital city in 1258. On March 21 the sun enters Aries, blossoms suddenly explode like fireworks, the day and the night are equal, and everyone prepares for serious entertainment.

On that day the Persians, having planted wheat or lentils in pots to sprout by the 21st, appeared in new clothes. All who were able to gave out thin golden coins and kept open house in their drawing rooms, where each of their small tables was loaded with delicacies, seven of which began with the letter 's': examples would be sirkih (vinegar), sabzí (greens), sumáq (sumach), samanú (malt and flour candy), sikanjibín (a soft drink), sawhán (disk-shaped candy) and sír (garlic bulbs).

On the thirteenth day, because the demons were loose in the city, everyone departed on long picnics outside the walls, past the dry moat, up to hidden gardens and mountain villages along streams in the cool north – for this was the day of Sízdah-bih-dar, Thirteen-Out-the-Door.

The impromptu orchestra at Khan's parties generally consisted of Khan and his friends. He was in love with music but unable to sing (in Kás̲h̲án they said a Zarrábí who could sing was illegitimate). He could not play the tár, a six-stringed guitar played with a plectrum, or the sitár, or other stringed instruments such as the santúr, the steel strings of which are struck with two padded hammers. After long practice, however, he became a demon on the one-headed drum (dumbak) which is tucked under the arm and requires virtuosity with all the fingers and the heel of both hands.

He also wrote lyrics for the others to sing, voicing his new philosophy of life, which was nothing but a protest against the world as he knew it in Persia, with no place for the talented and the educated to go – a response to a life which he saw coiling on ahead of him as a maze of emptiness, a useless wandering, leading nowhere.

How, in the conditions they saw around them, could the educated young, the observant, the patriotic, look for any opportunity to serve in their homeland? Their numbers were minuscule; their weak, unheard protests against their debauched leaders and the imperialist powers now dividing up their country only blew away in the wind.

In after years Khan believed that the shared fun and wit, the parties, even the composing of perfect but meaningless poems, were preparation for a future when some of them would play a significant role in the regeneration of Persia. There were perhaps a hundred of these youths, all told, and virtually without exception these reached ministerial rank and other important posts in the constitutional regime which followed the Revolution of 1906.

The Mad Mírzá's summer estate lay up in the foothills of the Alburz range, in Ja'far-Ábád, five miles north of Tehran. It enclosed rich gardens and orchards and plunging white mountain streams and mirroring pools. It boasted several pavilions, each with its terrace and its matchless view of sky and bare, turquoise and pink and amber-streaked hills. Down across golden plains, way to the south under a furl of dust and dark green trees, was the capital, and still farther below, a sun-like spark that was the solid gold dome of Sháh 'Abdu'l-'Azím. Above and behind the estate rose the white-roofed mountains of the Alburz range.

Here, Khan spent many a long, cool summer with his friends – listening to silence, breathing the crystal air: fresh air and silence and the sweet smells of the earth – three things that not all of modern Western technology has been able to provide. Surely, as legend had it, the very Garden of Eden was brought in being on the plateau of Iran. Magic is a Persian word, and not only the Persians but many a visitor too has felt the spell. The word goes back to the Magi, an ancient tribe and priestly caste among whom Zoroaster came, telling them to follow the star to Christ. (The fourth century Vulgate translates Magi instead of Wise Men.)

Once in a while the young men would vary their parties, card-playing, rides, swims, with a steep hike to To'chál, a glacier on the mountainside, and listen there to the echoes of rushing waterfalls. Climbing along those trails, they came upon groups of people out for pleasure, seated or lying about on rugs close to the stream, with a feast set around the samovar. Some would call to them and offer a share of the food: white mulberries and sweet lemons; lamb and rice; 'elephant ears', a thin pastry, cut in long strips; gaz, round powdery cakes of manna, honey and nuts. Without stopping, the youth returned to these offers the traditional thanks, 'May the food prolong your life (Núsh-i-ján)!'

At times the air was filled with odes from Ḥáfiẓ and Sa'dí, sung to the thrumming of strings and finger drum, and even the violin, newly imported from Europe, reinforced the age-old strains. Warm in the Persian sun that slanted through branches, came the spreading incense of wild white roses that grew along the path. When night came with its white, bright sweep of moon, the revellers had twilight all the way to dawn.

Was it his then youth or his love for the country he was born in that marked Khan forever with memories of those days? That time was all true, he would remind himself; it had not been a floating dream.

Back he would go in his mind to one particular night scene in a hill village, when he and the others were gathered by a rose bed under a blossoming tree, and their singer took to singing songs about freedom and love – songs that attracted a distant nightingale, so that it flew over walled gardens to perch on the tree above their heads, and set to echoing the singer, note by note.

Khan's band of youths not only repeated the classic sounds, but from their group new songs were born and new adaptations of the meters of Persia's eternal poets, which spread and found their way into the repertoires of professionals as time went by.

Down in front of one of the Mad Mírzá's pavilions lay a wide field of clover, and some huge boulders made a sort of clubhouse where the youth spent part of their nights. The clover field sloped downhill to a cemetery, treeless, sad, the graves unmarked, indicated mostly by stones sticking out of the ground, symbolizing the Persian's natural response to death. Death was ugly; if you spoke of death, a Persian would make a face and say, why talk of it? Like their graveyards in those days, death was to be raked out of the way. In the present case the cemetery stretched down to the village of Tajrísh, a center where people in neighboring resorts would shop for food. There, along a tunnel-like curving dirt road, roofed over with straw matting to keep out the sun, the shopkeepers displayed their fruits and vegetables and clay jars outside their doors.

The boys decreed that a hollow grave at the middle of the old graveyard led down to Hell, where the heroes of the hellish dead came and paid homage to the ruler, Sag-Shimr, and bowed before his throne. They would gather in a circle around that grave to celebrate a hellish feast with strange new songs, melodies born of 'black' 'araq, so untraditional as to make them roar with laughter, pealing across the dead.

From time to time a pipe, in which tobacco and hashish were blended, would be passed from mouth to mouth.

In those days the mystic language of the Ṣúfís and the hashish they smoked had become the vogue. Khan's friends burlesqued that terminology, and when a Ṣúfí chanced to join them, Khan would recite long, solemn odes of undetectably spurious mysticism of his own composition, to edify the guest.

A similar thing would happen when the youths were visited by some noted Shiah divine or holy man. Then too they had to appear respectable for the occasion. To prove that he was still a good Muslim in spite of having studied European culture and tongues, Khan would invent elaborate, faked verses, supposedly Arabic quotations from the Qur'án and the holy Hadíth.

He now found that he had gained a reputation for religious learning which was not deserved, and news of his prowess reached the older generation, some of whom wanted to judge the matter for themselves. All unbeknownst to the young company, the Prince invited some of his friends to sit concealed in a room near where the youth were gathered. All that the eavesdroppers could make out, besides laughter, was a conversation in the new language, and some incomprehensible recitations from Khan's bogus Persian and Arabic poems.

One of his favorite dodges was to ask a learned Muslim guest to explain the meaning of some 'Arabic' word or phrase which Khan had coined himself. The learned one's invariable answer would be that the term must have been among new contributions to the language made by Egyptian Arabic scholars at the Arab University in Cairo. Khan had to spend a lot of time prior to such solemn encounters training his friends not to laugh.

One memorable social occasion to outdo all others was put on in honor of a leading statesman's youthful kin. The night before, Khan and his friends, helped by many servants, ransacked the flower beds, collected thousands of roses and spread them over the half mile of roadway that ran alongside the cemetery from the village below, up to the entrance of the estate. An elaborate feast was made ready to be served around the fountain at their pavilion, and many thin glass bottles of Hamadán wine were set to cool in the open, turquoise-tiled canal of the downstairs reception room, while Khan composed a poem in classical style to welcome the guests.

Early the next morning, chanting this poem and strumming on their guitars, the host youths came out and greeted the visitors who rode up on their dancing Arab horses over the rose-covered road. This party went on for two days and two nights and was long talked of, down in the city.

The life which this band of teenagers led was actually one long party, going on from day to day, week to week, month to month, with breaks for sleep or hibernation. During such intervals Khan would return to his books and re-study what he had learned at the Royal College. He thought of those breaks as 'lucid moments' and would take up new subjects as well, such as further readings in classical Persian poets, and would compose new odes on events of the day.

Superficially one can see a similarity between the debauchees around the Atábak and Khan's youthful lotus-eaters. Both drank and caroused; but Khan's friends were young, with some hidden promise, some art, some intellectual quality in their games, while there was no redeeming feature in the brute-beast carryings-on of the libertines who ran the country.

ELEVEN

With Hashish through the Keyhole

Members of Khan's band would, on occasion, frequent the Ṣúfí headquarters of Prince Ẓahíru'd-Dawlih, a son-in-law of Náṣiri'd-Dín Sháh. This prince had become the successor of Ṣafí-'Alí Sháh, his mentor and the most eminent Ṣúfí Shaykh of the day. Among his followers, besides some prominent individuals, had been many run-of-the-mill dervishes and mendicants to be met everywhere, chanting and invoking blessings, begging in the streets and bazaars, or living in groups here and there across the countryside.

Because they disregarded the principles of religious practice as set forth in Islam, the Ṣúfís, who followed the path taken by mysticism in the Faith of Muḥammad, were condemned as heretics and infidels by the orthodox Shiah clergy. Readers of Fitzgerald's *Rubaiyat* are well acquainted with the Ṣúfí view of mystic truth, 'the one True light', which could be encapsulated in his lines:

> One Flash of It within the Tavern caught
> Better than in the Temple lost outright.

In ages past, leaders of the Ṣúfís had been put to death by clergy-incited mobs, but by the second half of the nineteenth century, the fanaticism of the mullás could not be so indulged against them. These days, in Ṣúfí gatherings were chanted the great classical mystic poems of Persia, and wine – symbol of the inebriating quality of man's adoration for God – was partaken of in the non-symbolic sense, as a means of release from the sorrows of life.

After the death of Ṣafí-'Alí, Prince Ẓahíru'd-Dawlih (Europe-educated, his Paris visiting cards engraved with dervish rosary and beggar's bowl) greatly improved the status of his following, and Ṣúfism also gained in numbers, for he opened his doors and now even the lowliest from the bazaar could frequent the house of a prince of the blood, a poet whose verses and songs circulated widely about the land.

Khan's circle did not fail to sing these songs, or to adopt the Ṣúfí terminology now popular since the Prince's rise to power.

Along with Ṣúfí songs and language came the hashish. Ḥashashín, users of hashish, is an Arabic word reaching into English through the 'Assassins', those doped, killer followers of the Old Man of the Mountains, members of a secret order which he, Ḥasan-i-Ṣabbáḥ, founded in Iran about 1090.[37]

Wine and 'araq were no longer enough, hashish was not enough, some of Khan's band, but clandestinely, took to opium as well. Khan formed the habit of using hashish and, before long, to excess. It seemed a pleasant stimulant, for while continuous drink stopped the appetite, with hashish one was always hungry. Also, it entertained the user with strange fantasies, adventures of the mind. If the user was alone, once under its influence he might be struck with panic and would run away from imagined terrors. If, as he tried to escape, he came to a narrow gutter or brook, he would halt abruptly, for the rivulet was suddenly a great river or a chasm opening beneath his feet. If the hashish was smoked between strong drinks, a user might lie senseless for days. The one thing that Khan's natural ambition and energy saved him from was opium, and he avoided parties where this was smoked – providentially, he thought in after years, since his tendency was always to go to extremes, and before long he would have died of it.

A Persian tale that shows the different states of mind brought on by alcohol, opium and hashish goes like this: A drunken man, a smoker of opium and a user of hashish were out for a walk, when they found their way blocked off by a wall with a locked door. The drunken man charged the door, but all in vain. The opium smoker said, 'Let us lie down right here and go to sleep.' The user of hashish said, 'Let us become very small and pass through the keyhole.'

That Khan and his friends managed to weather their continual parties and their use of hashish was due to their regular exercise – they swam, rode, hunted, hiked. Khan also practiced athletic exercises, although he did not go to the House of Strength, the zúr-khánih, where professional athletes worked out. Some of his young friends were eventually used up by their way of life, but Khan, pessimistic or not, still kept an eye on the future and would not allow his habits to take over and control his powers, whether mental or physical. He still believed he would need all his faculties for some task at a later day.

The use of opium was common in those days, both East and West.

In America, the patent medicines popular with women were mostly wine and laudanum, and anyone asking could purchase morphine pills from jars on drug store counters. Even babies were dosed with paregoric – camphorated tincture of opium, and British orientalist E. G. Browne describes 'the chain which I had allowed Sir Opium to wind round me . . .'[38] 'Fortunate are they who never even speak the name of it,' wrote 'Abdu'l-Bahá of this walking-dead drug.[39] Its use is forbidden in the Most Holy Book.

The little band's favorite games were cards, backgammon and chess. Some took to gambling and became addicted to that, devoting part of their weekends and certain evenings to it, almost as a business. Khan tried it, but only for small stakes, to show he could play.

On one occasion, two of the elder Prince's cousins came on a visit. Their father owned several villages and produced fodder and grain for the market. Khan and the young prince soon observed that whatever the cousins' field of expertise might be, it was not cards. He and the young host, in the course of a few evenings, won all the visitors' jewelry and ready cash. The cousins, however, kept doggedly on, and issued a flock of IOUs, redeemable at harvest time in fodder and grain. Thus, for one whole season, the Prince's horses ate for free.

Years later when Khan was a member of Persia's Peace Delegation to the Conference at Versailles, he spent some time on the Riviera with his family. Several cousins and uncles of the Shah were there, and having heard of Khan's gambling success as a youth, they felt that here, surely, was an individual who could provide them with a system whereby they could win at the gambling tables in Nice and Monte Carlo. Khan told them he had, actually, devised such a system, one that could never fail. Urged to reveal it, he said, 'It is very simple. Don't play.' They replied that from living so long among Americans he had lost the cleverness of his early youth. (Persians still believe that Americans, being so frank, open and non-devious, are as naive as little children.)

As the season wore on, the royal relatives lost heavily at the casinos and found to their sorrow that Khan's system was best. One of them who had brought along his three wives was reduced to staying over in Nice for months, running up a huge hotel bill until he was bailed out with money from home. Those in the know, enjoying their morning walk along the sea on the Promenade des Anglais (frequented in those days, before paid vacations, mostly by the elite) would glance up at the Prince's suite in the hotel as they passed by, and would see, each framed in her separate window, a blonde, a brunette and a redhead – the stranded wives.

TWELVE

Bottle in Hand to the Bahá'í Faith

During the period when Khan and the young prince and their friends used up the nights and days in feasts, in composing poetry, in bouts of drinking, and in smoking hashish, the last thing Khan was interested in was religion.

His schooling had opened his eyes to the causes of progress in the Western world. At the same time it made him aware of what the benighted Shiah mullás had done to Persia by creating a hopeless, self-perpetuating situation and shutting out every new idea of value, whether it came beating at Persia's doors from Europe, or arose within the country itself.

The Bábí, later Bahá'í, teachings, arising some thirty-five years before Khan was born, had, at the cost of unnumbered martyrs and hideous persecutions, injected new life into the heart of the body politic. But leading religious and government authorities proclaimed from the rooftops that the new religionists were taking the axe to Islam; and there were other, more subtle forces attacking the new Faith from the outside. The two imperialist nations, England and Russia, eager to take over the destiny of Iran, always favoring divisions, did not care to see the successful establishment of a modern religion, born in Persia, which had proved capable of bringing together every element of that sect-ridden, much fragmented society – Zoroastrians, Jews, Christians, Shiahs of all stripes – and setting a unified people on the road to progress.

There were indeed European scholars who hailed the new Faith and condemned the persecution of its followers. But still and all, under the surface many continued to support the policy of their governments, which was to keep the Iranians divided, deprived, and ignorant, the better to exploit them.

Besides, the Westerners enjoyed their sense of superiority. Occidental performance in the twentieth century, known worldwide, has shorn them of this; but at that time they were arrogant, thought themselves highly civilized and spoke of the Persians much as anthropologists might describe primitive tribes.

The Westerners could see that their nations were superior to Iran in every material way and some Iranians also were aware of the disparity. Being inordinately proud, having a magnificent heritage, the Iranians resented this, especially as, very brilliant, they felt they could think rings around the Occidentals.

Khan's American wife used to tell a story of foreign imperialism in Persia, which she said she had heard from 'Abdu'l-Bahá. According to this fable, there was an old paralyzed beggar, seated down in the dust beneath a balcony. A stranger, leaning over the balcony railing, contemplated the beggar. Increasingly curious, the stranger leaned farther and farther over the railing, till at last he fell. He landed across the beggar's paralyzed legs, and the blow awakened the nerves to life, and the beggar rose and walked away. But the stranger broke his neck.

Khan was only one young man; he clearly saw how his country's very existence was threatened, but did not see what he could possibly do to save it. The result was he turned to indifference, to his festive friends, the ecstasy of composing poems, and the oblivion of drink and hashish.

Khan's brother, a rigid Shiah, lived in a different world. He carried out all the rites and ceremonies, attended the passion plays that told, in the month of Muḥarram, of the Imám Ḥusayn's martyrdom, wore mourning two months out of the year to commemorate the same sad event. An event of which Gibbon, off in England, and certainly not over-emotional, had once written: 'In a distant age and climate, the tragic scene of the death of Hosein will awaken the sympathy of the coldest reader.'[40]

During Muḥarram and the following month, Ṣafar, the people were immersed in the lives of the Imáms. From Gobineau, Matthew Arnold described one of the passion plays in his *Essays in Criticism*, and told as well of the Báb's advent. During the wildest, highest pitch of the mourning period, when frenzied men in white garments symbolizing shrouds practice self-mutilation, and run through the streets shrieking and chopping at their shaved heads with knives till all down the front their white garb is slick with blood – it still is at such peaks of fanaticism that minorities, mostly the Jews and the Bahá'ís, are especially at risk.

Outside the wall of their houses, beside the gate, fellow Shiahs seeking to gain merit would put up a large container of a cooling drink, and the bleeding ones might briefly stop in their wild race and drink, leaving the contents stained red, and go shrieking on. Other groups, unbloodied, would beat themselves as they ran, and one could hear the heavy thuds of the blows echoing across the countryside, together with the reiterated shouts of the two Imáms' names, 'Hasan!' – the brother who was poisoned at Medina in 670 – and 'Ḥusayn!' – the one who was betrayed and martyred ten years later on the plains of Karbilá.

Most of the friends of Khan's brother were sportsmen and

wrestlers, frequenting the zúr-khánih or House of Strength. One was a powerful wrestler, by profession a mason, brother-in-law of the well-known Bahá'í architect, Ustád Ḥasan, whose house was opened day and night to the believers, his meetings dangerously, openly held. The young mason, Ustád Qulám Ḥusayn, became an ardent Bahá'í. As with the businessmen in Persia then, men of this class were not supposed to have any education or culture – but to the surprise of many, he soon converted his friend, Khan's brother, the devout Shiah, to the new Faith.

Ḥusayn Kalántar immediately gave up his old rites and rituals, so stringently practiced before. Not only that, but he began to convert Khan's friends, who belonged to the great houses of Persia and normally would have avoided a man who now had so many associates among classes other than their own. To Khan's astonishment, many of his friends became Bahá'ís. Khan himself would never listen to his brother's exhortations, for Khan was that sought-after youth whose company only chosen members of the well-born were permitted to enjoy. Only such as these were allowed to enter the circle of constant festivities and poetry recitations and music and song, up in the hill villages and down in the stately mansions of the throne city.

To his further surprise, his old associates began to avoid him, and gave him up to attend the many gatherings which met at night, where famed Bahá'í teachers would expound the tenets of Bahá'u'lláh. His friends did, indeed, try to attract Khan to these same meetings, but he laughed at them and called them stupid. Religious meetings simply spread falsehoods, he told them. But the other youths ebbed away from him; his leadership was gone, and he finally decided he must attend those meetings himself, expose the teachers and their superstitions, and win back his friends.

The converted ones, trying to persuade him to come, said that if he, better educated and more aware of the world than they, considered them to be wrong, it was surely his duty to come along and refute the new doctrines. And Khan, who wanted to guide them back into his own fold, saw merit in the argument and began to attend. These meetings were clandestine, and one's presence there might be a matter of life and death. They were down twisting, walled and unlit lanes. As the youths passed silently along, they might glimpse a wider street and see, by the yellow light of his oil lamp, some shopkeeper sitting on the ground among his piled-up melons. Or, lying along the path, a sleeping form might be observed, 'abá-wrapped and settled in for the night. The youths walked single file in the darkness, and if the leader happened to stumble into a hole, he was careful not to warn those coming behind, so that they might stumble in too.

Once inside a meeting, Khan pretended to listen to what was being said. But every half hour or so he would leave the gathering and go quietly into another room where he had an attendant entrusted with a bottle, who would pour him out a sustaining amount of 'araq, after which, fortified, he rejoined the audience.

One night he spoke up to the two great Bahá'í teachers, Nayyir and his brother, Síná. 'Is it fair', he asked them, 'to invite me here and talk to me hour after hour, and then, for a reward, to give me, at midnight, a small portion of meat and rice?'

The gentle answer was that before long he would understand that he was getting, as a reward for his patience, not earthly food but a heavenly feast.

Khan smiled back at them and said, 'The unfortunate truth is that I have been paying you no attention at all, and I have no idea what you are talking about.'

They were not offended in the least. 'Your seeming indifference does not discourage us,' one of them said. 'We know you are a true son of your late Bahá'í father. We know that in due time you will follow in his footsteps.'

And one night after several months, as Khan used to tell it, the teachers suddenly began to make sense. He thought it must have been the teachers' prayers that finally made him a Bahá'í. Anyhow, on that special night, he listened to every word. They told the story of the young Báb, the Herald of Bahá'u'lláh, and how He was banished from His home and jailed and executed, and how His followers were taken captive and tortured and killed, and how, after Bahá'u'lláh's Declaration that He was the one foretold, the followers were still being persecuted and still suffering as they had suffered before, and still, wherever they were, proclaiming and serving the new Faith.

They said the Bahá'í principles were the only hope for Persia, her regeneration and progress – and not only for Persia but the entire world.

Khan rose up, took the teachers in his arms, and wept, both for joy and despair. How, he wanted to know, weak as he was, could he ever use what he had to serve Bahá'u'lláh? After all his strugglings he had been given no way of serving his country, he told them, and that was why he had turned to a cynical philosophy and strong drink. How could he ever be of use to a Cause which required purity and sanctity and utter devotion? For only such qualities would serve, if this Faith was to spread worldwide.

Their answer was that the Manifestation of God would give him the strength so that he would abandon his old ways and become a successful servant in His Cause.

Khan used to describe that night as his resurrection from the dead.

Khan knew almost nothing about Islam, out of which, like Christianity out of Judaism, the Bahá'í Faith had come – beginning, as he learned later on, with a handful of students who belonged to the Shaykhí school, itself a sect of Shiah Islam. The Shaykhís heralded the Báb, who in His turn heralded Bahá'u'lláh – that much he knew.

But what, actually, did he know about Islam? He had been taught its popular tenets and rites as a small child, and as a matter of duty had read parts of the Qur'án which, since it was in a foreign tongue, he could not understand. He had no information on how to prove the truth of a religion. The Bible and other sacred Scriptures were only names to him, and so were their Revealers. In his mind, too, were scattered Ṣúfí concepts from the Persian classics, and terms that had much influenced his vocabulary and style; but here again there was little that was organized or in any way coherent, or meant to be. As more than one scholar has observed, what the Ṣúfís had was endless ways of saying the same few things.

Khan had long been a student and also a teacher. Vague notions, staying on the outer fringes of a subject, were not enough for him. He had to get on a solid base of scholarship if he were to demonstrate the truth of his new belief. His friends had accepted his leadership and entered his philosophical orbit without question. Now he faced an entirely new situation: the teaching of a Faith serious, weighty, not to be presented without satisfactory proofs. The public in general was ruthless. The people were reluctant to come and listen. They were complacent, mechanically following the rites and the priests who had created most of the rites. They thought they had what they wanted. Not seeking. Many were secularized, as Khan had been, and sick of the subject of religion. 'I have a little religion of my own,' superior Americans would tell the Bahá'ís in after years, shutting them away. It did not occur to them that their little religion could influence no one else, and barely themselves, and answer virtually nothing, and never bring harmony and peace to the hate-filled billions seething across the planet. The public as a general rule has dealt with the Bahá'ís *de haut en bas*. So had the haughty Arabs treated the Muslims in the early days. And before that, a Roman philosopher, Celsus, had called the early Christians worms holding a conventicle in a swamp. 'He means us,' wrote Christian apologist Origen.[41]

Khan believed that a root cause of public indifference was nothing but indolence. For any new idea would provoke thought, and thought might force the thinker out of his protective shell of passivity. Khan was, furthermore, inordinately shy – a shyness taught in Persian families similar to his. With close friends he was voluble enough, full of bright remarks, philosophy, and stories to laugh about, so that they always asked for more. But to him the notion of presenting a serious subject to serious people outside his orbit was unthinkable. Looking for a solution, he went over this problem day and night, mostly alone. The key to it finally appeared: he should study the Bahá'í Teachings and their proofs, beginning with the prophecies of Scriptures gone before. Then he must pray continuously to the one Source of all Truth, and ask that spiritual strength be given his heart. He saw that he would need the memory he used to have, before he took to drink and to mixing hashish with his tobacco. Hashish, he believed, destroyed the memory.

Khan's conversion must have taken place in 1895, three years after Bahá'u'lláh was gone from the earth. Though he knew the program he had set out for himself was the right one, Khan did not immediately walk forward on the new path. Some of the believers wondered why he did not at once become a teacher; but he needed time to give up the old ways, and this was provided by an invitation from the Mad Prince to go on pilgrimage to Shiah Muslim shrines in Iraq.

THIRTEEN

Journey to the Muslim Shrines

In the days when the life and death illness of the little prince, Qulám-'Alí Mírzá, had been at its height, his father made a solemn vow: if the boy survived, the whole family would go on pilgrimage to the Shrines of Ḥusayn, 'Alí and other holy ones out of Baghdad. He now, in fulfillment of the vow, began to order preparations for the long journey to foreign parts. Traveling in his caravan would be about sixty men and women, the whole family with their servants. Extra horses and pack mules had to be purchased; howdahs and litters and carts were readied. Not only people but furnishings had to be transported: tents, bedding, bulging trunks, cases full of kitchen utensils and other objects to supply every household need. Several trunks were packed with Kashmir shawls and robes of honor and other precious stuffs to be bestowed as gifts upon personages such as the custodians of shrines and those who would entertain the family and their entourage along the way.

The little prince told his family that he would not go unless Khan could come with him. Khan was easily persuaded – he had never set eyes on the outside world, and he prevailed on his widowed mother and other relatives to let him go. His uncle, in the beginning, would not grant his consent to such a long absence, for he had only recently placed Khan in the Prime Minister's cabinet as a translator of foreign newspapers and periodicals for the information of the Chief of State. But Khan insisted and was allowed to go.

Most travelers in that time and place went on horses or on muleback. Even the Shah and the royal ladies could use their carriages only in a few sections of the country where the roads were passable: springed vehicles with wheels made for Europe's boulevards could not survive on rocky paths above the chasms. In this case the Princess and her daughters would travel in a 'going throne' (ta<u>kh</u>t-i-raván). This was a small, wooden house with door and windows, mounted on two long, horizontal shafts, one mule tied up forward between the shafts, and one behind. The distance from one mule's tail to the other one's nose was about twenty feet. Inside, the two-mule-powered conveyance was furnished with a comfortably-stuffed mattress and cushions, accommodating two ladies, who, when sitting up, would be on their knees, face to face. Since chairs and sofas were seldom used at all, the Persians were at ease on the floor, in this case a mobile one.

Lesser travelers rode in the kijávih (that which hangs crooked) – two large, open boxes or panniers, roped together and placed to either side over the back of a mule. True to their name, they hung at a slant, the single inmate of each one gravitating toward the center. The muleteer persistently tried to get them even, coming up from behind without warning, as one observer had it, hitching up this pannier or the other one, adding cooking pots or heavy stones, perhaps a skin water bottle, to the lighter passenger's weight.

Howdahs, more elegant versions of the kijávih, were less precariously balanced and gave an easier ride. In general, each would have a curved roof to shield the traveler from rain and sun, not unlike that of an American covered wagon, but much smaller.

Khan and the three young princes were ecstatic about going on the journey, the more so as they all had new hunting jackets, riding breeches and boots, and each was provided with a hunting rifle, a cartridge belt and a whip. The servants were likewise mounted and armed, with their extra clothing packed in saddle bags and tied behind them.

At last the day came. As the travelers left the garden, a Qur'án was held high over their heads to bless them and give them a safe journey.

Every morning they broke camp early in the dawn, to reach a halting place before high noon, since heat would then put a temporary stop to the caravan. The food for the midday meal – meat, game, delicate saffron-colored rice – had all been prepared after dinner the night before. Following a siesta, the caravan went on again till sundown. They covered from about ten to fifteen miles a day.

It was early spring. Mountains and valleys, cultivated fields, budding gardens, a few mud villages along the roadside were spread

JOURNEY TO THE MUSLIM SHRINES

out before them in the soft air.

When they reached an area where there was game, they would ride away from the road up to the valleys and hillsides, and hunt for quail, partridges or gazelles. If, at the evening stopping-place, the caravan found no caravanserai (kárván-saráy, caravan house; English 'van' is from caravan), the servants would pitch tents to accommodate humans and animals alike. The tents for people were room-size pavilions, large, hand-embroidered; precious rugs were strewn on the floor, and well-stuffed mattresses laid down.

To guard against the ever-present danger of bandits, some of the attendants kept watch all night long.

Whenever the caravan neared a city, the governor would come out of the gates to meet and greet the elder Prince and his household and lead them to a suitable place to stay.

They went through Qazvín, said to date from the fourth Christian century, the Casbeen of Milton's *Paradise Lost*; Hamadán, ancient Ecbatana or 'concourse of many ways', where Esther and Mordecai and Avicenna and the dervish poet Bábá Ṭáhir are buried – with its yellowish sandstone lion, a great beast lying on its side now, even as it was a thousand years ago.

After two or three weeks the party reached Kirmánsháh, with its great parade ground and Governor's Palace, about halfway between Tehran and Baghdad. Most of the inhabitants were of Kurdish blood. The elder Prince's father and grandfather, directly descended from Fath-'Alí Sháh, contemporary of Napoleon, and donor to him of the white Arab horse often seen in paintings of the Emperor, had both ruled as governors of this city. Here, the Prince was received with special pomp: from the city walls his brother and other kin came out to greet him on horseback, bringing lavish gifts of sweets, fruits, and many a sheep to be sacrificed as thank offerings for his safe arrival, and with them, on Arab mounts, were riders in Kurdish headgear and dress. To entertain the new arrivals, these riders showed off their extraordinary horsemanship, meanwhile firing off their guns in mock battle and shouting in their high-pitched voices.

Kirmánsháh lies between the provinces of Persian Kurdistán and Luristán and the inhabitants speak a dialect containing many words out of ancient Persian. It was encircled by lush gardens, among them that of the Prince's grandfather, Muḥammad-'Alí Mírzá.

The night before arriving in the city, about six miles out, the travelers had stopped at a caravanserai virtually at the foot of Bísutún (the pillarless) Rock. Unknown to the pilgrims, a few decades before their visit (beginning the task in 1835), Britain's George Rawlinson had risked his life, climbed the death-dealing rock face and transcribed the cuneiform inscriptions carved for Darius, five hundred years before Christ.

The fame of this place has spread around the world because it is haunted by two Persian lovers, Khusraw and Shírín, and the sad heart of a third, named Farhád. Their tale, which varies with the teller, is found in the pages of poets like Niẓámí and Jámí, and goes like this: One day the Shah, Khusraw, was out hunting on a deserted mountain slope when he caught sight of a woman, bathing back of greenery in a stream. He had never looked at anyone so fair, and being Shah, he sent out a messenger to learn her name and claim her for his own. The word came back that her name was Shírín (honey-sweet), but she was already spoken for. She was betrothed to a sculptor named Farhád. The Shah called for him and reasoned with him, to no avail. Finally the Shah decreed that Farhád must prove his love for Shírín by taking up his sculptor's axe and splitting Mount Pillarless so a river could pass through. The sculptor toiled away on the rock and at last the task was done, the river poured through, he had proved his love. But kings sometimes betray. The Shah despatched an old woman out to the work place with a lying message for Farhád: Shírín was gone. His beloved had died. She had left the earth. And Farhád turned his axe on himself and leapt from the cliff.

The poets have written that after his death, the air of that region was changed, and ever since, the clouds will shed down tears of rain on passing caravans.

As Sa'dí has it,

> When I got to Bísutún,
> Down came the rain.
> Would I be wrong if I should say
> These drops were lovers' tears,
> Yet once again?

Khan, a poet himself, said afterward that the moment he reached there, he saw the rains fall on Mount Pillarless, and he could not control his own tears.

Their caravan put up for three weeks at the estate of the elder Prince's grandfather, located on the banks of the River Qara-Sú (Black Water). In all, the party remained in Kirmánshāh for two months, living in palace rooms and buildings in various gardens, all arranged by omnipresent relatives for their comfort well in advance. The stay here was due to the Prince's being so long absent – years – and having business matters to talk over with his kin.

Entertainments offered them by grandees and city officials went on forever in the usual way. Leading singers, guitar and flute players and other musicians were in attendance for the younger element. The best wine from local vineyards as well as cases of the well-known wine of Hamadán were continually served, the bottles first cooled in fountains supplied by mountain streams. Beginning at sundown, the revels, the delicacies, the roasts, the game, the music, the wines, took over till dawn.

There was a special garden, to the west outside the city line, and spread out against the mountains, which was known as Heart's Delight (dil-gushá). The Prince's party slept in buildings of sun-baked brick giving on the garden, but spent waking hours on its terraces or along its many streams and flower beds. Khan could not remember, in after years, any spot on earth so filled with freshness and fragrance and with joy enough to raise the dead. Thinking back to the place and time, he could only lament the unchanging law of change, and remind himself that while it ends all things, while it is the doom of all delight, it is at the same time a beginning, perhaps even of new bliss – this inexorable law of change that in the same instant both creates and kills.

Centuries ago, Sa'dí put it this way:

> Whoever came here built him a new house,
> Left, and to another passed it on . . .
> Woo not a faithless love,
> This world's a charlatan,
> Unworthy to be won . . .
> Life is but melting snow
> In summer sun.

At last it was time for the caravan to move onward. The elder Prince duly distributed among relatives, other hosts and dignitaries, some of his robes of honor and other costly presents he had brought. The city leaders on their Arab mounts rode out as an escort for several miles, till at the Prince's courteous bidding they returned to their homes. The travelers went on, from one mountain caravanserai to another, and came to the last Persian village on what in those days was the Persian-Turkish frontier – for Iraq, till the close of the First World War, was part of the Turkish Empire. This place was called the Castle of Shírín (Qaṣr-i-Shírín) and Khan saw the huge rocks which formed the foundation wall of that ancient Sásáníyán abode – their temperate winter resort, some eighty miles westward of Kirmánsháh. Across the border was the Turkish–Arab town of Khániqín – years later this would be the terminus of the railway built from the city of Baghdad to the Persian frontier.

Then Khan was in Iraq, so unlike his familiar Persian north. For the first time he was in a foreign country, and saw date palms and citrus trees growing in the open, their fruits more delicate and sweet than those of other lands. Iraq, or Mesopotamia as the Greeks called it, 'Between Two Rivers', the Bible rivers of the Euphrates and the Tigris. Here, except in mid-summer, the climate is good. This region is what legend calls the site of the Garden of Eden, land part and parcel of the Persian Empire for long centuries, since it had been wrested from Assyria in the days of Cyrus and Darius. Those two rulers toppled down its throne city of Babylon, near today's Baghdad (founded in its turn in the late eighth century AD), but long after that, Iran lost the region to the Ottoman Turks.

The caravan spent several days on their journey through Iraq, and finally reached the Shrine of the two Imáms, Kázimayn: the two Kázims were the seventh and ninth Imáms. This Shrine city, pictured in *The Dawn-Breakers,* is close to Baghdad on the Tigris River, and is known for its beauty all over the East.[42] The tomb's golden dome, with its exquisite tile-work facade, is at the center of a vast courtyard. Surrounding the inner Shrine are outer buildings, used by pilgrims for their daily prayers. The inner Shrine, beneath which lie the sacred remains, glitters with gold and silver and jewels. Pilgrims of every stripe, beggars, princes, whatever, from all over the Shiah world, especially India and Iran, gather there each year seeking blessings. Islam is a brotherhood of men of all colors, races and conditions, all equal in the sight of God. In His sight none outranks another, and in spite of all the sects and schisms that have shattered their Faith, and all the corruption that has sullied what began as a pure and true religion, all Muslims still promulgate this principle of men's equality before the Lord.

Every morning and evening at prayer time, the men and women of Khan's caravan, in separate groups according to sex, joined thousands of other pilgrims, entered the inner Shrine and clutched with bare hands the square, golden lattice-work enclosing the sarcophagus, and prayed for health and Divine help in all their doings. Looking back, Khan used to marvel at how most of the party survived infection. He said that in that holy Presence no one gave a thought to infection or germs or hygiene, nor would have, even had the pilgrims been abreast of science. Since the Imáms were thought to heal, every now and then an astounding miracle would be announced by the custodians of the Shrine: the healing of an incurable, or the blazing out of a dazzling light before the blurred eyes of certain pilgrims. And it is true that because of great faith, and the fact that the Imáms were holy beings who gave up their lives and received gifts and powers in return, and could surely intercede in the next life and bless, some of the pilgrims did see signs and miracles, and received answers to their prayers.

Khan used to say that the real miracle performed by a Prophet of God and His close successors is His transforming word that changes the age-long way of life of humankind. But he taught that lesser miracles by holy ones such as the Imáms are more than probable.

Some of the spiritual loot bought in the holy places, that pilgrims took back home with them included the rosaries of a hundred beads, fashioned of clay from the vicinity of the Shrine – for it was believed that by saying the prayers, counted by the beads, those prayers would be fulfilled. From a custodian, they would also purchase a small quantity of the dust of the Shrine, and it was believed that many, dangerously ill, were healed by drinking a mixture of this dust and water. Still another object purchased by innumerable pilgrims was a smallish, round seal made from the sacred clay of the Shrine city. Back at home, while saying his prayers five times a day, the worshipper would kneel and bend down his forehead and rest it on the holy seal.

The caravan spent about ten days in this place, also visiting the great mosques and other points of interest in neighboring Baghdad, and then set out on a three-day journey to the Shrine of the martyred Imám Ḥusayn in Karbilá.

This city also has the shrine of the Imám's brother 'Abbás and a young martyred son, 'Alí-Akbar. The structural beauty and embellishments of these buildings are even lovelier than those of Káẓimayn. As offerings to these shrines at Karbilá, great Shiah kings and rulers and others fabulously rich have sent their costliest jewels. Some, no doubt, were rivals even to the Shah's ruby, that Ambassador Benjamin saw in Tehran: 'One ruby there is in that mine of splendor', he says of the Shah's treasury, 'which, on being placed in water, radiates a red light that colors the water like the blood of the vine of Burgundy.'[43]

Not only their jewels have been sent here, but their dead bodies come from distant places, arrive here to be buried in outer buildings and courts and the vast cemeteries stretching out endlessly beyond the city; for this is sacred ground, and Muslims believe that who lies here will rise among the very first to quit their graves when the trumpet sounds on Resurrection Morn.

These processions of dead, not always welcome, threaded the Middle East. Arminius Vámbéry, renowned Hungarian traveler and orientalist, tells how – journeying across a desolate Persian desert on a moonlit summer night, a night of flitting shadows cast by the wind-driven sand – he, disguised as a dervish, and with fellow travelers, heard the sound of bells. A caravan, they told him, ahead of us in the dark. Hurrying to overtake it for company, they soon regretted their haste, for they found themselves caught by the throat in its sickening, choking wake. The nearer they came, the more poisoned the air.

'Hurry up!' the others cried. 'Hurry up! This is the caravan of the dead!'

Urging on their mounts, they reached about forty horses and mules, loaded down with coffins, some four to a beast. Briefly spoken to, the caravan's leader – his eyes and nose wrapped, the parts of his face that showed, ghost-white under the moon – said he had already been ten days on the way and must go another twenty to reach Karbilá, so the pious dead could lay them to sleep by Imám Ḥusayn. The animals, Vámbéry says, went head down, as if to bury their nostrils in the sand, while the horsemen shouted them along.[44]

Vámbéry is the same noted man who wrote with reverence to 'Abdu'l-Bahá: '. . . every person is forced by necessity to enlist himself on the side of your Excellency, and accept with joy the prospect of a fundamental basis for the universal religion of God, being laid through your efforts . . . and if God, the Most High, confers long life, I will be able to serve you under all condition[s]. I pray and supplicate this from the depths of my heart.'[45]

When Khan saw the great silver doors of Ḥusayn's tomb, and thought of the teeming millions who came humbly to this place, and considered that an evil Muslim Caliph, sworn foe of the Imáms, once smashed Ḥusayn's Shrine to the ground, turned a water course over it, and forbade, under dire penalties, any pilgrim to approach this spot he understood how futile human opposition is, when confronting the Lord.

The caravan's final visit in this area was to the tomb of 'Alí, son-in-law and rightful successor of the Prophet, first of the Twelve Imáms – deep scholar, strong warrior, the 'best-hearted Muslim'. He was murdered in 661 as he prayed in the mosque at Kúfa, his killer being Ibn-i-Muljam, a Muslim, member of a splinter sect.

Khan was present at Najaf when they commemorated the martyrdom. All one night, pilgrims from everywhere in the Muslim world – men, women, rich, poor, city dwellers, peasants, members of remote Arab tribes, a hundred thousand strong – packed every inch of the vast enclosure that surrounds the Shrine, also gathering on the rooftops of the outer buildings and at the base of the great dome. Never before had he seen such a congregation, praying, supplicating, calling out the name of him who was both First Imám and Fourth Caliph – chanting, singing, keeping their vigil through the night and the morning until it was noon.

FOURTEEN

A Bridge of Boats

About now came a crisis in Khan's life, for the great motley crowds at the pilgrimage centers took their toll: the holy cities were potent sources of infection at pilgrimage times, and cholera and other diseases targeted their victims by the hundreds or thousands. A number of those in Khan's caravan came down with fevers, and he himself was laid low by cholera and raved in delirium for nights and days. The Prince's doctor gave him up, but finally he rallied and slowly recovered. After this, Khan felt that God had spared him for some important task.

Then another crisis, which might well have been predicted: all through the journey, offsetting the pleasures and palaces and many delights, Khan had to suffer from the elder Prince's mad, non-human ways, that capital of cruelty in him, a portion of it allotted to almost everyone he saw. Finally Khan went and stood before him and spoke out, protested against what the man was doing – with the result that the Prince's rage was now directed toward Khan as well as the rest. Khan could not put up with it, and in spite of the young prince's pleas and the urging of the boy's mother, begging him to stay on at least till they should reach Persia again, Khan left one and all, joined a party of Persian pilgrims and returned to Baghdad.

Meanwhile, the Prince's caravan went on to Sámarrá, about a hundred miles away, to visit the well into which, the Shiahs believe, the Twelfth Imám disappeared in the year AH 260. They say he never died, that he and a chosen band live on to this day in the two secret cities of Jábulqá and Jábulsá; and at the end of time, when the earth is filled with unrighteousness and the faithful despair, he will issue forth, heralded by Christ Jesus, defeat the non-believers, and establish justice over all the earth.

As among the Christians, where educated and uneducated accept their Faith at different levels (Mary does, or does not, go bodily up into the sky; Eve was, or was not, made from Adam's rib), so the intellectual Muslims hold that what must have happened was this: at a time when the usurping Caliphs were killing Imáms, descendants of the Prophet, and the Shiah cause was weak in the extreme, the vanishing of the Twelfth Imám, who died early, if born at all, was kept a secret shrouded in darkness.

Baghdad, where Khan had gone after leaving the Prince's caravan, was a post of much importance for Persia, since many Iranian subjects lived there and in other cities of Iraq. Iran maintained a Consulate-General built in a garden right at the edge of the Tigris River. It happened that the post of Consul-General was occupied at that moment by a brilliant member of the Qájár house, who had served before as Under-Secretary for Foreign Affairs. He was about forty years old, cultivated, outwardly an ardent Shiah Muslim. A close friend of Khan's uncle in Tehran and other members of the family, he knew of Khan by reputation as a language student and an honor graduate of the Shah's College. The result was that when Khan dismounted at the Consulate and entered the garden, he was received with open arms and invited to stay as long as he wished.

Khan, still unhappy at being cut off from family and friends and separated as well from the young prince, found the Consul-General both a stimulant and a comfort. He began to enjoy the life in Baghdad. The country changed before his eyes. The Tigris, at first very low, began to rise after a heavy rainfall, and the palm and orange groves and other fruit trees flourished. Khan spent time wandering through the groves that stretched all the way to the Tigris. He also passed many a solitary hour, leaning against a railing and watching the river flow by. He had never seen an ocean, or even a wide body of water, and to him the great mass of the river was the same as a sea. By the hour, he watched thousands of small, round, basket boats, quffih, in which passengers were rowed to the opposite bank. He watched men transporting their goods downstream to the city, floating on the water, bobbing up and down on wooden rafts that rested on blown-up sheepskins tied together. Stopped by the boat bridge that stretched across the river, these men would disembark, sell their goods, then sell the wooden parts of the rafts, then let the air out of the sheepskins and sell them too. He learned that, afterward, these Arab traders would use their funds to buy other merchandise, as well as camels or donkeys to transport themselves and their baggage by land back to their homeplace upstream. There were only a few bridges across the Tigris in those days – built over a series of boats tied together and chained down on each bank of the river. These bridges were as astonishing to Khan then as was New York's Brooklyn Bridge years later when he first laid eyes on it.

As he watched the river hurrying past and thought of his plight, how lonely he was, how far from relatives and friends, he would lean above the water and weep, and then console himself by making up poems, and he kept these in his papers afterward, throughout his life. In one he wrote of the seasonal increase of the river, and told how it was swollen by his tears.

It was precisely at this time that shocking news came from Tehran. The Shah, Náṣiri'd-Dín, on Friday, the first of May, 1896, was shot dead, the assassin a revolutionary who luckily was a known bitter foe of Persia's new Faith – 'luckily' because otherwise a blood bath might have followed. In 1852 when Náṣiri'd-Dín sustained slight wounds from birdshot fired by two disturbed Bábí youths, unable to bear any longer the killings and the persecutions of their brethren, a reign of terror had followed, with the torturing and the slaughtering and the jailing of people (including Bahá'u'lláh) who were totally innocent of the crime. As to the youths, one was killed on the spot. He was cut in two and the halves hung up at a city gate. The other, tortured, refused to speak a word, and they poured molten lead down his throat. Of the horror going on in the streets, an Austrian officer wrote home, 'Would to God that I had not lived to see it! . . . At present I never leave my house . . .'[46] It was immediately after the royal murder, the Bahá'í teacher and poet Varqá (the Dove), was slashed to death before the eyes of his twelve-year-old son who, still refusing to recant, was strangled.

This time when the mullás and populace tried to pin the assassination on a member of the new religion, the murderer himself publicly denied any Bábí–Bahá'í involvement a few months before he was hanged.

Náṣiri'd-Dín was the only ruler Khan had ever known. He had mounted the Peacock Throne in 1848, more than three decades before Khan ever came into the world. He was, in his own person, King and state. He had ruled with none to curb his hand, at his sole whim, for almost fifty years and with the slightest gesture meted out life, meted out death. Now it was not only he who went, but centuries of unfettered kingly rule went with him, crashing down.

Hearing the dire news of the Shah's assassination, the Mad Prince, Khan's patron, felt that his caravan must hasten (although hasten is hardly the word) back to Tehran to see to his affairs in what might well be chaos. On their way the travelers came through Baghdad, and the Prince's young son persuaded Khan to accompany them back home.

So Khan returned to his mother, brother and sisters, and a different Shah, Muẓaffari'd-Dín, ruled for the first time for as long as almost anyone could remember.

On the journey to the Shrines Khan had come to believe more firmly than ever that the Godless world on one hand, and the priest-ridden world on the other, would in the end yield to the principles of human unity and global civilization enunciated by Bahá'u'lláh. His pilgrimage had seemed to be a leaving and a forgetting of his new Faith, but in reality it was a time when the seeds sown in his mind and soul by those he called his glorious teachers could germinate.

The new Shah, forty-three years old, son of the one who had reigned seemingly forever, got rid of most of the officials who had served under his father. Náṣiri'd-Dín, only sixty-five and vigorous, in perfect health, might well have stayed on the throne another decade or longer. During most of the long reign his son had pined in Tabríz, capital of Iran's northwestern province, traditionally the seat of government of the Qájár Crown Prince. A new day now dawned for his own people, who had stood by him as Crown Prince and Governor of Ádhirbáyján in precarious times, as they waited and waited for fate to bring about a change.

Now it was the turn of the new men, called 'Turks' because Turkish is the language of Ádhirbáyján, and they were all scrambling for office. Names little known in Tehran began to fill the highest posts. The old governors were recalled and the provinces acquired new ones from among the 'Turks'. A few old officials were left in their positions, however, for having served the interests of Muẓaffari'd-Dín at the capital when he was in de facto exile as Crown Prince. Some wealthy, provincial Kháns had married his daughters, and now that he was Shah they were also rewarded with high rank, in the army or as governors.

His sons were sent out to be Governors-General to the most important provinces. One of these was a youth of sixteen, Sálári'd-Dawlih, who became Governor-General of Kirmánsháh.

Then there were the members of great families who, just for the honor of it, became officials and courtiers and enjoyed new titles. One of these latter was a close friend of Khan's, a young man named Náṣir-Qulí Khán, grandson on his mother's side of the renowned Mukhbiru'd-Dawlih, a title meaning 'the Empire's Chief of Communications'. When Mukhbiru'd-Dawlih was still a youth he had helped supervise the installation of the British East India Telegraph that connected the various cities and provinces of Persia – a great thing, for the country had never had any modern means of communication before, and the late Shah gave him the title which in various forms was later conferred on several other members of the family.

This grandson of Mukhbiru'd-Dawlih was now invited by Prince Sálár to go with him to his post in Kirmánsháh as chief of his chamberlains, these latter being sons of noble houses who attended the Prince in the hope of future advancement to great heights. They received a nominal salary, but mostly used their own funds, and had their own servants and horses. Náṣir now persuaded Khan to go along to Kirmánsháh. He accepted the invitation as a stepping stone toward what had become his only goal, his only objective in life.

Khan had been shown a photograph of Bahá'u'lláh's son, 'Abdu'l-Bahá. It was the portrait of a youth, the head-dress a white fez with a white scarf wound about the base, the 'abá dark, the black hair long, to the shoulders. The seated figure was confident, in command, the young face grave but serene. The large dark eyes looked as if they had already seen through the material world and were easily holding its powers at bay. Khan was accustomed to watching many a noble young face, but compared to this one they were only the faces of creatures who were dupes of the world. He knew that soon, as age drew on, their features would thicken and their bright eyes grow dull, because the world abandons its own and they would find this out. In the Qur'án Satan tells his people: 'I deceived you . . . I only called you and ye answered me. Blame not me then, but blame yourselves . . .'[47] 'Abdu'l-Bahá has written that the serpent in Eden is 'attachment to the human world'.[48] Here was a face detached from material things, measuring this world by the world of the spirit. Khan saw that what he and his friends had was nothing. He wanted what 'Abdu'l-Bahá had – what he found in this pictured face.

'Abdu'l-Bahá, exiled long since with family and friends, was still being held a prisoner in 'Akká on the Mediterranean Sea. Náṣir promised Khan that after a time he would give him a letter of introduction to his father's family and relatives in India, including the great Áqá Khán, the head of the Ismá'ílí Muslims. From India Khan could embark for the Holy Land by way of the Indian Ocean and the Red Sea. Though roundabout and not immediate, this was a way of reaching his goal.

FIFTEEN

A Prince Accepts the Faith

Thus once again, Khan took leave of his Muslim mother, very dear to him, and his many connections, and the little Prince, Qulám-'Alí, his companion on the pilgrimage the year before. It was hard for both young men, close friends for years, to say goodby, and the other did what he could to dissuade Khan from leaving, and Khan would have listened, except that the lure of the holy city of 'Akká was more than he could resist. He particularly had in mind to serve the Master in 'Akká with the foreign tongues he had acquired, and spread Bahá'u'lláh's message to the peoples of the West.

The party leaving for Kirmánsháh with Prince Sálár numbered several hundred people, courtiers and others, each with various functions and duties, and most on horseback. The Prince himself went by carriage. The others had their fine Arab mounts. Khan was among them, as a guest of Náṣir, and once they had arrived he, Khan and several attendants took a large house with many rooms and a central garden with a pool fed by mountain streams. Every night until the early hours of the morning they enjoyed their parties and the best singers and musicians that the city provided. Then, before noon, Náṣir would dress and ride to the Government palaces that housed Prince Sálár. Khan would stay behind, entertaining all his friends from the year before when the caravan had stopped some two months in this city of poetry and pleasures. Weeks went by, and when Khan looked back on them later, he remembered them as friendly and happy, yet somehow lonely.

Then one day a messenger appeared and Khan was summoned to the Prince's palace. With considerable pomp and royal airs the Governor-General addressed him, saying, 'Ever since our arrival here, we have had no tutor with whom to continue our study of French, interrupted when His Majesty appointed us to govern in this city. We have recently heard that you are the leading linguist in the country, especially in English and French; and further, we recall that your uncle was our royal father's Chief of Chamberlains when His Majesty was Crown Prince at Tabríz, and we used to play with your cousins. We now wish you to attend upon us every day at Court, to teach us languages, and also to go riding with us and accompany us to the hunt. You shall receive sufficient salary and expenses while with us, and in due time reach a high post, as have your uncles, in serving our house.'

Khan wrote all these things home to his family in Tehran. He felt that, at least in his worldly career, he had arrived.

In the days when he was Crown Prince, the new Shah had appointed one of Persia's richest landowners as his deputy. This was Ḥisámu'l-Mulk of Hamadán, a member of the Qaraghuzlú family, who owned more than a hundred villages. This personage had a sixteen-year-old son, Iḥtishám-i-Dawlih, for whom the father had secured a daughter of the Shah as his bride, and who with a large suite of attendants had accompanied his parent to Kirmánshád.

The youth, the brother-in-law of the Prince Governor, was also the latter's rival, and from the start the two were at daggers drawn. Iḥtishám-i-Dawlih, indeed, arrived with more servants and blooded horses than the Prince Governor.

Every morning Khan went to Court and gave the Prince Governor his French lesson. Afternoons he rode out with the Prince, who had provided him with two fine horses. This went on for a few months, but the conflict between the Prince and Iḥtishám-i-Dawlih embarrassed Ḥisámu'l-Mulk to the point where he felt they must be separated. So, putting his son in charge of the family's vast holdings, he sent him back to Hamadán with his family and a crowd of attendants.

Before this happened, young Iḥtishám and Khan had struck up a friendship. They got along so well that Iḥtishám made it a condition of his leaving that he take Khan with him. The condition was virtually impossible to meet: first of all, the Prince Governor did not want to dispense with his French teacher and riding companion; second, he hoped that with Khan's help, Khan's uncle, a favored member of the Shah's Court, would give him his eldest daughter in marriage. The Prince was very eager to marry this young girl, who was known for her beauty, and whom the Prince had known when she was a small child and his father the Governor of Tabríz.

Meanwhile, Khan had found it increasingly difficult to remain in the Prince Governor's service. The main reason was this: a Persian ruler and those under him, to establish authority and strike terror into the rebellious, would conduct their business in tyrannical ways. They would mete out terrible punishments to murderers and bandits. For instance, they might have the victim bound to the mouth of a cannon and literally blown to fragments. The Prince attended these butcheries in person, almost every week, and his Court was expected to be present as well. Khan was not able to bear such sights and had made up his mind to leave as soon as escape was possible.

Now that the Prince Governor's rival was being sent away, Khan's own departure became possible. Iḥtishám's father bought Khan off from the Governor with several Arab horses and costly shawls, thus wresting permission for Khan to take a month's leave.

Khan remembered his departure as a wonderful day. He and the youthful prince led a group of some fifty horsemen, while the princess and her ladies, unable to travel by carriage on account of the mountain roads, proceeded in their litters and palanquins.

The young Iḥtishám, aggressive, reckless, preferred the most spirited of Arab mounts. He would wear out one horse after another in the course of the day, galloping after wild game; and by the time they reached the stopping place for the night, his attendants would be exhausted as well.

When they reached Hamadán they crossed the city and rode out some three miles to a village called Shivírím, whose inhabitants were Armenians. Hamadán was known for its fine grapes of many varieties and the wonderful fruits that grew on the mountain slopes. Here on the slopes was the young prince's residence: a series of buildings with the usual high walls, fruits, flowers, blue-tiled streams feeding pools and fountains, gardens famed as the loveliest in all Iran. At the center of them was a great mansion with many-roomed reception quarters for the prince and his continual crowds of guests. Sometimes there were a hundred guests at once occupying the main house and its various annexes.

Khan, too, had sleeping quarters in the mansion, but sleep was not easy to come by. As day followed day, he realized that by changing patrons he had only dug himself into a deeper hole. The life here was one of continual entertainments and feasting which used up most of the hours. In Kirmánsháh there had been a measure of reality and intellectual activity; here, strong spirits distilled by the Armenians, together with a wide variety of wines, local and imported, kept everyone in a haze of oblivion. The feasts as described by Persia's mystical poets, with their symbolic wine and love and roses and nightingales, were acted out in real life, and one never knew when day dawned or when night drew on.

Besides guests, the young prince's personal entourage included some one hundred individuals, some permanent, others transient: priests, dervishes, mystics, poets, physicians, secretaries, winesellers, elders from the villages bringing in gifts, wrestlers, grooms, magicians, philosophers, sages, each with some claim for attention. During intervals of lucidity, the poets recited their odes and competed for prizes, and many of Khan's odes were memorized and sung by professional musicians. Not only was the drinking virtually continual, but a great number smoked hashish and opium. Theoretically, Khan was to teach the prince English and French, but the moment never arrived. Although very intelligent, the prince was uneducated and could hardly write a line free from errors.

The prince was fond of Khan but the only way he knew to show his affection was to ply his friend with strong drink. The more Khan tried to refuse, the more insistent became the prince, and finally he would draw his revolver and threaten to shoot Khan unless the potion went down.

Those days and nights continued on for a number of months. Afraid for his life, Khan tried to escape, but he was watched at all times and could not break away.

The people of Káshán are not famed for courage, although Khan had proved himself braver than most. They tell among other tales how a caravan from Káshán was once attacked by bandits. The robber chief drew a circle around the Káshí in charge, and said, 'We will kill you if you step outside of that circle.' When the bandits had stripped the caravan and gone with their loot, the Káshí leader told the others, 'I certainly showed him up. Once when he wasn't looking I put my toe outside the circle.'

Khan finally despatched a letter to Tehran, to his friend the son of the Mad Mírzá, and asked him to send along a favorite servant of Khan's. This servant was a boy from Khurásán, very resourceful and brave, and his arrival made things easier. He watched over Khan at all times, drew him away to his sleeping quarters when the parties got out of hand, and would sit by him, revolver at the ready, threatening the attendants whom the prince sent, one after another, to get Khan back.

Luckily, after a few months Iḥtishám's father, who had remained in Kirmánsháh with the Prince Governor all this time, returned to Hamadán, and the continual drinking parties were stopped. Khan was then able to come closer to his young patron and warn him of the perils of his way of life. At the rate he was going, Khan told him, life was passing him by. Iḥtishám replied that he was weak and was in such a state from strong drink that he would never be able to take life seriously. Khan replied that God had given him great wealth, and with it responsibility. Since in Persia there was no freedom and little or no chance to exercise initiative, Iḥtishám ought therefore to look after his own well-being, for the sake of the people dependent on him, the thousands of villagers and farmers whose very existence was at his mercy. Through prayer, Khan said, the youth, only seventeen years old now, would find the strength and the will to stand on his own feet.

During long walks and rides at this time, alone except for a few attendants, Khan spoke openly to him of the Teachings of Bahá'u'lláh, not easy to do in a country where fanatics controlled the minds of the people and exercised their crippling influence over the rich landowners. But Khan had moral courage, and told him plainly that under no circumstance would he stay on, unless he could be of some help in making the prince a leader of men. Through Khan's persistence and continual prayers, the young man came into the Faith of Bahá'u'lláh, and wrote his letter of acceptance to 'Abdu'l-Bahá in 'Akká – a letter Khan forwarded by special and safe means. A wonderful Tablet from the Master came back to this youth, addressed in his name, and brought the prince great joy. At the same time Khan received a Tablet in Arabic in which 'Abdu'l-Bahá prophesied Khan's future services to the Cause, throughout the world.

Here was a son-in-law of the Shah, a young man of great wealth and power, whose future influence would protect many Bahá'ís in a country where the believers were hunted down. During the remaining months he spent with the prince, Khan entertained many a Bahá'í traveling teacher, among them the famed dervish Ḥájí Múnis and several of his dervish companions, all of whom Khan introduced to the young prince. In this way the new recruit's knowledge of the Teachings was deepened, and his faith grew strong.

Another individual there whom Khan was able to attract was a prince who acted as chief secretary to the Vice-Governor. His name was Muḥammad-Mihdí Mírzá (Mir'át-i-Sulṭán) and he was also a poet. He went on serving the Faith for many years, long after Khan had left for 'Akká and the United States. In later years Khan's nephew, 'Abbás Qulí-Khán Kalántar (whom Khan took to America to be educated, along with his brother, Alláh Qulí-Khán Kalántar, in 1914), became administrator of railways in Persia, and married a niece of Prince Mir'át.

During his stay in Hamadán, Khan was in constant touch with the believers in the city and the surrounding area, and constantly taught the Faith. Bahá'ís of Hamadán have proved themselves to be among the most devoted of all, and from earliest days many have been imprisoned and put to death. Khan's letters to 'Akká and also to his family in Tehran documented their activities.

It became apparent that Khan's long stay with the prince and his family would not provide for his future, and he was happy to return home when the Shah summoned the prince to the capital. Khan's Bahá'í experiences in Kirmánsháh and Hamadán had deepened him and increased his fervor, and he looked about for wider fields of service. By now Khan, using no caution, refused to conceal his beliefs, and was known in Tehran as a Bahá'í teacher. The name Bahá'í closed all the doors, even to one who was better educated than most and who had a foreign language equipment that excelled most of the others'. Even Khan's own uncle, highly placed, was afraid to introduce him about, for fear of being identified with the new religion. Restless, and in a risky situation, Khan decided to leave the capital. His dream was to get to 'Akká, but lacking the money to travel, he left for the province – not the country – of Iraq. This came about because he met a leading courtier of the late Shah, Fakhru'l-Mulk, who had been appointed Governor of that province. Its principal city was Sultánábád, focus of the rug-weaving industry in the central southwest. This Governor had two sons, to whom Khan had been teaching French. One, very intelligent, was destined to become a member of the cabinet and a Governor-General of important provinces. His mother, a Qájár princess, was the daughter of 'Izzu'd-Dawlih, a younger brother of the dead Shah. This boy urged his father to take Khan along, and Khan accepted, although the post was certainly not lucrative, and the new governor was known as frugal to excess; still, this again looked like a first step toward 'Akká.

Arrived in Sultánábád, Khan located the Bahá'ís and arranged for regular teaching meetings to be held in the different homes. In that city many Armenian Christians and Zoroastrians had accepted the new Faith and were anxious that their friends and relatives should be taught as well.

Meanwhile, a Muslim high priest, Hájí Áqá Muhsin, and his sons, had their grip on both city and province. They owned hundreds of villages and whatever they said was law. The Governor himself could keep his position only with the approval of Áqá Muḥsin.

When Khan had been in Sulṭánábád about two months and was into the third, his Bahá'í activities were reported to the high priest, who directed the Governor to send the young man back to Tehran. The Governor tried to pacify the priest because he wanted his sons, especially the promising one, to keep on learning French. At that point the Bahá'ís brought word to Khan that the high priest was planning to have him killed some dark night as he returned from a meeting.

Khan was not afraid and told them it would be a blessing for him to be put to death for his Faith. Their view, however, was different. They told him the Bahá'í Faith had reached America and that there was almost no one to interpret when Americans came to visit 'Abdu'l-Bahá, or to translate the Teachings into English. Why throw away his life in Sulṭánábád, when he could offer himself to 'Abdu'l-Bahá as a translator and interpreter. (By 1896, hundreds of Americans had reportedly accepted the Faith and clearly the Bahá'í grapevine had carried the news of this even to remote Persian villages. Thornton Chase, the first American believer, had been converted in 1894; and on December 10, 1898, the first Americans reached 'Akká, members of a band of pilgrims invited to join her by Mrs Phoebe Hearst, the publisher's mother.)

Khan thought this argument made sense, and he decided that he must set out for the Holy Land at once. Since his funds were meagre, and not nearly enough to travel on, he hit upon the plan of setting off on foot, garbed as a dervish or wandering mystic, and, as they did, living off the land.

SIXTEEN

Khan Becomes a Dervish

When they heard of Khan's plan, two youths, both valued members of the Governor's suite, insisted on coming with him, whatever the hardship and the danger. They were recent converts to the Faith, whom Khan had taught during his brief stay in Sulṭánábád.

With help from the Bahá'í friends there, they had several outfits made of the coarse white material which dervishes wear, and bought the kind of shoes they would need on rough paths up the mountains and across the plains. Then each packed his bundle and set out to say goodby to the believers at a special gathering called for the purpose. Afterwards, in the middle of the night, by a relatively little-used trail, they walked out of the city.

The three kept on until dawn, slept, and started out again while there was still daylight. Their method was to walk all night, climbing the rocky trails, until they could walk no more. Then they made camp near a small village, spreading their thin cloth mats by a running stream or mountain spring. One of the youths had managed the Governor's commissary and was also an excellent cook. After they had slept, this one would go into the village, buy a chicken and other food, return to the camp and prepare it. The other had a fine singing voice and could play on the stringed instrument which he had brought along. Entertained by him, they could forget their aching muscles and blistered feet. This youth also wrote down the poems which Khan composed along the way, poems telling the story of the journey and their hopes of reaching the goal.

After eating and resting, they would pack up again and set off, always avoiding the traveled roads because the Governor had sent out his men to catch the three and bring them back.

They made their way in this fashion along the paths of Iraq province for at least a week, through many a small village and past huddles of tribesmen's tents.

Khan had seen early on that he must instruct the other two as to the very real perils they all faced – three unarmed youths in the wilderness, with no police at hand, no bodyguards, no one to defend them. One ever-present danger lay in meeting groups of professional dervishes wandering about in search of shelter and food, hating any intruder on their territory, jealous of their privileges. Since Khan had studied the terminology and knew the philosophy of the desert mystics but the others did not, he told them that for their own safety they should neither identify themselves nor state which of the mystical orders they belonged to, for the dervishes of Persia and elsewhere in the Middle East were affiliated with numerous denominations and bore allegiance to different saints.

The custom was that when a strange dervish came upon other dervishes, he went up to the spot where food was on the boil and addressed the man in charge. Khan carefully coached the youth who served as cook and to whom he had given a mystic name, Paríshán, which means one lost in an ecstasy of love – and also refers to the Beloved's tangled hair. Paríshán was always to tell the stranger, 'We two are under a vow of silence. Our murshid, our mystic leader, is Ishti'ál.' Ishti'ál was Khan's pen name, also his Bahá'í name, blessed and conferred by the Master – it means aflame or blazing fire. The real dervish usually accepted this excuse, for he knew that a novice must subject himself to his leader 'like a dead body in the hands of an Imám'.

The stranger would then approach Khan, seated under a tree with his kashkúl. This was the alms bowl carried by dervishes, a receptacle with a chain for a handle. Originally it was made from a sea-coconut, a huge bi-lobed nut, the seed of the fan palm. Hanging above Khan's head would be his book of mystic odes, and he also had some French and English books and pocket dictionaries spread out before him.

Khan could appraise the stranger at a glance. He probably would be what dervishes call a s̲h̲utur, a camel, that is, an ignorant attendant who acted as burden-bearer to some murs̲h̲id. In Persian and Arabic, Khan would overwhelm the visitor with quotes from the classics and the Qur'án and with mystic lore, not excluding many important-sounding expressions that had no meaning at all, then conclude with prayers and taper off into silence.

This was the signal for the other two to summon the visitor and indicate that their murs̲h̲id was now in a state of ecstatic trance, which would probably last for some time. The stranger would then, at least temporarily, depart.

If, however, Khan thought that the stranger was a professional of the kind that preyed on travelers and other dervishes out in the wilds, and could rob or even murder and go on their way unscathed, another tactic had to be used: the young cook would tell the fearsome visitor, standing there by the cooking pot, to go off on his begging rounds through the neighboring village, that supper would be ready by the time he returned. And hope he never would.

The begging was traditional; in fact, the word dervish (darvísh) is said to come from 'door' and 'beg'. (In Arabic-speaking countries, a dervish is a faqíh, poor one.) The three youths, of course, had no door. No wall, no roof, no constable patrolling out in the wilds.

One evening a giant of a man, muscled, shaggy-bearded, bristle-browed, came up and stood unbudging by the cooking pot. He was told somewhat shakily that if he cared to go off on his rounds, supper would be readied for him. He turned away, but was soon back, fixing the three youths with his fiery red gaze, as if he knew they were impostors and he was going to take action.

Khan saw there was only one hope for them, and that was hashish. The drug went by many names in Persia: 'Parrot of all mysteries', or plain 'Mysteries'; or 'Secrets', or 'Master Siyyid' – it being green, and the Siyyids, descendants of the Prophet, wear a turban as green as parrot feathers. (An ode of Ḥáfiẓ which must have puzzled translators is addressed to hashish and begins, 'O thou parrot, speaker of secrets, may thy beak never lack for sugar!')

Persians are adept at communicating by signals. With a gesture, Khan told the cook to drop a large ball of hashish into the visitor's stew. They knew he would be taken care of for at least twelve hours, and while he slept they packed up their bundles and vanished.

After they had journeyed twelve days they called a halt because they could walk no more on their blistered and bleeding feet. Luckily their stopping place was near a pasture with a great flock of sheep, and one of the shepherd boys befriended them, ran errands for them in the village and brought food.

The country people hereabouts, isolated from any centers of civilization, were simple and credulous, but always truth-telling and resisting evil because they lived in the fear of God. Khan thought they were like good soil in a wild place, never cultivated, and for that reason capable of yielding a rich harvest.

They had enormous respect for dervishes, believing them to be holy, and when, for one reason or another – rains, injured feet – the three could not get to the village, the inhabitants would come out in groups and ask for prayers. Prayers alone were not enough for them, however; they asked for miracles too. Infertile couples would beg for a child, others wanted the youths to heal their trachoma or their malarial fevers. Khan found himself obliged to lay in a stock of roots such as ginger and various wild herbs in the hope the visitors would derive some benefit from them, however small.

As soon as they could travel again, the youths pressed on toward Kurdistán. The valleys were turning lush and green, carpeted with thick grass, but in some areas clouds of mosquitoes made sleep impossible. To defeat the insects, as well as innumerable grass snakes which liked, quietly, to ease up to human bodies for warmth and shelter in the open fields, they gathered dried cattle droppings and spread them in a wide circle, and when night fell set fire to the circle and lay down on their mats at the center.

When it rained they had to bed down with sheep and other animals in their rough shelters, but mostly they slept under the stars.

After they had walked about three weeks they reached Sanandaj (Senna), the principal city of mountainous Kurdistán. The Kurds are Sunni Muslims, orthodox; while the Persians are Shiahs, followers of the twelve Holy Imáms, believers in 'Alí – First Imám and 'Guardian of God' – and 'Alí's descendants, as heading the Faith of Islam. The Kurds are devoted to the dervishes, and follow Ṣúfí leaders who live in caves and high on mountains, as for example in Sulaymáníyyih, a district near the Iraq border where Bahá'u'lláh spent two years in seclusion before resuming His exile in Baghdad.

Somewhere along the journey the three travelers had purchased a colt to serve as a pack animal and at times to be ridden. Their trail over the mountains was rocky and narrow, with a sheer drop of hundreds of feet to the valley below. The colt refused to stick to the mountainside on the right, stubbornly choosing, despite all persuasion, the extreme edge over the drop. It was then they discovered that the poor beast was blind in the left eye. That explained why they had

KHAN BECOMES A DERVISH

been able to buy it so cheap – for even less than a debilitated donkey would bring in the bazaar. At the next village they sold the animal, and more than recouped the purchase price.

The Governor of this province was Mírzá Maḥmúd Khán, former Consul-General at Baghdad, whose guest Khan had been some two years before. He decided against calling on him, afraid the Governor would insist that Khan abandon his dervish costume and stay on at the Governor's palace to act as an assistant. Instead, when the three reached Sanandaj near sundown, they rented two empty rooms where they could stay the night.

The next day they made enquiries, hoping to find Bahá'ís, and discovered quite a number. This fairly large community was made up of former Jews, Christian Armenians, Ṣúfís, Shiah Muslims and Sunni Kurds. They included poets, musicians, merchants, government servants. These Bahá'ís had already heard of Khan and, overjoyed to find him in their midst, told him he would be a great help in attracting various leading men to the Faith. Many invited the three youths to stay as guests in their homes, but Khan explained the goal of his journey, and stated that it would be better if the three could live in their own separate quarters and thus be available to every type and class of the population. The believers replied that they would rent and furnish a separate house for them, one suitable for the reception of important guests. Khan thanked them but said all they needed was a house with a few rooms and a courtyard – they would need no furniture at all. At last the local believers yielded and rented him just such a house on one of the town's high hills.

It was in this city that his longing for 'Abdu'l-Bahá reached the point where he sat down and addressed to the Master his 'Ode From Senna':

> Save me, great Mystery of God, I faint and fall.
> Save me, without Thee I only burn and sigh.
> Save me, I am as nothing in the eyes of all,
> Save me, in every city: 'He is mad!' they cry,
> Of this lost, distracted wanderer in the desert of Thy face.
>
> O Thou, O Thou from whose sunbright brow the moon hath
>   drawn her rays,
> The thought of whom illumines many a weary lover's soul,
> But to behold Thy face I have no dream in all my days.
> Then fulfill my hopes, in grace, grant me leave to reach my goal,
> A desert wanderer I, and yearning for the garden of Thy face.
>
> Without Thee, only a prison to me is Heaven and its flowers,
> Without Thee, only a place of thorns, the blissful bowers.

O Thou whose brow so moonlight fair is the envy of spring
   hours,
In his love for Thee,
He is torn free,
Is Ishti'ál, from all that be,
And again and again,
Cries this refrain:
I am lost in the glory of Thy face.[49]

SEVENTEEN

Escape from Sanandaj

Word began to spread through Sanandaj that here were three dervishes unlike any they had seen before: that one, very young, knew European languages and had several books in French and English, and also books of Persian and Arabic prayers; that he knew chapters of the Qur'án and whole Persian mystic poems by heart, and was familiar with the deepest lore of the mystics; that of the other two, one was a fine cook and the other sang and played the odes which Khan was composing. Sanandaj had no newspaper in those days but obviously did not need one. Even the tiniest details of their doings and sayings were reported.

The three ordered wood, and the Bahá'ís loaned them cauldrons, cooking pots and two large samovars. These were kept on the boil and tea was served from dawn till midnight to the many groups who came to visit. Kurdistán was known for its young poets and other literary personalities, and some were great landlords and heads of noble houses who guarded the frontiers and were singled out by the Shah for his royal favor.

Not even a week had passed when the Governor-General had his curiosity aroused, sent several members of his court to call on the newcomers, and on the same day found out who the leader of these dervishes was. The next day, by letter, he requested Khan to take his midday meal with him, also sending along horses for all three. Khan decided to go there alone, in his dervish clothes. His skin had been burned dark brown by long exposure to the hot sun and his hair had grown very long.

When Khan entered the large reception hall the Governor rose from where he sat in the seat of honor (ṣadr-i-uṭáq), walked toward him, embraced him and placed him at the head of the room by his own seat. He then turned to the distinguished guests who were present and told them about Khan's family and his education and knowledge of languages (pitiful, looking back, to note how rare and precious such an education – elsewhere taken for granted – was in that time and place). The Governor was a great liberal at a time when few dared admit to favorable views on progress and democracy; and he openly told his guests that interference from imperialists, together with a fanatical clergy, made it impossible for a youth of Khan's attainments to serve the country. And that Khan had therefore turned his back on a life of luxury, assumed the garb of a dervish and was traveling toward other lands where there was freedom to express one's opinions without fear.

As Khan had foreseen, he then requested him to change out of his dervish clothes and serve at Government House. Khan excused himself on the ground that he had made a vow never to live in comfort again until he had achieved his heart's desire – which, he did not add, was to be in the presence of 'Abdu'l-Bahá. He promised, however, to pay frequent visits to the Governor's mansion while in the city, and to be at the disposal of anyone who sought him out. Then, attended by several horsemen of the Governor's court, he rode back to the rented house.

When he got back his two companions hurried to greet him. They had been wondering what had taken place, for that afternoon they had received, from various donors, a gift of sheep and lambs and quantities of provisions, besides beautiful rugs and weaves. It turned out that a number of the Governor's guests, hearing Khan so highly praised, and feeling they should cultivate one so much approved of by the Governor, had gone home and sent off the gifts.

Khan wondered what they could do with so many live sheep. A large landowner solved the problem by taking them to one of his farms, and sending back a sheep each day. By this means the three young men were able to feed the large number of all sorts of people who daily called to see them.

The Bahá'ís usually brought new seekers in the evening, while the others, including grandees and landowners of great wealth, called in the course of the day. To groups of these, Khan expounded the principles of the new Faith, together with interpretations of the verses of the Qur'án and various mystic poets which pointed to the advent of a new, universal Manifestation of God.

There were among the visitors a number of men of culture and distinction, and some of these invited Khan out to their gardens in the countryside where they enjoyed less formal meetings. Here Khan disclosed special, particularized truths of the Bahá'í Faith.

Although widely known as warlike, and certainly old enemies of the Persians whom they regarded as seceders from Islam,[50] the Kurds were far more than bandits and marauding tribesmen. They included many cultivated individuals, well-known state secretaries, and good writers with their own distinguished style. One of the most famous was the statesman and soldier Ḥasan-'Alí K͟hán of Garrús, with the title of Amír-i-Niẓám (General of the Army) given him by Náṣiri'd-Dín S͟háh. He had governed various provinces during the latter's reign and possessed such innate power that even those warring bands of Kurds who from time to time came raiding down out of the mountains, scattering death and destruction, shuddered at his very name and took temporarily to peace.

Busy as he was with the duties of his office, the Amír-i-Niẓám never neglected to teach literature and calligraphy to chosen individuals wherever he went. His style was the Nasta'líq, for which he was famous.

A few years before, when Khan was returning from the shrine cities, this man had been Governor-General of Kirmáns͟háh, and Khan had been presented to him at that time. He was seventy-five then, tall and cadaverous, with face and hands as wrinkled as a mummy. His eyes, though, were bright and keen, and he expressed interest in the fact that Khan, although so young, had completed his education at the Royal College and knew both French and English. A liberal, he stated that the salvation of Iran depended on sending the youth to Europe to learn the modern culture of the West.

This man had educated another, a poet and brilliant literary figure, who was in his service as secretary for many years. This was Ḥájí Máliku'l-Qalam, now the Governor's Chief of Secretariat. Not a day passed but he came to see Khan and took him off to one or another of the beautiful gardens of various princes. Each day Khan read him a new poem of his own composition, and he replied in kind. Khan considered himself particularly fortunate to have met this man, one of the leading lights, and they were not few, of Senna.

Since Khan and his two companions continued to wear their white dervish clothes of coarse linen, the poet called them white-plumed birds of Heaven.

Many years afterward, when Khan was in Tehran as head of the Crown Prince Regent's Court (1921–4), a son of that Ḥájí was attached to the Court, with the title of Prince of Calligraphers (Amíru'l-Kuttáb). Khan invited him to visit the family several times a week and teach calligraphy to his daughters, Marzieh and Hamideh K͟hánum. Unfortunately, they, American-born, did not take kindly to his strict discipline, misbehaved, and were especially apt to giggle when he described his domestic trials and sad life as the husband of several wives. By then, his illustrious father had been dead a long time. He himself passed from the scene during Khan's final visit to Tehran (1949–50).

A special event during Khan's stay in Sanandaj was the visit of a renowned mystic whose followers in Kurdistán were numbered in the hundreds of thousands. This was Ḥájí S͟haykh S͟hukru'lláh. He too had heard about Khan and now requested to call. He arrived one day with a number of attendants, and when he had embraced Khan after the fashion of a high mystic, very humbly knelt down before him, which greatly impressed the many onlookers. (Persians invariably watch to see how one individual is evaluated by another.) The S͟haykh was a man over sixty, with flowing white hair and a white beard. His face was fair, the eyes brownish-gray, and his accent broad Kurdish. He exuded joyousness, and his purity and sincerity were clearly genuine. When he spoke, he did not prove to be a man of deep learning; rather, a man of prayer and true faith. Before leaving, he had one of his people undo a bundle in which was the large skin of an Angora goat (murg͟hurz) with exceptionally long hair and inches-deep wool. This precious gift he offered to Khan for use as a rug on which to sit when guests came, or a prayer mat when saying his prayers. Such a gift meant to the watchers that the donor held the recipient in great esteem.

Shortly after this Khan came down with cholera again. He blamed it on being run down from the long journey, on disregard for rest both while traveling and here in Sanandaj, and on lack of plain, nourishing food instead of the elaborate feasts at which he was so often the guest. He was ill for weeks but still refused to accept the Governor's offer of a comfortable home in the government compound. One day the Governor, distressed, told Khan, 'I do not feel that you have many more days to live.' His concern was not entirely personal, for he was planning to open a school for the study of European languages and culture, which he wanted Khan to direct. This did not appeal to Khan, for he felt it would fasten him to Iran and a remote area of the country at that; and he made up his mind to leave as soon as he was able to travel and an opportunity offered.

This came when some tribal quarrels, typical of Kurdistán, involved the Governor in continuous negotiations and kept him from learning what the three visitors were up to.

To raise money they sold some of the gifts they had received: rugs and textiles, a few sheep and two of the horses. Then, one evening, after having said goodby to close Bahá'í friends with whom he always shared his plans, Khan and his two companions packed up, loaded their belongings on the gentle horse they had kept and set out at midnight, following a mountain trail toward Kirmáns͟háh. This particular area, stretching to frontiers with Asiatic Turkey and Iraq, and the home of several large, important tribes, was governed by Khan's relative, his parents' paternal and maternal cousin, Iqbál-i-Dawlih, head of the G͟haffárí branch of the family.

It took them about eight days to walk from Sanandaj to Kirmánsháh, where Khan led them to the garden of Dilgushá (where the heart rejoices), owned by the government and outside the city limits. He knew it well, having often been entertained here on previous visits, and soon found the place he was looking for, where a spring of cool water bubbled out of the ground. Here, on the bank of the stream under tall shade trees, the three unpacked and spread out their sleeping mats.

The Governor was off on a tour of tribal districts, attempting to restore peace, and the Lieutenant-Governor, also a cousin of Khan's, had been left in charge.

On the day after their arrival Khan sent a message through one of the gardeners to this man's son, a youth of about fourteen. That afternoon the son rode out and called on the newcomers, being very much surprised to find Khan in the garb of a dervish. He urged him to change his clothing and move to his father's quarter of the city, but Khan told him that in the garden here the three would be easily available at all times to the dervishes and Bahá'ís who might wish to come and visit. The boy said he would see to it that provisions were brought out to them every day and that he himself expected to spend many hours in their society.

The next day he and his father both came calling because the Lieutenant-Governor had recently received a message which he wished to convey himself: when the Governor of Kurdistán learned that the three had left and were headed for Kirmánsháh, he had wired Khan's cousin to this effect, 'I have completed plans to establish a school and I desire Khan's immediate return to Sanandaj.' The Lieutenant-Governor had forwarded the telegram to his chief, who replied, 'Request Khan to await my return, and accept post of director and teacher of a school which I myself desire to establish in the capital, a center of far greater importance than Sanandaj.' He added that Khan was to be properly looked after till he returned.

Khan promised to wait, and meanwhile got in touch with many Bahá'ís who came out to the garden, bringing seekers for instruction. While there, Khan learned that a group of four Bahá'í dervishes, friends of his from a few years back, when he had been in Hamadán and Tehran, were by chance in Kirmánsháh. Their leader was Ḥájí Múnis, an elderly man who, as a professional dervish, had traveled throughout the Middle East, finally accepted the Faith and visited 'Abdu'l-Bahá in 'Akká. Ḥájí Múnis was anxious to have Khan join him in his wanderings, especially to India. But Khan said no. He knew that the Bahá'í Faith forbids a monastic life, and too, would not sanction his wearing the dervish dress. His adopting the garb had been a temporary thing, done out of sheer necessity, for it seemed the only possible way he could reach 'Akká and the presence of the Master.

Ḥájí Múnis, though a devout believer, had not yet abandoned his dervish ways, and Khan realized this when one of the Ḥájí's attendants, a youth of about twenty, came to him and complained: 'I am enduring terrible hardships as the Ḥájí's companion. For example, you see that I am thinly clad and the nights are very cold. The other three have good warm cloaks and sleep comfortably all night till sunup. Then, come day, as we travel in the broiling mountain sun, they pile their heavy cloaks on me, and I must sweat and suffer all day long.'

'Why do you put up with it?' Khan asked him.

'I am an apprentice dervish,' he replied. 'The course has lasted several years. All during these years I have been the camel (the shutur, as the dervishes had it), and I have carried the loads. It seems to me the time of my apprenticeship should have reached its end by now, and he ought to give me proof that I am a dervish full blown: the Ḥájí ought to confer on me the dervish Robe, the Garb (Kisvat). The time has come, indeed it is gone, when I should, by rights, have all the privileges enjoyed by a full dervish and be able in my turn to impose obligations on other apprentices.'

'Then why do you stay?' Khan asked.

'Because he keeps refusing me the Kisvat,' the young man wailed. 'He won't give me my dervish garb.'

'Listen,' Khan told him, 'the Kisvat is nothing but a garment worn by a dervish. You did not have to suffer so much just to put on the garb. In any case you are a Bahá'í now and thus not bound by rituals and rites. You should go your way.'

Khan heard later on that the youth parted company with the Ḥájí and his friends, who had to find themselves another camel. He left the wandering, ascetic life and became an active follower of Bahá'u'lláh.

Still another of the Ḥájí's group was a dervish named Mustamand (poor, weak). He too left the Ḥájí, and traveled to 'Akká, where 'Abdu'l-Bahá gave him the title Tavángar (opulent, mighty). This man wrote Khan many letters, even after Khan had been sent to America by the Master in 1901 – and also sent on photographs of himself and some of his Bahá'í associates.

After a month the Governor returned from his journey to the tribes and discussed the projected school with Khan, assigning him a suite of rooms above the main gate of the garden created by Muḥammad-'Alí Mírzá, one of the many sons of Fatḥ-'Alí Sháh. (This prince, who had been appointed Governor of Kirmánsháh, also governed the frontier areas of Iraq and Luristán. His title was Dawlat-Sháh.)

A friend of Khan's childhood, Prince Mujallal-i-Dawlih, was a descendant of Dawlat-Sháh. He would enter history for giving his daughter in marriage to Reza Shah Pahlavi, and their son Muhammad Reza became the Shah so widely known in the West.

For two or three months, Khan taught classes in French and English in that series of rooms. The pupils were specially chosen, as Khan had once been himself, from leading families. He also started classes in the Bahá'í Faith, to which inquirers were brought by the local friends. One of the books which he expounded there in his quarters was the *Íqán*, the *Book of Certitude*, which Bahá'u'lláh had revealed within two days and two nights near the close of His stay in Baghdad (1862). A 'model of Persian prose', the book sets forth the 'Grand Redemptive Scheme of God' for humankind, and in all the vast Bahá'í literature is second only to the Kitáb-i-Aqdas, the Most Holy Book of His laws.[51]

The days passed and as usual the rumors started up: a dervish, a close relative of the Governor's, who had been put in charge of the Governor's school, was busy spreading the Bahá'í Faith. Alerted, the mullás, in a body, demanded that the Governor expel Khan from the city, and threatened that unless he complied, they would arouse the populace and have Khan put to death.

The Bahá'ís felt that the Governor could not possibly stand up to the mullás, and that Khan and his companions would certainly die at their hands if they stayed on – the three should leave at once. They believed, too, that since the Cause of God had reached America and few in the Middle East knew English, and Khan was one of them, he should be kept safe to translate the Holy Writings for inquirers far away, across the sea.

They left. The plan had been to cross into India and board a ship for 'Akká, but they learned that there was a plague in Baghdad – 'political plague', that is, which recurred periodically when the British wanted to shut off the traffic to India. Willy-nilly, they joined a caravan headed for Qum and Tehran.

The day before they left Baghdad, one of the Bahá'ís reported that he had overheard some mullás discussing a plan: they would send a band of killers after the three to get rid of them on their way west to the frontier. The plan fell through when the young men headed for the north instead.

Meanwhile, at the urging of the believers in Kirmánsháh, the three had abandoned their dervish garb and were now wearing the flowing robes adopted by the learned classes, although they retained their white fezzes with white cloth wound around the base.

Along the way to Qum were various halting places where the youths visited with local Bahá'í friends. A fellow traveler from Qum to Tehran was the distinguished believer, Mírzá Mahmúd Furúghí, a learned mullá who had become a Bahá'í and because of this had endured much persecution and imprisonment here and there throughout the country. Khan had already met this teacher in Tehran some three years before, when Khan had first become active in spreading the Faith.

Back in the capital, Khan happily rejoined his family and close friends. They all thought that this time they could keep him at home, experiencing the peace and quiet of family life. His mother and sisters knew nothing of all he had gone through as a dervish, wandering across the mountains and desert wastes. Uncles and friends hoped he would now listen to them and set aside his Bahá'í activities in favor of a post with the government such as innumerable generations of his ancient house had held, feeling that such service was both a duty and worthy of their qualifications.

Even his Bahá'í friends wanted Khan to conform somewhat more to custom. They had learned through the grapevine of his dervish exploits in many places, and appreciated all the teaching he had done, but now felt he should leave off his dervish fez and wear a hat like other Bahá'ís. This was the black felt or lambskin 'flower pot' brimless hat. It was worn at all times, both in and out of the house, and was becoming to almost every face. Having no brim, it did not interfere with a worshipper's bowing his forehead to the earth in prayer. In after years when Reza Shah (who rode roughshod over the mullás and their ways, thus perhaps helping to bring on the strong clerical reaction under Khomeini) introduced an unbecoming version of the chauffeur-type peaked cap, there were hat riots in some areas, while the more peaceable of the Muslim worshippers simply turned their caps back to front when they prayed.

It is clear from many accounts how important types of clothing were in the Persia of that day – they symbolized one's rank, beliefs, pursuits. As in the Christian Middle Ages (and again under Hitler), you were what you wore. According to medieval Church decrees, a minority member had to declare himself publicly by some badge or hat. And there were, too, sumptuary laws which forbade persons 'of low degree' to wear expensive dress.

EIGHTEEN

The Point of No Return

Khan found the political situation in Persia worse than ever, with England and Russia still more firmly entrenched. Concession-seekers came into the country, couching their requests for special privileges as if they were idealists whose sole aims were the welfare of Iran and the safeguarding of her independence.

As for the country's pitifully few enlightened statesmen, the moment they proposed a liberal or progressive measure, the mullás and their mobs would shriek it down. Key mullás were well-financed by agents of the imperial powers, whose one and only program was to subjugate Irán in the furtherance of their normally, but not always, conflicting interests. Khan could not breathe in that poisoned air.

Meanwhile, waiting eagerly for his chance to escape, he attended many a Bahá'í meeting, and the believers could all feel, he wrote afterward, the 'fire of longing' which blazed in his heart. At this time, Mírzá 'Azízu'lláh Varqá (son of the martyred Varqá whose twelve-year-old son Rúhu'lláh was killed with him) had opened a shop on Tehran's fashionable Lálizár Avenue, where he sold merchandise imported from Europe. It was here that crowds of young Bahá'ís would come to listen to Khan's stories of his dervish experiences in the provinces.

At these evening meetings Khan addressed his young friends with that fire and eloquence which later on and far away brought so many into the Bahá'í Faith:

'In this greatest Day of Days, when the Faith of Bahá'u'lláh, your Faith, is the one and only remedy provided by Almighty God for the healing of nations, what good is it to follow material and ephemeral pursuits in a country that is yours in name only, where you live out your life at the sufferance of your foreign masters?

'This is the great, long-promised Day. This Faith of Bahá'u'lláh is entrusted to its followers. Let us arise as one body and hold high the torch of Bahá'u'lláh! Let us hasten to the presence of 'Abdu'l-Bahá and, guided by Him, offer up our lives in the service of humankind.'

One night a blizzard raged outside and drifts of snow piled up in the streets. On a sudden impulse, Khan told them:

'My friends – no more talk, no more lip service. The time has come to seek Him out. No more postponements, no more thoughts of preparation for the journey. Let whoever is willing, follow me!'

Ten young men rose up and followed Khan into the night. They fought their way in the dark, through the snow, till they reached one of the twelve city gates. About a mile beyond lay a post house where travelers could rest and change horses. In those days, Siyyid Ahmad Báqirof of Rasht and Bákú, a member of the prominent Bahá'í Báqirof family, had recently obtained a concession to keep the road from Tehran's gate to the Caspian Sea in good repair. Using the new carriages and wagons instead of animal caravans, he transported passengers and merchandise between Rasht on the Caspian and Tehran. He also established about ten post houses along the route and put each one under a Bahá'í manager.

By midnight, Khan and his band had reached the first post house, about a mile outside the Qazvín Gate. The brilliant young Bahá'í manager, Mírzá 'Abdu'l-Ḥusayn, entertained them so joyously that night that Khan never forgot it, nor the love which fired the whole group.

They slept in their clothes, just as they were, until dawn broke, when they set out through deep snow.

Sometimes a horse-drawn wagon creaking past would pull up and give them a lift; but mostly they walked, chanting holy Tablets as they went, singing mystical love songs, and the hard miles swung by. Also of help was the presence of Mírzá 'Alí-Akbar, son of the famous Bahá'í calligrapher, Mishkín-Qalam, one of the earliest companions of Bahá'u'lláh, with Him in exile from Baghdad to Constantinople and on through the years in Adrianople to the prison-city of 'Akká. This young man was not of the learned class, and had none of his father's talents, but was brought up to be in trade. As they trudged along, he entertained them with sidelights on the journeys his father had shared with the Manifestation.

The last post house before Qazvín was Yangí-Imám, and here a notable Bahá'í was in charge. He was a muleteer and illiterate, but he had served many years transporting the goods of two brothers, merchant princes of Iṣfáhán, Mírzá Muḥammad-Ḥasan and Mírzá Muḥammad-Ḥusayn. The highest mullá of that city owed the two a large sum of money, and rather than pay his debt, preferred to denounce them as Bábís so that they would be killed. They were seized, chained and decapitated, and their bodies were dragged out to the great public square, and left to be desecrated by the mobs. The authorities confiscated all that the two had possessed. Their rich homes were sacked, stripped to the walls, even the flowers and trees of the gardens demolished. Many were revolted at the fate of the two innocent men, and even the Christian priest of Julfá wept over them that day.[52]

Mashhadí Ḥaydar, the manager of this post house and former employee of the martyred brothers, told in his simple speech of early Bahá'í days and his accounts were so moving that his listeners often had to wipe away tears.

They had reached Qazvín on the fourth night of their journey. Not far from the city is Alamút, stronghold of him whom the Crusaders called the 'Old Man of the Mountains', who once conquered the city.

The young people stayed there three days as guests of the Bahá'ís. One of these was Jináb-i-Samandar, who lived in the very house where the beauteous poet, Ṭáhirih, once had lived. Except for minorities and peasants, she was the first woman in the Persia of her day to unveil her face in the presence of men, and she became the first woman in the world to die for women's rights.[53]

Khan also met the noted Bahá'í physician, Ḥakím-Báshí, here in Qazvín.

Resuming the journey, the youths climbed through mountain country and encountered more snow and severe cold than any of them had lived through before. One night they had to put up in a stable where there were no animals to provide warmth. They had no bedding, only their heavy overcoats, Khan's being lined with fur. (The Persians often used fur as a lining, fur in, skin out; and seeing a European's coat with the fur showing, they would say, 'You are only warming the weather.') That night the travelers lay down in a row under their coats, with a ladder across the coats to hold them in place.

Nearly a week passed before they reached Rasht, a town which a Western visitor has described as having an English look. Because of the rainfall, mud-adobe was not used for building here. It had other special features, one the manufacture of embroidered saddle coverings, another, malaria.

The Bahá'ís of Rasht had been alerted by a telegram from Tehran to expect the would-be pilgrims. A telegram was not then the routine affair it is today, for Persia had only single-wire lines between cities, and when, as often happened, the rickety poplar poles were down on the ground, the telegraph agent would simply tell you, 'The line does not speak today.'[54]

The day after their arrival Khan, his brother Ḥusayn and one other from the group called on the Governor, Muḥammad-Valí Khán, later Commander-in-Chief of Mázindarán. He would play a leading role in Persia's 1906 revolution, six or seven years down the road. He was one of Persia's great landlords, and was also a Bahá'í but known as such only to his fellow believers.

Khan requested the Governor to order passports for the youths, since they were to travel through Russia, but he refused.

'Your uncle and various prominent relatives of the rest of your group have informed me by telegram that you must not be permitted to leave the country,' he told Khan. (The families had obviously concluded that, with no preparations for the journey, the hardships would be too much to endure.)

'You are therefore directed to go back to your homes.'

That seemed to be that. Khan, however, approached him and whispered in his ear, 'The Bahá'í Faith has reached America and they need translations of the Sacred Writings into English. I would therefore be useful to 'Abdu'l-Bahá in 'Akká. It is urgent that I should go to Him.' The result was, the Governor issued one passport: for Khan.

The others, except for the son of Mishkín-Qalam, who already had a passport, stayed on in Rasht until they received funds from Tehran for the trip home.

Khan, though virtually without money, determined to leave for Bákú at the earliest moment possible. The morning he left Ra<u>sh</u>t stayed in his mind through all the years. He walked with his brother to the public square and hired a horse to ride to the lagoon, where he was to go on by rowboat to the port of Enzeli, board a steamer and cross the Caspian Sea. As Khan was about to ride away, his brother put some silver coins in his hand, about one dollar in all.

Khan does not describe the trip to Enzeli, but early in this century Ella Sykes says the lagoon was 'teeming with fish and waterfowl', and tells of a 'rickety native boat'[55] – who knows, perhaps it was the same one used by Khan to reach the port.

Bahá'í friends met him at Enzeli, and they visited together till late that afternoon, when it was time for a second boat to take Khan and the other passengers to the steamer, about a mile away. In those days the port was not deep enough for steamers to tie up at the pier. The Caspian was rough and stormy and the boat ride to the ship was excruciating agony, especially for Khan, who had never seen such a wide expanse of water or such tremendous waves. The ship was the *Soura Khan* and she belonged to a Turk, one of the business leaders of Bákú. Small, not over a couple of thousand tons, but to Khan she was a whole village afloat.

That night of anguish aboard her came back in bad dreams. The Persians are not a maritime people, and Khan was sure, from moment to moment, all night long, that the ship would founder. He suffered so much that he would crawl to the captain on his hands and knees and repeatedly ask, 'Is she going to sink?' To which he always received the same answer: 'Oh yes. Pretty soon now. Pretty soon.'

The next morning, ecstasy: Khan saw land. In after years he and his wife Florence always thought the sailing and docking of whatever ship they were on was a great event, a cosmic time, a time for prayers and tears, like birth and death. Perhaps this had its beginning in Khan's trip across the Caspian.

Within an hour he was embraced by Bahá'í friends who had been informed of his arrival. But there were problems. One was a lost satchel. In Ra<u>sh</u>t he had been given a satchel with some clothing and quinine packed in it, and this was to have been carried to the *Soura Khan* in another rowboat; but when he looked for this satchel among the pieces of baggage, it was not there. He arrived in Bákú with nothing but the clothes on his back.

Another problem was much more serious and had been worrying Khan even when still in Tehran: he had not received permission from 'Abdu'l-Bahá to come to 'Akká. He had composed his 'Ode from Senna', a love poem addressed to the Master, begging to be allowed to serve Him in the prison-city, but although the Master lovingly replied with a Tablet, no permission had ever come. He was still hoping for it when he set off into that winter's night a few weeks before. Would it be waiting for him when he reached Bákú? It was not.

For the moment, the warm welcome of the friends in Bákú put this worry out of his mind, or at least drew a veil over it. Although they were used to Bahá'í travelers, for these came here from distant places – from Persia, Turkistán, India – on their way to and from the Holy Land, Khan found quite a number of the believers waiting for him at the pier. One of them was Ustád Áqá Bálá who with his brother and elderly father owned a large construction firm in the city. They were all strong Bahá'ís, and the year following this the Master gave the father and one of the sons the privilege of working on the excavation and preliminary construction of the Bab's Holy Shrine on Mount Carmel.

Many of the friends offered Khan the hospitality of their homes, but he had made a vow never to sleep in a comfortable bed until he reached the holy presence of the Master. Consequently he was taken to the Bahá'í Centre, a building not yet completed except for the ground floor. During the week that he was in Bákú, Khan slept in a corner of the meeting room, on the floor and with only his fur-lined coat for a cover.

The renowned Bahá'í teacher, Ḥájí Mírzá Ḥaydar-'Alí, was spending several weeks here at the Centre, holding meetings and then making his bed in the same room where he taught, the room in which Khan also slept. Ḥaydar-'Alí was on his way to Tehran, and when the Bahá'ís learned that Khan was without funds and did not yet have permission to visit the Holy Land, they requested Ḥaydar-'Alí to take the young man back to Tehran where he could wait at home for word from the Master. But no, Khan would not turn back.

Every night, in that room which they shared, Mírzá Ḥaydar-'Alí taught the Bahá'í Faith to travelers and townspeople. Rich and poor would come, including the famous oil millionaire, Áqá Músá Naqiof, whose executive secretary, Mírzá 'Alí-Akbar Naḵhjavání, came to the United States in 1912 as a member of the Master's suite.

Mírzá Ḥaydar-'Alí was a remarkable Bahá'í. He had been an early disciple and companion of Bahá'u'lláh and had suffered long years of imprisonment in Persia and elsewhere, particularly the Sudan, because he insisted on teaching the Faith. He had already written a book, embodying proofs and evidences of the new Manifestation of God, supported by sacred writings of previous Faiths, especially Islam. He was one of the staunchest upholders of Bahá'u'lláh's Covenant, and when he stood in the presence of 'Abdu'l-Bahá, was as nothingness itself. He was to spend his last days in the Holy Land, on Mount Carmel, and meet many American Bahá'ís, who used to call him the Angel of Carmel. He is buried in the heart of it now. Hand of the

Cause A. Q. Faizi later translated into English his *Stories From the Delight of Hearts*.

We may imagine how Khan felt when such a man asked him to address the meetings also – in fact, would not take no for an answer.

Although without means, virtually penniless, Khan made up his mind to go to Tiflis, capital of Georgia, in the central part of the Caucasus. In that city there lived a Bahá'í of the well-known Mílání family from Persian Ádhirbáyján, who had accepted the Faith from the Báb Himself while in prison. This man, whom Khan had known before, was a textile merchant. Khan wrote him, explained his situation, that he was waiting and hoping for the Master's permission to make the pilgrimage. The reply was an invitation to come and be his guest.

With a few rubles Khan bought a third class railway ticket for Tiflis. He sat awake all night, crowded in with many kinds and conditions of people, listening to different languages and observing young and old, their manners, looks and ways so strange to him that they drove out the memory of the enormous variety of human beings he had seen at the Muslim shrines.

The next day, in the forenoon, he was met by Hájí Mílání and conducted to his shop at Serai-Aslán, in the quarter of the cloth merchants. The Hájí led him upstairs to his apartment over the shop and told him to rest. But here again, because of his vow, he refused the comfort of a bed and slept on the floor.

Here in Tiflis he spent several weeks, meeting Bahá'ís and also looking up a college friend from Tehran, Abu'l-Hasan Khán, now a clerk at the Persian Consulate-General. This friend wished him to meet the Persian representatives here, and accept a position.

'No,' Khan told him, 'I have burned my bridges behind me. I shall probably have to return to Tehran, but only to prepare for 'Akká, and there I shall learn the plan whereby I am to be guided all through my life.'

His friend urged Khan to stay on and teach French and English, both in demand, instead of returning to Tehran. Although he did give an occasional French lesson, Khan did not feel it would be fair to start classes only to abandon them when word came that he could go to the Holy Land, as, daily, he hoped it would. Still, the days passed and nothing came.

NINETEEN

In Sight of the Goal

With only the fur-lined coat and his one suit, as spring came on Khan bartered the suit for lighter clothes, and bought a kind of pasteboard shirtfront with attached collar, discarding this for a new one when it was soiled.

The Ḥájí, his host, showed him much kindness and, knowing he could not set out for 'Akká without permission, suggested that after his visit in Tiflis he go on with the caravan to Tabríz in Persian Ádhirbáyján and stay with the Ḥájí's relatives in that city. Perhaps, he said, it was not God's will that Khan should go to 'Akká at this time.

Khan gave in, but bitterly, and wrote his family in Tehran of his changed plans. He asked his uncle to write him a letter of introduction to the Crown Prince, Muḥammad-'Alí, son of Muẓaffari'd-Dín Sháh, now (as was customary for the heir to the throne) governing in Tabríz.

The caravan was due to leave in just a few days, and Khan with it. But then a miracle happened, as so often, he felt, throughout his life: a letter came to him from Bákú, and in it was a letter from Ḥájí Siyyid Muḥammad-Taqí Manshádí, the Master's secretary in charge of dispatching the mails. It told the believers in Bákú of 'Abdu'l-Bahá's telegram saying Khan should leave at once for 'Akká, and asked for an early reply as to the time of his departure so that they would be prepared for his arrival. The Bákú friends, in their letter, requested Khan to leave for Bátúm, the port on the Black Sea, and there join the noted Bahá'í teacher Mírzá Maḥmúd Furúghí and four others from 'Ishqábád for the sea voyage to Constantinople.

That very night Khan left by train for Bátúm and arrived the next morning with the party from 'Ishqábád. One of them was a woman from Kirmán named Rúḥání (Spiritual) who, on that journey, set them all an example of courage and devotion. Another was the young son of a prominent merchant of Jewish background, Mírzá 'Azízu'lláh, who made very generous contributions toward erecting in 'Ishqábád the world's first Bahá'í House of Worship.

The pilgrims boarded an Austrian steamer which immediately eclipsed Khan's memory of the one in which he had crossed the Caspian. En route to Constantinople, she made four or five stops at Turkish ports. At Trebizond the ship was held up for over an hour by a raging storm which kept her from entering the harbor. In all Khan's young life he had never been through anything like this. He and his fellow passengers in the steerage were in mortal terror, except for Rúḥání, who assured them that pilgrims with permission to come would reach 'Akká in safety. Meanwhile, the other believers, pale with fright, trembling, were fervently reciting the Greatest Name, *Yá-Bahá'u'l-Abhá*. This woman's calm in all the turmoil was to Khan a sign of her great faith.

Once they had reached Constantinople they were conducted to a small caravanserai located under the bridge and close to the Bosporus, that rough and narrow strait between European and Asiatic Turkey that joins the Black Sea to the Sea of Marmara. Here they stayed about a week. The reason for the delay was Jináb-i-Furúghí's insistence that they should wait and board the Austrian steamer for Beirut and Haifa, because Bahá'u'lláh had always praised the ships of that line.

Jináb-i-Furúghí made his fellow travelers stay off the streets, penned in the caravanserai, sleeping in quarters so miserable that Khan, for the first time in his life, was attacked by bedbugs. The reason for their forced seclusion was that the always-terrified Sultan, 'Abdu'l-Ḥamíd, sat on the Turkish throne. He went in fear of his life and thought there were spies all through the city, seeking to murder him. Bahá'í travelers were suspect, particularly now, when the Faith had reached the United States. Enemies from various Muslim sects, jealous of this success and knowing that the new religion was constantly gaining adherents in the Middle East as well, spread slanderous stories about the peace-loving, government-obeying Bahá'ís.

The Sultan, whom Gladstone called the 'Great Assassin', had faith in no one. On one occasion, when he had ordered two men executed, he insisted that their heads be embalmed and sent to him in Constantinople, so he could be sure. This was the ruler who had his tailor devise strangely-placed pockets in his clothing, to hold not only the reports from his secret agents but also his three revolvers. No one, in the Sultan's presence, was allowed to put a hand in his own pocket: documents were brought to him in hands outstretched and bare. In every corner of his apartments there were washbowls because he felt called upon to wash his hands every few minutes.[56] This was the jailer with life and death powers over his Prisoner, 'Abdu'l-Bahá – the man to whom the violators of Bahá'u'lláh's Covenant reported that 'Abdu'l-Bahá, aiming to usurp the Sultan's throne, was fomenting a rebellion against him, was building a fortress and vast ammunition depot on Mount Carmel and had secretly raised up an army of 30,000 men.[57]

Khan related in after years how the Sultan, panic-stricken at the thought of real or imagined enemy spies, forbade the installation of modern utilities such as electricity and the telephone in Constantinople, except in a very few places, continually under guard. Khan would say that the Young Turk Revolution of 1908, which brought the 'Great Assassin' down, proved that his constant terror of plots and plotters was not without its basis in fact.

During the monotonous days in the caravanserai, the pilgrims received a number of Bahá'í visitors, who came discreetly and invited them to their homes; and somehow the time passed.

At last the Austrian ship was due to sail. Of the same line as the one they had boarded in Bátúm, this one was much larger than the last, and Khan might have taken this as an omen of greater things to come. She made stops along the way, sometimes putting in at two or three Turkish or Greek ports in a day, discharging passengers and cargo, so that it took about a week to reach Beirut. The pilgrims traveled steerage, on the open deck. Khan kept to his vow, and when fellow believers offered bedding, refused, lying out under his coat, sometimes in pouring rain. He had very little money to spend for food, and whenever the ship lay at anchor and Turkish, Greek and Arab vendors came aboard with dates and other edibles to sell, he would buy bread and cheese and an occasional raw egg, swallowed down for strength. As with bedding, he steadfastly refused the others' offers of food.

He was skeleton-thin by now, but so filled with joy at realizing the hope he had cherished so many years, a dream at last within reach, that he had no room to dwell on his physical condition.

The pilgrims had written ahead to the noted Bahá'í merchant Muḥammad Muṣṭafá Baghdádí telling him the time of their arrival, and he had sent a number of believers to meet them at the dock and escort them to his home. This man, so kind and welcoming, was the father of Dr Zia Bagdadi, later well known to the American Bahá'ís, who practiced medicine and taught the Faith in Chicago for many years, till, while teaching in Florida, he passed away.

Only those who have experienced Bahá'í hospitality in the East could appreciate the love and tender care that was showered upon the pilgrims at the Baghdádí home. The new arrivals and the welcoming party then shared a sumptuous meal with their hosts, and Jináb-i-Furúghí spoke memorably of his teaching experiences in Persia and Turkistán, where he had been repeatedly persecuted and thrown in jail.

The host duly thanked the speaker and told the gathering that he had known of the services and achievements of this great teacher for a number of years. He went on to say that he wished those present to hear the story of the dervish wanderings of Ali-Kuli Khan (Ishti'ál) and how the young man, educated beyond most, had given up what would have been a distinguished career in Persia and dedicated his life to the Faith especially at this moment when the Sacred Writings had to be translated into English, the holy Cause having reached America. He told them, too, that Khan had converted the son-in-law of the reigning Shah, and as a result had received a remarkable Tablet from 'Abdu'l-Bahá.

Hearing all this, Khan was trembling and could not hold back his tears. It had never occurred to him that anyone would know of these things in this distant place. And, especially, he thought, how wonderful it was to hear such words from this great believer, who when young had run alongside the parasoled howdah of Bahá'u'lláh Himself on the exile from Baghdad to Constantinople.

Although reluctant to speak about himself, Khan was persuaded to tell something of his wanderings, and ended by chanting his 'Ode from Senna'. As he spoke, he saw tears of happiness and sympathy glistening on the faces of the friends.

That evening the pilgrims boarded the ship again and sailed away down the coast to their final port. It was still dark the next morning, some time before dawn, when the ship anchored about a mile off Haifa. In those days Haifa was a town of negligible importance, and the harbor was not deep enough to permit a steamer to come in any nearer. A number of believers, with Ḥájí Muḥammad-Taqí Manshádí, came out by rowboat to meet the pilgrims and get them ashore. Everything was still dark, and the outline of Mount Carmel barely visible.

Once on land, Khan knelt and kissed the earth, and offered thanks to God for granting him his dearest wish.

TWENTY

The Arrival

Since it was still so early, Khan was taken to the coffee house of Ḥusayn Effendi, a Bahá'í who regularly greeted and served refreshments to newly arrived pilgrims.

'The Master is right here in Haifa,' someone said.

At this, Khan, terrified, broke down and wept. 'How can one such as I,' he cried, 'one with so many shortcomings – how can I stand in the presence of One from whose all-seeing eyes nothing whatever is hidden?'

The believers offered words to quiet him down.

'You'll see,' they told him, 'He is not like that. He is all bounty and mercy. He will make it easy for you to endure the awe of His presence.

He has invited you to come and once you see Him you will have no more worries.'

Then, as the sky brightened, they led him about a quarter of a mile away to a house near the sea, and while they walked, Khan kept weeping and voicing his fears.

Centuries before, the English mystic, George Herbert, had described an experience such as Khan was about to have.[58]

> Love bade me welcome: yet my soul drew back,
> Guiltie of dust and sinne . . .

Invited to be Love's guest, the lover answers,
> Ah my deare,
> I cannot look on Thee.

Whereupon Love, smiling, takes his hand and says,
> Who made the eyes but I?

And at the end,
> You must sit down, sayes Love, and taste my meat.
> So I did sit and eat.

The arriving party climbed the brick steps leading to the courtyard. Khan was shaking and his heart pumped too fast. What sort of Being was he going to see? He had known but one photograph of the Master, the youthful one taken at Adrianople, in the days when veiled women, gazing down from their latticed windows, would throw roses at His feet. When he dared to look, there, standing tall before him, was One in turban and robe, One with a full beard, dark but with much gray intermingled, and a face just as Khan had always visualized the countenance of Bahá'u'lláh.

'I saw this was Bahá'u'lláh,' he said in after years. (Dídam Bahá'u'lláhst.) Khan collapsed, fell to the floor.

'He lifted me up,' Khan would say, 'put His arms around me, and kissed me on both cheeks. Noting the state I was in He told His attendant to take me to another room and give me some tea.'

Ustád Muḥammad-'Alí helped Khan to the corner room where the pilgrims would rest.

Within a few minutes 'Abdu'l-Bahá sent for him. By now, to his surprise, Khan felt strong enough to stand in His presence. The Master said:

'Marḥabá! Marḥabá! (Welcome, welcome), Jináb-i-Khán. You have suffered much on your wanderings, but welcome! Praise be to God, you have reached here in safety.

'The Blessed Perfection, Bahá'u'lláh, has promised to raise up souls who would hasten to the service of the Covenant, and would assist me in spreading His Faith. His Cause has now reached America and many in the Western world are being attracted to His Teachings. You, with your knowledge of English, are one of those souls promised me by Bahá'u'lláh. You have come to assist me by translating His Sacred Writings as well as my letters to the friends in America and elsewhere in the West.'

The room seemed charged with His words. They resounded ever after in Khan's mind and heart.

Then He said, 'You must reside with me and assist me in my work.'

He stretched out His hand to the table and took up a pack of folded papers, the sort He used for Tablets, and passed them over to Khan.

'These are the answers', He said, 'that I have written to some of the American Bahá'ís. Go and translate them into English.'

Khan unfolded the top ones. They were Tablets 'Abdu'l-Bahá had written in His own hand. They were in Arabic.

'But my Master,' he cried, 'these are not in Persian! These are Arabic! In my college I studied European languages, but not Arabic!'

No one had ever in his life looked at Khan with such loving eyes and such a smile. Still smiling, 'Abdu'l-Bahá reached for His rock candy on the table. Filling both His hands He told Khan to cup his palms for the candy. Then, His eyes mysteriously solemn, and His voice taking on a new, strange tone, 'Abdu'l-Bahá said: 'Go, and eat this candy. Rest assured, the Blessed Perfection will enable you to translate the Arabic into English. Rest assured that as time goes on you will be assisted to translate from the Arabic much more easily than from the Persian.'

They both remained standing throughout the whole interview, Khan before the Master, within a few feet. Dismissing him, the Master pointed to the bedstead in the room and said He had taken a house in the German Colony and was no longer using this bed.

'This is your bed,' He told Khan. 'Sleep in it.'

TWENTY-ONE

Working for the Master

When night came, Khan did not have the courage to sleep in the Master's bed. And so, once again, as in all through the two years just passed, still keeping on with his vow, Khan lay down on the floor. This went on for three nights. On the morning of the fourth day Ustád Muḥammad-'Alí, the Master's attendant, entered the room and said, 'Jináb-i-Khán, you have wandered many weary weeks and months, and all that time you have lived and longed for the day when you might enter the Master's holy presence. Now that your wish has been granted and your goal reached, are you aware that you are disobeying the Master?'

Khan was shocked to hear him. 'What on earth do you mean?' he asked.

'I mean that you have not slept in the Master's bed, as He told you to do.'

'I did not intend to disobey Him,' stammered Khan. 'I simply was not brave enough to sleep in a bed in which the Center of Bahá'u'lláh's Covenant had slept.'

But he promised Ustád that from now on he would obey, although it was only with fear and trembling that he finally crept into the bed which had been 'Abdu'l-Bahá's. For two years he had passed his nights comfortless on the floor or the ground. He thought of his secret vow and wondered if maybe this was what had come of it.

The Master's house in Haifa where Khan first saw Him was a 'block' or so from the beach and from the embarcadero built for the arrival of Kaiser Wilhelm II the year before, in 1898. The house was not isolated, there were other houses around it and it gave on a street roughly parallel with the sea and extending to the German Colony street – the place where the German adventists once lived, looking for the Lord to appear on Mount Carmel, the Mountain of God.

In those days 'Abdu'l-Bahá's confinement in 'Akká, not yet reimposed as it would be later because of the never-ending plots of the Covenant-breakers, was less strict. Every week the Master could go to Haifa and spend a few days there in order to supervise the excavating for the foundation of the Báb's Tomb on the slopes of the mountain. The family remained in 'Akká and the Master would spend the night in His rented house.

As the work required more and more of His time, He came more often to Haifa. He therefore rented a second small house on the avenue known as the German Colony, lined by stone houses with sacred Scriptural verses over their doors, about the coming of the Lord. This avenue led directly from the sea front to the foot of the mountain. And here Khánum, His sister, the Most Exalted Leaf, or one of His daughters and a son-in-law, could stay and look after Him, and He would pass the night.

At the time of Khan's arrival, the first rented house was used by 'Abdu'l-Bahá as an office and a place where He could receive the pilgrims and other visitors. A flight of brick steps led up from the street to an open courtyard surrounded on three sides by rooms; and a door giving directly on the street was the one to the Master's reception room. Here there was an iron bedstead where He sometimes rested in the daytime. (At first there had been two beds here and Jináb-i-Furúghí slept in one of them.) Besides several chairs, the room's other furniture consisted of a large table at one side, on which 'Abdu'l-Bahá kept writing materials, papers, some flowers, rose-water and a plate heaped with rock candy. (Why the Master liked to give the Bahá'ís rock candy we do not know. Perhaps it was because it would last and they could save it, as Khan did throughout life. Or perhaps, as we sometimes think, it was a symbol, because in the East candy is put in the mouth of a sheep before it is ritually sacrificed.)

The room next to this one, measuring about fourteen by sixteen feet, was a kind of store room for household and other articles – brooms, odds and ends. Against the wall, beside a barred window giving onto the courtyard, stood a table of plain wooden boards with a raw, wooden backless bench, on which Khan was apt to lie down and sleep at night, and wooden pegs for his few spare clothes dotted the rough wall. In one corner, away from the window, rested a large sarcophagus especially built to order by the Bahá'ís of Rangoon, Burma, and sent by them to the Master, to hold the sacred remains of the Báb, which as directed by the Master had recently been brought out from their hiding places in Persia. This sarcophagus was to be transported to the Tomb of the Báb as soon as the Tomb was completed and ready to receive the holy dust. This, the room's most prominent feature, was in a sort of wooden packing case, and Khan himself was greatly surprised when told – in after years by a trusted attendant of the Master's – that as he sat at his table near the window and did his translations month after month, the sacred remains of the Báb and His companion, so recently brought out of Persia, may well have been here in this very room. His informant was apparently Muḥammad-'Alí, and looking back over the room in memory, Khan gathered that, for a time at least, the sacred remains could have been hidden in the beautiful, carved – he thought empty – sarcophagus. The date of Khan's tenure was sometime in 1899, perhaps late spring. [See Appendix]

At the back of the house was a room where travelers could stay temporarily, before leaving for 'Akká, and next to this, also with barred windows on the back street, was the room of Siyyid Taqí Manshádí, to whom all the mail was assigned by 'Abdu'l-Bahá. His room was piled high with letters, papers and packages relating to his perennial task of reaching out to the world and linking the Bahá'ís to their heart and center. He allowed no one except Khan to enter this room. Manshádí would carry the mail to the post office or ship, and in his famous, child-like handwriting – well-known everywhere – he would enclose a brief, bare account of Bahá'í news with the Tablets – laconic, but all the news. A small chá'í khánih (pantry where tea was prepared) was adjacent to this room.

Khan thought how wonderful it was that the Master wished to keep him in the Holy Land. He had feared that, like other pilgrims, after all his long journeying, he would be permitted to stay only a while, and then would have to leave for his own country or some other place that the Master would indicate. He said he could not describe the power with which 'Abdu'l-Bahá's welcoming words and the gift of rock candy suffused his whole being. And now, almost night and day for over a year, he would be in 'Abdu'l-Bahá's presence.

Often the Master would stop, on His way to the excavations where the Carmel Shrine would one day rise, and dictate Tablets, so that Khan had to stay prepared at all times, to write swiftly on his lap or the palm of his hand.

Khan said the believers thought it a privilege to talk to him then, because of his close association with 'Abdu'l-Bahá, but that he was too busy to notice the attention.

Asked what he wore in those days, he said a red Turkish fez such as the local Bahá'ís wore (it is, we think, one of the handsomest hats in the world) and a white jacket. White had been favored by believers since the days of the Báb.[59]

The Master's usual clothing, Khan said, was a long, straight coat (qabá) with narrow sleeves. Over this came His long robe with sleeves (labbádih) of heavy woolen material which folded over the front like a wrapper, and over this His 'abá, heavy in winter, light in summer. At home He often wore only the qabá and labbádih, without the 'abá. His garments worn beneath the qabá – materials varying with the season, – were a thin linen shirt, a woolen undershirt, and woolen drawers, over which came the outer shalvár (trousers). The colors He wore often were light gray and beige.

As for his difficult new task, Khan said that from that first meeting some new power was created in him, and he set to work with dictionaries and other helps and began to translate. During the several months spent in His presence, Khan translated the Master's Arabic as well as His Persian (and other language) Tablets, and afterward, through the years in America, he continued this work, and it did indeed become easier for him to put Arabic into English than to translate from his native tongue.

Unlike Persian, which is Indo-European, Arabic is a Semitic language, so difficult that the Master, an expert in Persian, Turkish and Arabic – His writings taught as a model by scholars in the East – reportedly called Arabic a 'bottomless abyss'. English-speaking readers of Bahá'í Writings are fortunate, receiving them all in English, and not conscious that to Persian readers the same page may suddenly slip into Arabic, a foreign tongue, much as if an English text should suddenly pass into Latin. On occasion, Bahá'u'lláh Himself has translated the Arabic into Persian, so that the English reader reads the same text twice.[60] Khan did, of course, work with helps and in the beginning for some months he studied the Occidental translators of Bábí and Bahá'í Writings, among them E. G. Browne, the distinguished orientalist who was the guest of Bahá'u'lláh at Bahjí (April 15–20, 1890). While these offered some assistance, he eventually found them wanting in many ways and he tried to produce new expressions and combinations of words to convey implications and shades of meaning. He reached the conclusion that a profound study of the languages involved was not enough to present an adequate rendition of the creative words of Bahá'u'lláh and the Master – for these are in themselves a new language with new connotations. No matter how great the scholar, Khan decided, unless he or she is a true believer, devoted to the Faith, the translation will fall short. This was also along the lines of Mírzá Abu'l-Faḍl's comment, that when he first read the *Íqán*, as a non-believer, its deep meanings remained obscure to him, but when he read it afterward as a believer, it was the key that unlocked all the holy Scriptures of the past.

Khan tried to follow the literal sense of the original as closely as he was able. On many occasions, verbally and in Tablets, 'Abdu'l-Bahá called Khan His best translator. This was long before the superlative achievements in the field by Shoghi Effendi, with his perfect English, Arabic and Persian, and his French so accomplished that he had to make a decision, Laura Barney said, as to whether he should put Bahá'í basic literature into English or French.[61] The Master told Khan not to worry, expert translators would come in the future, and assured him his work showed a deep and intimate knowledge of the inner meaning of the creative words.

Sometimes a Westerner will ask, why do we need a new translation when we have one already? One might as well ask, why didn't we stay with the Model-T Ford? Anyone looking at the first English *Íqán* vis-à-vis the original can see how closely it does adhere to the Persian, even if, as Horace Holley remarked, it confused him to the point that he wanted to throw the book across the room. Khan was the best available then, for the time and place. He was almost, you might say, with so few to help, a Crusoe without a Friday. And he was never one of those translators with no sense of right and wrong, no conscience, a tarjumán-i-bí vujdán of which the Master writes. He wore himself out trying to be faithful to the original, especially because he was afraid he might inadvertently cause divisions in the Faith. Meanwhile, the Master continually encouraged Khan, and told him to simply do his best. And let us not forget that 'Abdu'l-Bahá has written, '. . . translation is one of the most difficult arts.'[62]

Writing of Khan's work as interpreter for Mírzá Abu'l-Faḍl, Hand of the Faith H. M. Balyuzi says his 'services were invaluable, as he also contributed to the compendium of the Scriptures of the Faith available in English, by undertaking copious translations.'[63]

It was, so far as we know, not Khan who set a great eagle in pursuit of humankind in that early version of the *Hidden Words* from the Persian. Later on, removing the eagle, the Guardian rendered the words as 'grievous retribution'.[64] Persian does not write in the short vowels (for example, cat would be written ct), and the average reader has more or less to guess at them: here, the original word, 'iqáb (retribution) is, on the page, indistinguishable from 'uqáb (eagle).

On Fridays and Sundays in the early afternoon, the Master, accompanied by many Eastern and Western Bahá'ís, would go to Bahjí, the mansion where Bahá'u'lláh's latter days were spent, and visit his Tomb. Sometimes 'Abdu'l-Bahá would ride in His carriage or on a white donkey. As His correspondence with the United States and Europe increased, He would stay behind in 'Akká and work with Khan, and then, taking Khan along, would drive to the Holy Tomb, and enter it, surrounded by the crowd of pilgrims. Going inside the glass-topped enclosure, the Master would stand beside the entrance to the room which is the resting-place of Bahá'u'lláh, in the Shrine adjacent to the Mansion. Here, in His beautiful voice, He would chant the Arabic Visitation Tablet (which many Western Bahá'ís know so well today in the Guardian's translation and is the same Tablet chanted in the Shrine of the Báb), as the pilgrims would remain silently grouped about Him.

What was it like, working so long as the amanuensis of 'Abdu'l-Bahá? There were occasions, Khan said, when he could speak to Him, but other occasions when he did not dare. Sometimes the Master was most approachable; at other times He was inaccessible, remote in His majesty, and then Khan hardly dared breathe. Khan never saw Him in the same condition twice. Much like the ocean, one reflects. Members of the Family sometimes compared Him to the ocean. He always showed great dignity, but with courtesy and consideration. And when He wished to impress an individual with the need to improve his way of life – to sacrifice the self, to see no fault in others and so on – He always said, '*We* must do thus-and-so', not '*You* must'.

It was in the Master's carriage from Italy, called a karrúsih (no doubt carrozza), which was entered from the back and had benches along the two sides, that Khan first came to 'Akká. He told how the river poured into the Bay during part of the journey, and for a long stretch they went through water which sometimes rose to the carriage floor.

There was a caravanserai within the prison-city from the days of

Bahá'u'lláh. It was a walled, square courtyard where grain was unloaded from camels and mules, and with rooms for the drivers giving onto it. One flight up was a balcony facing the courtyard from all sides and here was a row of rooms, each with its door to the balcony and one long window to the outside to catch the fresh air. By day the travelers' belongings, their mattresses and such, were rolled up and bundled to one side as in Persia.

For a few weeks Khan slept in this caravanserai. Its head was a believer, Áqá Muhammad-'Alí, and he kept the upstairs rooms primarily for Bahá'ís. Mishkín-Qalam, the great calligrapher, and Jináb-i-Zaynu'l-Muqarrabín, whose skilled hand penned so many Tablets of Bahá'u'lláh, and Hájí Mírzá Haydar-'Alí, 'the Angel of Carmel', used to stay here, some living here with wife and family.

Every day Khan would go to the Master. 'Abdu'l-Bahá would say, 'The ship is coming on such and such a day. These Tablets must be ready.' And they were. But if the Master made no such comment, Khan took more time.

As the work load increased, the Master had Khan move over to His house (the former home of 'Abdu'lláh Páshá which He had rented in November 1896, and where Shoghi Effendi was born March 1, 1897).

It had a large courtyard with pool, flowers and trees. You went up a flight of stairs along the side of the house and on your right entered 'Abdu'l-Bahá's day reception room, with windows on the sea. Next to it was a smaller room with a table at the center and a bare wooden takht (bench), also with a window on the sea. This was Khan's room, where he lived and worked, translating letters from Europe and the United States and the Tablets answering them. The Master would dictate to him in Turkish, Arabic, Persian and Old Persian (for the Parsees). Khan would speedily write down His words in copy books, keeping many reed pens at the ready and many pots of powdered ink.

The Master had given His pen case of carved boxwood to Khan. Made in Shíráz, it was a light yellowish-brown, hand-carved with flowers and birds. It had a sunken inkpot of silver, filled with silk fibre to prevent spillage, and a tiny silver spoon for adding water to the ink, glossy black like India ink. The pens were thin brown reeds from Japan. They came about four feet long and would be broken at the knots and cut to about ten inches with a fine English knife, the Roger knife, called in Persian Rájis. The cutting would be done to measure on an amber-colored, dried artery of a sheep. (With an English pen it was not possible to make the sharp angles necessary for Persian calligraphy. Modern pens have endangered this great art.) Mishkín-Qalam used the Japanese reed as described, and also a long nay – bamboo – for the Greatest Name design, that says Yá Bahá'u'l-Abhá (O Thou the Glory of the All-Glorious), a design which he created, and is now seen worldwide on the walls of Bahá'í homes.

The Master also gave Khan a pure gold pen-holder, spiral-shaped, with a pearl at one end. This was a gift to the Master from one of the believers, probably Elsa Barney as she was then known, later Laura Dreyfus-Barney.

Lunch would be taken in that smaller room, served on that table, and the meal would be eaten in 'Abdu'l-Bahá's presence, Khan being there, with one or two sons-in-law including Shoghi Effendi's father, Mírzá Hádí, and the younger brother of Bahá'u'lláh, Mírzá Muḥammad-Qulí, who had a long beard and a gentle voice, and was utterly self-effacing before the Master. Sometimes a few Westerners also ate at this table, occasional visitors like Mr Remey and Lua and Edward Getsinger. Usually, both in 'Akká and Haifa, Khan also had his evening meal with 'Abdu'l-Bahá.

Next to his work room was another with windows on the sea, the bedroom of the Master Himself. Then followed a series of family rooms giving onto an open, roofed gallery – a mahtábí – and down below was a large room where, morning and evening, 'Abdu'l-Bahá and the pilgrims and others prayed together. Next to this was a small room where the tea was prepared.

The tea had to be exactly right, full in color, hot from the samovar, in gleaming glasses with silver holders.

Some of the old believers would chant the Tablets of Bahá'u'lláh. These were early Bahá'ís who had accompanied Bahá'u'lláh from Iran to Baghdad and over the long journey to Constantinople and Adrianople and ultimately to the Most Great Prison – 'Akká. These included Jináb-i-Zaynu'l-Muqarrabín, with his long hair and beard, who had suffered years of imprisonment for the Faith. Once the high priest of Iṣfahán, he was noted for profound scholarship, both in Islamic culture and in the Bábí and Bahá'í Faiths.

TWENTY-TWO

Red Ink for Martyrs' Blood

In those days of being with the Master, Khan wrote a number of letters to his brother, using red ink to symbolize the blood of the martyrs. These letters describe the joy he was experiencing day and night, and the work he was doing for 'Abdu'l-Bahá. He tells of being continually in 'Abdu'l-Bahá's presence in 'Akká and Haifa, even sleeping in the bed 'Abdu'l-Bahá had slept in, after sleeping nowhere but on the floor or the open deck in his long journey to reach the Master. He writes that part of his work consisted of translating Tablets revealed by the Master with the swiftness of driving rain that floods the fields; also that he was at work translating the monumental book, the *Fará'id*, by Mírzá Abu'l-Faḍl, and *The Hidden Words*, and *The Book of the Covenant*, and the Tablets related to the same. How his tasks are constantly on the increase as more and more persons write from America, acknowledging their acceptance of the Faith. He writes that, without exaggeration, during the few months he has been with the Master, over four hundred of these letters have come in from America. He tells his brother he begged God for help, and that 'Abdu'l-Bahá always strengthened and confirmed him.

'So this is my life here now,' he writes in his red ink. 'I do not see when and how I shall return to Persia or be sent anywhere else, for I haven't time even to think. All I know is, I must serve the Covenant while life lasts. Lately my nerves became so weak the doctors ordered me to stop work, but God be praised, the beloved Master blessed my forehead with His hands and comforted me and said He has great plans for my future and is preparing me for great things, that I must make progress day by day because my destiny is to be one of those souls that the Blessed Perfection had promised to send Him.' Khan ends the letter by saying that even to have written it was wasting the time he urgently needed to do the Master's work.

He also wrote of his one great concern: that 'Abdu'l-Bahá was hemmed in by enemies. 'Still,' he told his brother, ''Abdu'l-Bahá overcomes them with His ever-moving pen. The way he bears their hostility with peace and joy is the very proof of His heavenly powers. While all the members of His household are devoted in their service to Him, the one outstanding member is His sister, the Greatest Holy Leaf, tireless in her continuous service, ministering to all.'

Another memory of Khan's days in the Holy Land was the coming of a pilgrim, an elderly Bahá'í teacher, formerly a dervish, whose name was Ḥájí Qalandar. He came from Cairo, and was tall, with a long gray beard and still wearing his dervish hat with a light turban around the base. This man had known Khan's father forty years before in Káshán. When he left he traveled to Bulgaria to teach the Faith and wrote Khan from there that he had met Khan's cousin, Mírzá 'Alí-Muḥammad Khán, who was with the Persian consular service there, and had given him the Bahá'í Message. The cousin had accepted the Faith and wrote Khan, telling him (besides family news of the death of Khan's paternal aunt), of his great joy at becoming a Bahá'í, and saying he hoped to receive permission to visit the Master following the Naw-Rúz.

The epistles and Tablets which 'Abdu'l-Bahá gave Khan and directed him to translate included the manuscripts of *The Seven Valleys*, the *Ishráqát, Tarázát, Tajallíyát*, the *Tablet of the World*, the *Words of Paradise*, the *Glad Tidings*, and *The Tablet of the Most Great Infallibility*. These were Writings which the Master had had Jináb-i-Zayn go over. The Master also told Khan, later, to translate the *Íqán*. This came about through a cousin of Miss Bolles, Helen Ellis Cole, who, visiting the Master, asked Him for a special favor, which He granted: that He should have Khan translate the book of *Íqán*. The Master placed an authenticated copy of this text in Khan's hands and he began translating it while still in the Holy Land, asking the Master to explain its inner meanings. His work, completed a few years later in the United States, was the pioneer appearance in the West of Bahá'u'lláh's 'unique repository of inestimable treasures' wherein He has 'laid down a broad and unassailable foundation for the complete and permanent reconciliation' of the followers of the world's high religions[65] – and must have helped to ready the believers for the great symphony to come, the Guardian's own rendition of *The Book of Certitude*.

Khan never doubted that his work was provisional – others in future would do better. As Emerson put it about his own poetry, he would write poetry 'in this empty America' until the poets should come. Meanwhile Khan agonized over every word. Long years after, Willard Hatch, on pilgrimage, told the Guardian how readily Khan had put aside his own now-superseded translation of the *Íqán* in favor of the Guardian's, and Shoghi Effendi had responded, 'His faith is firm.'

Khan finished the various works in the United States. His introduction to the *Íqán* (in the translation of which book he was assisted by Howard MacNutt), brought out in New York by George Blackburne Co. in 1904, states that he worked from a copy 'revised in the presence of Bahá'u'lláh and approved by Him'. Other data as to the background of this book, included in his introduction, were provided by Mírzá Abu'l-Faḍl.

It was a totally new experience for Khan to meet Occidental Bahá'ís. One of those who came to see 'Abdu'l-Bahá as a pilgrim from the United States was Mrs Emilie Dixon of Washington DC, accompanied by her sister and her two daughters, Louise and Eleanor. Khan had never seen an American family before (the era of hordes of tourists taking over the planet was far in the future, although wars, trade and pilgrimage had always made some nationals known to others). Louise was a blonde of medium height, and Eleanor, the younger one, was a brunette and tall. (Khan's memoir does not describe Mrs Dixon or her sister.) When, in the following year, 'Abdu'l-Bahá sent Mírzá Abu'l-Faḍl, and also Khan, to America, Khan became close friends with this family.

Another pilgrim was Charles Mason Remey of Washington DC, Admiral Remey's son, who arrived from Paris where he was studying architecture at the Beaux Arts – a tall, slender young man with reddish goatee and red-blonde hair – and very eager to learn of the Faith. A mother and daughter named Kelting arrived from Chicago. From London came Miss Ethel Jenner Rosenberg, a descendant of the physician Edward Jenner, discoverer of vaccination (d. 1823), who immunized subjects against smallpox by infecting them with cowpox, hence the name, vacca being the Latin for cow.[66]

Ethel Rosenberg was well educated and proved a real help to Khan with his translations of the holy Tablets during her stay of several months. Another believer, a Californian who had married a British colonel and lived in London, was Mrs Thornburgh-Cropper. Her elderly mother, who was a friend of Mrs Phoebe Hearst of California, also arrived and made a long stay in Haifa in the Master's house; for, during the last half of Khan's stay, the Master spent most of His time in Haifa where work on the Mount Carmel Shrine was in progress.

Another distinguished American Bahá'í, who came from Paris, was a sister of Mrs R. H. White of Brookline, Massachusetts, and the widow of a Frenchman, Jackson by name. With Mrs Jackson was a boy of fifteen, Sigurd, the son of a noted American actor named Russell. Sigurd's mother had married Richard Hovey, the poet, and following his death she had become known as a teacher of elocution and trained many fine actors for the American stage. (Some years later Khan would meet and marry one of Mrs Hovey's pupils.)

Still other pilgrims from the West were two Californians, Mrs Helen S. Goodall and her daughter, Ella Goodall (Cooper) of Oakland and San Francisco, lifelong devoted servants of the Faith with whom Khan corresponded for many years.

And there were many more.

Every evening pilgrims from East and West gathered in the large corner room of the prison house in 'Akká, the house of 'Abdu'lláh Páshá, near the house of 'Abbúd, and visited together. Here, too, the old believers exiled with Bahá'u'lláh would chant. One, with an exceptionally beautiful voice, adding to the joy of those days and nights, was Mírzá Maḥmúd of Káshán. All of these, when in the presence of 'Abdu'l-Bahá and even in their contacts with Bahá'ís in general, were exceptionally humble and devoted and courteous, a fact which Khan, accustomed to the self-importance of Persian grandees, found most impressive of all. Once or twice a week the Master Himself would attend these gatherings.

After the meetings the assemblage would scatter, and certain European or American pilgrims whose stay was to be short would dine with the Master in His quarters upstairs, Khan being present to translate. Some wrote down the answers to their questions, and these notes, when approved by the Master would then be spread among the friends in the Western world. Such pilgrim notes, however, did not have the authority of the translated Tablets.

During his first months there, Khan was extremely nervous when the Master called on him to translate for the visitors at the meals and other times. He knew the English words and normally could translate at ease, but the fact that they were the spoken words of 'Abdu'l-Bahá made the process almost impossibly difficult, and there were times when he had to struggle with himself both mentally and physically to obey. He would far rather have the ground open and swallow him than go through the ordeal, and he prayed hard not to break down on such occasions and make a scene.

One day (it was 1900 by then – the century had turned) when no one else was there, 'Abdu'l-Bahá called Khan over and said He knew why Khan was having so much trouble translating His spoken words.

'It is not that your English is not adequate to the task,' He said in effect. 'It is your fear of misleading the questioners and the others to whom they in turn will speak later on – fear that you will not correctly impart the meaning of my words. It is this fright which causes you extreme nervousness.

'Be absolutely confident', the Master continued, 'that when you translate my words, whatever you say in English will convey the exact sense of them. This will enable you to overcome the difficulty.'

Then the Master looked at Khan with a wonderful, loving expression in His eyes and, smiling tenderly, He said, 'You cannot conceive what power is going to be yours in the future when you speak of the Faith. Forget your present difficulty. The day will come when, without any preparation, you will speak to large gatherings. The more numerous the people, the better you will speak. You will deliver the Message to hundreds, to thousands, no, to millions!'

Khan accepted this on faith, because 'Abdu'l-Bahá said it, but for the life of him he could not imagine how one individual could ever speak to millions.

A quarter of a century later, when he and his family had been away from the United States for six years, one of New York's broadcasting companies – the radio was new then, so new that the family wrote back to Persia about it – asked Khan to speak. He rose up, faced the microphone and realizing he was, incredibly, about to give the Bahá'í Message to millions, he began his talk with this account of what 'Abdu'l-Bahá had told him in 'Akká long before.

This instruction of the Master to Khan for his lectures on the Faith is reminiscent of the great words of the Master, specially addressed in a Tablet to Dr Grossmann, the noted Hand of the Cause: 'When you speak, do not think.'[67]

From that day on, Khan could face any audience whatever, with no hesitation, no fit of nerves. The larger the audience, the easier it was for him to speak. The Master directed him never to prepare any notes before speaking, but to rise and, as the Master said, open his mouth, and whatever would be required by the needs of the audience would come.

This was a special instruction to Khan from the Master, a personal gift, Khan said, and did not imply that a speaker must not use notes. We have often heard this or that individual, not yet deeply versed in the Sacred Writings as Khan was and, lacking his years of serious, general studies, rise and give a less than valuable speech. There is still truth in the saying that 'extemporaneous is extemperroneous'. Besides, everyone knows that many, seemingly speaking impromptu, have memorized their talks beforehand – and they should be thanked for it. Abraham Lincoln prepared ahead, while on the 'railroad cars' going to dedicate the cemetery at Gettysburg. He borrowed a pencil and a bit of paper and jotted down the world-famous speech.

Looking back into the mists of past ages, and trying to measure the relative life of the arts, we note that the Word was immortal from the beginning, and carved stone lives a long time, and color or outline on clay and some other surfaces too, but until this day song died with the singer, the voice with the speaker, and when the dancer was blotted out, so was the dance. Now, even though Khan is no longer in the world, and that thin and burning young man who somehow and so long ago got himself to 'Akká is only an image on the air, still his recorded voice exists, and can still be heard by millions. In particular there is a recording that Daisy Pumpelly Smythe had made in New York City in which Daisy, Juliet Thompson, the two Kinneys, and Khan and Florence each describe their first meeting with the Master. Daisy included in this recording a chant by the Khans' younger daughter, Hamideh, and also 'Abdu'l-Bahá's chant taken from the 78 RPM record on shellac made during His visit to America in 1912. All of this has been copied on tape, safely preserved this far, and can be heard by millions as the years go by.[68]

Returning to the year 1900 when Khan was serving in 'Akká and Haifa as amanuensis to 'Abdu'l-Bahá: one of the Master's tasks was writing or dictating replies to letters from all parts of the world. He had several secretaries to whom he dictated. Among them were his sons-in-law and Mírzá Ḥabíb, son of one of the early companions of Bahá'u'lláh, named Áqá Muḥammad-Riḍá Qannád of Shíráz, trained from childhood by the Master. In the beginning, only Tablets replying to American believers were dictated to Khan, who took them down in Persian or Arabic; they were then read over and corrected by the Master and then translated by Khan. 'Abdu'l-Bahá would sign the originals and Khan would get them ready to mail. As time went on and the work load increased, the Master would also dictate to Khan Tablets – besides the Persian and Arabic ones – in Turkish and pure Parsee, the latter for Zoroastrian believers. Turkish, be it said, is very difficult. As the Master would tell scientist Hudson Maxim in New York later on, 'In the East it is thought that acquiring Turkish is equivalent to the study of three other tongues.'[69] The Master would revise the Tablets, writing in any words that Khan had omitted, and Khan (in his then beautiful hand) would recopy and return them for His signature before they were mailed.

In these Tablets the Master dealt with abstruse questions of scriptural, philosophical and cultural import which had for long ages gone unanswered, and He revealed them with such ease that one would have thought He was reading His answers out of a book. It was done with miraculous spiritual power and an unbelievable memory. On one occasion when a number of letters had to be answered at once to meet a deadline and catch the mail, the Master called in two of His sons-in-law and two other secretaries besides Khan, and began dictating a different Tablet to each of the five. He started out dictating one paragraph to each, then returned to number one, dictated the second paragraph, and so on down the line. The addressees, subjects, and in some cases the languages were different, one from the next.

TWENTY-THREE

The Covenant-Breakers Attack

'Abdu'l-Bahá, meaning the Servant of Bahá, had adopted servitude for His 'crown of glory'. He fulfilled in His daily way of life what the Prophet and the Saints of Islam meant by the saying, 'Servitude is a substance the essence of which is Divinity'. This servitude was second nature to Him. He showed it in all His acts and deeds. For over a year Khan was privileged to observe this life.

In the 'Akká residence where the Master lived with His family, Khan was, as said before, assigned a small room between 'Abdu'l-Bahá's bedroom and His day reception room, with windows on the Mediterranean Sea. Here Khan worked, and here he slept on a cot. He did his translations at a wooden table in the center.

This was the time when Muḥammad-'Alí, the half-brother who broke the Covenant made by Bahá'u'lláh, and was next in years to 'Abdu'l-Bahá and in rank second only to Him, having tried but failed to create a schism among the believers, was particularly active with his younger brother, his brother-in-law and their families, in constructing their vicious plots against the Master. For they saw

Bahá'u'lláh's testament as pertaining to their own personal family interests, while He saw it as a document addressed to all mankind.[70]

'Abdu'l-Ḥamíd, Sultan of Turkey, then in control of the countries of Asia Minor, used 'Akká as a prison for political rebels, and self-appointed among the Sultan's spies were these close members of the Master's own family. The result was that 'Abdu'l-Bahá, already a prisoner, although by this time less confined, now went in continual peril of His life. He was to be sent away, the rumor was, to die in the Sahara, or He would be hanged, or He would be drowned off 'Akká in the sea.

The Sultan's spies were, Khan believed, well compensated for sending in their reports, whether false or true. Lavishing bribes on various Turkish officials, the Covenant-breakers represented the visits to the Master of American and a few European pilgrims as the arrival of agents with whom 'Abdu'l-Bahá was plotting to place Syria and the surrounding area under British rule.

Whenever these enemies – including Mírzá Áqá Ján, who, after forty years of devoted toil as the amanuensis of Bahá'u'lláh, threw in his lot with the Master's foes – would meet local Bahá'ís or visiting pilgrims on the street, the Covenant-breakers would make loud and insulting remarks, in the hope of starting a quarrel and then laying the blame on the followers of the Master. Since Khan was known as a Bahá'í from a prominent Persian family who had come to serve the Master as secretary and interpreter, and whose translations would surely bring in still more Americans to follow 'Abdu'l-Bahá, he was a frequent target of the Covenant-breakers' loud and vicious remarks. And they well knew what it meant to a Persian, proud and sensitive, to take public insults, and never respond. Khan simply ignored them, and passed on by.

Those people were devoured by their envy of the Master's holy being and the love He attracted, and the great success He was achieving though a captive Himself and, in the beginning, with virtually no one to help Him. He, forsaken, assaulted by His relatives, His parents gone, with no son of His that survived, and sustained, except for His aged uncle, only by ladies living in seclusion: Khánum, his unmarried sister; four unmarried daughters; and His consort, Muníríh Khánum.[71]

To cite just one example of the relatives' unrelenting hatred and their no-holds-barred struggle to destroy 'Abdu'l-Bahá, there was the way they behaved during the visit of a certain noted pilgrim: Among the distinguished Persian Bahá'ís who came to see the Master four months after Khan's arrival, was Ibtiháju'l-Mulk of Gílán. He was a man of considerable wealth, a well-known landowner of that province, staunch in his loyalty to the Covenant, unswerving in his love for 'Abdu'l-Bahá.

While in the Holy Land this man asked the Master's permission to give a banquet for all the pilgrims and resident Bahá'ís. A great feast was accordingly arranged, and the Master attended and served the believers with His own hands. Several American and other Occidental believers were present too. Two were Mrs Kelting and her daughter from Chicago. Another was the loyal Miriam, English wife of the Syrian doctor, Khayru'lláh, who on his return from teaching the Faith in the United States had joined forces with Muḥammad-'Alí the murderous half-brother of 'Abdu'l-Bahá.

About twenty days before this banquet, Mírzá Áqá Ján, now a Covenant-breaker, had written a letter to Ibtiháj, hoping to make him a prey to doubts and shake his faith in 'Abdu'l-Bahá, appointed Center of the Covenant of Bahá'u'lláh. Since Ibtiháj was already informed about the violators of Bahá'u'lláh's Will and their traitorous doings, he had returned the letter to Mírzá Áqá Ján unopened.

The banquet took place on a Sunday and after it the Master led the assemblage to Bahjí. Prior to entering the Tomb, a water jar filled from a neighboring stream on His shoulder, and they following with their jars the same, 'Abdu'l-Bahá watered the flowers growing outside. Then, at the door, He anointed each guest with attar of roses.

Inside, and for the first time in Khan's hearing, the Master Himself chanted the Tablet of Visitation in the Shrine, His voice so strong and sweet, the air of the Tomb so holy, that the believers were carried away from themselves to realms undreamed of before.

After the Tablet was chanted, 'Abdu'l-Bahá requested the Western believers to sing a hymn in English. And many there shed tears, hearing the Western strains following the Eastern, their echoing voices fulfilling the prophecy that, with the coming of Him Who lay there in the Tomb, East and West would embrace each other like unto two lovers.

Soon after, Khan wrote his brother how on another occasion one of the Covenant-breakers had shattered the peace of the holy Shrine. One day Khan had remained in the Master's presence in Haifa, while Ibtiháj, with other resident Bahá'ís and visitors, had gone on pilgrimage to Bahjí. They entered the Shrine, and as they waited to pray silently in the fragrance of the flowers under the gentle light sifting down through the glass roof, Mírzá Áqá Ján crept in among them. Breaking the stillness, he harshly demanded that Ibtiháj and the others listen to his words. To cover the disturbance, the famed calligrapher Mishkín-Qalam lifted up his voice and began to chant a prayer. At this Áqá Ján ran up to the venerable man and clapped a hand across his mouth to stifle the prayer. Then he began to belabor them all:

'You infidels! You idolaters!' he cried, in terms habitually used by the Covenant-breakers when denouncing the faithful. 'For forty years I toiled to serve Bahá'u'lláh, and now I ask but a word with you, and you refuse me your ears!'

To avoid a quarrel the pilgrims quietly tried to leave the holy Tomb. But Áqá Ján ran over to the entrance, stood in the open door and barred the way, hoping for an exchange of blows and bloodshed, which he could then report to the Turkish city officials and have them punish the Bahá'ís. No one raised a hand against him, and at that moment a police officer hurried to the scene. (As a rule, on pilgrimage days, a policeman would be stationed by the Shrine to prevent just such attacks.)

The officer, seeing that Áqá Ján was deliberately barring the door, told him to stop making trouble and take himself off.

'These merciless people', shouted Áqá Ján, 'will not permit me – I who served Bahá'u'lláh forty years – to say even one word!'

'Your forty years all went for nothing', the policeman told him, 'because of your foolish trouble-making now and your trying to force these people to listen against their will.'

The officer's report, Khan wrote his brother, convinced the authorities that they should no longer tolerate such goings-on by the violators at the Shrine, their preying on the pilgrims and interrupting their worship. Still, the secret, incessant plottings went on.

As for Ibtiháj, he concluded his pilgrimage and left for Paris, and in later years this great Bahá'í nobleman extended loving hospitality to Khan, Florence and their children on their visits to Iran.

At last, from continuous overwork, Khan was worn out. He was raised in the fine dry climate of Tehran, on its high plateau, and now, close to the sea, he grew so weak he could hardly walk.

'Abdu'l-Bahá and the family, especially Khánum, did all they could to help. Both native and European doctors were called in, and one recommended treatment was that he should bathe every day in the seaweed along the beach. The Master's house in Haifa was only a short distance from the beach, but Khan, even supported by a helper, had to sit and rest several times before he got down to the water. This and other treatments proved useless. Young Khan was broken-hearted: here he had toiled and struggled so hard to get to the Holy Land so he could serve the Master, and in however small a way relieve Him of at least some of His burdens, and now he was himself another burden of the Master's, a stumbling corpse.

It took a miracle to heal him. Those were the days when the foundations were being laid for the Shrine of the Báb, and the whole site, a few acres, was covered with a vineyard that bore excellent varieties of grapes. One day a large number of local and visiting Bahá'ís were gathered in the courtyard when the gardener arrived and presented to the Master a basket of those succulent grapes.

The Master called each believer into His room and with His own blessed hands gave each one a bunch of grapes. Khan had propped himself against a wall and was wishing he too could have some of the grapes. 'Abdu'l-Bahá looked over at him and asked if he wanted a bunch. Khan made a polite gesture, meaning yes.

'Is it not true', the Master said, 'that your doctors have forbidden you to eat fruit, saying the fruit might make you even weaker? Come here, I will give you a bunch.'

One of the friends took Khan's arm and helped him over, and the Master gave the sick young man a lavish cluster.

'Go,' the Master said as He handed them over, 'eat these grapes and the blessings of Bahá'u'lláh will heal you.'

Someone steered Khan back to the tea area and he sat down and devoured every last grape.

As is well-known, Bahá'ís do not offer accounts of miracles as proof of the Bahá'í Faith, for Bahá'u'lláh teaches that the real miracle is the transforming power of the Manifestation's words. It is these creative words of the Manifestations of God which are the miracle, ever-present and eternal. Still and all, many and many a person, including Khan, bore witness to miraculous events.

From the day of the grapes, Khan went back to work, his services often beginning before dawn and going on till the middle of the night.

The Master's activities were virtually continuous. As Khan's work load increased, his usual program was to get up and take tea and a light breakfast around six before starting to work. On waking, he would have heard 'Abdu'l-Bahá already returning from His daily round of visits to the poor among the Jewish, Christian, Muslim, Arab and Turkish inhabitants of 'Akká. On these visits to the elderly, the deprived, the sick, He would minister to their requirements, comfort them, when needed, give them funds. This He would do almost daily between four and six in the morning – while each Friday a large congregation of poor men and women would flock to the courtyard before His house.

These people were among the neediest, the most miserable, of any human beings on the face of the globe, and they saw the Master as their only friend and his ever-present care their only hope.

'Abdu'l-Bahá would often praise and bless Khan's efforts and his (normally) undefeatable energy – and how indeed could Khan avoid nearly around-the-clock labor when he had such an example in the room next door? The Master would always reward Khan with appreciation, saying he was being made ready for a great service to the

Faith, a service that would go on in a worldwide field for many years.

Whenever there was a ship in port and about to leave after its usual short stay of a day or two at Haifa, the Tablets would have to be prepared for mailing – all dictated, translated, signed, and the mail 'closed'. The pace was very fast. One day the Master came in and found Khan working at top speed to meet the deadline, and having skipped his midday lunch.

'Abdu'l-Bahá smiled, His luminous eyes twinkling, and said: 'There was once a blacksmith in Iran, and to keep his fire going and get the iron red hot so it could be hammered into shape on the anvil, he had a boy apprentice to blow and blow the bellows. Finally the boy, half dead from toil, cried out, "I am dying! I am dying!" And the blacksmith shouted back, "Die and blow the bellows! Die and blow! Die and blow!"' The Master said that now He was like the blacksmith driving on that boy, but He told Khan, 'It is in a good cause, a cause which the future will reveal.'

TWENTY-FOUR

A Crisis of Faith

Khan, rather than quote from many other pilgrims' accounts, liked to relate those things which he had experienced himself. He would say that the closer one comes to the Source of Light, the more likely it is that one may be assaulted by the forces of darkness. In his case, he was subjected to trials unforeseen, and test after test. Many persons, he said, living close to the Master, experienced such tests, and only those survived who were helped through by the Master Himself. Khan was able to survive where many did not. As the prayer says, 'How many the leaves which the tempests of trials have caused to fall, and how many, too, are those which, clinging tenaciously to the tree of Thy Cause, have remained unshaken . . .'[72]

He survived, Khan said, not because of any merit he had, but only because of the bounty of 'Abdu'l-Bahá.

Among the prominent Bahá'í teachers of that day was Mírzá Asadu'lláh of Iṣfáhán. He was a brother-in-law of the Master Himself, married to Munírih Khánum's sister, and lived in 'Akká with his wife and children. Khan had often met him as he traveled and taught in Persia. Around 1898, on the teacher's last visit, Khan had attended meetings in Tehran where he spoke.

Khan had also learned from a confidential source that during this visit Mírzá Asadu'lláh had been entrusted with a secret mission by

'Abdu'l-Bahá. This assigned task was to meet with certain Persian Bahá'ís and receive from them a box containing the holy remains of the Báb, carefully hidden ever since His body and that of His companion, crushed by the bullets into a single mass, had been cast out onto the edge of the moat at Tabríz on the day of the martyrdom (July 9, 1850) and removed by the faithful in the middle of the second night. To protect the sacred dust from the ever-watchful mullás of Shiah Islam, the remains had been concealed in one place after another: here in a private home, there in a shrine, finally in and near the capital, until 1899. Let alone the mullás, the believers themselves were also a danger to the holy remains, because they were irresistibly drawn in great crowds to whatever spot was rumored to be the hiding place.[73]

When Mírzá Asadu'lláh, together with his son Amínu'lláh, later known as Dr Farid, was on his way back from Persia and, still obligated to exercise the greatest precaution, had stopped in Beirut, he called in six other believers, so that there would be eight with himself and his son, and had a group photograph taken, together with the sacred box. Beneath the group he wrote this verse from the Qur'án: '. . . on that day eight shall bear up the throne of thy Lord.'[74] This photograph Mírzá Asadu'lláh showed about everywhere, and the believers rewarded him with funds.

That very year, however, 'Abdu'l-Bahá had, in a Tablet, interpreted this verse, from the Súrih of 'the Inevitable'. The Master's words were to this effect: that the throne is the temple or body of the Manifestation of God, and that the Manifestation is symbolized by the number one. And according to the abjad reckoning – the numerical value of the component letters, used everywhere by Persian and Arabic scholars – 'Bahá'' is eight plus one. ('B' in the abjad is two, the short vowel is not written in, the 'h' is five, the long vowel is one, and the symbol called a hamza, represented by the apostrophe, is also one.) The verse thus means: on that day Bahá will bear up the throne (the body) of thy Lord. On that day eight will bear up one.[75]

Khan had already studied this Tablet when he was back in Persia. He was therefore amazed to see Mírzá Asadu'lláh's fabricated fulfillment of the verse, a statement entirely other than that revealed by the Interpreter appointed by Bahá'u'lláh. There were the eight of them, standing behind the coffin containing the Throne – body – of the Báb, as self-created fulfillers of the prophecy. And furthermore, this act of his violated the requirement for extreme secrecy on the mission.

From that day on, Khan became suspicious of the renowned Mírzá Asadu'lláh.

One day when no one else was by, he mentioned this to 'Abdu'l-Bahá and would have gone further into his doubts of the Mírzá's loyalty. But the Master stopped him.

'No, no!' He said, smiling. 'Mírzá Asadu'lláh is a philosopher, a metaphysician! No, this is not the time to say anything further about him!'

Some years later Mírzá Asadu'lláh, his son and family were declared violators of the Covenant, and this did not come to Khan as a surprise.

The son, Amínu'lláh, then about fifteen years old, visited the Master's household almost daily, the daughters being Amínu'lláh's cousins on his mother's side. (Except for family members, because of the strictures of the time and place, the ladies did not meet the men and lived in seclusion.)

He was small and there was something about his face and the look in his eyes, something furtive as he glanced quickly from side to side and lowered his voice as if confidentially, which made Khan feel uneasy whenever he was around.

He started coming in to see Khan, and from then on, frequently and in a casual offhand way, would tell Khan that yes, even though Khan was a hard worker and devoted to the Master's service, the Master's daughters did not really appreciate his labors, sincerely motivated though they were, and the importance of the tasks he was performing. At first, Khan ignored the hints. But every day, almost, the boy worked on Khan in this way, using different words but always saying the same thing. A Persian might even have thought he was conveying some kind of a message. Anyone who has lived in what is often the viper's nest of a Shiah household – where threats and insults, meant to be decoded, are conveyed by indirection, where members cease addressing each other for months, only to join forces and intrigue together later on against other members, formerly apparent friends, and truth does not exist, and servants come and go with hostile messages – will see the picture.

Very depressed, Khan thought the situation over and came to the conclusion that while 'Abdu'l-Bahá was the divinely-appointed Center of the Covenant, this did not pertain to members of His family; they might, for all Khan knew, be less than perfect in certain ways, like other humans. But then a new doubt invaded him: he asked himself if it was fair that, after all his struggles to reach 'Abdu'l-Bahá, and all he was going through to do the very best he knew how, he should be subjected to this, by the Master's own kith and kin.

Khan said nothing to anyone else. Then he found that this young boy had approached several other resident believers, devoted servants of the Faith, in much the same way. One of these was a young man whose Persian parents had been exiled out of Baghdad with Bahá'u'lláh, going on with Him to Turkey, Adrianople and the Holy Land. This youth's name was Mírzá Ḥabíb. 'Abdu'l-Bahá Himself had trained him in Persian, Arabic and Turkish, and the sacred

Writings of the Faith. He had a beautiful singing voice and was often asked to chant. He was, although highly emotional, both courteous and gentle, and spoke with earnestness and zeal on Bahá'í themes, and his companionship was a real pleasure to Khan.

Mírzá Ḥabíb also turned despondent, and began to say he was dissatisfied with the situation in 'Akká, and spoke of his growing desire to leave for some other part of the Turkish empire. It turned out that Amínu'lláh had been after him too, with tales of his being disapproved of by the Master's daughters.

Still another devoted servant, subjected to the same sly treatment, was Áqá Ḥusayn who had the coffee shop in Haifa and received and entertained at his establishment all the new pilgrims and visitors as they came off the ship. Amín's venom was injected into this good man as well. The three were continually manipulated, their feelings exacerbated from day to day, until all three reached a crisis of faith and were near collapse.

If anyone cares to ask why the violators of the Covenant should be avoided by loyal believers, this one sad episode would be answer enough. Khan came to see from this and other episodes that the violators are the serpent, the believers the hypnotized dove. Or to use another metaphor, the violators are sick with a mortal disease, and if the believers, by associating with them, hope to bring them back to health, all that happens is the believers are infected themselves. He noted that once the Covenant-breakers had won over a soul, they would cast that soul out. After all, what had they to give? Loyalty and love? They would not be faithful to anyone else, he reasoned, those who were not faithful to Bahá'u'lláh. And they were not outside enemies of the Faith, Sauls who might one day become Pauls. They were not those backsliders, ineffectuals, who quietly drop away. These were contaminators and killers – they were what the Qur'án calls 'the diseased of heart'.[76] '. . . guide into the torment of the Flame', the Qur'án says of Satan, 'whoever shall take him for his Lord.'[77] Satan, the dark side of man, will seize a soul, then cast him out, and tell him, 'I cannot aid you, neither can ye aid me. I never believed that I was His [God's] equal . . .'[78] Nor should anyone imagine that these persons are stupid: English has preserved a tribute to their mental powers in such expressions as 'fiendish ingenuity' and 'diabolical intelligence'.

Áqá Ḥusayn committed suicide. Mírzá Ḥabíb of the singing voice, who owed his training and indeed his very life to the Master, could stay close to Him no longer, and begged permission to go away. From Constantinople he went on to Persia, entered the consular service of that country, and served in Arabia and elsewhere in the Middle East. On a future trip when Khan and his family passed through Damascus they paid a visit to Mírzá Ḥabíb, who was the consul there, but he was only ashes now, no longer the bright fire which had so cheered and companioned Khan at Haifa and 'Akká in the early days.

As for Khan, he always felt afterward that it was only 'Abdu'l-Bahá's power and love that saved him from perhaps physical, surely spiritual, death.

Khan never could hide his feelings, and the Master used to say that to read Khan's heart you had only to look at his face. It was clear that although Khan did his work and never failed in his duties, for some months 'Abdu'l-Bahá had noticed a change in him. The great happiness that had brightened Khan's face from the very day of his arrival was now extinguished. His face was shadowed with grief, his soul in torment. Those were terrible days. He thought that by obtaining permission and leaving the Master, that vestige of his belief which had once called forth from the Master the title of Ishti'ál (blazing flame), would at least burn on in memory within him to console him throughout life. God, however, willed otherwise.

One day the Master entered the courtyard and called for Khan, who was up in his room, and at once hurried down the stairs. To the right of the courtyard there was a passageway that led to a small, square piece of ground which the Master had had cleaned up and planted to shrubs and flowers. Here He sat down and told Khan to sit down in front of Him. He lifted His hand and touched Khan's hair and touched his face. Then He asked Khan, His voice pleading, to speak out.

'Oh my Ishti'ál,' He said. 'Empty out your heart. Let all be told. Do not grieve any more. 'Abdu'l-Bahá understands. He knows. But these are tests you have to undergo, to develop your faith and prepare you for a great work that God has destined for you, joining with 'Abdu'l-Bahá in the service of the Faith.' He went on this way, in that anxious, eager, loving tone of voice.

Khan shook and trembled and burst into streaming tears. Raising up his voice till he wailed, folding his hands in prayer, sobbing, he begged 'Abdu'l-Bahá to send him away, to let him go, to let him be no more, just so he could keep by him a remnant of that wonderful faith in Bahá'u'lláh which had completely transformed his early life, till it became a paradise, lost now – that joyous faith which had smoothed away the toil and sorrow of long, rocky wanderings that had led him to the Master.

He wept out the whole thing, and what the youth, over and over again, had whispered in his ears. 'Abdu'l-Bahá replied with the exact truth, and reminded him of all the kindnesses which the ladies, led by Khánum, His sister, and Munírih Khánum, His wife, and also His daughters, had showered upon Khan, in response to his daily, unselfish and devoted service.

That day was Khan's baptism of fire. Completely reassured, he felt born again. Or as if his dross had been burned away, leaving him something supremely precious at the core. And as time went on, he only grew stronger and braver when assaulted as he would be in future by many tests.

It was only a year later that, having come via Paris, London and New York, he reached Chicago and again met Mírzá Asadu'lláh, who was later joined by his son. Khan then discovered that Asadu'lláh, through a course of lectures, which he called 'The School of Prophets', intended to found a sect which would acknowledge him to be its all-powerful leader and chief.

Khan also discovered what had brought on the maneuvers of Amín against Ḥabíb and himself in 'Akká. Amín's motive was simply to get rid of the two young men and make them leave 'Akká so that he could be the one to marry Munavvar Khánum, the Master's not yet married daughter. For Amín had heard the ladies praising Khan so highly that he feared they were thinking of him as a husband for their young lady.

The Master once told Khan that when the disloyal wished to put doubts into a believer's mind, they did not come to him with any criticism of the Center of the Faith. To this, they knew, a believer would not listen. What they did was, with the person they were manipulating, create perplexities by criticizing this or that Bahá'í.

For Khan, in the Holy Land, there were still other tests to be endured.

Studying the Epistles of Bahá'u'lláh and the Tablets of 'Abdu'l-Bahá which he was translating day and night, Khan was particularly impressed when he considered the human characteristics of the holy Manifestations. For only through these world Prophets, Who were also human, could the invisible Essence manifest itself, its exalted names and attributes, to humankind. This, he understood. But then he began to feel that these world Prophets, even in a physical sense, must be far other and apart from human beings. And yet . . .

He would ask himself about these things during his brief periods of rest, or when he walked in the fields outside 'Akká, or in Haifa, across Mount Carmel.

For example, he would ask himself how it could be that Bahá'u'lláh had so highly praised a man like Mírzá Áqá Ján, His amanuensis – had called him Khádimu'lláh (Servant of God) and 'Abd-i-háḍir (Servant in Attendance).[79] For this was a man who, after having been for so long a channel through which the revelations of Bahá'u'lláh went out to all the world, had, after Bahá'u'lláh's ascension, turned away, disobeyed the Will of the Manifestation, and violated His Covenant: that instrument provided by Him to canalize the might of His Faith throughout the world.[80]

A CRISIS OF FAITH

Or Khan would ask himself how it could be that the Master, omniscient, Center of the Covenant, vested with His authority by Bahá'u'lláh, made by Him the sole exponent of His words, would ask a newly-arrived pilgrim whether he had had a happy journey.

When one comes to understand the basic function of a Manifestation of God, or of the Heir to His authority, doubts of this kind seem trivial and groundless, but they took over every moment of Khan's leisure time – to such a point that he appeared to others as lost in thought and people had to address him more than once before he responded.

On one of the visiting Sundays to the Bahjí Shrine, Khan's work load was so heavy that the Master let him remain at his desk, to follow and join Him later. But 'Abdu'l-Bahá and the pilgrims had been gone hardly an hour when Khan was again assailed by his perplexities: what could possibly be the relationship between the Divine Essence and the Manifestation? He stopped work and fell into deep meditation.

Suddenly, he heard footsteps on the stairs, and Mírzá Hádí, the Master's son-in-law, father of Shoghi Effendi, entered the room. He called out that 'Abdu'l-Bahá was downstairs and asking for Khan. How could the Master and the others have returned from Bahjí so soon, Khan asked.

'On His way to Bahjí, the Master suddenly stopped, turned back, reached the courtyard and said you should be sent for.'

Khan left the room and, as he hurried down the long flight of stairs, he could hear the Master addressing him by name, and saying in a loud voice words which Khan had been repeating to himself for days and which had become a terrible test:

'Yes,' He was saying. 'Yes, it is true that notwithstanding human limitations, the Invisible Essence has chosen man to be the Manifestation of His names and attributes for the guidance of humankind.'

Khan was so startled at hearing his secret thoughts voiced aloud by 'Abdu'l-Bahá, that he fell down and fainted.

When he came to himself he was in the servants' room where tea and coffee were made ready for the guests. He was given something to refresh him, went back upstairs to his work, finished what he had been doing, and joined the Master and the pilgrims at sunset in the Shrine.

From that day forward, Khan never again had a recurrence of those particular tests.

TWENTY-FIVE

The Goal of the Living Martyrs

In the rainy season the fields at 'Akká were shades of jade green, and the plains roundabout, especially in the Bahjí olive groves and about the Shrine, were studded with ruby-red anemones. From all over the East, besides many from Europe and the United States, large numbers of pilgrims would visit the Master. He ordered a big tent to be set up near the Shrine where assemblages of Bahá'ís would gather and the Master would welcome them and have them served with refreshments and tea.

One day, when the visitors had come together in the holy precincts of Bahjí, 'Abdu'l-Bahá withdrew from the crowd and had Khan follow Him into the tent – Khan did not know why. But as he entered the tent, following 'Abdu'l-Bahá, the Master addressed him in words which spoke to the core of his soul. Khan suddenly fell to his knees before Him and, with streaming eyes, begged to do what would win him the Master's good pleasure, and begged for the strength to dedicate to Him all the days of his life. The impact of the words uttered by 'Abdu'l-Bahá in that tent was, to Khan's heart, like what the disciples underwent when the Son of God was transfigured before their eyes on the mountain and they fell down in terror. His past was blotted away. A new world was born to him, a world lit by the light of conviction absolute. It was told to his soul that nothing at all is real except God's divine Will, and its source in this age is the revelation of Bahá'u'lláh, and its establishment on our earth today is in the hands of the Center of that Covenant He made with humankind.

Throughout his years of wandering up and down the mountains and over the deserts in hope of reaching 'Abdu'l-Bahá, Khan had often written the Master and petitioned Him for the gift of martyrdom. His replies brought Khan many blessings, but made no mention of that special bounty, Khan's dream and dearest wish. Then one day in the Holy Land, when no one else was by, the Master spoke of those numerous requests. He said: 'While suffering death on the pathway of God is the highest attainment, still, that dying which continues on throughout life, giving life to other souls, is the station of "living martyrdom". The death of a martyr means the immediate end to all his afflictions and tests: martyrdom is the easiest way to enter the Kingdom of Heaven. But those who rise up to serve the Cause, to bear afflictions and undergo tribulations and trials in order to draw souls into the holy Faith – those are living martyrs, their labor goes on and on, and their noble work, the regeneration of all humankind, will win them the highest of rewards, for ever and ever. My prayer for you [the Master said in Persian, for thee] is that you will reach that goal, the goal of the living martyrs.'

There was an aged believer who lived in 'Akká and Haifa and performed various services in the Master's house. He was past eighty, and there came a time when he fell ill and took to his bed. One day as the Master was concluding His weekly visit to Haifa, the old man's son begged 'Abdu'l-Bahá to bless his ailing father, because he did not think his father would still be alive when the Master returned the following week. 'Abdu'l-Bahá went into the sickroom and placed His hand on the man's forehead.

'Do not worry,' He said to the son. 'Your father is going to be all right.'

The next week when they reached Haifa, Khan saw the aged father outside 'Abdu'l-Bahá's house. Broom in hand, he was vigorously sweeping up the street. He lived and worked years longer.

Such incidents, and they were many, were trivial when compared to the divine power that pulsated in the Master's creative words, spreading Bahá'u'lláh's message to far away parts of the globe.

Once in a while Khan would be homesick for the friends of his childhood and youth in Tehran. In spite of his present life, he could not totally forget the old, joyous days with those young companions out of the past.

One day in Haifa 'Abdu'l-Bahá had gone out to return the calls of some Turkish officials, and Khan went for a lonely walk on the slopes of Mount Carmel. As he walked, he recited to himself lines from poems, telling of sad partings from cherished friends, long gone. 'Stay,' the Arab poet Imru'u'l-Qays has written, 'let us weep over the memory of a beloved one and a place at the edge of a sand-hill between ad-Dakhú'l and Ḥawmal.'[81] But Khan was reciting that day from Persian poems.

It was late in the afternoon when he walked back to the house, and found that the Master had returned from His round of visits.

Smiling, 'Abdu'l-Bahá looked at Khan and said, 'You have been thinking of your friends in Persia this afternoon. You have been lonely and reciting Persian poems.' Then He proceeded to repeat the very lines Khan had recited to himself, in a secluded, empty place, with no one near. Khan's memoir says, let the reader take these experiences as he pleases, but for himself, they were printed forever and ever on his soul.

There was no special time set aside by the Master for dictating

Tablets – to Khan a superlatively important work. 'Abdu'l-Bahá simply used odd moments for this, moments He could spare from all His engrossing occupations. One day in Haifa the leading Muslim Turkish judge had called on the Master, and while the attendants were serving tea, 'Abdu'l-Bahá sent for Khan, told him to sit down, and dictated a long Tablet in Arabic. In His service, Khan had become so used to rapid writing that as he hurried along he would connect up the words in a long chain which no outsider could read.

The judge sat, marveling at this performance, then said to 'Abdu'l-Bahá, 'But can he read back the words he has written?'

'Yes, he can,' the Master assured him. 'Khan, read the Tablet back.'

To the judge's surprise, Khan obeyed, with never a pause.

Among all the things he witnessed in that holy Presence, one phenomenon which particularly impressed him was the complete naturalness and the great wit displayed in the Master's conversation. There was no artificiality. There was no attempt to show superior learning or any particular spiritual authority. This in itself was to him a miracle. 'Abdu'l-Bahá was continually teaching the deepest, the most abstruse of lessons, but in the plainest of words, with smiles, with humor, unfolding the most complicated of themes. He never referred to Himself with the pronoun 'I'. He placed Himself in with all the others who, as their highest, their overriding duty, served the Cause of Bahá'u'lláh. He always said, '*We* must do – *we* must obey – *we* must act . . .' The most eminent Bahá'í teachers who entered His presence demonstrated their complete nothingness before Him; the greater the teacher, the more humble in that Presence. Foremost among them was the Bahá'í savant and historian, Mírzá Abu'l-Faḍl, who, beginning in 1901, would become Khan's mentor and companion during a stay of four years in the United States. This great man was the teacher of some of the leading professors at al-Azhar University in Cairo, Islam's foremost seat of learning, yet in the Master's presence he was the humblest of creatures. He would tell the believers that the Center of Bahá'u'lláh's Covenant was the mighty sea of divine knowledge, and he himself but a pebble on the shore.

Khan was often present at meals, at the luncheons or dinners in 'Akká or Haifa. Various dishes would be served the guests, but 'Abdu'l-Bahá Himself would have a bowl of ábgúsht, a stew of vegetables and lamb, very simple, and this plain stew was often the diet reserved for Him alone. He would on occasion spoon out some of that stew into Khan's dish, and then some remaining pieces of bread that had been mixed in with the stew would be served him with the Master's own hand. One day, after He had served Khan a portion of this food, He remarked, 'Sometimes material food confers spiritual sustenance and strength.' He prayed that Khan would be sustained with the spiritual strength conferred by the power of Bahá'u'lláh.

Khan needed all the divine assistance that might be sent his way, for tests came, one after another, often from the Covenant-breakers, sometimes from the believers, though these were less serious.

For example, there was Mrs Thornburgh of California. She had visited the Master before, in that first group of pilgrims brought to the Master by Mrs Phoebe Hearst in December 1898. During Khan's stay she returned for a visit of several months. She was present at all the meetings in 'Abdu'l-Bahá's house. She and Khan became close friends and she nursed him herself when he was ill. However, as the number of Western pilgrims increased and he had to translate for every one of them, he did not have much time to place at her disposal. Furthermore, Mrs Thornburgh was almost totally deaf, complicating the problem. Khan made it a point to sit by her at table, so that she could hear him better, but frequently he could not overcome her deafness. When she saw the joy on the others' faces as Khan translated the words of 'Abdu'l-Bahá, while she herself missed so much, her own face would cloud over. Finally she went to the Master and complained that Khan mumbled on purpose, and deliberately addressed her in a low voice so that she could not hear. This distressed Khan very much, especially as he had tried so hard in the awkward circumstances to overcome her poor hearing.

'Abdu'l-Bahá saw Khan's predicament and told him to be patient with Mrs Thornburgh, and that He understood.

Much more difficult to deal with were the machinations of the Covenant-breakers. One thing sprang up after another, for it was always there, the dark at the base of the lamp. In their unceasing efforts to destroy 'Abdu'l-Bahá, His brothers and their people spread malicious rumors against Him, the extent of which He finally disclosed in His Will and Testament after enduring their hatred of Him in silence for many long years.

Some of their calumnies were aimed, not at political power centers, but at Muslim and Christian religious communities. They spread the word that 'Abdu'l-Bahá had announced that He was God, or was a Prophet of God outranking every other. This, although the only station He claimed was that of servitude, and His very name, 'Abd, means servant. In Tablet after Tablet He emphasized this fact. Yet people came to ask Him about such matters. One was an American missionary from Beirut, very patriarchal with a long white beard. Striding into the Master's reception room, he addressed Him without any preliminaries:

'I hear you claim to be God. Do you?'

'Abdu'l-Bahá, who was greeting the man with His usual gentle courtesy, was told again, His welcome ignored:

'I hear you claim to be God.'

With great dignity the Master denied ever making such a claim, but to no avail: the missionary continued, as roughly as before.

Khan said the scene made him think of Christ, hungry in the wilderness, and taunted by Satan, who told Him: 'Command that these stones be made bread.'[82]

Or again, told Him, if He was the Son of God, to cast Himself down from the pinnacle of the temple.[83]

Khan felt that the Master's sister, Bahíyyih Khánum, the Greatest Holy Leaf, embodied all the qualities of a true great lady. It was she who directed the servants when they had to prepare food for the crowds who visited. She was extremely loving and kind to all the pilgrims. Her dignity was next only to the majesty and dignity of 'Abdu'l-Bahá, but there was also an indescribable humility and gentleness about her. It was her silence that impressed Khan the most. She never spoke at any length, and this deep silence contrasted with the eloquence of her brother, the Master, and was almost as impressive.

She treated Khan with special kindness. Because she knew that in Persian households, during the summer season, watermelon and other fruit juices would customarily be drunk, she had such drinks prepared for him. She even sent him a white umbrella to carry when he was out in the sun.

To Khan, the Master was the speaker and revealer, while Khánum felt her mission to be continual silent service.

Khan was not sure she could write letters, because every week she would send over to him numerous letters addressed to her from European and American pilgrims, ask him to answer them on her behalf and even sign them with his own name. (Khánum would, in future days, as virtual regent of the Faith, write many an eloquent letter, but that time was almost a quarter of a century away.)

Despite the enormous press of work, the Master found time once in every week to hold a class for small Bahá'í children. Here they would recite the short Tablets they had learned by heart and bring samples of their handwriting to show Him. He loved them. He showed great concern, wishing them to learn the principles of Bahá'í conduct. Although He was firm, He strictly forbade anyone to strike a child or use the customary rod or harshly punish them. He told their parents and teachers to emphasize the importance of good conduct and said that in this way, if the child failed in some particular, the very reminding the child that he had failed would impress that child as a severe punishment. The child would thus learn to avoid even the slightest failure in good conduct and grow up to recognize good conduct as the true mark of a Bahá'í.

TWENTY-SIX

Prayer is not Enough

Meeting and observing the men and women visitors and pilgrims who came to 'Abdu'l-Bahá from all over the world was a valuable experience for Khan. Those who came to Him from the Occident were either Bahá'ís already or seekers who wished to hear the Teachings from 'Abdu'l-Bahá Himself. Today's Bahá'ís, with the magnificent source books available, can hardly understand what it was like to have only a few scattered platform lectures, or accounts of returned pilgrims, or those acres of thin, closely-typed pages that appeared nationwide through the struggles of devoted believers who, whatever else they might lack, were certainly eager and indefatigable.

Knowing little of Bahá'í history, and less of the Báb, the early American believers repeated the same few facts over and over again. Indeed, the young women members of Ella Goodall Cooper's Peach Tree Circle in San Francisco would, meeting by chance on the street, greet each other tongue-in-cheek with the opening of Mrs Cooper's usual speech on the Faith, 'In 1844 a radiant Youth . . .' Or a speaker might start out with, 'Before I tell you what the Bahá'í Movement is, let me tell you what it is not.' By the time they had finished telling what it was not, the hour had passed.

Teachers sent over from the East began to deepen the believers; but a few of them failed because they were so dazzled by the wealth of the West and the ease with which starry-eyed followers would transfer some of it to them, that they turned aside from the Faith, choosing from it a little preserve ('heresy' comes from the Greek for 'choice') for their own selves: savoring the things not of God but of men.[84] It is obvious why the Master, traveling eight months in the United States, paid His own way and would accept no funds at all, nor any costly gifts.

Some of the visitors from the West would arrive with notebooks at the ready, containing lists of questions. They would ask their questions, and Khan would translate the replies of the Master, and they would write them down. Some would come with special questions relating to their study of prophecies from the past about the Coming of the Lord. Others would come to Him with questions, but once seeing the Master, they had no questions to ask. They knew.

These last would offer themselves to carry out whatever tasks He wished, and would leave with only one aim: to dedicate to Him all the remaining days of their lives and work like Him to weld together all races and faiths.

Khan used to tell how 'Abdu'l-Bahá would classify the different souls who learned of a new Divine Revelation:

At the word of the Advent, some would arise, seek out its source, and surrender themselves to the will of the new Manifestation. Others would be distraught to learn that God's Manifestation had been again and swiftly gone. They had missed His coming. These two classes were chosen by the Lord Himself as heralds of His Faith. But most would be those who, hearing of His advent, would believe in Him and dedicate their lives to Him only after they had received logical, intellectual proofs of His claim. The first two classes would be protected when undergoing tests and trials; but those who, relying only on reason, accepted Him only through logical proofs, and the weight of convincing arguments, would have great difficulty with those tests and trials which are the inevitable lot of the believer. As Rúmí said:

> The reasoner
> Has wooden legs.
> Not stable he
> Whose leg's a peg.[85]

Lines which describe the mystic's age-old contrasting of cool brain and burning heart.

'Abdu'l-Bahá teaches that there are four ways of testing what you hear and reaching a conclusion. All must be brought to bear. Reason is only one of the four. The other three are sense perception, traditional authority and inspiration.[86]

Far from considering himself saved for being a Bahá'í, Khan believed that 'none knoweth what his own end shall be';[87] and remembered what the Prophet Muḥammad had also said: 'neither know I what will be done with me or you.'[88] Bahá'ís have the example of many devoted servants who served for years and fell and were forgotten. The Bridge, the Sirát, sharp as a sword blade, narrow as a hair, is always there for every soul to cross.

Faith was a mystery and seemed to depend entirely on the grace of God; a human being's faith, like everything else he has – eyesight, brain, bodily health, length of days – is always in God's hands, and the believer's lot is to accept God's will for him, as best he can. For Khan, this called to mind Rúmí's story of the bitter melon, told so many centuries ago:

Luqmán, a sage identified with Aesop (i.e. Aethiops, Ethiopian), had a master who gave him a slice of bitter melon. Luqmán ate it with pleasure, as if it were sugar and honey. He was given another slice, and then another, and swallowed them down with delight. Then his master tried a slice himself and found it was so bitter that it blistered his tongue.

'Why, Luqmán,' he asked, 'did you eat this with such pleasure?'

'Because, O Master, thou hast given me so much that was sweet in my mouth and honey on my tongue. Should I now refuse one morsel that is bitter? Love makes the bitter sweet.'

Repeatedly, in the Qur'án, the Unknowable addresses the Prophet, telling Him that tests of faith are ineluctable, and that the more firmly they are withstood, the stronger faith will grow.

The Master told Khan that meditating and praying were not enough – in this day the believer's paramount concern should be to teach the Faith. There being no Bahá'í clergy, the believer takes over that function (certainly this concept is like the Protestant Christian teaching of the priesthood of all believers). No Bahá'í should assume superiority over another, every believer is a teacher, not only in words but deeds. Compared to a Bahá'í's behavior, his way of life and conduct, the most convincing proof he has to offer is of the least importance.

'Abdu'l-Bahá would quote the words of 'Alí, First Imám and Guardian (Valí), successor of the Prophet Muḥammad. Asked 'What is truth?', 'Alí replied, 'When the True One is made manifest, His signs and verses are His evidence, His presence is His proof.' 'Abdu'l-Bahá would go on to say that every morning when the sun comes up, it does not first send out a herald to wake up the townspeople and tell them to rise and go to work. It needs no herald; it is its own proof. They see the light and they rise. In the same way a believer cannot prove he is of the faithful simply by announcing himself to be a Bahá'í. Only by serving and sacrificing, and by dedication to the needs of others whether they are Bahá'ís or not, can a Bahá'í prove that he is of the people of Bahá.

'Abdu'l-Bahá would also use another way of stating this. He would tell of a man who appeared among the townspeople and announced that he had just returned from a garden of roses. There was no smell of roses about him, however, and the people were not convinced. Then another man came to them, with a rose in his hand, and its fragrance all about him, and the people needed no words to tell them he had been in the garden.

He would quote the Blessed Beauty, Bahá'u'lláh, to the effect that the true helpers of the Faith are righteous acts, and that the Manifestation had bidden His followers to storm the citadels of the hearts of men with the battalions of good deeds.

Many who wrote or visited 'Abdu'l-Bahá would ask this question:

God being omnipresent, why would it not be enough to concentrate on His presence in the natural world, rather than to believe in a man, a Prophet, claiming to be the intermediary between man and God? As, for example, Jesus claimed, when He said, 'I am the way . . . no man cometh unto the Father, but by me.'[89] As His Tablets and addresses show, the Master gave many answers to this question. When Khan was in the Holy Land, 'Abdu'l-Bahá made this reply to an American inquirer: There was once an Arab traveler who had lost his way in the desert. He was dying of thirst and, humbly, he begged God for water. Suddenly on the far horizon he saw an oasis with waving trees, and he knew that there could be no trees and greenery unless water was present too. When he had somehow dragged himself across the sands and reached the oasis, how did he go about quenching his thirst? Was his conviction enough for him, that growing things meant water? Or did he search avidly for a source, a crack in a rock or an opening in the earth where water could get through and he could drink and live?

Believing that God is present in nature has never been enough. This belief has never founded, and could never found, a civilization. But belief in God's Chosen Ones, His Prophets, through Whom come the living waters of His revelation, has created structures in the life of man that the revolution of many ages and cycles could not destroy, and brought him holy light that time could never dim.

'Abdu'l-Bahá always emphasized the importance of education, indeed of life-long study, for man and woman alike. As the Muslim tradition had it, 'Seek ye after knowledge, though as far away as China.' But He assigned paramount importance to the knowledge that comes from the Unknowable through His Manifestation on earth. Acquired, worldly knowledge would help to establish a material society, but 'in material civilization good and evil advance together and maintain the same pace.'[90] To consolidate all human achievement, man needed what the Master called 'immediate knowledge'. Acquired knowledge is limited, but the immediate knowledge transmitted by the Manifestation to the faithful is infinite. It is boundless in fruitful results.

Many asked the Master to explain to them what was the sin against the Holy Spirit, which Jesus said shall never be forgiven. As Matthew has it: 'And whosoever speaketh a word against the Son of Man, it shall be forgiven him: but whosoever speaketh against the Holy Ghost, it shall not be forgiven him, neither in this world, neither in the world to come.'[91]

One day while Khan was walking with the Master in the streets of Haifa, he asked about this teaching. 'Abdu'l-Bahá answered him to this effect: This sin means to challenge the Divine authority of the Messengers from God, Who are the Manifestations of God's holy names and attributes – and to attack the Messengers' spiritual rank and function.

'Today, for example,' He said, 'if someone stops me on the street and strikes me a hard blow because, as a human being, I have somehow offended him – I can forgive him. But if he comes up and attacks me because I am the appointed Center of Bahá'u'lláh's Covenant, that is my spiritual function, and he has committed a sin which I cannot forgive; I can only ask God to forgive him.'

The Master was not claiming to be a Prophet, only using an analogy. He was referring to His spiritual station as disclosed in the Will and Testament of Bahá'u'lláh. As every believer would know, He was the Master, the Exemplar, the Interpreter – and His station was 'radically different' from that of the Manifestations of God.[92] His Father had bestowed on Him the title of the Mystery of God (Sirru'lláh); He was a unique phenomenon, occupying as He did an office not known in the world's religious history before.

TWENTY-SEVEN

The Frightening Change

Khan had begun to hear that by special request of Elsa (Laura) Barney of Washington DC, the Master had agreed to send Mírzá Abu'l-Faḍl to America to unfold the true teachings of Bahá'u'lláh and interpret the prophecies of the Holy Scriptures, the key to which Mírzá had found in the book of Iqán.

Mírzá could not speak English and his going to America without an adequate interpreter would have been of little use. Khan himself was not disturbed by the problem. In the past 'Abdu'l-Bahá had often stated that He could not dispense with Khan's services. However, Khan began to notice certain changes in his daily routine.

As has been said, his workroom, where he also slept, was upstairs in the 'Akká house, between 'Abdu'l-Bahá's bedroom and His day reception room. One night he was awakened by a gentle touch. He sat up and saw the Master was there, wishing him to go with Him into the reception room next door. It was then three or four o'clock in the morning. Khan rose and followed the Master, who began giving him certain instructions, quite out of the ordinary.

'We are both so busy during the day and evening hours,' He said, 'and there is then no time for the special instructions I wish to give you. That is why I have gotten you up so early.'

This happened a number of times: the Master would waken Khan, have him come next door, and begin to instruct him.

Finally one day 'Abdu'l-Bahá spoke to him along these lines: 'During all these long months that you have worked for me, I have been preparing you and now you are sufficiently prepared. The time has now come for you to leave me and go to America with Mírzá Abu'l-Faḍl. There in America he will write a book called *The Bahá'í Proofs* and you are to translate that book. In addition, you are to translate his oral and written teachings, and his lectures to the many groups in the United States which are eager to hear him.'

For Khan, this came as an earthquake shock. He had been so busy, night and day, in the Master's company, that (except during his almost unbearable test) he had never for a moment given any thought to a future time when he would no longer be in the holy presence of the Master. He broke down and wept. In after years he would point to a picture of the long, outside stairway leading up to the Master's day reception room, and tell how, in his anguish, he had hammered his head against that outside wall.

Lovingly, the Master consoled him. He had taught Khan all he needed for service in the wide field that was America, a land chosen by God, inhabited by a people whose mission it was to establish peace and justice throughout the world. This would be a great service for Khan to render, and also a great opportunity, for he would be living in intimate association with a man of unbounded faith, of great erudition, and in such company would become even better prepared for his task.

Khan finally was reconciled to this new situation, but dared not even hope he could survive away from the Master, unless he was supported by the Master's own strength.

Khan dearly loved his Shiah Muslim mother. However, in spite of her pleadings, as soon as he became a Bahá'í his sole aim was to go to 'Akká and serve 'Abdu'l-Bahá. She wrote him constantly to the Holy Land, begging him to come home and establish a career like the rest of the family. In one of her letters she asked Khan to tell the Master of her wishes and obtain His permission to go back to Persia.

When an opportunity offered, Khan told the Master of his mother's letter. 'Abdu'l-Bahá said, most lovingly, 'Write your mother and tell her you will surely return at a future time, when your coming will rejoice her heart. But you should also make it known to her', the Master said, 'that now you are about to be sent on a long journey, to a far away country where you will do a great work that will bring you fame, for it will identify you with a great Cause, a Cause devoted to the welfare of all humankind. You will come back to her in a matter of years, tell her, when your name and fame will confer blessings upon her and on all the family.'

'Abdu'l-Bahá added that Khan should keep in close touch with his mother wherever he went and, as a token of his affection, should send her and the family gifts of money whenever his means allowed. Khan told the Master that for then his mother was being looked after and was not actually dependent on him, but the Master repeated what He had said and Khan promised to do as bidden regarding his mother and family as long as he lived.

On his long journeyings to come to 'Abdu'l-Bahá, Khan had made do with very small amounts of money. He reached the Holy Land with nothing but the clothes on his back. From time to time, 'Abdu'l-Bahá would supply him with gold Turkish and English pounds so that he could buy light garments, suited to the climate, and also have a little pocket money. Strangely enough, whenever the last coin had been spent the Master gave him more – Khan never had to ask.

One morning in Haifa, 'Abdu'l-Bahá sent for Khan to meet Him at the little house on the German Colony street where He had passed the night, attended either by His sister or one of His daughters.

He told Khan that two American ladies had arrived from Paris and were staying at the German hotel near the sea, and Khan was to call on them and escort them to the house. They were cousins, Elsa Barney and Ellen Goin (pronounced Goween), the first from Washington DC, the other from New York.

Khan walked over to say that 'Abdu'l-Bahá had sent him to fetch them.

They were two beauties, dressed in the latest Paris fashions, and Khan, already abnormally shy, nearly sank into the ground. He had never before seen such strikingly beautiful American girls – or many lovely girls of any kind in those veiled Middle Eastern societies.

He could hardly get his message out. Years later, whenever Elsa – by then called Laura, that name being used by her father in his will – would recall their meeting, she would tell him, 'Khan, you were so shy that all the time we were talking to you, you were looking at your shoes. You must have had on a brand new pair that day, and were more interested in them than us.'

Two other pilgrims, Edward Getsinger and his wife Lua, spent several months in the Holy Land during Khan's stay. Lua was young, eager, a brilliant, ardent teacher of the Faith. Born Louisa A. Moore, the Master named her Livá (Banner) and called her 'the Mother Teacher of the West'. Lua brought many into the Faith, including Miss May Ellis Bolles, later Mrs Sutherland Maxwell of Montreal. Edward, a German-American and also a noted Bahá'í teacher, was studying various branches of science.

The Getsingers stayed at a house in Haifa that the Master had especially rented for His American Bahá'í visitors. Edward was very fond of pork and this to Khan's surprise, for he writes that the Bahá'ís he knew did not eat pork. There was only one butcher in the German colony who sold it, and Dr Getsinger would buy pork from him and cook it at the American pilgrims' house.

One day Khan asked him, 'Don't you know that we shouldn't eat pork?'

'You'll have to eat it too', he replied, 'when 'Abdu'l-Bahá sends you to America. That's the only kind of meat they've got.'

At lunch, Khan reported this to 'Abdu'l-Bahá, who said, smiling, 'If that's the only meat they have, it doesn't matter – the time will come when people won't eat meat anyway. You have only to examine human teeth. Human beings are not flesh-eaters, like the carnivores. Human teeth are better adapted to such foods as fruit, grains and nuts.'

Khan's understanding was that Bahá'ís, like Jews and Muslims, should not eat pork. He never produced a text on this, however. But he used to say that even if there was no text about it in Bahá'u'lláh's Most Holy Book, His Book of Laws, the Aqdas – still the laws on matters not therein would be dealt with according to the relevant laws of previous Scripture.[93] Most Occidental Bahá'ís eat pork – although, clearly, not only Bahá'ís but others are slowly becoming full vegetarians. One has only to compare a seventeenth-century menu, say in Samuel Pepys' diary, or even a turn-of-the-century menu, with a modern household's to see this. A gradual, not a sudden, change from meat to vegetarian foods, was recommended to Bahá'ís, since humans have been meat eaters for long generations. Meat was always served to Bahá'ís in the Holy Land. Tea was served too, and Turkish coffee, both delicious and impeccably presented. The offering of courteous hospitality is so important in the Bahá'í Faith that a reference to it is included in 'Abdu'l-Bahá's beautiful prayer for the dead, where the newly-arrived soul is described as the guest of God: 'I testify, O my Lord, that Thou hast enjoined upon men to honor their guest, and he that hath ascended unto Thee hath verily reached Thee and attained Thy Presence. Deal with him then according to Thy grace and bounty! By Thy Glory, I know of a certainty that Thou wilt not withhold Thyself from that which Thou hast commanded Thy servants . . .'[94]

Anyway, no pork was ever served in Khan's household and he avoided it elsewhere. Once as a young man in America he was served a delicious meat course.

'What was that good meat?' he asked afterward.

'Pork,' his hostess replied, grinning.

Khan darted away from the table and got rid of his dinner.

Over the years, when no one else was available to cook Persian food for him any more (Florence was always taking courses in cooking, and finally, near the end of her life, achieved a roast duck), Khan became an excellent cook, although at the beginning his family had to eat many a scorched eggplant and burnt-black crust of rice, and billowing smoke and loud wails and exclamations of indignation would issue from the kitchen, while the family cowered elsewhere.

One thing he could not put up with was the American version of Persian food. Whenever his Occidental hosts would ask what he wanted for dinner, he would beg, 'Please! No Persian food.'

Living as they did in a Muslim country, the Master and His household observed the local customs. This made for good relations with the local people. Among these customs, 'Abdu'l-Bahá, and hence the others, kept the long, thirty-day Muslim fast, the Ramaḍán, but at that time He did not wish the believers to keep the Bahá'í fast of nineteen days, ending on Naw-Rúz. On the other hand, the family remembered Khan's telling them that the Master kept both fasts.

Khan was not used to keeping the Ramaḍán. In fact, as a youth he had been completely alienated from Islam, and he and his fellows, the story went, had even killed a crow out on the plains north of Tehran and deliberately eaten it by daylight to flout the Muslim fast. Furthermore, 'Abdu'l-Bahá's Muslim fast in the Holy Land was quite different from that observed by well-to-do Muslims of Persia, who slept most of the day and ate most of the night. The tiny minority of the elite had lavish parties and gambled the time away until sun-up.

Here it was different: the believers fasted and worked. But those with the Master enjoyed one great privilege during the Ramaḍán: they broke their fast with 'Abdu'l-Bahá Himself, and He, with His own hands, passed around the tea and the food.

Despite all the work and the continuous tests, the more than a year that Khan lived so close to the Master was the happiest period of his life. Now he would have to go out in the world and face life as it would be without his Lord. To console him, 'Abdu'l-Bahá would tell him, 'I will be with you at all times. You must go forth now and give to others the bounties that have been given you here.' But the Master's words of comfort and promises for Khan's future triumphs could not make up for the loss of His physical presence, His love, His forgiving, all-embracing, mother-love.

Through all the tests, what Khan had experienced there in the Master's home was continual ecstasy, supernal delight not to be put into the language of any beings on earth. Now he was like a wild fledgling, swept from its nest on a cliff, either to fly or else drown, way down, in the deep sea.

When the time of Khan's leaving neared, Edward and Lua Getsinger were told that they must leave the Holy Land and return to America. To them, the Master had given certain instructions which in their case He considered most important. 'Abdu'l-Bahá told them that as they traveled from place to place and taught the Faith, they should not stay a long time in any one city. They should above all visit smaller towns and places unfrequented by other Bahá'í teachers and give the glad-tidings of the Advent to plain and ordinary people. He also gave them precious necklaces and other jewels that Elsa Barney, on her visit, had begged Him to accept. 'Sell these,' He told them, ' and use the money for your return to the United States.' Accordingly, Lua and Edward planned to go to Cairo, there sell the jewels, and leave for Paris.

A letter from 'Akká, written to his brother in the spring of 1901, turned up in Khan's papers, in which he says the Getsingers left for Port Said before he did and that Lua wept bitterly at her parting from the Master, for she loved Him much. Many pilgrims would be overcome in this way, when they had to leave Him. In 'Akká and Haifa tears were not in short supply. 'Abdu'l-Bahá told Khan to accompany the Getsingers to their steamer, and this departure meant another separation and more sorrow, for he had become much attached to them during their stay.

It was their intention to accompany Mírzá Abu'l-Faḍl to Paris and from there, later, to the United States. While Mírzá was in Paris, a Syrian Bahá'í, Anton Haddad, would be his translator. As for Khan, he went on with his work for the Master, knowing he would soon have to leave, but not knowing when.

Apparently, the Getsingers did not go on to Paris at this time but returned shortly to 'Akká and stayed on until, with Khan, they left the second time. Another letter to his brother in Persia, dated the nineteenth of Muḥarram, 1901, from Port Said, told Ḥusayn that the Master had directed Khan to sail with the Getsingers, and how the three of them had wept. By reading still others of his letters it is clear that Khan finally did leave 'Akká for Paris with the Getsingers and reached Port Said two days later. They were all in tears at leaving 'Abdu'l-Bahá, and to make things worse the sea was rough and all three were sick. It was the European look of the Port Said waterfront that gave Khan his first notions of the Western world.

They were entertained at the home of Aḥmad Yazdí, a Persian Bahá'í merchant who was also Honorary Consul for Persia. He and his two brothers, who carried on business in Haifa and Alexandria, were very active in serving the Faith, receiving and entertaining American and European Bahá'í pilgrims.

Aḥmad Yazdí located these three in a building many stories high, the first tall building Khan had ever seen. It was not skyscraper high, but Khan was a convinced acrophobe, as his children were quick to learn and put their knowledge of it to use in later years. He dreaded even the thought of heights. He would make a face and cringe away if you mentioned mountain climbers to him, or talked about Harold Lloyd, popular, horn-rimmed-spectacled film actor of the day, whose apparent forte was scaling the outside of skyscrapers, and clinging to dizzy ledges, hanging on by his fingernails. Two other phobias of Khan's were peach fuzz – his children would cry 'peach fuzz!' to him and run away laughing – or anything to do with snakes. He seemed to enjoy being teased and would take them on his lap afterward and let them play with a lock of his hair, twirling it around; or they would finger his sálak, the scar that marked most Persian faces in those days – in Khan's case, a black dot high on the left side of his nose.

TWENTY-EIGHT
Paris and Natalie

The travelers were told that the first ship which would sail for Marseilles would arrive in eight days and it would take them five or six days to cross the Mediterranean, while the trip north by rail from Marseilles would take about eight hours.

Another letter to his brother, which turned up in Khan's papers, was dated May 27, 1901, and said they had arrived in Paris on May 26. The ship had made the crossing in four days, not putting in to other ports on the way. The letter had a long account of the grandeurs of Marseilles, it being the greatest city Khan had ever seen. He told Ḥusayn that a second class cabin from Port Said was ten English pounds per person and the second class rail fare to Paris had cost sixty-five francs. Instead of eight hours, the train had taken twenty (perhaps they had been sold tickets for a local, stopping at every way station). They had passed many great cities, Khan reported, and he described the beauty of the green fields and mountain slopes as contrasted with the dry lands of Persia. Every single foot of ground was cultivated, he wrote, and he assured his brother that the Paradise on earth of which they had heard was this lovely France. As for Paris, he said that only the insane would try to describe its wonders.

The travelers found rooms in one of the inexpensive hotels, where they got room and board for half a pound Sterling each. (They apparently stopped first at the Hotel de l'Arcade on the street of the same name, later at 7 rue d'Assas.) That afternoon, May 26, the three of them took a carriage and went off to call on Baháʼí friends. Some were out of town, but they finally obtained the address of Mírzá

Abu'l-Faḍl and hastened to call on him and his interpreter, Anton Haddad.

Mírzá expressed delight at seeing Khan, for he had been a long-time friend of Khan's father. (The two men, Mírzá and Khan, would have their ups and downs later on. In fact when Khan's small daughter Marzieh – who never met Mírzá, not being born when he was in the country – had one of her tantrums, Khan would call her Mírzá Abu'l-Faḍl. Still, Khan's devotion to and great respect for Mírzá were always in place.)

Mírzá had now been in Paris for a number of months, Khan wrote, and already some thirty new believers had come into the Faith and were firm in the Covenant. A number had gone to visit the Master in 'Akká. Some were people of means, others average citizens. Khan was to call on a few that very afternoon of the letter.

At the close of this letter, Khan asked his brother to give this message to his uncle, together with his love: 'Tell him that I left my country in order to devote my life to 'Abbás Effendi [this was what the Master was called in Persia]. And now, let all wait and see who would be the winner, Khan, or those who stayed at home, fastening themselves to the skirts of this or that nobleman, and seeking to accumulate the gifts of this world.'

Khan was not sure how he would spend two or three weeks in that great city, but expected he would have to stay on in Paris until his companions, the Getsingers, would be able to arrange their affairs.

As the days passed, Khan found several of his friends from home – obtaining their addresses at the Persian Legation – young men who were now studying in Paris. Among them were the two sons of the well-known Minister at Tehran, Mukhbiru'd-Dawlih. He also met Naṣru'lláh Khán Bakhtíyárí, a youth of exceptional brilliance, with whom he had become acquainted something less than two years before, at Bákú.

The two brothers showed great interest in the Faith and the elder, Ḥasan-'Alí Khán (whose title later on was Naṣru'l-Mulk) went with Khan to call on Mírzá. But the younger, Muṣṭafá-Qulí Khán, prevented him from ever going there again, warning him that any association with Bahá'ís would harm their future careers in the higher circles of Persia. As for Bakhtíyárí, he became a Bahá'í, but his strong addiction to alcohol and opium boded ill for his future.

In another letter, dated June 11, to his brother, Khan blessed the kindness of the Master for putting him in touch with the wonderful Bahá'ís in Paris. He referred in particular to Miss Elsa Barney, who was there with her older sister Natalie. Both had been educated in Paris for years. Natalie was a fine poet in both French and English, and her work was published in France as being that of a Frenchwoman. In later years she would frequently be mentioned in the wrong memoirs, and in addition to other biographies, a full-length book about her by Jean Chalon has recently been published in French and English. Meanwhile her sister Elsa (afterward Laura Dreyfus-Barney), whose name will go down the ages because of her 'imperishable service',[95] the collection and transmission to posterity of *Some Answered Questions*, is almost unknown.

Natalie was tall, blond and graceful, and Khan came to meet her through her sister Elsa and her cousin, Ellen Goin. Natalie was, to put it mildly, not inclined toward religion. She was a pagan in the Greek sense, and worshipped beauty. But in the event she was much affected by Khan's fiery yearning when he spoke of the Bahá'í Faith and especially of his being with the Master during all those long months on the shores of the Mediterranean Sea. It was not the Faith which attracted her, but Khan's yearning love for 'Abdu'l-Bahá.

Khan's meeting with her came about in this way: one day when they both were with Mírzá, Elsa told Khan that Natalie had a great wish for Khan to attend her birthday dinner.

'Please accept,' Elsa said. 'It might draw Natalie to the Faith.'

Natalie had a house in Paris near the beautiful Parc Monceau, and the next day Khan took a carriage in the late afternoon and was driven there, to attend the dinner. As a Persian poet who had won many prizes in annual poetry contests at home, he was excited at the thought of meeting a beautiful young lady poet. But he was not at all accustomed to the society of beautiful young women and was almost too shy to speak to them. It was only the hope of attracting Natalie to the Faith that made him accept her invitation. If that happened, the awful embarrassment would be a small price to pay.

He arrived too early, rang the doorbell and was ushered into the empty drawing room by a maid. The ladies would be downstairs directly, she said. Khan was admiring some of the oil paintings when he heard a rustle. There on the staircase stood a young woman dressed in a gorgeous evening gown of light-colored silk. When she had reached the floor, the train of her gown was still on the lower steps. It was many a long day before that picture lost its bright colors in his mind, if it ever did.

At first, when Natalie spoke to him, Khan could not answer. Then Elsa and Ellen and some other women joined them; and for some reason it was a relief to see that they were all in gowns something like Natalie's. Perhaps that mitigated her effect.

At table, Khan sat to the hostess's left, Elsa to her right.

Khan tried to control his feelings but soon found himself pouring out his soul about 'Abdu'l-Bahá and the Bahá'í Faith, and the tears were pouring down his cheeks. Natalie showed no reaction whatever, except that she never took her eyes off him, and studied his gestures, and began to make personal remarks about his 'piercing eyes and dark, dark brown tousled hair and white, even teeth'. Her words nearly killed him.

When, late that night, he was permitted to leave, he thanked God for having escaped an impossible situation. He ought, he told himself, to run away from Paris at the earliest moment, to avoid a pitfall – otherwise he could not go on in his chosen field, or win the good pleasure of the Master, obtaining which was always his chief goal in life.

On the following afternoon when Elsa came to Mírzá's class, she delivered to Khan an envelope from Natalie, and he took it with trembling hands. When, later and alone, he opened it, he found a long poem, written in her own hand, that she had composed for him.

Natalie's poem, written to Khan in 1901, and a yard or so in length, inevitably reminds us that Wilde had just died the year before, and that at sixty-four, Swinburne was already past it. Here, in part, is the poem:

To a Believer

Calm Oriental eyes full of stilled fires,
Eyes that hold deeper lives than ours can know,
Eyes that have seen the light of souls, and glow
In silent speech with more than world's desires
Or passing pleasures of a world that hems
The Infinite into a lapse of time . . .
Oh patient God-lit eyes, you bring a chime
Of peace to our unrest, you shine as gems
Upon truth's coronet, and troubled years
Shall pass as streams into the quiet sea,
And wave-tossed moments of Eternity
Take to her tideless shore our ill-spent tears . . .
Your joys and faiths and hopes come from afar,
Yours is a caravan that passes by
The desert of our sterile cares, your sky
Holds still the radiance of a guiding star!
And so you move on heedless of our strife . . .
Bright purple sheaths of splendor cross the gray
Dense space . . .
Earth's colors waken from their beds of shade.
The East has poured from out her jeweled gown
The hoarded wealth of centuries – to drown
The temples of dead Gods who like leaves fade

And fall into their autumn and are lost –
Oh shivering spectre of a spectral past!
Oh moaning monks of churches, chant your last
And let the Spring-time rise from out the frost
Of your cold Faiths, melt, you have stayed too long –
The world's a mouldering graveyard, incensed air
Cannot wipe out the fetid smell nor spare
One error from your heap of hidden wrong –
The heaven-hells you offer each are lies:
A mirage of the desert is the light
That burns and does not know the wrongs of right,
The rights of wrong!
Oh merciful dear eyes, let my soul lean as wanderers to the cool
Pure waters, – and let me see my face . . .
Let me be mirrored in you – let me sleep
And by your peaceful lights forget to weep . . .

We know exactly how Mírzá Abu'l-Faḍl and Khan, and Laura and Natalie and some others looked in those days, because Alice Pike Barney, a talented artist, left their portraits, some in oil, some in pastel, to the Smithsonian Institute in Washington.

The three young women, Elsa, her sister Natalie, her cousin Ellen, were members of one of America's wealthiest families; and yet Elsa and Ellen, since accepting the Faith and meeting the Master, had no thought except to serve, and Elsa would gladly have given up everything for the Master had He so wished. Khan felt it a great honor to have spiritual sisters like these – and knew it was through no merit of his, only the bounty of 'Abdu'l-Bahá.

Another who was in Paris during those early weeks in June was Juliet Thompson, and she recalled (in January 1951) how, 'entering my first Bahá'í meeting, I was strongly impressed by two figures: the wise and saintly Mírzá Abu'l-Faḍl and, translating for him, a fiery, strikingly handsome young man – our beloved Ali-Kuli Khan.'[96]

Khan also wrote in one of his letters to Ḥusayn of the Shah's imminent visit to Europe, and said that even if the Shah spent millions on the journey, and met all the world's great ruling personages along the way, he would never have the experiences Khan was having, in meetings where he was arising and proclaiming, in English and French, the Message of Bahá'u'lláh.

The last week of his three weeks' stay, Khan was a guest in the studio of Charles Mason Remey, and the friends took him about to suburbs and neighboring towns where he spoke of the Faith to many inquirers. He then received a cable from Aḥmad Yazdí in Port Said, sent by the Master's orders, which said, 'Khan vite Chicago'.

There is some confusion in the memoir about dates at this point, for it says the cable was received at Paris on May 26, which was the date of his arrival there. Khan says he left Paris 'June 13–14', presumably not many days after he received the cable, and he is definitely located in London on June 14 and 15 by his bill at the Portland Hotel. There is also a letter from May E. Bolles, dated June 14, from 100 rue du Bac, Paris:

My dear Brother,
    I am so very sorry not to have seen you to say goodbye . . . but I am sure Lua explained to you that I felt very ill this afternoon, and I could not eat any dinner – but just had to give up and lie down. Then I prayed and asked God to give me strength to go over and see you – and I got up and went quickly over to Mr Remey's in a cab – but I was too late – you had already gone . . .
    Dear Brother, it has been a great joy to me to know you, to see the fire of love burn in your face, to be strengthened and inspired by your words.
    I know how hard it is for you to start off alone in this way. I know that it is your great love and devotion to our Lord (rouhie fedah) [may my soul be sacrificed to Him!] that has enabled you to follow His Command, and make this voyage. I thank God that you had the strength to do it, and I know that your blessing and reward will be very great.
    Always remember . . . that this action of yours will be a wonderful example to others, and that the hidden influence in the lives of others – of our pure and noble actions of sacrifice is very great.
    I shall pray for you always – that Our Glorious God will bless and strengthen you, will protect you every hour of your journey, comfort and sustain you, and that every trace of fear, anxiety or dread will disappear from your soul thro [sic] the blessed love of Our Great Master, and His constant presence with you, His faithful and obedient servant . . .

Obviously Khan was much disturbed at having to set out alone, and face an unknown life across the redoubtable sea. When one thinks back, knowing that this life of his would take him from his days as a wandering dervish to receptions at the White House, one can only feel surprise at where the Bahá'í Faith will toss its followers.

Believers in Great Britain had already asked Khan to visit them before he left for America. Mrs Thornburgh-Cropper had written June 4 from her London home, 5, Gloucester Terrace, Regent's Park: 'Dear Young Friend . . . How you must enjoy beautiful Paris, speaking the beautiful language like a native . . . being with so many dear believers – are you coming to England . . .? Please answer these questions . . .'

TWENTY-NINE

No One at the Dock

In London Mrs Thornburgh-Cropper had Khan to dinner. First, a friend met him and accompanied him to the hotel, they driving the several miles in a public carriage. Khan noticed, as they rode, that a man, breathing heavily, was running along beside the cab. He asked his companion about this and was told that such men would loiter around the railroad station and follow a passenger to wherever he was going, so as to earn a shilling or two for carrying in his luggage. Khan was astonished to find a situation like that in the capital of a country which exercised colonial rule over so many nations and was so rich. He stopped the cab, got out, and handed the man a couple of shillings, to spare him from running any further.

When the unfortunately-named but popular ship *Minnehaha*, an Atlantic Transport liner, sailed on June 16, Khan was on board and completely alone. Originally, Khan had expected that the Getsingers would accompany him to the United States, but for whatever reason, they had remained in Paris. As it turned out, he might have had the companionship and guidance of Emogene Hoagg (the one who later, working closely with the Guardian in Haifa, typed *The Dawn-Breakers*) had she known of his departure soon enough.

The *Minnehaha* was a steamship of only some twelve thousand tons but to Khan she seemed to be the largest ship that could ever have been built. The journey took twelve days and, mostly, the sea was calm and the weather sunny. Still, this being an ocean, Khan did not trust it, and thought the ship would founder if a storm blew up, so every night at bedtime he prayed fervently for his life. What sustained him was the belief that Bahá'u'lláh had promised a safe journey to 'Akká pilgrims, provided they had first asked for and then received permission to come. Surely, he thought, a similar protection would be accorded one who was crossing the ocean at the direction of the Master in order to spread the Faith in America.

One of Khan's problems on board was that he could not read the ship's menus, which embarrassed him much. As a sample, he once asked for toast when he thought he was ordering dessert. When it came to choosing the right cutlery to use, he watched the others and did what they did.

At last the voyage neared its end. As the ship came into harbor and prepared to dock, Khan was in a turmoil. He had never imagined New York would be so huge. From his previous experiences in the Middle East he assumed the crowd waiting on the dock were all Bahá'ís. But when he set foot ashore with his luggage, not one person asked for him. He was amazed that with all the eagerness to meet him that they had expressed in their letters, and their wanting so much to greet the amanuensis who had been closest to the Master, nobody was there.

A fellow passenger (possibly a Samaritan?) approached him and asked if he could help. Khan told the man his New York address, the Bahá'í headquarters on West 57th Street, and the man called a cab for him and Khan was duly delivered.

It was very warm, late June. He took the elevator up to the floor where the Bahá'í hall was located. And there in the hall he found a couple of hundred men and women, all eager to welcome him. He then learned that a large delegation had set out to meet the ship, but the passengers had all been landed much earlier than expected.

Khan stood up, faced the audience, gave them the Master's messages, and launched into a fiery address which, even decades later, those still living remembered.

Khan wrote his mother, back in Tehran, ten days after arriving in New York. (Exact dates are not always at hand: people live their lives, and do not think of themselves as recorders of history.) He told her in that letter that night and day he appeared before audiences of more than two hundred persons and spoke to them of the Cause and the blessed Covenant, and that all were happy to see and hear him. He could never have dreamt, he wrote, that some day, in a great country like America, he would stand up and face hundreds and hundreds of well-educated, intelligent men and women and raise up his voice and prove to them the greatness of the Center of the Covenant. He said this was due solely to 'Abdu'l-Bahá, who had let him stay in the Holy Land and had trained him for thirteen months, transforming him into a new being. Without that, he would not have been able to speak.

Early on he must have met the mother of Elsa and Natalie Barney for there is a letter, hastily written in pencil, apparently hand-carried, from Elsa to her. The letter is addressed to Mrs A. C. Barney, Waldorf-Astoria, or 582 Fifth Ave.:

Mother Dear,
  I am more than happy to be able to ask Ali Kuli Khan to meet you. I admire him immensely for he has such a fine intel[l]igence – large heart and rock like faith.
  I am sure that you will both have the greatest pleasure in knowing one another. And I only wish that I could be there too . . . I am in wild haste – I

cannot speak too kindly about Ali Kuli Khan – but you will see for yourself –
With deep love to you Mother Dear, I am your Devoted Daughter –

A New York letter of June 29, 1901, from Helen Ellis Cole indicates Khan's talks, however impassioned, were not always as successful as he thought. Apparently he had not yet properly gauged the American audience. She writes: 'I was so sorry for you the other night. At first I fear you will have many trials, because American people must always have everything made very clear to them. But patience dear brother all will be well.'

This is the sort of comfort a speaker least enjoys.

As time passed, Khan would be able to handle any audience. His platform eloquence was even compared to Woodrow Wilson's. He never seemed to feel that he was giving the talk – it came out of the blue. Afterward he would say, 'Oh, I wish someone had taken it down!' His daughter Marzieh, not having had the benefit of 'Abdu'l-Bahá's guidance, and dependent on careful preparation, used to sit through his talks dreading that the spirit would let him down. She did not believe the rumor that Florence Khánum, perhaps relying too heavily on the spirit, had once given a talk on 'Xerxes and Anti-Xerxes'. She did, however, get her own talks pinned down on paper beforehand, and lived in fear that her notes would blow away. Khan's family, one way or another, were all public speakers. It was impossible to say a word at their table without interrupting.

After ten or twelve days in New York, Khan took the train to Chicago, where he was to translate for Mírzá Asadu'lláh and await the arrival of Mírzá Abu'l-Faḍl from Paris. He was astonished at the train, far more splendid than any he had seen in Europe or the Caucasus. Other marvels to him were the Brooklyn Bridge, a modern wonder then, and the most famous skyscraper in the world, the Flat-Iron Building.

Khan knew of the situation in Chicago. About a year before, the Master had sent Mírzá Asadu'lláh there. He had also sent Ḥájí 'Abdu'l-Karím and the merchant prince Ḥájí Mírzá Ḥasan Khurásání, both from Cairo. The mission of the three was to correct the false teachings which Dr Ibráhím Khayru'lláh of Syria, first to establish Bahá'í classes in America, had given the seekers. The Master had promised this man a great station in the Faith if he would study the Teachings carefully and convey them to inquirers without interposing any materials of his own. The Master had warned him of this some years before at 'Akká, but on his return to Chicago Dr Khayru'lláh wrote a book, supposedly Bahá'í, but embodying his erroneous views and with no sanction from 'Abdu'l-Bahá. This resulted in Covenant-breaking and created a division among the new Bahá'ís. The above three individuals had been sent to correct the problem.

However, there had been one obstacle. They had as an interpreter a young Egyptian boy whose English proved far from adequate. The two believers from Cairo were therefore being called back, while Mírzá Asadu'lláh was to continue on in Chicago.

Meanwhile Mírzá Abu'l-Faḍl had left for Paris with his Syrian interpreter, to be there for a few months prior to leaving for the United States. That was why Khan was ordered to leave Paris and go on to America where he would join Mírzá Asadu'lláh in Chicago and work there, awaiting the arrival of the great Mírzá Abu'l-Faḍl, who was to teach in that city. Khan's function, besides translating for the teachers, would be to translate the Master's Tablets as they came in, and see that they reached their due recipients.

A number of believers met Khan's train in Chicago and escorted him to the Bahá'í house on West Monroe Street, the headquarters here of the Faith. It was directly across the street from a splendid park. Hundreds of Bahá'ís had gathered to see and hear the young interpreter of the Master, who came with messages of greeting from Him. One of these was Thornton Chase, the first American Bahá'í, a pillar of the community, a fine-looking businessman, tall and imposing.

A few minutes after Khan had finished speaking, he felt much exhausted by the heat and Thornton Chase asked him to come out to a drugstore nearby. Khan looked at him in surprise, wondering if Mr Chase thought he was ill.

'I am quite well, thank you,' he said.

'Never mind,' said Thornton Chase. 'You will see what I mean when you get there.'

Khan was not yet aware that only a fraction of an American drugstore had to do with drugs.

They sat down at the soda fountain and Mr Chase ordered Coca-Cola. Khan had never heard of it. For all he knew there might be alcohol in it. He hesitated to take a sip.

'Taste it!' said Mr Chase.

Khan tasted it. After all, he told himself, we are in a drugstore, so it is not surprising that this tastes like some peculiar drug.

'You must learn to like it,' Thornton Chase told him. 'You'll have to drink a lot of it as time goes on.' And he was right.

Later on, Khan was taken to his room on the second floor of the Bahá'í center. Ḥájí 'Abdu'l-Karím and Ḥájí Mírzá Ḥusayn Khurásání, and their young interpreter, Ḥusayn Ríḥí, were still living there. Mírzá Asadu'lláh also had rooms in that house.

That evening after dinner, Mírzá Asadu'lláh had his meeting for Bahá'ís and seekers, and paragraph by paragraph, Khan had to translate what he said. The class, who had only heard Asadu'lláh before through the young Egyptian boy with his limited English, thought Khan, with his rapid translation, one of the wonders of the world. They were astonished at the many-syllabled, philosophical terms Khan used; especially because, like many at that age, he believed it would impress the public more if he made use of words that were very long and even obsolete. He favored such words as 'atrabiliar' and 'subfusc'.

Soon after the meeting, his earthly life nearly came to an end. In the Middle East of those days, the well-to-do lit their rooms with oil lamps, while the rest used tallow candles or oil with a wick lying in it. In Paris and London they did have gas light but Khan never had to deal with it himself. That night in Chicago, conducted to his room around midnight, exhausted from his long day, he simply blew out the gas and fell into bed.

Perhaps an hour later he woke in the dark and found he was choking to death. He ran from the room, banged on a door and screamed for help. One of the men came to his aid, turned off the gas, and told him that except for an open window he would have suffocated. The effect of the gas on his throat kept him hoarse for weeks. He felt once again that God had saved him for some destiny (which he knew he must work hard to achieve).

Gradually, through constant observation, he began to learn American ways. For example, he learned to comment on the weather: 'Nice day, isn't it?'

Nobody ever said that, as a conversational gambit, in Persia. You would have been thought stupid. Everyone could see what the weather was.

Another question that seemed unnecessary to him was, 'How did you sleep?'

'Why, Madam,' he wanted to answer, 'I put my feet up on my bed and I stretched myself out and I slept.'

He had already learned that American and Persian sleeping hours are different. Persians are awake early in the morning, even having business appointments at eight. They sleep during the early afternoon, and their next sleep is after a late dinner, perhaps at ten or so. They say the food gives them a good, natural sleep. (World sleeping habits would be interesting to look into, sleep being one of the most mysterious experiences in life.)

It did not take Khan long to sort out the situation in Chicago. The Syrian Arab, Dr Khayru'lláh, had arrived in the United States in December 1892, and by 1894 had communicated word of his unusual success to the Master. By 1896 there were, reportedly, hundreds of Bahá'ís in Chicago and Kenosha, and many who later on became prominent servants of the Cause first heard of Bahá'u'lláh through him.

Dr Khayru'lláh was identified with various kinds of so-called New Thought teachings, including Spiritism and reincarnation (defined by one of the Bahá'ís, Howard MacNutt, as reincarnotion) and even, some thought, black magic. It was from such points of view, fads of the day, that he would present the Teachings of Bahá'u'lláh, he himself not being well-grounded in the Bahá'í Faith. He had organized his ideas on the Faith into a series of lessons intermingled with New Thought and the like. The climax of the course came in the last lesson, vouchsafed in a hermetically secret, special meeting, where he announced the Greatest Name, Alláh-u-Abhá (God is All-Glorious)..

A number of young Americans, men and women who had heard him, traveled to 'Akká to see 'Abdu'l-Bahá and on their return reported on the notes they had taken, which of course differed markedly from what they had heard Khayru'lláh teach.

One of these was Ella Goodall, later Mrs Charles Miner Cooper, whose legacy in after years would give San Francisco its imposing Bahá'í Center. On May 5, 1940, she told Marzieh how she herself had come into the Faith. Lua Getsinger was, Mrs Cooper said, Khayru'lláh's best pupil, but he taught such non-Bahá'í subjects as reincarnation, lore of the Orient, and that the Master was Christ. He called the Bahá'í part, the famous eleventh lesson, 'the pith of the Teachings'.

Lua had recently married Edward Getsinger, and it was he who had the idea of taking the Teachings to Phoebe Hearst. He went to Pleasanton, a few miles south of Oakland, in California, and eventually received an appointment at the Hacienda. Lua was sent for to explain about the Bahá'í Faith.

Afterward, classes were held in Mrs Hearst's San Francisco apartment on top of the Examiner Building at Third and Market Streets. Nell (Helen) Hillyer (later Mrs Philip King Brown), a friend of Ella Goodall's, invited her to the Hearst apartment one evening; but as only initiates were allowed to attend the classes, Ella had to wait in a bedroom until one o'clock in the morning. At that hour, Lua came in – radiant, vital, hungry. Nell sent out to Gobey's saloon for an oyster loaf, and they also shared a little white wine, drinking from the one available glass. Lua gave Ella Lesson One of the Khayru'lláh series, but there was nothing in it about the Bahá'í Cause.

Nevertheless, feeling somehow that here was something important, something that should be investigated, Ella and Mrs Goodall traveled to New York and there Anton Haddad began to give them Khayru'lláh's series of lessons.

Nell Hillyer, in New York at the time, and unable to wait for

Haddad to give Ella the eleventh lesson, 'the pith of the Teachings', sprang it on her the night before.

Mrs Goodall returned West, but Ella obtained permission to make a secret visit to 'Akká, she and Nell Hillyer together. Ella went on the pilgrimage already believing, and was confirmed at once.

On the way, stopping in Cairo, 'Abdu'l-Karím told her, 'Empty your cup. You are going to the Source.'

Invited to 'Akká, Khayru'lláh came with several Western pupils, including Miriam (also called Mary and Maryam), his young English wife. He asked permission to spread his course of 'Bahá'í' lessons, but 'Abdu'l-Bahá did not allow this because they did not represent the true teachings, would mislead the seekers and finally harm Khayru'lláh's own status as a Bahá'í.

Later on it became known that while in 'Akká as the Master's guest he met secretly with Muḥammad-'Alí, arch-breaker of Bahá'u'lláh's Covenant, arch-foe of 'Abdu'l-Bahá, the plotter who, unless God had stopped him, would have shattered the Faith destined by God, so the Bahá'ís believe, as the sole instrumentality for unifying the world. Muḥammad-'Alí, who was, as the Master's Will ('the Charter of the New World Order'[97]) informs us, 'as an axe striking at the very root of the Blessed Tree'. And, the Will goes on, referring to him and his followers, 'Should they be suffered to continue they would, in but a few days' time, exterminate the Cause of God, His word, and themselves.'[98]

Khayru'lláh, lured away by the fleshpots of America, disregarded the Master's counsels, and on his return to America precipitated a 'devastating crisis' in the Faith, but as the Guardian has written, successive teachers from the East (including Ṭihrání, Khurásání and Abu'l-Faḍl) dispelled the believers' doubts and held them together.[99] Nevertheless, Khayru'lláh continued to attack the Master and the Faith for twenty years, was divorced by his wife (who stayed loyal to the Covenant) and died abandoned and forgotten, his great chance blown off on the winds. As for those who, on his account, left the emerging pattern of World Order, they vanished like cloud-shapes.

THIRTY
Visions, or Vision?

Khan's instructions were to translate for Mírzá Asadu'lláh at his classes and also translate the regular lessons that he prepared in Persian each week. Khan said he faithfully carried out these tasks, since the teaching had to go on until Mírzá Abu'l-Faḍl should arrive. But inwardly he was much distressed at the striking contrast between what he had heard from the Master and what Mírzá Asadu'lláh was giving out, the latter's lessons supposedly interpreting Scriptural prophecies concerning the Advent of the great Manifestation. Asadu'lláh included along with this a good deal of misty metaphysical jargon, which later he insisted was necessary to attract the seekers in Chicago.

It was the Master's expressed wish to Khan that there should be true harmony between Asadu'lláh and Khan, and that they should present a united front in their teaching work. Also, Asadu'lláh received a Tablet from 'Abdu'l-Bahá soon after Khan's arrival in which the Master stressed the importance of harmony, especially at this time of the confusion brought about by Khayru'lláh. If matters were to be straightened out, a united front was now an urgent need. This Tablet of the Master's read in part: 'Ali-Kuli Khan is unique as interpreter and translator . . . He is, however, highly sensitive and thus, regard for his feelings is essential.' This had to do with the matter of Mírzá Asadu'lláh's journey to Persia and his return to 'Akká while Khan was there, and the group photograph which Asadu'lláh, the box containing the Báb's remains in front of him, had taken with seven others to fabricate his interpretation of the Qur'ánic verse, 'on that day eight shall bear up the throne of thy Lord'.

'Abdu'l-Bahá on several occasions had remarked that if anyone's acts or words seemed of a nature to harm the Cause of God, Khan would become so wrought up that he could not keep silent. The Master's warning in the Tablet to Asadu'lláh now seemed to Khan prophetic, for he had already begun to feel that the classes and lectures showed a distinct tendency to build the speaker up as a leading teacher and impress his hearers – at least those 'mystically' inclined – with the teacher's 'wisdom' and 'spiritual vision'. After all, when he was a youth in Persia, Khan had delighted in concocting a fake mystical vocabulary which was equally impressive.

As time passed, Asadu'lláh began to call his series of lessons 'The School of the Prophets', and planned to publish them under this title some day.

Khan struggled to be patient, and a faithful translator. It was not easy, but he knew the situation was only temporary, until Mírzá Abu'l-Faḍl should come, so he did not, he said, 'outwardly groan', but carried on as best he could.

About two months after Khan arrived in Chicago, Abu'l-Faḍl, often referred to by American believers simply as Mírzá, landed in New York, and after a few days, accompanied by Elsa Barney, came to Chicago. The rooms assigned to him in the Bahá'í house were on the second floor at the right front corner, while those of Asadu'lláh were on the same floor at the opposite corner.

VISIONS, OR VISION?

Abu'l-Faḍl's arrival in Chicago created a great stir, not only among Bahá'ís and seekers but the general public. The press gave detailed accounts of his background, his great erudition, his various long terms of imprisonment in Tehran at the hands of the Persian government who were the tools of the Muslim clergy, fanatics trying in vain to destroy the Bahá'í Faith. Especially stressed was his high standing among the intellectuals of Cairo, achieved through his published books on the Bahá'í Faith and his proofs of religious truth as opposing the atheistic beliefs then current in Europe. Erudite professors at Cairo's university of al-Azhar, Islam's greatest seat of learning, would often submit their works to Abu'l-Faḍl for his criticism before publication.

Khan would say that in all his life, and all his long association with learned persons in America and elsewhere, and all his reading, he knew of no one East or West (the Prophets and 'Abdu'l-Bahá always excepted of course), even centuries back in history, whose knowledge, erudition, critical faculties, exceeded or even equaled Abu'l-Faḍl's. He was not only a historian, Khan would say, of religion, philosophy and world politics, but 'a true philosopher of history'. And his devotion to the Faith of God within every great religion was matched only by his selflessness and his (not typical of scholars) humility. Mírzá well knew, Khan used to say, that all humanity's acquired learning is nothing but a drop when compared to the ocean of the Manifestations' and Holy Ones' intuitive knowledge. This was the reason, Khan said, for Abu'l-Faḍl's utter self-effacement in the presence of 'Abdu'l-Bahá.

Every day local Bahá'ís and others from distant cities came to classes given by Mírzá Abu'l-Faḍl. He also spoke at a weekly meeting, usually held in the Masonic Building downtown in Chicago's Loop. At his public meetings he never spoke from notes, but at his classes he worked from notes, answering questions that had come in the mail or been asked by listeners. Khan, of course, translated for him. Many intellectuals came to hear Mírzá, including Catholics and members of Protestant denominations. His presence and his beautiful manners impressed them all. Khan was also with him when hostile religious leaders attempted tc oest Mírzá in argument, trying to disprove the revelations of Bahá'u'lláh. These he would drive into a corner, wall them up with his logic. If sincere inquirers, they would give up and admit the soundness of his arguments; if there only to dispute and not to reason, they soon took themselves off, defeated.

Believers in large numbers came to the classes, particularly those who wished to be deepened in the Faith. On the other hand, Khan noticed quite a few, the majority of them women, choosing instead to go to the classes held by Asadu'lláh, for he would interpret their dreams and visions as well as present his cloudy explanations of the Faith. After a time Khan found that the latter group was circulating the rumor that Asadu'lláh conveyed the 'really spiritual' side of the Bahá'í Teachings, while Mírzá, though a great and learned man, could teach only matters relating to the intellect.

Khan was much disturbed at what he called 'this unhappy phenomenon', the separating into two camps, that of the 'spirit' (Asadu'lláh's dreams and visions) and that of Abu'l-Faḍl's 'intellectual matters'. As Mírzá became aware of his new reputation as a brain divorced from the spirit, he was much amused.[100]

Despite the situation, Abu'l-Faḍl never once made a derogatory remark about Asadu'lláh, and always showed him courteous attention and deference, as to one who was older than himself and had been longer in the Faith.

Khan, younger and of a different temperament, felt they faced a serious threat to the development of the Faith in Chicago, one that might divide the friends and make it impossible to lay a firm Bahá'í foundation in that community.

'You may remain silent', Khan finally burst out to Mírzá, 'and exercise restraint, but I cannot bear to see all your labors going to waste under these conditions. I must do my duty as I see it.'

Thereupon Khan wrote a letter to 'Abdu'l-Bahá describing the situation. He asked the Master to allow Amínu'lláh (Faríd) to come to the United States to translate for his father, so that Khan could give his full time to Abu'l-Faḍl's important work. Khan stated clearly that it would do great harm to the Cause if Asadu'lláh stayed on in the same city as Mírzá, for this might create further division and convey an entirely erroneous impression as to the meaning and purpose of the Faith.

'Abdu'l-Bahá favored this request and wrote a Tablet back to the effect that Asadu'lláh had often asked for his son to come over and be with him. While this had not been possible before, now, in view of the situation in Chicago, He would have Amín go there. Later, Amín and his father were to return to the Middle East.

Some weeks after the Tablet was received, Amín arrived. His knowledge of English was limited at that time, but he carried on and his father was able to resume his classes on a more regular basis than before. The (mostly) women pupils, delighted with what Asadu'lláh told them about their dreams and visions, flocked to him in still larger numbers. They would climb the stairs, hurry past the room where Mírzá and Khan were at work, and get to Asadu'lláh, each time with a fresh dream to be unraveled.

Khan soon realized that his suggestion about Amín had been unwise. It had enabled Mírzá to accomplish a great deal more work than before, but the basic reason for Mírzá's coming to Chicago was being subverted. 'Abdu'l-Bahá had sent him to replace the false teachings of Khayru'lláh with the true Bahá'í Faith. For this, the Master had dispatched Mírzá and Khan to this city in the heartland of America. But now Asadu'lláh's occultism and improper teachings were gaining ground, making for still more division among the believers. Instead of one chief obstacle to spreading the real Faith of Bahá'u'lláh, there were now two.

Khan knew that Mírzá clearly saw the damage that was being done, and was suffering. But Mírzá told him, 'I cannot write the Master about it. I cannot add yet another burden to His heavy load.'

Khan felt, however, that for the protection of the Faith he must write to 'Abdu'l-Bahá again. He could not endure to be silent. He described the confusion among the Bahá'ís and begged that Asadu'lláh and his son should be removed from Chicago and sent to teach in other cities. (Khan's reasoning may well have been that this would dilute Asadu'lláh's influence and prevent him from staying long enough in one place to make a party for himself.) With Asadu'lláh gone, Mírzá would be free to solve the problem created by Khayru'lláh – to show the believers that only on genuine Bahá'í principles, as interpreted by the Center of Bahá'u'lláh's Covenant, could world unity be established.

The Master issued a command to Asadu'lláh and his son that they leave Chicago, teach in other cities, and as soon as possible return to the Holy Land. Early in 1902 Asadu'lláh wrote to Khan in New York that the Master had directed him to return to the Holy Land with his son.

However, when the time came for Asadu'lláh to go, the son remained in America. The father had told some of his close pupils in Chicago that they should arrange for Amín to stay in the United States, where he could become well-educated and equipped to serve the Faith. Instead of going to 'Akká with his father, as the Master had ordered, Amín stayed behind with these friends to attend school, and they, thinking it was the Master's wish, kept him and provided for his education. He went on to study medicine, and as Dr Ameen U. Farid practiced in Los Angeles until his death in 1954 or 1955.

It is well known how Asadu'lláh defected and broke the Covenant, and that both his son and daughter (who married an American Bahá'í) severed their relations with the Faith and opposed 'Abdu'l-Bahá. The American, Sidney Sprague, returned to the Faith and died a loyal believer.

One of the confusions created by Asadu'lláh, and symptomatic of his incorrect teaching, had to do with the administrative body of the Chicago believers.

In those days the Bahá'ís of Chicago had elected, with the help and suggestions of Khayru'lláh, a body of nine, which they called the Board of Council, to deal with the general affairs of the community. Members included Thornton Chase, Charles Ioas, Albert Windust, Mr Greenleaf, Mr Agnew and Dr Bartlett.

With the arrival of Mírzá, these men became firmly grounded in the Bahá'í principles and actively served the Master. Mírzá, with Khan, also taught Dr Getsinger and Lua, although they, especially Lua, were busy travel-teaching in different cities.

Asadu'lláh, working toward his plans for his own future, these being to build the Bahá'í Faith around himself, changed the name of the Board of Council to the House of Justice. This suited the members of the Board very well, for it pleased them to become members of the House of Justice. In the Book of Aqdas, Bahá'u'lláh decrees that there should be a House of Justice in every town or city,[101] as well as a supreme House of Justice ('sole legislative organ'[102]) for the entire Bahá'í world. 'Abdu'l-Bahá, authorized so to do in the Will of Bahá'u'lláh, which left the Faith in the Master's hands, added in His own Will and Testament the 'Secondary Houses of Justice' (i.e., the present National Spiritual Assemblies) to the world system, also adding the power of the Universal House of Justice to reverse its own previous decisions.[103] In future, present-day Local Spiritual Assemblies will be called Houses of Justice.

When Khan learned of what Asadu'lláh had done he was astounded. How could Asadu'lláh have conferred such a title on a body of believers in Chicago, on his own, and without sanction from 'Abdu'l-Bahá?

Exceedingly upset, Khan talked this over with Abu'l-Faḍl. Mírzá only smiled, very gently, and said such matters would be corrected by the Master.

Despite this assurance, Khan's agitation continued. Like many another Bahá'í worker, Khan was frustrated when he saw the Cause being held back by purely human obstacles. He did not lose his faith, but came to think he could no longer stay at his tasks when his efforts to spread the Message as rapidly and widely as he had hoped were blocked by others. Now, impatient over the corrupting influences of Asadu'lláh and Khayru'lláh, beset by problems arising from his situation in an unfamiliar environment, and certainly not finding Mírzá, saintly though he was, too easy to work with, Khan wanted to give up.

He suffered so much at this time that he wrote the Master and asked permission to withdraw from the work. He said he would always be a Bahá'í but he could not endure the situation any longer. 'Abdu'l-Bahá replied, telling him, 'You are a leaf on the tree. When the tree is shaken, the leaf is shaken.'

Also, things turned out as Mírzá had said. When Asadu'lláh wrote the Master that he had formed the House of Justice in Chicago, 'Abdu'l-Bahá wrote back that the Chicago body should, for the present, be called the House of Spirituality. Other cities followed Chicago in using this name.

THIRTY-ONE

Mírzá and Khan Stop Smoking

In December 1901 a telegram arrived for Mírzá and Khan from Elsa Barney. Miss Barney had engaged quarters for them in Washington DC. Their first address in the capital was on De Sales Street, a street only one block long, between 17th Street and Connecticut Avenue. In after years the Mayflower Hotel was built there and the fine old red brick houses came down to make way for a parking lot, but Khan believed the house where they lived was still standing in the 1950s. It was a boarding house, so they were able to take their meals there. Khan and Mírzá had rooms on the top floor – because Mírzá, scholar, author and bachelor needed absolute quiet, away from the sounds of traffic, or the cries of babies, or those of cats (though he was fond of children and partial to cats).

The Bahá'ís would call on Mírzá by turn, and several times a week public meetings were held at the old Corcoran Building opposite the Treasury Department on 15th Street. Charles Mason Remey, back from Paris, was active in Washington. Among others whom Khan had already met in the Holy Land were Emilie Dixon and her two daughters, Louise and Eleanor.

Abu'l-Faḍl's instructions from the Master were to begin by writing his book, *The Bahá'í Proofs*, with Khan translating whatever was written each day. Mírzá wrote in Arabic, in a style and depth which he alone could command.

In addition to all the other work, they held a class for seekers each afternoon at three.

As for their food, Mírzá ate very little, but drank tea all day long, preparing it himself. He ate an occasional biscuit, and continually smoked cigarettes – a brand imported from Egypt, like his excellent tea.

About two years later, 'Abdu'l-Bahá revealed the message called by American Bahá'ís 'the purity Tablet', and addressed it thus: 'O Friends of the Pure and Omnipotent God! . . . although bodily cleanliness is a physical thing, it hath, nevertheless, a powerful influence on the life of the spirit.' Some prohibited things, the Master wrote, are 'so loathsome that it is shameful even to speak their name', while with others, 'the injurious effects . . . are only gradually produced . . .' and these were not absolutely prohibited. Smoking tobacco was not absolutely prohibited, as the Guardian also explained in later years. But 'Abdu'l-Bahá wrote, in a book first published in May 1916, 'one of the components of tobacco is a deadly poison and . . . the smoker is vulnerable to many and various diseases. That is why smoking hath been plainly set forth as repugnant from the standpoint of hygiene.' The Master explained that in the days of the Báb 'every individual who abstained from smoking was exposed to harassment, abuse and even death – the friends, in order not to advertise their beliefs, would smoke'. Furthermore, since in Bahá'u'lláh's Book of Laws the prohibition of tobacco was not specifically laid down, the friends did not give it up. He said Bahá'u'lláh 'always expressed repugnance for it', but smoked a little in the early days and later abandoned it. The Master emphasized that smoking is 'filthy' and is, 'by degrees, highly injurious to health'. He said also it was 'a waste of money and time'. He said that renouncing tobacco 'will bring relief and peace of mind' and 'make it possible to have a fresh mouth and unstained fingers, and hair that is free of a foul and repellent smell.'[104]

One should add that smoking never has been prohibited to Bahá'ís, since as the Guardian told the present writer, 'We cannot forbid what Bahá'u'lláh has not forbidden.' Nevertheless it is clear that the Master wished the Bahá'ís to give it up.

Mírzá, the chain smoker, gave it up. No more imported tobacco from Egypt. He said if his smoking was a test to the believers, and they saw it as a weakness in their teacher, he would stop. Khan, too, who had smoked since the age of fourteen, gave it up. Khan as a direct result of the Tablet, Mírzá perhaps even before.

Khan achieved abstinence through gradualism. He cut a steadily diminishing number of cigarettes into four pieces each, and filled in the gaps in his day with peppermints, with which he seemed to be supplied all through life. (These mints and 4711 cologne were the two scents his children would associate with him.)

Mírzá was a devout, a saintly man, and when, all alone, he said his prayers he could be heard through the door weeping and begging God to forgive his sins. He used to say that the closer one came to God the more one saw his own imperfections. Khan worried over the intensity of Mírzá's devotions, and also his frugal way of life, due not to economies but his delicate constitution. Khan felt that unless Mírzá was careful of his health he would not be able to write his daily segment of *The Bahá'í Proofs*, the book which all concerned were anxiously awaiting.

But because of Persian etiquette and a promise Khan had made to Mírzá, Khan was not free to speak to him about his long devotions, his diet and his taking so little rest. Soon after Mírzá had arrived in Chicago, he and Khan had discussed their collaboration, and Mírzá of his own accord had said he would accept any of Khan's suggestions as to ensuring the effectiveness of their work – but that Khan must give Mírzá his word of honor about one thing: 'You must promise that you will never interfere with my personal affairs.'

'How', Khan asked him in surprise, 'can you ask such a promise, when you knew and greatly praised my late father the Kalántar, and are aware that the members of his family were brought up to be courteous and well-mannered? How could I ever presume to meddle with the personal affairs of such a great man as yourself?'

Khan had promised, but did not realize at the time what Mírzá meant by his personal affairs, which was mostly that Mírzá, working hard at his classes and his book, would be allowed to live on tea, tobacco and a few crackers.

Since Elsa Barney had requested the Master to send Abu'l-Faḍl to the United States (as her guest), he felt he must go to her and to her mother Alice, whom he considered marvelous, both as a woman and an artist. Khan knew that Mírzá also held Mrs Barney in high regard, and that he much liked Elsa and would even listen to her suggestions. So Khan went to Elsa and told her how hard it was to manage Mírzá for his own good.

Khan's worries were soon justified. Although entitled to full board, Mírzá did not order any meals for days. One day when Khan had been out, he came back, knocked on Mírzá's door, but received no answer. Khan hurried downstairs to ask if Mírzá had gone out. The landlady said Mírzá must still be in his room; so the two of them climbed the stairs, forced their way in, and found him unconscious on the floor. They called the doctor and Mírzá was revived, but Khan knew he must take action.

That evening he brought word of the crisis to Elsa Barney. Obviously, Mírzá needed to eat. Elsa, knowledgeable, said all must be accomplished with great caution, otherwise Mírzá would say that Khan had broken his promise. They decided to consult with her mother, consultation being a prime Bahá'í method for solving problems.

Her mother knew what to do. The next morning she had her chef prepare a chicken for Mírzá, but to throw him off the track, she stopped downstairs at the boarding house and asked the housekeeper if Mírzá had been ordering food. No, he had not. Accordingly, around noon Alice Barney rapped on Mírzá's door. Khan opened it.

After greeting the two, Alice said, 'I have learned from the lady downstairs that you, dear Mírzá, are not ordering any meals, and so I have had a nice chicken cooked for you in my own kitchen.'

Mírzá, with his supreme intellect, was not deceived, and before thanking Alice, turned his gaze on Khan as if to say, 'Is this how you keep your word of honor that you would not interfere in my personal life?'

Khan pretended to be filled with remorse but actually exulted, knowing he had won a victory as Mírzá would not go against the wishes of Mrs Barney, who watched while he downed a portion of the nicely-roasted bird.

Another embarrassment that Khan, still very shy, endured from Mírzá had to do with shopping. If they were out and Mírzá purchased something, he would not allow Khan to carry the package. Here he would be, solemnly dignified in his oriental flowing robes, his turban and his full beard, walking along loaded down with a package, while young Khan in Western dress, and disencumbered, walked along with him. No member of a high-placed Persian family was to carry his bundles, Abu'l-Faḍl insisted.

Nor would he ever let Khan pour his own tea – Mírzá himself served Khan and any others present with his own hands. The story was that when, having returned to the East, he was provided by 'Abdu'l-Bahá with a servant, someone called on him and found Mírzá waiting on his servant.

Realizing that Mírzá needed someone to look after him more closely than Khan himself could manage, burdened as he was with hours of translation each day, he began to cast round in his mind for some Persian who would be able to deal with Mírzá's special requirements as to food, and in general to keep a careful watch on his well-being.

Khan said that he took a step at that time which, unaware and innocent though it was on his part, did harm to the Bahá'í Cause in America. It was something which he thought would preserve Mírzá's health for his important book and thus benefit the Faith.

When, in 1901, on his way from the Holy Land, Khan had visited Aḥmad Yazdí's establishment in Port Said, where general merchandise and European apparel were sold, he had seen a number of young men serving as clerks in the store. One of these, about fifteen, was from Iṣfáhán. This one told Khan he had come from Persia to 'Akká the year before, along with one of the older pilgrims, a teacher of the Faith, and afterward had entered the employ of Aḥmad Yazdí. This young boy begged Khan to ask 'Abdu'l-Bahá to send him to America to study so that he could serve the Cause. Khan promised he would do his best.

Now that Mírzá so urgently needed someone to be his attendant, to make sure he did not neglect his health, to take care of various chores, while Khan, already overworked, had neither the time nor Mírzá's permission to do any of this, he thought of Aḥmad Yazdí's clerk. He talked the matter over with Mírzá, and the upshot was, Khan wrote the Master about the situation in Washington and about the young boy from Iṣfáhán. The latter was told to go to America, serve Mírzá, and once Mírzá's work was finished, return with him to the Middle East. The boy's name at that time was Aḥmad-i-Iṣfáhání. Later on he took the name of Ahmad Sohrab.

Khan did what he could to help the new arrival, who knew very little English, supplied him with clothing and helped with other needs, in addition to which Ahmad received his expenses from Mírzá. His being there gave Khan more time to work, both on *The Baha'í Proofs* and on translations from works of Bahá'u'lláh, including *The Seven Valleys*, the *Ṭarázát* series of Tablets, and the *Íqán*, as directed by the Master. Khan was also traveling frequently to New York then, staying with the Howard MacNutts and Mr MacNutt was helping him to perfect his translations.

Howard MacNutt was the well-known Bahá'í teacher who, later, collected and brought out the Master's discourses in America, titled by 'Abdu'l-Bahá *The Promulgation of Universal Peace.* 'Abdu'l-Bahá wished him to write the introduction to this work 'when in heart he is turning toward the Abhá kingdom so that he may leave a permanent trace behind him'.[105]

With the coming of Ahmad, Khan took rooms outside Mírzá's house, but close by so that he would be available for the public meetings, the classes, and when visitors came to see Abu'l-Faḍl.

Every week brought Khan a large packet of Tablets from the Master, sent by Him in response to many letters from America. Khan had to start work at six in the morning to translate these Tablets and get each one ready for mailing with a covering letter from himself. They went out to all parts of the United States. Khan also received a great deal of mail, sometimes hundreds of letters, from American Bahá'ís asking him questions to present to Mírzá, then translate and mail back the answers. (Small wonder that as the years wore on, Khan's right hand developed a tremor which he believed was writer's cramp and ascribed to his virtually continuous writing tasks for the Faith.) What with all this, and the classes in Mírzá's rooms, and the public meetings, and continuous other Bahá'í work, Khan reached a state of exhaustion and had to consult a doctor in order to keep going.

Clearly, he had little time for personal friends, but did see Elsa Barney every day when she came to ask after Mírzá or attend a class. In addition, there were evenings when she invited Khan to her home to teach her Persian. She was the believer he saw most often, and she encouraged him to tell her his troubles and ask her advice. She was a very wise person, looked at a problem from all sides, and then offered a solution. She was young, dark, and strikingly beautiful (as her mother's portraits of her show) and a great comfort to him, but the love she inspired in him was, he said many years later on, that of a child for its all-wise grandmother.

He was also invited to the home of Mrs Emilie Dixon, who lived with Eleanor, her youngest daughter. Louise, the other daughter, was married, Khan thought, and did not live in the capital. He found it a pleasant respite to call at the Dixon home.

He also chose another friend, a young Bahá'í girl whose parents were German-Americans. They owned a store on 7th Street where they sold musical instruments, and lived in an apartment upstairs, over the store. This girl's name was Lydia Helbig. She was a blonde with blue eyes, and two delightful dimples when she smiled, which of course was pretty much all the time. Khan and Lydia finally drew close enough to visit the zoo together on Sundays. They used to board the trolley car on Connecticut Avenue and ride out to Chevy Chase Circle. There were no real estate developments out that way then; there was only Rock Creek Park, with the one trolley heading north.

Khan continued to be extremely shy, and except for close relatives had had little contact with women and no experience with the life led by American youth. Quite dark, he was not the plump-and-pink type so much admired in Persia, and he was surprised that Occidental women admired him. He wrote back to the family, 'I have come to a country where the women think I am handsome.' Old photographs show a slender, engaging young man, and as for his clothes, most of the European and American clothes of that day (not the Eastern ones with flowing robes) look funny enough now, but he did have a foreign appearance. One time when Francis, Florence's always-amused brother, was out for a walk with the newly-met young Persian, Francis dropped behind and said to his sister, 'What *is* it, Floss?'

Visiting with Eleanor, walking with Lydia, Khan's talk was only of the Master and the Faith, or of poetry, mysticism and philosophy. He would recite his poems to them and give on-the-spot translations. The young ladies were impressed, but he never gave them a chance 'to make amorous remarks', and never felt bold enough to offer any himself.

THIRTY-TWO

When the Lights Went Out

Eleanor, with her keen intelligence, drew Khan out beyond all personalities, so that he would launch into the vast Bahá'í scheme of human unification and world peace. He began to feel that he could not bear to miss a single evening in her company, and wondered what the outcome might be. Talking with Eleanor was such a pleasure, and Mrs Dixon made him so welcome and so much at home as she prepared tea and refreshments in the room next to where they were sitting.

In their own homey room, he began to have glimpses, through lifting mists, of a place where his heart could be at rest. He could pass over boundaries and enter a mysterious country whose inhabitants numbered only two. The sun always shone there, the only season was spring. It was a protected country like the world in a paperweight, the two shut in together for always in a translucent carapace.

The visits went on for some time in this timeless peace.

And then came an evening which Khan would never forget.

Eleanor, now and then, had spoken to him about a man who would call on her occasionally, a man twice her age. He was a government worker, apparently with few intellectual interests, and not at all drawn to the Faith. To Khan, he sounded old and dull, certainly not a rival, and he would tease Eleanor about him whenever his name was mentioned.

One evening it was Mrs Dixon who opened the door instead of Eleanor.

'Where is Eleanor?' he asked.

'Now, Khan, you sit down and have some refreshment and I'll tell you the whole story.'

Not knowing why he expected a terrible revelation, Khan sat. He turned to her and begged her to speak out.

Very slowly, she replied, 'She's gone to the country to visit some friends. I don't know just when she'll be back.'

Then she handed Khan a package, which he tore open. Inside was a note from Eleanor, and a Bible. On the flyleaf she had written lines in memory of their friendship. In the letter she wrote to this effect: that the visits could no longer continue because she was becoming so closely attached to him that she was afraid the relationship might lead to marriage, a marriage that would interfere with the mission laid out for him by 'Abdu'l-Bahá and bring unhappiness to them both.

'I have no ambition along such lines,' she told him, more or less. 'I want to live a quiet life in a small town, and that is where I shall be – as the wife of the gentleman of whom I spoke.'

Khan felt she had cut him off at one blow from life itself. He could never, never subject himself to such anguish again. Dazed, unseeing, he said goodnight. From now on he would have no friendships whatever with any young women, except for casual encounters at the public meetings.

Many and many a night after that he would walk, all alone in the dark, around the block off Fourteenth Street, and look up at the top floor windows, the Dixons' apartment, where the lights were, and feel the tears on his face. He confided in no one except Elsa Barney, his advisor and friend.

That was the Washington summer of 1902. Early that year he wrote his brother that again two Bahá'ís had been martyred at Abargú and a cable from Iṣfáhán asked the American Bahá'ís to appeal to the Shah, then in Europe, to stop the persecutions. Accordingly, the Bahá'í Board of Council had cabled the Shah to this effect, and the American believers were also going to write an appeal to him.

It was also in 1902 that Khan's right hand gave out from having written so much. It was 'almost lifeless' and he had to dictate for two or three weeks. He was then at the MacNutts, with Mírzá in rooms close by.

That year he had to upbraid his brother for quarreling with their uncle, and told him that as Bahá'ís they must endure all things with patience.

Khan and Mírzá devoted the entire summer to preparing Mírzá's book, to Khan's other translations, including the *Íqán*, and to continual visitors and classes.

One day a cable was received by Elsa from Natalie in Paris, saying their father had suddenly died.

Elsa asked Mírzá and Khan what the Bahá'í teaching was on cremation, and learned that it was to be avoided except in such a case as a general epidemic, when it might be essential. Elsa wrote to 'Abdu'l-Bahá on the subject, stating that Western scientists endorsed cremation because of the many advantages.

The Master then revealed a Tablet, and Khan translated it in New York on June 18, 1902.

HE IS GOD

The handmaid of God, Miss Barney, had asked a question as to the wisdom of burying the dead in the earth. She said too that scientists in Europe and America, after prolonged and wide-ranging research and debate on this subject, have concluded that according to the dictates of reason, the benefits of cremation have been fully established – and wherein, then, lies the wisdom of the Holy Religions requiring burial in the earth?

As thou art aware, this servant doth not have the time for a detailed explanation, and therefore can write only a brief reply. Where universal phenomena are concerned, no matter how long and hard the human intellect may struggle to find the right procedures or the perfect system, it can never discover the like of the divine creation and its order of transferences and journeyings within the chain of life. For the transferences, the compositions, the gatherings and scatterings of elements, and of constituent parts and substances, proceed in a chain that is mighty and without flaw. Observe the effective universal laws and see to what a degree they are solidly established, secure and strong.

And just as the composition, the formation, and growth and development of the physical body have come about by degrees, so too must its decomposition and dispersal be gradual. If the disintegration be rapid, this will cause an overleaping and a slackening in the chain of transferences, and this discontinuity will impair the universal relationships within the chain of created things.

For example, this elemental human body hath come forth from the mineral, the vegetable and the animal worlds, and after its death will be entirely changed into microscopic animal organisms; and according to the divine order and the driving forces of nature, these minute creatures will have an effect on the life of the universe, and will pass into other forms.

Now, if you consign this body to the flames, it will pass immediately into the mineral kingdom and will be kept back from its natural journey through the chain of all created things.

The elemental body, following death, and its release from its composite life, will be transformed into separate components and minuscule animals; and even though it will now be deprived of its composite life in human form, still the animal life is in it, and it is not entirely bereft of life. If, however, it be burned, it will turn into ashes and minerals, and once it has become mineral, it must inexorably journey onward to the vegetable kingdom, so that it may rise to the animal world. That is what is described as an overleap.

In short, the composition and decomposition, the gathering and scattering and journeying of all creatures must proceed according to the natural order, divine rule and the most great law of God, so that no marring nor impairment may affect the essential relationships which arise out of the inner realities of created things. This is why, according to the law of God, we are bidden to bury the dead.

The peoples of ancient Persia believed that earth-burial was not even permissible; that such burial, to a certain degree, would block the coursings and journeyings required by nature. For this reason they built Towers of Silence open to the sky, on the mountain tops, and lay the dead therein on the surface of the ground. But they failed to observe that burial in the earth doth not prevent the natural travellings and coursings which are an exigency of creation – that rather, earth-burial, besides permitting the natural march of phenomena, offereth other benefits as well.

And briefly stated, beyond this, although the human soul hath severed its connection with the body, friends and lovers are still vehemently attached to what remaineth, and they cannot bear to have it instantly destroyed. They cannot, for example, see the pictured face of the departed blotted out and scattered, although a photograph is only his shadow and in the end it too must fade away. So far as they are able, they protect whatever reminder they have of him, be it only a fragment of clay, a tree, or a stone. Then how much more do they treasure his earthly form! Never can the heart agree to look on the cherished body of a friend, a father, a mother, a brother, a child, and see it instantly fall to nothing – and this is an exigency of love.

Thus the ancient Egyptians mummified the body that it might remain intact to the end of time, their belief being that the longer the dead endured, the nearer they would draw to the mercy of their gods. Yet the Hindus of India cremate the body without any concern, and indeed the burning is a solace to their hearts. This lack of concern, however, is fortuitous: it deriveth from religious beliefs and is not a natural thing. For they suppose that the more rapidly the body is destroyed, the nearer it will come to divine compassion. This is the opposite of what the ancient Egyptians believed. The Hindus are even persuaded that, as soon as the body is with great rapidity disintegrated, forgiveness will be assured, and the dead will be blessed forevermore. It is this belief which reconcileth them to the cremation.

Greetings be unto thee, and praise. I did not have the time to write even a line, but out of regard for Miss Barney, this has been set down.

(signed) 'Ayn-'Ayn[106]

HE IS GOD!

Another point remains, and it is this: that in case of contagious diseases, such as the plague and cholera, whether cremation of bodies with lime or other chemicals is allowable or not? In such cases, hygiene and preservation is necessarily more important; for according to the clear Divine texts, medical commands are lawful, and 'necessities make forbidden things lawful' is one of the certain rules.

Upon thee be the glory of the All-Glorious!

(signed) 'Ayn 'Ayn

Apparently our bodies are a debt we must repay to the earth.

Elsa had cabled her sister in the meantime not to cremate the body of their father, but Natalie cabled back that cremation had already taken place and that she herself was bringing the ashes to Washington. From then on Elsa used the name Laura, that being the way she was designated in her father's will.

Another important event of that year, 1902, was the arrival of Phoebe Apperson Hearst, the widow of Senator George Hearst, a '49er from California. She maintained a house in Washington, a large building on New Hampshire Avenue a few blocks to the south of Dupont Circle. So far as Khan could remember, it was still standing in the 1950s.

Her son, William Randolph Hearst, who lived in New York, still unmarried, had already begun the building up of his publishing empire.

Now, with Mírzá and Khan in Washington, Mrs Hearst was anxious to discuss with them various plans for promoting the Faith. For one thing, she felt Khan should enroll at Harvard, the better to equip himself for future services. Khan explained that the Master had sent him to America to translate Bahá'í writings, including Mírzá's book, and that he was working at least fifteen hours a day. Since, however, Mrs Hearst had been accepted as a Bahá'í by 'Abdu'l-Bahá Himself and had received from Him the title 'Mother of the Faithful', Mírzá thought her suggestion should be communicated immediately to the Master.

Sponsorship was not new to Mrs Hearst for she had sponsored work in Chicago when Khan was there with Asadu'lláh, had written them often, and provided them with a monthly sum to defray their expenses.

'Abdu'l-Bahá approved Mrs Hearst's suggestion, provided the sum to be made available was moderate. So far as Khan could remember, he was to receive fifty dollars each month while at Harvard.

Circumstances intervened, however; matters which had nothing to do personally with Mírzá and Khan, but which caused both Harvard and the projected monthly sum to be dropped.

About seven years later, Khan learned what had happened. Through San Francisco friends of Florence Khánum's, Khan was invited to give a course of lectures on Persia in their city. It was then that he again met Phoebe Hearst and learned that certain believers had asked her for funds to bring out Bahá'í booklets, and had apparently used the money for other purposes. This, of course, had made her feel that she was being exploited and she had drawn back, disillusioned, from a number of projects, including the Harvard one.

Khan was able to convince Mrs Hearst that irresponsible acts by individuals could hardly be blamed on the Bahá'í Faith, and that Bahá'ís were not interested in her because of her fortune, but because of her being a believer. From then on until she died, she remained firm in the Faith, and it was through Khan that she carried on a correspondence with the Master until her death in 1919.

THIRTY-THREE

The Trials of Mrs Cole

More important for Khan than any course at Harvard could have been was the work he was engaged in: translating Mírzá Abu'l-Faḍl's *The Bahá'í Proofs*. The Master had sacrificed Khan's services in order to send him to work with this great scholar, knowing that He Himself had no one in the Holy Land to take Khan's place as a translator. That is a measure of the importance He placed on Abu'l-Faḍl and the task in America.

The first edition of Mírzá's book is titled *The Behai Proofs*. This was a misleading spelling contributed in the early days by E. G. Browne, and corrected by 'Abdu'l-Bahá. The second edition (1914) corrects the spelling. Obviously, the Guardian's adopting for the Western friends the transliteration system selected by a congress of orientalists was a great boon to the Faith. He asked the believers, in March 1923, to 'adhere scrupulously and at all times to this code in all their writings'.[107] A non-uniform spelling among orientalists was a great time waster and readers could not always be sure of the intended original word. Think only of the many different spellings of the name Muḥammad, which include Mahomet, Maumet, Mehmet, Mehmed, Mohamed, Mohammed, Mahound. The system is not phonetic; it could not be, as pronunciations vary all over the Middle East. But one advantage of the system is that the scholar can easily put the letters back into the original and discover just what or whom he is reading about – a great relief, especially when dealing with names.

In the Translator's Preface to *The Behai Proofs*, Khan describes it as 'an introductory work to a forthcoming book which he [Abu'l-Faḍl] is writing in compliance with the Command of the Center of The Covenant . . .'[108]

The first edition came out in New York City (April 1902). It was printed by the J. W. Pratt Company and the copyright was owned by 'A. P. Barney of Washington DC', undoubtedly Elsa's mother, Alice Pike Barney.[109]

Of this work, Khan told his daughter Marzieh, 'I <u>pulled</u> *The Bahá'í Proofs* out of Mírzá Abu'l-Faḍl. It's all introductions because he never felt he got it started.'

In his early days in the United States, one of Khan's patrons seems to have been Helen Ellis Cole. On July 2, 1901, she wrote him from Stoneacre, Newport, Rhode Island. Her letter shows that she was sponsoring his translation of the *Íqán*, sending funds to him in Chicago (at 475 West Monroe Street) and also to Mírzá Asadu'lláh.

How welcome her 'arrangements with a great learned man, a Mr Dresser to help you with the translation of the *Ighan*' were, we do not know. As soon as she received permission from 'Akká, Khan was to proceed to Mr Dresser in Eliot, Maine, and she would send him the travel money, although just then she could not 'send that which I hoped to Mirza Assad [*sic*], as I am a little short'. She was sorry Khan was so lonely in Chicago. Not surprising, but the great sacrifice he is making 'is for our dear Lord (que mon âme lui soit sacrifiée)' she added. And closed with: 'Dear brother you will soon be among firm believers in Eliot, – so be patient and brave.'

A month later, August 19 (Khan was already in Eliot and her letter was forwarded from Chicago and Kenosha to Sarah Farmer), she wrote vividly: 'Please tell me *at once*, if the thirty pages which you told me you had still to translate of the Kitab-I-Ighan are thirty Persian pages, or thirty English pages?'

That is one question you would think stood in no need of being asked.

The clearly harassed Mrs Cole, raised up by the Divine Plan to deal with all those impossible foreigners, and worse, to see about publishing a book, for as we all know, dealing with *anyone* about bringing out a book – author, publishers, printers – is enough to make you send for the man with the wet sheets, went on to say, 'I must know this. I want to get the Book out by Dec. 1st . . .'

She also wanted Khan to come to Boston for three weeks, beginning September, if Mírzá Abu'l-Faḍl could spare him.

She closed with: 'Please dear brother, address my letters, *Mrs Hugh L. [?] Cole*, and don't put 9 on the envelope. You know I have to be careful, and this might make trouble for me.'

Putting 9 on their writings, nine in the abjad reckoning meaning Bahá', was a custom of early believers. Mrs Cole put 9 on her letters, not her envelopes.

Their letters crossed, because on August 20 she wrote again, thanking Khan, and telling him he must, if he could, 'bring a good Persian–English Dictionary with you when you come? If not, where can we get one . . . Shall I send to London by cable for one?' She would send Khan fifty dollars for his trip to Eliot. Apparently his work was to be kept a secret, for she went on, 'No one here knows why you are coming here except Miss Farmer. So please say nothing about it, or about me in connection with the translation. Dear brother may I caution you to be so careful about speaking of people. For this reason – we cannot always tell just *when* the Truth of God enters the heart – so we must not say so-and-so is not a Believer. This is only for God to pronounce.'

We do not know when the first translation of the *Íqán* came out. Our copy is dated 1904, and the book was published in New York by the Geo. V. Blackburne Co., 114 Fifth Avenue. But since this handsome presentation copy – green leather and gold, number nine on the spine of it and the Greatest Name monogram on the front – is signed by forty-two early believers it may have been a special edition.

What became of the great Mr Dresser we never heard. We do know that Khan was not particularly impressed with American translators from the Persian. He told of one such, unnamed, who asked his help with a translation he was making of the quatrains of 'Umar Khayyám. Persian words, like ants, come in segments, and the man had translated a considerable number of separate segments, taking pieces of words for whole words.

One who helped to ease Khan's loneliness and became in some ways a surrogate for his mother, so far away in Tehran, was Josephine Cowles. She called on Mírzá and Khan in Washington, grieving over the loss of her only son. Receiving the Faith, her heart was less burdened and she transferred some of her maternal love to Khan, calling him 'Son', while he called her 'Mother'.

She went on pilgrimage to see the Master later on, and by the time He came to America in 1912, she had married a distinguished southern colonel named de Lagnel. The Master visited them several times in their large apartment at the Mendota, near Calorama and Columbia Road.

Another mentioned by Khan in his memoirs is Mrs Jackson, a prominent Bostonian who had married an officer of that name in Paris, where she lived in a magnificent house on Avenue d'Antin. She had come to Washington and taken a house, Lua being her guest and companion.

Yet another Bahá'í family were the Joseph Hannens. Pauline, the wife, was tiny and young, and looked even younger. Mírzá and Khan had moved by then to a house between Scott Circle and Thirteenth Street on Massachusetts Avenue, where Mírzá had rooms on the second floor. This little Mrs Hannen would come upstairs to be taught the Bahá'í Faith, leaving her baby in its carriage downstairs, outside the front door. (Innocent days, those!) She visited a number of times, and sat quietly while Mírzá explained the Bible prophecies about the coming of the Lord. Just sat and listened, accepted a cup of tea from Mírzá's hands, said goodby, went back downstairs and pushed the baby home.

One day Khan said to Mírzá, 'Does this little girl understand what we are talking about? Is she really interested?' They both decided that since she kept coming back, she must be interested, although she said nothing. Impatient, Khan made up his mind to find out for himself whether she was receiving the Message or not. On her next visit he simply asked her, was she satisfied with the explanations or did she need more answers in order to become convinced?

She suddenly beamed at them. 'How could there be anything more wonderful than this great Faith?' she said. 'After you have received this, what else in the world would you wish to possess?'

She and her husband and family served the Cause all through life, and her husband was a great help to Khan when he returned from Persia in 1910 as head of the Washington Legation.

Marzieh used to think of Joseph Hannen, who wore a black ribbon on his pince-nez, as her first Bahá'í teacher. At crowded meetings, Mr Hannen taught the children to memorize the principles, and over the years Marzieh could still hear her own high voice piping the lesson: 'Every human being has the right to live. He has the right to rest, and to a certain amount of tranquillity . . . Science and religion go hand in hand, and any religion that is contrary to science is not the truth . . .'

Joseph Hannen even died while serving the Faith. He had gone to the Old Post Office Building on Pennsylvania Avenue to get the mail from 'Akká and was killed by an automobile, his blood spattering the letters.

Pauline Hannen was the sister of Fanny Knobloch, and the Barnitz family of Washington was related to the Hannens. The minuscule Leona Barnitz was called Jújih Khánum (Little Chick Lady) by the Master.

Another Bahá'í young lady, destined to become a great servant of the Faith, was Mariam Haney. She arrived in Washington during the early years of Mírzá's and Khan's stay: beautiful, tall, with a head of Titian hair. Her fine Bahá'í husband, Charles, was strong and well-built, but a few years later he succumbed to Bright's Disease. Widowed, she continued ardently to serve as before. Their tall, handsome, red-headed son Paul, their only child, was in after years Chairman of the National Spiritual Assembly of the United States. He was later made a Hand of the Cause of God by the Guardian, went to Haifa with his wife Marjorie and served there the rest of his life.

Khan would think of these and other outstanding early believers who came to meet Mírzá and himself in a golden haze of memory. Mírzá, like Khan, loved Washington. The quiet, the sunshine, the flowering springtimes, the inviting parks. The two of them were familiar figures in the northwestern section of the city: Mírzá, old, with his patriarchal beard, white turban and flowing robes; Khan, young, in his carefully selected Western dress. Even as a dervish, Khan had been a good dresser. George Spendlove, curator of the renowned Chinese collection at Ontario's Royal Museum, once remarked to Khan's daughter, 'Marzieh, I always think I'm well dressed until I see your father . . .'

THIRTY-FOUR

The Prime Minister Cometh

Khan's gravitating to the Persian Legation in Washington was simply the pattern of his life repeating itself – Persians in high positions asked for his language skills. His half-American children used to think they perhaps owed their existence to Dr Johnson's *English Dictionary*, committed to memory, at least in part, by Khan when he was a young boy.

The Persian Minister to the United States, Isḥáq Khán, arrived in Washington the same year as Mírzá Abu'l-Faḍl and Khan – 1901. He was a General – a title bestowed on him by the Shah, and in addition he had his state title, Mufakhkhamu'd-Dawlih. Later on the Shah made him a Prince. A distinguished man, he was also, though a Shiah, tolerant of other peoples' religions. Before his Washington post he had been Persia's Minister-Resident at Cairo and there had become a friend of Abu'l-Faḍl.

The Minister came to call on Mírzá and Khan, and had tea, and it turned out that he was also a friend and had been a close associate of Khan's uncle, Niẓámu'd-Dín Khán.

Isḥáq Khán knew French but no English, and he asked Khan to serve at the Persian Legation and also be his personal secretary. Khan told him that he had heavy responsibilities as a Bahá'í translator and had been sent to America by 'Abdu'l-Bahá to translate Mírzá's teachings and also the important book Mírzá was then writing.

At this point Mírzá interrupted and said that the two of them would write the Master at 'Akká, explain the situation and say how kind the Minister had been to the Bahá'ís in Cairo.

'I am sure', Mírzá said, 'that His Holiness will permit Khan to help you as much as possible.'

As Mírzá expected, the Master replied that it would be well for Khan to assist the Minister, providing he could spare the time from his Bahá'í duties.

That was how Khan came to resume his official life, begun some years before at the Foreign Office in Tehran and carried on later as chamberlain and French tutor to the Shah's son, Sáláru'd-Dawlih, Governor of Kirmánsháh.

Early in the fall of 1903 the Minister received a cable from the Atábak, he of the one-time wild revels, who had been deposed and was on a trip around the world. This cable, from Japan, requested the Minister to meet the Atábak in San Francisco and accompany him to New York, from where he would sail for Egypt and Arabia and perform the pilgrimage to Mecca.

At first the Minister wished Khan to go with him and escort the party to New York. Then he decided Khan should go to New York instead and see to all the arrangements, securing hotel accommodations, staterooms on the ship, and the like, and then await their arrival. This was a great disappointment to Khan, as he would have liked to see the country on the journey West, and also to be with the Atábak whom he had served as interpreter some years before in Tehran. After all, he was very young, had been working day and night, had been rejected in love and needed the change. He found out afterward why the original plan was abandoned: by this time, back in Persia, Khan was well-known as the one who had ignored opportunities for rising in the government to become a Bahá'í, who had served 'Abdu'l-Bahá in 'Akká for more than a year, and had then been sent by Him to help spread the Faith in America. Time after time in the future, Khan would see doors closed to advancement because he steadfastly continued to follow the one great aim of his life, to teach the Cause of Bahá'u'lláh.

After the Minister left for San Francisco, Khan went to New York where he engaged the Presidential suite at the old Waldorf-Astoria on Fifth Avenue at 34th Street (quite possibly the very suite which, in 1918, would be assigned to Khan and Florence as guests of the US Government on their way to the Versailles Peace Conference). Khan also booked staterooms for the party on one of the ships of the British Cunard Line.

He learned in the meantime of the Atábak's financial difficulties. By the time the deposed Premier reached San Francisco he had run out of funds and the Minister had been obliged to arrange payment for the trip to New York. Khan read of the Atábak's plight in the papers and consulted with Miss Barney, suggesting that as a gesture of friendship from the Bahá'ís, a gift to the Premier might well prove helpful to the Bahá'ís of Persia later on, when he and his people were in power again.

The party arrived, and Khan was there at the station to greet them and escort them to the Waldorf. They were six altogether, including the Atábak and his son, 'Abdu'lláh Khán (a future Prime Minister), and the Atábak's head chamberlain, Abu'l-Karím Khán.

Khan was able to talk privately with the Atábak that evening. After asking for news of his uncle and family, Khan expressed regret that at this time, when Persians in many parts of their homeland were agitating for a parliamentary regime, the Atábak's enemies had brought about his resignation.

Thanking Khan, the Atábak said it was a consolation that there were still persons who appreciated his sincerely-rendered services to the country.

Next morning Khan was up early, unaware of what was ahead of him. The party had to leave in a few hours, otherwise they would be unable to reach Mecca in time for the annual pilgrimage. But first Khan needed to introduce Miss Barney and her cousin, Ellen Goin, to the Atábak. He took them up to the suite and in the course of the conversation Elsa graciously handed the Atábak an envelope. It contained between eight hundred and a thousand dollars.

Khan then took three of the men and all the luggage to the steamer while the other three decided on a leisurely tour of New York.

When the whistles started blowing for the ship's departure, the three were not there.

How Khan – young, unknown, with no official title – single-handedly held up the ocean liner *Philadelphia*, at high tide for over half an hour, so that Persia's former Prime Minister could board at a time more convenient to himself, left a lot of newsprint behind.[110]

One cannot help asking what he used for clout. Did he threaten war between Persia and America? Would Iran call out her navy – perhaps six or so lateen-rigged dhows on the Persian Gulf – or would she take on America with her army, mostly generals, and a few unpaid, skeletal soldiers in loose uniforms? (Some of those soldiers in the days of Náṣiri'd-Dín had even proved criminal: they had dared to petition the Shah for their pay, which their officers were far better acquainted with than they were themselves, and the Shah had strangled a dozen of them, as an example.) We do know that Khan appealed to the other ship's officers as well as the captain, to the newsmen, and by phone to City Hall. He said if the ship sailed without the Atábak there might be serious repercussions between the British and the Americans on one hand and Persia on the other, for the Atábak was sure to be re-named Prime Minister on his return home and would never forget that the Cunard Line had prevented his pilgrimage to Mecca.

Whatever he said, it worked. Thanks to Khan, Iran launched no attack.

One account of the episode is headed, 'He held up a Liner.' It says the Vizier overslept at the Waldorf-Astoria while the *Philadelphia* waited, and that the telephone wires from pier to hotel stayed red hot. The youthful Khan is referred to by various strange spellings, but the reporters did get parts of his name right, the closest perhaps being Ali Kuli Keri Khan.

The night before (says the unidentified New York journalist mainly quoted here, who obviously enjoyed producing his article, primarily out of thin air), Khan had thus addressed the Vizier:

'Know O most powerful and blessed,' said Kuli, prostrating himself before the vizier, 'that the ships of these strange people sail at the hour appointed, and so small is their regard for even the Favored of the Gods, O Light of Persia, that if thou dost delay thy arrival for so little as the space of but one hour, they will sail without thee.'

. . . But alas! how can one to whom hour-glasses serve for stop watches, be expected to run on standard time?

Thus it befell that after the old Khans, and young Khans, and middle-aged Khans as well had, heedful of Kuli Keri Khan's warning got early to the pier and had marched solemnly aboard, Ali Ashgar Atabek Asam, the King-Khan, had not appeared.

The hour of sailing approached – and the grand vizier did not . . . The court astrologer and official clairvoyant poured a little ink into the palm of his hand and went into a trance.

'Aha!' he exclaimed, gazing into the ink. 'Allah be praised! He is even now leaving the hotel . . .'

It was fifteen minutes past the sailing hour when an open landau, driven like mad, whipped through the gateway, and came tearing down the dock.

'Allah be praised,' cried the devout Kuli. 'He comes, he comes!'

The cry like a slogan was caught up, and the passengers to whom the grand vizier, and Persia itself, had been of vague and misty significance but half an hour before, joined with the faithful in the glad cry, 'He comes; he comes.'

. . . Leaning back complacently in the carriage, smoking a cigarette and as unruffled as though he were ahead of time . . . he sat chatting pleasantly with his son . . . and the Persian minister, Mehdi Guami Khan.

'Ah! We are here,' observed His Excellency. 'Shall we alight?'

Upon reflection, it seemed best to do so . . .

Grandly oblivious of the expectant cabby below, the vizier proceeded leisurely on his upward way . . . The coachman . . . waited patiently for a short while, but . . . became uneasy.

'Hey youse,' he called to the attendants. 'Who's settlin' dis bill? . . . Call the veezer back.'

Ali Kuli Keri Khan, the official interpreter, looked properly shocked.

'It is paid at the hotel,' he said. 'Profane no longer the adjacent premises with your detestable personality' (this last in Persian).

. . . and still the ship did not sail. 'He owes $2,000 for tickets,' said one man. The rumor spread.

There was many a grain of truth in the rumor. The San Francisco press would report later that the vizier was going around the world bankrupt, 'traveling like a nabob'. 'No more Persian visitors for me,' was the comment of Jules Clerfayt, railroad agent who piloted the party across America at the Persian Minister's request. It developed that His Highness could neither pay his bill at San Francisco's Palace

Hotel, about $200, nor his overland railroad tickets, some $760.

'I'll settle when we get to Chicago,' he assured the agent.

Alas, in Chicago no cash was forthcoming, only compliments, and promises of royal decorations for the future, and Clerfayt paid all.

'Write it all down and I'll forward the money from Cherbourg,' the Vizier assured him.

Obviously the Grand Vizier was living off the land.

In New York at the last moment, as told in the *Times* and some other papers, workers had already started loosening the lines that tethered the ship to the dock, and the lone remaining gangplank was about to be hauled ashore, when a 'very pretty' girl in a long raincoat, and carrying a sealed package, came hurrying along the pier. (In justice to the good, gray *Times*, it limited itself to calling her 'a young woman'.)

'Too late,' a patrolman told the girl, holding up his big palm. But at this point 'the ubiquitous Keri Khan rushed down the gangplank and spoke to the patrolman', who let the mysterious girl aboard. She proved to be Miss Ellen Goin, of 582 Fifth Avenue, duly chaperoned by her father J. D. Goin, and if both accounts, Khan's and papers', are correct, she and Elsa must have rescued the Prime Minister twice, once at the Waldorf the night before and once now at the ship.

However, it was surely Khan alone, with nothing but his eloquence and persistence, who kept the *Philadelphia* from sailing off minus the Grand Vizier. More sober than the rest of the press, the *New York Times*, January 31, says the ship was delayed for 'over a half hour'. According to the *Times* those in the suite, whom the *Times* believed had had a night on the town, were pretty helpless and responded to their Chief's non-appearance with 'a case of "nerves"'. The *Times* tells how 'various persons in high Persian lamb hats rushed up to the Captain, first requesting him to hold the steamship, then begging him to hold her, and finally threatening him . . .' There was only one of him, but he seemed like several. Also, Khan was evidently the 'young man' who phoned the Waldorf and returned with the Vizier's command: 'Tell the Captain to wait for him without fail.'

The mail had long since been loaded on, all the shorelines but two had been cast off, all the gangplanks were gone except one. The Captain delivered his ultimatum: he would wait only ten minutes more and then if the Prime Minister failed to appear he could follow by another ship. But only this ship would do, Khan told him, only this one would get the Vizier to the Mecca caravan in time for the pilgrimage!

The minutes ticked away. Scouts ran up the pier to make sightings and report back as soon as the Prime Minister should, Insha'lláh, heave into view. The Persian suite, having as best they could erased the signs of their night before, collected by the gangway, along with the other passengers who as by a contagion were now caught up in the excitement.

Then the time was up. Captain Mills ordered the last line off and the gangway was removed. At this point the interpreter – Khan – as relayed by the newsman who presumably was not present, turned his most powerful gun on Captain Mills: 'It is not', he said, 'for any man to slight the Grand Vizier, who sails on orders from His Majesty the Shah!'

At a future time the Master would call Khan 'Nabíl-i-Dawlih, Shadíd-i-Sawlih', the first his state title, the second meaning intense, strong, vehement to attack.

Khan's threats remained as frightening as before: the Captain was to hold the ship, or else. Khan apparently did not say or else what. But those in the family who had been subjected to his will power when aroused, would sympathize with the Captain.

Then suddenly the cry burst forth from many throats: 'He comes! He comes!' An open carriage rolled in (slower in the *Times* than in the other papers), containing a 'little stout man in a Persian lamb cap and dark clothes', lolling back on the cushions. 'Leisurely and as though he were about to board his own private steamship, he left the carriage, turning a deaf ear to the officers who were shouting to him to hurry.' He was halfway up the gangplank when the cabby bellowed, in a *Times* rendition somewhat at variance with the other accounts: 'Hey, send de guy back; he ain't paid me yet. Does he tink I'm workin' for love?'

The sensational last-second arrival of Miss Ellen Goin with her small package did not go unreported but, as suited to the paper's dignity, was made little of. Featured was the fact that the great steamship had, unbelievably, been delayed over half an hour beyond her sailing time.

In another unidentified New York clipping, dated February 1, the distinguished traveler was described as 'a Bab'. It described the arrival of Ellen Goin and her father at the pier and had the girl place the package in the Vizier's hand, the two then hastily departing, cutting short the eminent one's thanks. Unlike the romantic interpretations of some of the press, this paper explained that His Excellency, like the girl herself, was 'a member of the Persian religious sect known as Babs, or Behaists . . .' (not true of the Atábak). She and her cousin Elsa Barney had both visited 'Abbás Effendi at 'Akká, the article continues. 'Both being wealthy give liberally to the Cause . . . Miss Barney helps to support the Behaist Home for Women in Washington, Miss Goin gives the basement floor of her handsome home for meetings of the sect . . . The Behaists' movement in this country is not increasing rapidly. There are believers in the cities of Chicago and Cincinnati and a few at Keokuk [Kenosha], Wisconsin. In this city [New York] there are about two hundred . . . and in Washington a much smaller number.'

The writer adds that while Bahá'ís deny being Muslims their belief 'is nevertheless an offshoot of that faith'. They have 'put aside' some features of Islam 'and have a higher spiritual platform . . .' Looking back at the brittle yellowed newsprint from the vantage of today, when in Khomeini's Iran they have hanged college girls for being Bahá'ís, we find this particular paper's concluding paragraph of special interest: 'The Behaists believe that a greater prophet than Mahomet came in the person of BehaUllah, the father of Abbas Effendi and that to his Teachings, and not to the Koran, should the world turn for instruction.'[111]

The writer could hardly have known that Bahá'ís reverently study both Bible and Qur'án, and believe that all God's Manifestations are essentially the same, including Bahá'u'lláh, all being mirrors reflecting the one Sun. That it is the times and their separate needs which differ, and that today is a watershed time, because the world is coalescing into a neighborhood, thus requiring a universal message not previously delivered because not relevant in the past. That every authentic Messenger comes to humankind from the one unknowable Author of all things.

On the day he left New York, January 30, 1904, the Atábak had almost exactly three years and seven months more to live. Nor did he return to a rich country, for he found the Treasury in what W. Morgan Shuster describes as 'its normally void condition',[112] and tried for another loan from Russia. He had been recalled to office by Muḥammad-'Alí Sháh, the Shah who bombarded the Parliament with the members inside because he did not care for representative government. The Atábak would be assassinated August 31, 1907, by a youth who did, and the killer's suicide would be observed as a public holiday.

'He was', writes Shuster of that Prime Minister, 'the most intelligent and forceful personage in recent Persian history.'[113] Western visitors passing through Iran are inclined to deliver assertions of this type. His pronouncement becomes less convincing when we realize that Shuster did not speak Persian and could not have known the Atábak in any case, since Shuster arrived in Persia in May 1911, years after the Atábak had been removed from the scene. Percy Sykes calls the Minister 'able, if unscrupulous' and says the new Shah had reinstated him 'to overthrow the Constitution [of 1906]'.[114]

THIRTY-FIVE
Khan Meets His Fate

In 1903, writing from Green Acre, Sarah Farmer repeated her invitation to Mírzá and Khan, who had been too busy to attend the School during the previous summer. Miss Farmer had dedicated her property in Eliot, Maine – Green Acre (so named in a poem to her by Whittier) – as an international summer school for religious and spiritual studies. Here she offered a free platform to teachers from all parts of the East, who would come to her in America and speak on their various schools of thought.

Sarah was a Boston 'Brahmin', as members of old exclusive New England families were called, at least by non-members. She had been among the first Americans who visited 'Abdu'l-Bahá in 'Akká and accepted the Bahá'í Faith. The Master told her that spreading the many schools of Eastern mysticism and age-old superstitious beliefs could never bring about the peace on earth to which she had dedicated her school. Instructed by Him, she established Green Acre as a center for Bahá'í studies; and so it has remained, under the National Spiritual Assembly of the United States.

Florence <u>Kh</u>ánum used to speak of a Jain she had seen in the woods at Green Acre, who, believing all life sacred, sat during meditation with his arms bare and covered with mosquitoes from hands to elbows, which he forbore to swat. Luckily, after the change-over from gurus, mystics and swamis, the notorious Maine mosquitoes could be given back some of their own.

Mírzá and Khan spent July and August of that year teaching at the Summer School. They were allotted a frame house near the Inn (later called Sarah Farmer Hall) and held numerous classes, besides public meetings, under the pines and in the hall known as the Irenian (peace-promoting). Not only Bahá'ís but many inquirers were attracted, some from Maine and neighboring states – New Hampshire and Massachusetts – some from far away.

Khan had firmly resolved to avoid young women as much as possible, for he had never recovered from the pain of Eleanor's rejection. And so the moment classes were over, he would take himself off, in order not to encounter any girls. This he could do, as Mírzá would not be alone. Aḥmad-i-Iṣfáhání had arrived from Port Said and had been brought along to see to Mírzá's needs. Khan had discovered an old cemetery in the village and he would retire there with a volume of Byron's poems, read them for hours and cry to himself.

One afternoon at the close of a meeting, a little gray-haired lady came up to him and asked him to walk with her a hundred yards or so to a knoll near the Inn, overlooking the dancing sunlight on the Piscataqua river down the slope. She lived in a tent there during the summer, and cooked her own vegetarian meals instead of eating with the others at the Inn.

She began by praising Khan's good English, as he translated for Mírzá at the close of each spoken paragraph. Then she asked – he found out later that she was highly intuitive – 'Why are you so sad? Why do you always go away all alone after the meetings?'

She could not understand why anyone so glowing with energy and enthusiasm while translating for Mírzá could be so dark, depressed and unhappy afterward, and walk away alone.

Khan wept. He already knew this woman was a scholar, deep in art and philosophy, and also an author and a poet. In spite of himself he told her about Eleanor Dixon.

'I have been a poet all my life,' he said at the end. 'I cannot bear the thought of that much pain a second time. So I have made a vow never to meet alone with any young woman again.'

The little lady, famed in Bahá'í history, Mary Hanford Ford, understood.

'I have a daughter here with me, myself,' she told Khan, 'seventeen years old. But she is already engaged to marry a young man from the South, so you will have no trouble from that quarter.' And as she spoke, Lynette, the daughter (Tennysonians may like to hear that her brother's name was Gareth), came in. But she would be safe to know.

Khan's, and indeed his family's, friendship with Mrs Ford lasted from that day until her death.

The Green Acre season closed, but Mrs Ford told Khan it was still too early to return to Washington. She suggested that Mírzá return with Ahmad, while Khan could stay on and teach the Faith to some of the Boston intellectuals – 'scholars, professors, thinkers,' was Khan's interesting classification of them – for which the city was famed.

Mírzá was very fond of Mary Hanford Ford and he approved her suggestion. She and her daughter had an apartment on the fourth floor of a building on, so far as Khan remembered, St Botolph Street, and she helped him find two rooms about five blocks away.

Early every morning Khan would translate the many letters he received from Bahá'ís all over the United States to be sent on to the Master in 'Akká. He also had a heavy correspondence with friends asking him questions on the Faith and related philosophical matters. In addition, every week a large mail came in from the Master, bringing

His Tablets to be translated and forwarded to American addressees. This work kept him busy from six or so till after one. Then he would walk over to Mrs Ford's where they lunched together, discussing (as was her wont) 'cultural and poetic' topics.

Afternoons and evenings Khan might be invited to speak on the Teachings or to visit with one or another of the then few Bahá'ís in Boston.

One day Mrs Ford told Khan about a couple who had lost most of their fortune. The husband had been a rich industrialist, and the wife, 'a very great person, had played a leading role in the American Women's Club movement'. This couple, Francis William and Alice Ives Breed, would, she thought, welcome meeting with Khan and hearing about the beautiful Faith of Bahá'u'lláh. (We have preferred to use 'Faith' and 'Cause' most of the time, but the believers of that day often said Bahá'í Movement.)

Teaching the Faith was Khan's highest ambition and he agreed. The next day Mrs Ford told him Alice Ives Breed would be delighted to receive him one morning during the week. When the day came Mrs Ford and Khan presented themselves at a house, number 22 on Marlborough Street, just a block away from the Boston Public Gardens.

They rang, a maid opened the door and led them through a small room to a large reception room. The first thing that caught Khan's eye was a graceful ewer, brought from the Middle East, where such a utensil would only be kept in the toilet, never placed on a piano. Then as they took seats he noticed an oil painting on the wall – a portrait of a young girl with a face so sweet, so spiritual, he was sure it could not be of any girl then living, of anyone he was likely to meet in his day. He thought it must be the picture of a saint in the days of the Italian Renaissance.

The lady of the house came in. Khan was introduced. Making conversation, he told her he admired the painting, and asked who had been the artist in the long ago.

'Why, that's a portrait of my eldest daughter, Florence,' Mrs Breed said. 'She will be down to greet you, before going out.'

Khan was horrified. Mrs Ford had led him into a trap. She had given her solemn word that he would be kept out of situations like this. But she made little gestures to him, meaning to keep calm, so that Mrs Breed would be unaware of his agitation. His personal problems must not prevent him from giving a clear account of the Faith. He must not be the cause of her turning away from it.

At that moment the young woman in the portrait came down the stairs. Khan rose. He knew, somehow, that here was Fate.

A former debutante, a society beauty, she made an entrance, shook his hand and asked the usual American question, 'Do you like our country?'

Afterward, Khan and Mrs Ford went back to her apartment. He had no idea what sort of impression he had made. He was completely miserable, and nothing Mrs Ford said could quiet him down.

'Anyway, you are leaving for Washington,' she told him, 'and she is going to New York. You must calm down, just as if nothing has happened. No harm has been done.'

Little did she know, he thought, how much harm had been done.

Several days later Khan called at Mrs Ford's for their usual luncheon together, rang the bell, went in and found Florence Breed sitting at the table.

Matters must have gone reasonably well, for the Sunday following, Khan and Mrs Ford were invited to (midday) dinner at the Breed home.

There he met Mr Breed, a tall and distinguished man, though he limped badly from having been dragged by a runaway horse. Other members of the family present that day were Alice, next in age to Florence, married to an Englishman, Charles Godfree, in the hotel business; their son Charles; Florence's two brothers, Francis and Ralph, the latter being the youngest child of the Breeds, then about seventeen. Ruby, the third daughter, must have been absent, since she is not mentioned.

In after years, 'Abdu'l-Bahá presided at Ruby's wedding and gave her a diamond ring. Ralph would have the honor of meeting Shoghi Effendi in Paris and being photographed with him, Florence, her two daughters and their governess, in the wheat fields at Barbizon. Ralph became a Bahá'í, as did Ruby and Alice and her son Charles. Francis always said he himself was not good enough.

THIRTY-SIX

Florence

Alice's daughter Florence could have become a proper Bostonian – she had family connections, brilliant parents, had attended a Boston finishing school, met celebrities in her mother's home, become familiar with the culture of the Continent as well as of Turkey and Greece, spoke excellent French – but she obviously was not the type to become one. She did not lack for offers. A number of fine young men from Harvard and the New York and Chicago social scene wished to marry her, but she had decided to go on the stage instead. One of her discouraged suitors, Frank Boswell, a well-to-do Philadelphian, took a trip around the world to forget her, but never did, and died unmarried. Another, who became president of the American Radiator Company, did survive till the mid-1950s. Such were the kind of man one assumes she would have married.

But the one she chose (although they were never to marry) was a New England poet, a Harvard man, a minister's son, one time divinity student, later English instructor at Harvard and Secretary to the Librarian of the Boston Public Library – Philip Savage. Philip believed that 'what is true and beautiful is absolute; and what is stupendous and gorgeous and impressive and wonderful is inferior to it'.[115] He must have witnessed in Florence the true and the beautiful. The sonnet he wrote her, 'To Citriodora' (Lady of the Lemon Verbena) is a small classic, tender words which mean all the more because, unknowing, he was to go away from her so soon:

> I turn and see you passing in the street
> When you are not. I take another way,
> Lest missing you the fragrance of the day
> Exhale, and I know not that it is sweet . . .[116]

When he died she left the East Coast, the Atlantic Ocean they had looked at together and counted all its colors, the Boston streets where they had walked, and went away to the Middle West. She turned to spiritual studies. She investigated New Thought. She studied Christian Science and some of the members felt that she could become a healer. She took up Yogi breathing and levitated, or thought she did, a block.

The story of her future began one morning when she happened to notice the posted announcement of a lecture on Chaucer, to be given by a Mrs Mary Hanford Ford. Coming as she did from Boston, hub of the universe, Florence was apt to regard Chicago as through a lorgnette, *de haut en bas*. To her, as to many, it was still vaguely a town of the wild frontier. 'At that time I did not realize', she said, 'that Chaucer might be known west of Boston.' She decided to attend the lecture anyhow, a fateful decision which led irrevocably to all the events of her future life.

After the lecture she and the speaker – a small, trim, vital woman with a gentle voice – visited together. She learned that Mrs Ford, a banker's daughter, was born in Meadville, Pennsylvania, in 1856. She had married the owner and editor of a leading newspaper in Kansas City, the *Evening Mail*, and became known as a cultural influence in that city, speaking on art, literature, music, on labor problems, on new developments in science. She made trips abroad, visited museums, attended the Venice Biennale. Later on she had husband trouble (perhaps brought on by alcohol, but, as the Victorian ethic required, he was said to be recuperating from a long illness), and was left with a family of three to support. There was Roland, the oldest boy, about sixteen at this time, Lynette, twelve, and Gareth, ten. It is obvious from these names that their mother was literary.

As the two chatted, Florence confided that she was looking for a quiet retreat where she could do some in-depth studying. Immediately, Mrs Ford offered to rent her a room in her own old-fashioned house. It was on the south side, she said, facing Lake Michigan. She warned that it looked dreary from the outside, it needed a new coat of paint. Then, pausing, she added, 'The neighbors call it the Haunted House.' Florence said, 'Is that so very dreadful?' And Mrs Ford answered, 'I do not think you will be bothered.'

Mrs Ford thought it best to explain the household in advance. In the kitchen was a German woman with her young child. Mrs Ford was her only friend. This woman did the cooking and helped the children to learn German. Then there was an American woman 'in sad financial straits' who taught the children French. Then there was a young black who also helped around the place and was so dedicated to Shakespeare that he conversed in Shakespearian English. And now there would be Florence from New England, who had made her debut in this very city as the guest of social leader Mrs Potter Palmer, who lived in a castle (which seemed imposing then, but shrank to ridiculous proportions in after years, when viewed against the high rises. By coincidence, that mansion would be torn down in 1950, the same year that Florence would die).

Taken out to what she felt would be her new home, Florence was ushered into a magnificent living room, spacious and high-ceilinged. It ran the whole length of the house, and all four walls were banked, floor to ceiling, with books. Florence's bedroom gave right onto the lake.

She sat down to her first meal with the rather motley household. The meal was vegetarian and consisted mostly of lentils – not plain, everyday lentils, but described as 'the classic lentils, reminiscent of Greece and Rome'. There was a small, pasteboard box in the middle of the table. At one point in the meal, little Gareth made an unflattering remark about someone in the neighborhood. 'Aha!' said his sister Lynette. 'That'll be a penny in the box for you!' Mrs Ford explained to Florence that anyone who spoke ill of the absent had to put a penny in the box. She said the children did not like this at all, because the fine came out of their pocket money. (Members of the Austrian National Assembly, hearing this from Marzieh at a future time, established just such a box. It seems that one day a famed pioneer was visiting, and she told them, 'Oh, I've just got to say this', dropped in a heavy fine and had her say.)

Florence, so recently living in an atmosphere of death – and any mourned death seems to bridge the two worlds – did not feel rejected by the Haunted House. One night, however, she woke up in her vast, shadowy room with its deep pockets of dark, and found she was not alone. There, rocking away in her chair in a shaft of moonlight, sat a scowling old woman. The old woman hoisted herself out of her chair and shuffled purposefully over toward the bed, and stood contemplating Florence with small, angry eyes. Florence burrowed under the covers until she was gone. The next morning at table the family told her, 'Oh, that was old Mrs So-and-so, who used to live in your room.' Not much else happened during Florence's visit, except that sometimes, on the stairs, she could smell violets from an invisible source. And the Shakespearian scholar made her a proposal of marriage in sixteenth-century English.

Mrs Ford's Haunted House has apparently gone down in history, at least in the annals of the American Society for Psychical Research, because years later, in Boston, Mrs Ford reported on it to Dr Richard Hodgson of that Society, and he asked her to write it up for their archives. Today these phenomena are being studied scientifically, in laboratories, under controlled conditions when possible. This kind of study is not discouraged in the Bahá'í Faith, but Bahá'ís are told to avoid the seances once so popular, the ectoplasm, the flying trumpets, the sudden materializations of phosphorescent hands. (Khan himself was once induced to attend a seance presided over by a famous medium. She delivered to him a detailed message from his dead father, the Kalántar. Khan asked, 'What language did he speak?' 'Why, English, of course.' 'I am very sorry, Madam, but there must be some mistake. My father was a Persian, and he did not know a word of English.')

Florence was in a sensitive condition, what with her own nature and the sudden turn her life had taken at home. She confided to Mrs Ford that sometimes at night when she was dropping off to sleep, she heard heavenly choral music, sung by great multitudes of people. It was antiphonal – thousands of women's voices, answered by thousands of men's. She could even tell Mrs Ford the words of the song they sang. 'Why,' said Mrs Ford, 'you have heard the "Song of the Soul" by Jakob Boehme!' (She pronounced it Jacob Beemie, meaning the German shoemaker and pedlar, an inspired Lutheran mystic who was born in 1575.)

In her youth, Mrs Ford told Florence, she had lost her faith and become an atheist. Then, as she watched by the bedside of her dying father, she received 'a clear revelation of the continuity of a human being's life'. She began to study all aspects of religion. When Florence first met her, Mrs Ford called herself a spiritist. Her main interest was in leading a spiritual life of assistance to others. Like Swedenborg and Emerson, she also had what is called second sight.

Toward the end of Florence's Chicago stay, Mrs Ford announced that she was going to take a new and unusual course of study. 'In the ninth lesson', she said, 'we are promised a surprise – a new spiritual message, said to be the greatest message from God that the world has received since Christ.' We do not know who the teacher was, but Florence attended the first lesson. The next summer, 1903, Mrs Ford said she was going to Eliot, Maine and look into the Bahá'í Teachings. She said there was a Persian philosopher there, with his young Persian interpreter, and she was going to investigate, and would report back to Florence.

Early that autumn in Boston she told Florence, 'This is a true, spiritual Message.' She gave Florence a few pages of an early translation of the *Hidden Words* and told her to study them.

Some of those early translations were of course primitive, necessarily so, as few orientalists were available, not only in the Bahá'í Faith, but worldwide. It is obvious that the early American believers must have thirsted for the Faith, impatiently overlooking difficulties of language, English errors, floweriness, in their rush toward Him Who had brought them a message from the unknowable realms of God. Some decades later, when Khan was reading over early prayer translations, he said, 'Look at that grammar. No wonder God didn't answer these prayers.'

THIRTY-SEVEN

Attractions of Boston

Florence and Khan began to meet daily: at the Boston Public Library, the Gardens, at Harvard College and the Longfellow home; and gradually they went afield to Concord and Lexington, birthplace of the American Revolution. They walked by the quiet, dark river that winds, reflecting the sky, through wide meadows where the farmers once took their stand in battle, and 'fired the shot heard round the world'. It was then that Khan, visiting the seat of Emerson's Transcendental school of philosophy, Emerson's home in Concord, met his one living daughter, Ellen. She took him to her father's library and showed him Emerson's favorite corner – the corner with the Persian books.

For Khan, the weeks with Florence Breed went by like moments. Many a telegram reached him from Laura Barney, telling him to hurry back to Washington so that Mírzá's classes could be resumed. Each time Khan replied that he would come back as soon as he had fulfilled his Boston engagements.

Meanwhile, Khan continually taught the Faith to Florence. She became and remained a dedicated believer. Some who knew her tried to analyze her faith but failed. She was not necessarily a convincing teacher with words. Not necessarily reasonable. Marzieh used to think her mother could not have made a Bahá'í out of her – but that may be true of most Bahá'í parents in relation to their children. In a Bahá'í home the children are apt to catch the Faith by contagion, the air is Bahá'í, and this helps the children gradually to learn the Faith from others and also to teach themselves. Khan, of course, was extremely persuasive and convincing, and intellectually equipped from continually corresponding with the Master after being with Him over a year, then being with Mírzá, then having to find answers to endless questions about the Teachings. He also had the gift of confirmation, of bringing people into the Faith.

As for the quality of Florence's faith in after years, besides lifelong services, there were her daily, lying-down, floating, trance-like prayers (they both often prayed lying down, Khan moving his lips, Florence softly muttering), when the children knew she was in her other dimension. It was routine for them, they were used to it, and let her be. Of Florence's faith, 'Abdu'l-Bahá said, 'I testify that she is a true believer.'

Khan's return to Washington was finally determined by Florence's plans. Because of her interest in the theater she was going to New York to become an editor of the *Dramatic Mirror*, a magazine with offices on East 42nd Street. She was also to study acting and elocution with a Mrs Hovey. She was a poet, who, widowed, had married an actor named Russell and produced a little boy, Sigurd, who had visited the Holy Land at the age of fifteen with Mrs Jackson. Well-known as a dramatic teacher, Mrs Hovey had great faith in Florence's future on the stage, and even considered her potentially greater than Sarah Bernhardt. For one summer season Florence had been invited to join a stock company under the famous Elsie de Wolfe (later, Lady Mendl). Greeting Florence in her old age, a European admirer compared her appearance to Duse. She had a kind of natural presence.

Since, in late September or early October, Florence was due in New York and Khan in Washington, they arranged to travel on the same train. Convention being what it was in those days, they were not to board it together, since her family was going to see her off at Boston's Back Bay station. Khan boarded the train early, and as soon as they were out of the suburbs went looking for her.

When at last he caught sight of Florence and came up to her, his heart throbbing, there was no greeting, no invitation to sit down. She looked straight ahead. Hurt and confused, furious, he walked back to his own car. As often in years to come, he blamed Mrs Ford. It was all Mrs Ford's fault, taking him to meet this cold young lady. Once again, he renewed his vow to stay away from all nubile women for all time.

Because he was to stop over in New York at Howard MacNutt's to go over some translations with him, he left the train at the 125th Street station, nearer than the downtown one to the MacNutt home on St Nicholas Avenue. On the way there he thanked the higher powers that now, undisturbed, he would be able to devote himself entirely to his many Bahá'í labors.

But when he came down to breakfast the following day, a letter lay by his plate, brought in with the morning mail. He did not recognize the writing; had never seen it before. Khan tore the envelope open and at the end of the third page found the signature: Florence.

She wrote that the reason she had ignored him, had not invited him to sit with her, was that he had forgotten to remove his hat. (Filled with delight at finding her, trained all his life to keep his hat on both indoors and out as a mark of respect, he had totally forgotten his hat, or even his head.) She told him there were several Bostonian passengers nearby, friends of her family, and the sudden arrival of an 'Oriental-looking' young man with thick dark brown hair who did not even have the courtesy to take off his hat when greeting a lady, would have been hard to explain.

The letter asked him to meet her that evening at the home of Mrs Hovey. He met her at the class and was duly introduced to the (very dramatic) teacher. After class he escorted Florence to the Martha Washington Hotel for Women. In those days nice young ladies often stayed at hotels reserved for women, to be safe in person and reputation.

Days and evenings, during Khan's New York week, they would meet and discuss poetry and philosophy in the light of the Bahá'í Faith. At parting, they agreed to write each other and exchange thoughts every day. Khan's side of the correspondence did not omit the theme of love as reflected in Persia's classics, mainly Ḥáfiẓ and Saʻdí. His letters to her, kept in an old trunk, were burned later on, by someone who was theoretically taking care of them. But hers of 1903 and 1904, replying to his, he carefully gathered and had typed long after she was dead. He, biased perhaps, thought them superior to other letters he had seen of well-known women writers of England and the Continent.

Sometimes Khan and Florence would receive three letters from each other every day (the mails worked better then).

At last he did return to Washington, where Laura Barney had him to dinner on the evening of his arrival. She took one look at him and said with a smile, 'There must have been some other attraction up there in New England, besides all those intellectuals.'

Khan blushed. He tried to turn the talk to his many lectures in Boston and all the social gatherings he had attended at which he could tell about the Bahá'í Faith. But Laura kept probing. What had kept him away so long? He put on a serious expression and mentioned the Breed family and Florence. Made the mistake of praising Florence's lovely voice, her charm, her good manners. Hastened, also mistakenly, to say she should not judge this new friend of his by his own clumsy words. Quoted a verse from the mystic Niẓámí on Persia's Juliet and Romeo, Laylí and Majnún:

> If thou wouldst gaze on Laylí's loveliness,
> Then must thou hide thyself in Majnún's eyes.

Laura said she would be off to New York that very night on the midnight train and asked him to write a line to Florence and request her to lunch with Laura at Laura's hotel the next day.

A day later, back from New York came Laura.

'Khan,' she told him, 'you are right about Florence Breed's looks, but you are wrong about her voice. Her voice is artificial.'

'I beg your pardon!' he cried. 'I talked to outsiders who have known her from birth and they said she has always had that lovely speaking voice.'

Too late he knew he should have kept quiet. Laura changed toward him then and there. Or so he thought at the time. Events were to prove that the same attraction which caused her to rush off by midnight train to investigate this paragon from Boston must have been the reason for Laura's efforts to draw Khan back to 'Akká when she was there, working on *Some Answered Questions*. But so far as he could see now, that remembered night when she had come home from a dance at the White House and asked him to sit beside her on the sofa might never have been.

Luckily, his translations, being prepared for publication, required weekly or bi-weekly visits to Howard MacNutt in New York. In his free time he would often meet Florence in Central Park, and on occasional Sundays they would cross the Hudson and stroll along the Palisades.

The strength of the emotions begun in those days carried them forward together for forty-six years.

A series of faded letters has turned up, tracing, at least one-sidedly, the course of their romance.

THIRTY-EIGHT
A Victorian Love

On September 6, 1903, Florence wrote Khan – very much with white gloves on – about the visit from Laura Barney and Ellen Goin.

It was good of Miss B to come . . . She has a great deal of beauty and I found her greatly interesting. Miss G is so very pretty and charming . . . Miss B laughed and said she liked your enthusiasm, even if what you said were not always true, so I had to smile, as I then concluded she found me a disappointment . . .

From 30 Turner Street, Boston,
October 11–12, 1903, [signed] Florence Breed
Dear Khan,
I cannot be sure that I shall have the time to go to the country for an hour tomorrow morning to listen to the poetry I should so much like to hear . . .

October 14–15, 1903 [New York]
I wish you would tell Mrs Hovey [the drama teacher] of the new religion as she wants to hear about it . . . Do you care to bring any of your poetry?

October 20–21, 1903 [and now living in New York]
You are very generous and the tea looks delicious . . . Once, one of those horoscope people told me I had in past incarnations! been . . . a queen, an actress, a wicked enchantress, and a nun, and that in this present journey I was to live out, in little, each incarnation – that the reason men universally were so chivalric toward me was because of the Queen-phase when I did many favors!! – and because of having been very wicked in ages gone by. Mrs Hovey lectures this evening. You may hear the echoes of her 'R's' in Washington. She is really teaching me to read . . . I shall be glad to meet Miss B but it is particularly Mirza Abul Fazl I should love to see! . . . A man wrote me he had loved me for seven years, etc. etc. and I feel so sorry because I like him . . . but I cannot love him . . . I wrote him a nice letter and hope to cheer him up . . .

Mrs Hovey gave an interesting lecture this evening. There was a young Hungarian gentleman there, whose uncle was president of the House of Lords in Hungary and another uncle is the bodyguard of the King of Austria and the way he stared at Mrs Hovey, and the 'R's', made me laugh out loud several times . . . I was ashamed of myself, but it is all your fault. I never laughed at Mrs Hovey . . . until you looked so funny. [Khan had quite possibly made one of his faces when Florence mentioned her comely but mature and dramatic instructress.]

At the lecture, Florence did not dare look at her English friend, Miss T, as 'she and I have so many jokes about the awful sounds Mrs Hovey emits and thunders forth'. The young men did not please her 'for they say things to each other they should not say in the presence of gentlewomen. I cannot forgive vulgarity at any time, and nobles should be noble . . . as to American girls, I am only one-half American and I am not a pure type of American; I lack the virtues of the type, but I gain other things – my interest in metaphysics, poetry, I do not feel is American . . . but all my practices are largely American . . .'

The young Hungarian soon expressed passionate love and proposed to Florence during a 'very painful hour'. He also told her he said his prayers to her every night.

Florence and Mrs Hovey, sitting before the fire, had long philosophical conversations. Florence warned Khan, in case he was visiting New York, that he reminded Mrs Hovey of the late Mr Hovey, 'so look out'.

A Victorian, Florence loved – or liked – some men but was inclined to wish they were women 'because of the conventionality that I think has to be considered'. In acting, she wrote, 'It is the "publicity" that I shrink from and abhor – though I am quite sure I have the dramatic temperament and perhaps, gift . . . I love isolation . . . to live with Nature [she wrote transcendentally] where my nature leads me . . .'

She told Khan, 'Mother wrote me she has had "another adorable letter from Khan" . . .' and says further on, 'I think you are a very great person and pray do not talk of dying.'

These letters, guarded enough, were all signed on the order of 'sincerely your friend', and often only initialed F. M. B. (We do not know what the M stands for.) Florence's mother had warned her never to write a letter that she would not like to see on the front page of the New York *Times*. Contrasting with such non-committal endings, she often in later letters called Khan 'my child', 'dear little sweet person', 'cunning little darling', 'my own little angel'. These were playfully absurd – he was not little, for example, perhaps above average height for the time – but they tell us something of her inner state: a growing affection, and also, through the use of diminutive terms, a desire to deny the importance he was beginning to have in her life. After the loss of Philip Savage she may not have dared to fall deeply in love again.

And yet, unconsciously, she may have been wanting to tell Khan how strong her love could be when she wrote in the latter part of November, '. . . some day I may tell you how I love my Father – it is a wonderful glory to have a Father one can love as I love mine.'

In a letter of November 18 she says, 'I think I could write you letters all day and all night. Why don't you tell me not to?' Her winter pledge was no men, just work with Mrs Hovey 'and my beloved art'. And Khan's friendship.

'I fear the weathervane of my desires . . . I am not fickle but I get through with many people and lay them aside like novels . . . and alas! I'm not ready to leave my dreams . . . I fear tragedies, and I am too lazy for deep feelings – too tired, too surfeited with the seeming of them where they do not exist. I am bored with men; as a class they give me nothing but ennui . . . when they make love – goodby, as I am neither asbestos, a widow nor a lovelorn maiden. Now I will tell you something and then good night. It begins to dawn on me that I find something in you that I have really gone in need of for many years . . .'

Two days later she sent him an idea which clearly seems to be an echo of John Keats's 'Last Sonnet':

> Bright star, would I were steadfast as thou art . . .
> Still steadfast, still unchangeable,
> Pillow'd upon my fair love's ripening breast . . .
> And so live ever . . .

'How wonderful it would be if a man were so constant . . . so true to God and to humanity that the star of his wife's love . . . should shine in the heaven of his mind as unshaken, and beautifully burning, and as calm, as the evening star in the heavens of the physical universe . . . True love', she continued, 'seems to me like your Religion to only add to what one has . . . taking therefrom nothing.' She did not intend to marry, Florence went on, because she knew such 'beautiful and great and clever women in America . . . they would all fascinate my poor husband so, I should . . . be continually in tears . . . bitterness would be my constant food.' No doubt millions of women have felt the same.

A few days later she is writing, 'I have wished all day I might see you. I am so blessed with your friendship. I know this even more when I look around upon the rest of men . . . you are as sweet in spirit as the scent of the rose I am wearing. (If Mrs Hovey were to read this, the thunder of her "R's" when she could command her indignant feelings of Jove-like rage . . . would blow me to Washington, which would please me after all.)'

Many have noted a kind of imagined fragrance clinging to those early believers and their words, who had been in the presence of 'Abdu'l-Bahá. Like Sa'dí's bit of common clay placed in his hands at a bath house, that clay was sweet and scented because it had been close to a red rose. Mrs Hovey obviously did not want to see her prize pupil vanish into matrimony.

'You know so much for a little boy,' Florence went on, 'you seem about forty years old to me.' She told him how she had written her mother at home and addressed the letter to Mr A. K. Khan.

Like many women, like Laura, Florence seemed to enjoy giving Khan advice. Sometimes she pulled him out of a depression, but this time she wrote, 'I know you are eternally, inevitably, an optimist, even though I have not yet received the Teachings of Bahaism which reveal everything.' Apparently in those days the Faith was still being disclosed little by little. There is much in the letters of a philosophical turn, as one would expect from a New England transcendentalist. '. . . as to the human will,' she wrote, 'I found it was a straw in the current, but the Divine Will, omnipresent in man's divine nature will do all things.' She also quotes 'Mrs Browning' to this effect:

> God's completeness flows roundabout
> our incompleteness,
> Round our restlessness His rest.

Florence thought one could meet God 'even in the depths of hell'.

In several letters she mentioned her jealousy, understandable when one remembers his many women admirers. Her discreet use of initials effectively thwarts the biographer.

There is more about Miss B. 'Can't you love Miss B more? I hope you can't.'

Meanwhile the enamored Hungarian, rejected by letter, had replied with a cold postal card. Florence was sorry because 'He does make such fine bookplates but I hate to write him again even though I want my bookplate as he designed the best I ever saw'.

And a few days later: 'I am just in from the theater. I missed you so much all evening – between the acts I thought everything seems so empty . . .' In the usual ups and downs of love, she was not always sure. 'I hardly realize I am in love with anyone I am so busy; so it is fortunate I have so few holidays and Sundays. Dear me, I have heard a man makes love more, before marriage, and a woman after . . .' She continues ambiguously, 'Be assured I have never had so hard a time to get rid of anybody as I would have, if I wanted, but I do not – to leave you.'

That fall he sent her a ringstone, 'a glory and so yellow like the sunrise, the dawn of that new day of sunshine and joy, I feel when I recite the Greatest Name'. She ended with: 'You are many things that are lovely and interesting.'

On January 2, 1904, responding to a gloomy letter from Khan then undergoing trials in Washington, she wrote, 'Why do you not see that after every death comes a resurrection . . . and Life, not death, is omnipotent.'

By February 14, he was not Dear Khan any more but dearest Ali and she was Florence: '. . . for hours all day I have been living a love letter to you that I dare not write . . . you are all that I want in life . . . Dear, I love you. I *love* you. Please take all the love you want for I have it for you. I can stand everything, dear, if you will love me – or even if you do not. I have no words to speak of my heart's love to you tonight.'

Elizabeth Barrett Browning had died in 1861, but Florence was writing in the same spirit as the author of *Sonnets from the Portuguese*:

> . . . What I do
> And what I dream include thee, as the
>   wine
> Must taste of its own grapes.

One doubts if a girl could write such letters, or such sonnets as Elizabeth Barrett's, today, eighty and more years later. They imply restraint, dignity between the sexes, courtship – matters unknown in today's era of the pill, pornography, designer jeans and bikinis. One is not sure that, since the advent of modern psychology, any man or woman could be put on such a pedestal again.

On February 17 she asked him, 'These men – why do you try to make me love you, why do you not leave me alone? Well, I love you because I am so different from almost everybody I know, and I am so pleased to have so much more happiness in you than I ever can find anywhere . . . love . . . never did come to me before.' She was fond of others, she told him, 'But, this is like hate in comparison to my love for you.'

She found herself ill one day from one of her 'rare headaches and nervous fatigues. I am just like an animal when I feel ill or tired, I simply go away from everybody and not being able to eat grass, I rest until I am revived . . . You need not tell me you find me the best woman you have ever known, dearest, I dare say it cost you some effort to tell that lie . . . I am sixty-five persons in one and whatever it is, in love – one, one, one.'

Mrs Hovey was planning a trip south. 'Oh, dearest, don't you see her, if she goes via Washington. You may – not.'

On February 22 she wrote to him, 'I fully understand that there is nothing dear heart between you and Miss B.' Going back to his thwarted love for Eleanor, she says that she could hardly believe Khan really loved her, and refers to Eleanor's 'old gentleman', chosen instead of Khan. She now remembered Philip as belonging to the long ago. 'You know I don't mean to be disloyal to my first love – but you are more to me than any power of language can state . . .' And addressing him from her prim Martha Washington Hotel for Women she adds, 'Yes, truly if the bellboy is not in sight of course I shall kiss you as soon as I see you.'

And further, 'You came into my heart to stay.' No doubt similar words have been exchanged by lovers since the dawn of time, but in the event she meant exactly what she wrote, and there was never anyone else. Then a typically Victorian addition: '. . . ever since I sent you my handkerchief, the vibrations from Washington . . . are almost burning me up!'

She called him angel and little angel. 'I pray . . . that God may let me always be united to you in love, here and hereafter . . . Though some of the time I might want to be with Philip in the next life; but the other half with you . . .'

On a more mundane note she mentions how well he dresses, something people noted all through his life. 'You look awfully handsome in English clothes. I really hope you will always have enough money to buy very good clothes . . .'

She spoke of progress in her career. 'Well, yesterday Mrs Hovey went wild over my work. "My girl, you are an actress. It has come at last." Really she was overcome . . . buried her head in her hands, walked around, stood still and shivered in one cold chill after another, and then lay down exhausted.'

Florence herself was worn out – doing three days' work in one, having stagefright in advance of her spring recitals. But she said, 'I cannot bear the thought of dying without having done one great service to art, to religion, to humanity.'

And she tells him of a terrible experience she had at the hospital, on the day before Philip died. The sun was going down and she was alone with him. He was in great pain and great excitement from his fever and dread of the operation only a few hours away, which would cost him his life. And he poured forth grief at his 'unaccomplished work and life – all, everything he strove for unaccomplished'. She could never forget 'that flash of a great soul revealing its one word on its existence here, so soon to go out. I saw both the human incompleteness and the divine promise, and the sweet spirit . . . I tried to make a vow with myself then that I would go on and fulfill what his spirit had left unfulfilled . . .'

The Boston Herald had accepted an illustrated article by her mother, Alice, Florence wrote on February 23rd. 'She wanted to leave some record for us her children of her travels in Japan, Russia and China . . .' and she hoped to publish a book later. (Later, that time in the future when so many books do not get published.)

'My maid has just brought breakfast to my room, so of course one, this one is permitted to leave her heart's adoration. Now I have just eaten . . . one of four oranges, two chops, one potato, three cups of coffee, two rolls, the rest, alas, I had to leave . . .'

'Mrs Ford said to me last fall, Dearest, I have to smile, she said, "Florence if you will entirely cut out the men and work for the next two years devotedly to your art, you will make your name." . . . Mrs Ford said it was my test if I were worthy to be an artist. I can't be an artist unless you love me . . . If only I could be Salvini's leading woman this spring . . . I would gain at once a serious reputation with the (dear) public . . . Elizabeth Marbury, who is the greatest play-broker in the world, said she would make a star of me in three years! The usual time has been nearer ten . . . She and Elsie DeWolfe live together.'

Florence then confided, 'I love women as a class far better than men . . . the only friendships I so far successfully have are with women, for every man since I was seven has been in love with me, for a period, but they all get over it though they do tell their wives I am their second choice.' She also affirmed that 'heaven knows I always unconsciously stir up jealousy in many women . . . I see your beautiful religion harmonizes all such detached puzzles into one living, enlightened unity . . . I fear you will see there are countless many who have no use for me. My deeds alone must praise or dispraise me . . . sweetest darling, do not . . . tell Mrs Ford anything yet . . .' She told him not to come visiting, if it were not convenient, until June. 'You know I do not need to see you to love you.'

Some disturbance must have come up between them, since she wrote on February 25th, 'I want you always to believe in my loyalty to you, despite . . . gossip or anything; and always, dear heart, come to me and be true in friendship; for truth in friendship never killed true love, it kills only false love . . . I do wish you were here in New York today, but heaven will take care of us both until we meet.'

There are a number of references in the letters as to Khan's difficulties, blue moods, lack of appetite – health problems attributed to hard work and 'nerves'. 'Please, dearest, be very calm; there is so much time for love . . .'

She continually tried to buoy him up: 'As a strong body shakes off illness,' she told him, 'as a pure mind shakes off evil thoughts, so a wholesome spirit or nature shakes off morbidness and blues, despondency and sorrows . . . I shall continue to think of you as the best and loveliest Bahai I ever saw or ever shall see, except the three Teachers . . .' a reference to the Báb, Bahá'u'lláh and 'Abdu'l-Bahá. 'When I saw you I felt my life had come to an end, so far as its quest for love . . . I ask for so little; truly, all I want is love . . . I . . . see nothing in world riches . . . even in friendships; only here and there a spirit gave me the light of God, in the dark, and Mrs Ford is one . . .' She said she tried, as Khan told her, to keep 'in the flow of spirit . . . God alone is "friend of the friendless"; with one as with all . . . death, sorrow, losses, release our spirits that they may rise to higher ethers . . . God and one's soul, are the only two sure things; their eternal relationship, the one sure thing [her arithmetic is a bit dubious here] . . . After I am completely broken down to truth, I begin to learn to live . . . No, I will not pray for you to die . . .'

February 28, 1904. 'In all the rain of a dreary day I went to Mrs Hovey for a lesson. Do you know, dearest, she is so good, generous and sweet to me the major part of the time. I feel more than wicked to get so mad with her, the rest of the time. She is having an angelic streak, these days.'

Florence and Khan, separated, were looking forward to a momentous talk, 'and then many things will be settled'.

On February 29 she told him, 'You are such a dear, lovely embodiment of all that I love.' Of his sorrows she wrote, 'You know, I think we have a gratefulness to sorrow, as time carries us on to a point when we may look back . . . as salt to insipidity.'

He was besieged by attractive women and Florence repeatedly told him she was jealous. She said jealousy was 'an unworthy thing . . . a medieval evil . . . anyway I am jealous at present and I may never get over it . . .'

About the Faith she writes, 'I am so pleased to see the [Bahá'í] message at last given to the general public . . . It seems so strange, yet beautiful to me, to see the Greatest Name in an ordinary newspaper. Now I can send this article to the Hungarian.'

Of his 'great traits ever since I met you,' she says, '. . . inside three minutes I was pleased with the first thing that struck my attention, your faultless breeding . . . the very flower of courtesy . . .'

March 5. 'I only want to stay as near you this Summer as possible . . . my most beautiful joy – and I do not want to go away from you . . . I have just given up a chance to play Ophelia through the West, as a leading woman in a company . . . So this hopeless tragedy is avoided . . . You too will go to Acca some time; I wish you might go with Mirza A[bu'l]-F[adl] or Miss B. How happy they must be.'

Earlier, March 2 or 3, his letters had stopped coming for several days. Evidently he was away for a whole month.

A dramatic critic proposed to her, 'which of course gave me a headache'. The man's wife had been gone nine years 'and she may be insane', but even so 'I wrote him I was astonished at him'. Florence told the critic she cared for someone else and he asked her if she was sure. 'Not a man has called on me this winter but fell in love,' she adds.

She thought it was cruel that no man would be her friend. She complains that Khan had neglected her for 'nearly a week', and says that her sister Alice had just invited her to spend June to September at their place in Lake Geneva, Wisconsin, a place that she passionately adored – forest, villas, sailing, swimming – everything around a little lake seven miles long, 'but God knows if I can live down the memories', for she had spent 'one blissful summer there some years ago. Since when death and a broken friendship and the changing interests have brought a number of differences; and really only sorrow has filled the years since I left there, all radiant with life, hope, love, ambition.' We do not know what the bliss and disappointment was about – possibly Philip Savage and her later estrangement from his family after he died.

'Don't you think two letters a week are best? Your telegram came just in time to save me from death.'

'I often write you letters and do not send them . . . I write too much from the heart, then I tear them up.'

Early in March she again wrote of 'fighting to overcome stage-fright. The most awful sensation, next to absolute sin, I dare say, there is!' Mrs Hovey planned that at first Florence should act and read before selected audiences.

Florence informed Khan she had been out to tea 'with some very sweet people; they met at a tea where I was too, last year; and inside three weeks they were married and never before that Sunday did either know the other existed. It is such a beautifully happy love affair . . . Neither life had been quite harmonious before . . . He always had wealth, but not love. She always was rather poor. Now she has love, and she is enjoying throwing her husband's money around (which, in my private opinion, is the only thing to do with money!).'

She wrote of her current life in New York, the varied lives she had to live, as 'a strange, queer thing . . . entirely upside down from the way I was brought up to be and to live and to do . . . I do not like it . . . but I see there is a unity in diversity. I hope you are the unity of all my diversities . . . I find the universe in you . . . you are like the sun and I am like nature, and when you don't shine . . . then I don't reflect any joy.'

The drama critic was apparently still on the scene and she had gone to the theater with him again. 'There is no crime in studying my art . . . you unconsciously insult me with any suspicions . . . Of course, if a man kisses one's hand with dignity or chivalry . . . one has to be conventionally gracious, but if a man slobbers all over it, the way the Hungarian did once, neither he nor whoever does so, gets a chance twice . . .'

'I am so grateful to God for bringing you into my life.'

'Mrs Hovey "dies to know of Sigurd", but you have my word. May she not know this? She will be happy to.' This must mean that Sigurd Russell, Mrs Hovey's son, had accepted the Bahá'í Faith. Florence continues, 'For the first time I heard the Babbies' Faith laughed at. I was so deeply shocked, and so upset at first; but I see now, what it is to suffer persecution for one's faith. I mean I see, from afar, what it is . . . the person spoke of "Miss B's Persians" in such a ribald way . . . My sister sent me an adorable picture of the baby [Charles Godfree] this week . . . If only men . . . would retain the angelic beauty of childlikeness and women too.'

On a Tuesday, perhaps in May 1904, she wrote from Boston, 'Pray for my success Thursday evening when I read, dear. [This recital had been planned for May 9. There is nothing further on it in the letters]. Today again I had no strength . . .' She looked forward to another winter season in New York City with lots of reading engagements, so that she could act at the new theater in New York.

A letter dated only Tuesday noon sends her greetings to Mírzá. 'I shall never forget him; but I confess to you I am so lost in my thought of you and for you and about you I had quite forgotten Mirza. You know I don't like the honors of the world, or great state about living. I care more for the picture than the frame.' Florence said her work was only the frame and Khan was the picture. Mrs Ford had both cheered her and made her nervous when she said the present two or three years were Florence's crucial test as an artist . . . 'That I need not be discouraged if I fail in the life of an actress and she thought it was awful anyway for me to take it up, and that Mother would never have permitted it had she truly known the practical status of stage machinery and its politics.' (Deliberately ambiguous here, perhaps?)

She wished Khan was 'a little farmer' if he would only have her there on the farm (and an absurd couple the pair of them would have made, about 180 degrees away from American Gothic). Showing Florence's ignorance of farm life she went on, 'Isn't that very lazy of me? To wish for idyllic love in the midst of the great century? And that is all I ask of life . . . that is why I shall have everything else but that, I suppose, one of these days . . .' But she adds, '. . . even the little I have heard of Bahaism brings so much peace and assurance . . .'

Judging by her letters they still worried the question of Eleanor between them, and Florence sympathized 'in your grief over E . . . if God spares the life then one must continue to live, one must be comforted by the knowledge that there are more perfect services to render, there is more sympathy to give, there are deeds to do, words to speak, and new trial to make towards redemption . . . live, and be of good courage and like a nightmare, a bad moment, you will yet forget your sorrows . . .

'Angel; for heaven's sake, the critic just walked in and asked me to marry him . . . weeks ago I told him I cared for someone else. He said, "I remember you said you were happy because someone cared for you; and I thought I should drop dead on the spot! It was as if someone stabbed me." Then he said, " I love you very much, but I will never speak of this again."'

Florence told him it was his dramatic criticism that she was interested in.

'He asked me to kiss him, just once. Now, I will not kiss even a man who is dying of love for me, I am ungracious; so I said, "No." Are you glad I would not, dearest, or . . . don't you care? . . . if in your sorrows, my love is only a cry in the dark to you and means little or nothing . . . I don't want you to allow me to love you . . .

'I am trembling in my shoes lest someone is making love to you, as I have a theory that what happens to me, happens to you . . .

'My luncheon tomorrow is at the home of the daughter of that (wretched) old man, that I wish would tell me the truth about my father.' Florence had always longed to know her father's antecedents, and apparently there was one man, a minister, who knew the facts. 'He and she are socially distinguished here. It is a queer world sometimes.'

Of the men she was seeing, she insisted that 'My eyes assume an expressionless glare when I look at all men save you!'

Florence was slowly becoming a Bahá'í and wrote, 'Dearest friend, I so want to read and inform myself more of this Revelation . . . talked a long time last night to my acquaintances and I love to hear about it – you will teach me yourself, won't you? I will perhaps promise you not to be in love with you at all if you will only give me the teaching.'

Khan must have been travel teaching as well as continually teaching classes in Washington. She mentions a trip he would take to St Louis. A hoped-for visit with him about now was indefinitely postponed. Unfortunately Khan remains voiceless throughout the dialogue, his letters not having survived. There seem to have been misunderstandings, none of which could be settled 'until we have had our talk'. 'I am sorry if I give you the impression of flitting from flower to flower . . .'

Their problem was many-faceted – it was not only to reconcile the East and West in them, but like all pioneers, each of them deviated from the usual pattern of the majority at home. Both were eccentric in the sense of not having the same center as the others of their kind. But they were beginning to find a merging of their conflicting pasts in the Bahá'í Faith. One letter ends, 'I thank you for helping me with those beautiful thoughts on religion.'

She would often tell Khan just why she was seeing this or that man, usually unidentified, '. . . partly in the hope of saying some things to him that he ought to hear, partly out of sympathy over his sorrow for his dissipated brother who died a few months ago, partly because he is one of my oldest friends . . .' Khan was, after all, used to veiled women who were kept behind supervised doors. To reassure him, she stated her position clearly, 'I love only you and I love you the best, now, always and forever if it is the will of God.'

On the Fourth of July, 1904, Florence was back in New York and they had gone on an excursion to Palisade Park across the Hudson. 'I am glad', she wrote the day after, 'we escaped the hideous noises of the town . . . the vista of the Hudson River and wooded shore lives in my eyes (or as Wordsworth says "flashes upon that inward eye, which is the bliss of solitude" – lines written by his wife, they say, and the best too in his poem, "Daffodils"). Such a glory of haze and breezes, sunshine and Ali today . . . You look the most beautiful in the woods or under the trees – that is a "real person" as Philip used to say . . . who grows beautiful amid Nature – whom she does not show up to be artificial . . . I find I come quickly to the bottom or end of most people; and for pearls or gold have a handful of gravel . . .'

On July 8 she wrote, 'I so much enjoyed seeing Miss [Juliet] Thompson last night . . . but it is hard for me to be natural or nice to anybody however lovely when you are in the room . . . I was sure you were really in love with Juliet, last night . . . She really has genius, but I have nothing like that at all . . .' All too human, she added farther on, 'Did you admire my new brown shoes? I pushed them half way across the room so you would surely see them . . . I love them. They make me feel gay.'

The next day she asked about coming to see Mírzá Abu'l-Faḍl. 'I should dearly love to go to see Mirza this afternoon about 4:00. Shall I intrude if I come?' She also thought of bringing along a Miss Pierson (unidentified).

August would be the final month of Florence's letters. On the 2nd, in Boston, she came down to breakfast happy and cheerful, out of the Slough of Despond. Her studies were going well. She asked Khan to address letters to her: 'Back Bay Post Office, Boston, General Delivery . . . I shall, of course, prefer to walk over there each morning, to having trouble here; guests, etc.' She asked him *en passant*, about his 'week with your lovely friends . . . Isn't it lovely to be the only man amongst so many women?'

That day she was 'glorying in' Emerson's essay on Compensation, getting more from it than ever. But she was less than philosophical about Khan's feminine entourage: 'Dear, please "shake" (get rid of) all those sweet females and go and rest; although the moon shines, go to bed . . .'

In the evening she was writing quite matter of factly about what was to become a classic – *The Bahá'í Proofs*: 'Thank you for telling me of Mirza's book – I hope to see Mrs. Ford tomorrow and shall get it if I can.'

Florence seems to have had a confrontation with someone that summer, probably Laura Barney, though as usual she blurs the identification. Doubtless it had to do with Khan. She advises him to go to 'Akká while the lady in question is still in America: '. . . do not go to that Heaven when she is there. Acca surely must be to your heart a Mecca of Peace . . . Of course, tests are God's affairs, but I rather think Miss — is *your* affair . . . The Master knows all things . . .' Florence evidently felt that the mysterious Miss Blank had a very strong influence over Khan. 'Are you in the power of Miss — ? No, you are not . . . Telegraph me care of Miss Clough, 253 Ocean St., Lynn, Mass. in case you can't meet me Saturday a.m. by eleven thirty at Newbury Port. I go to Lynn tomorrow, so I shall get no more letters from you, Dear.'

The last letter of the series is dated August 25. As usual she hoped Khan was not ill and not 'nervous'. She said she would like to remain in Boston all through the coming winter, if she could do that with a clear conscience. But she also said, 'In New York I have an opportunity to develop a gift . . . I have the freedom, the sympathizers . . . I am handicapped in Boston at every turn. At least in New York I have a breathing chance.' She delayed going to New York. It was not a personal wish to go but a sort of ambition to succeed. She asked if Khan could not write his books during the coming winter in New York. (Non-authors cannot be disabused of the belief that authors need only 'hole up somewhere for a couple of months' to produce a book.)

'Will you spend next Sunday at Green Acre? And come here Monday?' If she received no letter from him before leaving for Lynn, 'I shall feel very triste and cheated, dearest. For I do not return home until Saturday p.m. Oh, if you would be here then, but I suppose Green Acre claims you.'

A postscript says, 'Please keep well. Do be happy dearest Heart, for life is worth being cheerful in . . . let us hope.'

THIRTY-NINE
Vinculum Matrimonii

Mírzá Abu'l-Faḍl had at last seen his book, *The Bahá'í Proofs*, written, then translated by Khan, then published. He was old, delicate, and suffering from the climate, and 'Abdu'l-Bahá wrote him to return to the Middle East. Khan, however, had been directed by the Master in a Tablet written early in 1904 to remain in the United States and carry on the Bahá'í work begun with Mírzá.

After Mírzá left, Laura and her cousin Ellen sailed for Europe, and later obtained permission from the Master to come to 'Akká. Her purpose was to ask a series of questions of 'Abdu'l-Bahá, write down His answers, and then (Khan says, not quite accurately) have the resulting book published in the United States.

In the event, the first edition of her remarkable book, *Some Answered Questions*, was published by Kegan Paul, Trench, Trübner & Co., London, in 1908. The second edition was brought out by the Bahá'í Publishing Society, Chicago, 1918.

Laura herself says in her introduction that 'these answers were written down in Persian while 'Abdu'l-Bahá spoke, not with a view to publication, but simply that I might have them for future study. At first they had to be adapted to the verbal translations of the interpreter; and later, when I had acquired a slight knowledge of Persian, to my limited vocabulary . . . In these lessons he ['Abdu'l-Bahá] is the teacher adapting himself to his pupil . . .'[117]

Originally, she adds, these materials were in no special order, but later they were 'roughly classified' to help the reader.[118]

Kegan Paul published the Persian text as well. The scholar, Hippolyte Dreyfus, first Frenchman to become a believer, translated the work into French and it was published by Leroux, Paris.

Some Answered Questions was brought out by permission of the Master, and Laura said He went over the original Himself and thus the text was 'like a Tablet'. The work took from 1904 to 1906, but in addition, we assume, there was the background of teachings learned on previous visits. It constitutes, the Guardian states, her 'imperishable service'.[119]

'I have given to you my tired moments,' 'Abdu'l-Bahá once told Laura, rising from the table after answering one of her questions.[120] (Not only her questions, Juliet Thompson said, but the questions Laura had collected from others as well.)

Some time after Laura had gone to 'Akká, Khan received a letter from her that puzzled and disturbed him. She wrote that he surely would be very happy to be in the Master's presence again, and translate His replies to her questions. At the same time, she had written Ellen Goin, who had returned to America by then, to arrange for steamship accommodations so that Khan could make the trip.

Khan could not understand this new development. He had his instructions from the Master to remain in America. Now, without consulting Khan, Laura was suddenly deputizing her cousin to book passage for him on a ship to the Holy Land.

Reinforcing her daughter, Alice Clifford Barney had written Khan from 'Akká around this time that she would provide traveling expenses for him to come.

At once, he wrote the facts to Laura and to Ellen and explained that he was remaining in America because the Master had so directed.

Result: another letter from Laura to Khan and another to Ellen, to expedite his coming.

This was a serious test to Khan because, aside from his instructions, he was sure that if he had to leave Florence, he would go mad, perhaps even die. (This is not so far-fetched as it might sound. There was even an Arab tribe, celebrated by Heine, whose members died of love. Love has often, in history, been regarded as a dangerous disease.)

He talked the situation over with Florence and then wrote the Master that if, in spite of His previous orders, 'Abdu'l-Bahá desired him to leave America as Laura indicated He did, he would of course obey.

At this same time he received two letters from Persia. One was from that distinguished statesman, his uncle. 'I am getting old', the letter said in effect, 'and my many children are young. My wish is that you will return to Persia, marry my daughter and take charge of my properties and all my affairs.' The second letter was from Khan's mother, begging him to carry out his uncle's wish.

Florence had come to Green Acre for the day when Khan told her of the two letters.

'Of course you must return home', she told him, 'and do as your family has asked.'

'But I have already answered the letters,' Khan said. 'I told them I was getting a book of mine ready for publication and could not leave here at this time.'

Florence knew what he meant. She told Marzieh in later years that, hearing those words, she felt as if an iron portal were clanging shut across her future. She knew he could not go away from her. Meanwhile, the two of them waited to see what 'Abdu'l-Bahá's reply about Khan's departure would be.

Soon a Tablet came for Khan. The Master wrote that Miss Elsa Barney was there and had desired that Khan should come and share her happiness in the Holy City, but that insofar as He was concerned, He had already sent Khan His instructions to remain and serve in America.

Florence and Khan rejoiced. But then, still another letter came in from Laura, and one from Ellen, that Khan should prepare to leave for 'Akká. This time, Khan was angered. He wrote Laura that he had already told her of the Master's orders to him, that he was free and of age, and that she should know him well enough to understand that he could not put a friend's request above a command from the Master.

Florence and Khan had another of their long talks and spent some hours in prayer. Then they reached a decision. To prevent any further obstacles from family or friends, and in view of the Master's desire that Khan should stay in America, they would take a fateful step.

Slipping out one evening, they went to the house of a Reverend Smith who lived in a suburb of Boston. Having thoughtfully brought a license along with them, they presented it to the Minister, as the law required, and he married them.

This way (long before Bahá'í marriage in America), they believed they could spare the Breeds a lot of trouble and expense, and they also hoped to keep the matter quiet for the time being, and have a little time to themselves.

The next morning, however, the papers spread the word: international marriage, Boston society girl, distinguished Persian. The press cabled Persia for information about Khan and the story crossed the nation.

The two cabled the Master and were told that, hearing this news, 'Abdu'l-Bahá clapped His hands and sent for sweets, shared the word with the pilgrims, and celebrated with them this first fulfillment of Bahá'u'lláh's prophecy, that the day would come when East and West would embrace like unto two lovers. He blessed their marriage with a remarkable wedding Tablet, wishing them a life of achievement in both the material world and the spiritual.

Soon after, another letter, sent by Elsa [Laura] Barney from 'Akká, enclosed yet another Tablet from the Master, which stated that although He had already sent them a wedding Tablet, He now wrote this second one by Elsa's request.

That first Bahá'í marriage of East and West, born only out of love, with no thought for the future, proved a disaster in many ways, although it is often hard to tell calamity from providence, providence from calamity.

Khan would tell Marzieh in confidence that 'Abdu'l-Bahá had written him, now that he had made this marriage, he would suffer much, but the final result of it would be very, very good. But then, the Master had, Khan said, directed him to rub out those words. (Khan does not mention this in his written memoir.)

He does say that immediately after the marriage 'untoward events began to manifest themselves'. People did not feel like sponsoring his work, now that he was no longer a glamorous bachelor and had taken on a beautiful bride. The friend who had received 'Abdu'l-Bahá's permission for Khan to translate the *Íqán* and had planned another translation for him just after its publication, cancelled the second assignment once Khan's marriage was announced. He was now a married man, she wrote him, and he must look for sustained remuneration somewhere else. Mrs Hearst lost interest in sending him to Harvard, on the ground, as stated earlier, that a certain American couple had abused her generosity.

Florence and Khan were also unwilling to ask any help from her family. The family took it for granted that Khan had ample means. Florence herself – whose faith and optimism were often, to a skeptic, based on air, but worked for her (except where Rahim, her first born and almost lifelong crucifixion was concerned) – was neither a nail-biter nor a pacer-up-and-down. She floated, she was lapped in the grace of God. Her texts might well have been such as these from the *Gleanings*, where Bahá'u'lláh says, 'Put thy whole confidence in the grace of God . . . with Him are the treasuries of the heavens and of the earth. He bestoweth them upon whom He will . . .'[121] And also, 'Great is the blessedness awaiting the poor that endure patiently and conceal their sufferings . . .'[122] (Except that she never really felt poor.)

Through all that was to come, both the good and the bad, Florence continued to worship Khan – and by extension his country and his people. She had what she wanted, and in times of straitened circumstances never seemed to miss her former social life or her opulent youth.

The wide publicity their marriage had received helped them much. Reading in the papers that Khan was a scholar, sent to America by 'Abdu'l-Bahá to teach the principles of the Bahá'í Faith, William James, the noted philosopher, called on them and invited Khan to give several lectures at Harvard's Phillips Brooks House. Both president and faculty also attended, and some of the graduate students who heard him later became active Bahá'ís. One who did not embrace the Faith was W. H. McCracken, the future president of Vassar College, but, remembering those lectures, he helped to get Marzieh (who had the necessary credentials but was faced with a long waiting list) enrolled at Vassar during his tenure.

Khan then began to receive many remunerative lecture invitations from clubs, churches and other cultural institutions. One unusual opportunity was offered him by the Omar Khayyam Club of Boston, probably the first of its kind in the country. Its president was a Mr Burrage, a leading industrialist called the 'Copper King'. He was much interested in Khan's approach to the poet, for Khan gave a mystical and spiritual interpretation rather than the usual bacchanalian, tomorrow-we-die view. The newspapers reported on this new approach, for 'Umar was a household word in that time and place.

The audiences were delighted to see that Khan presented his subject spontaneously, without notes.

The money coming in from lectures helped him over many a bad patch but funds were in short supply for a very long time.

Directly or indirectly, Khan taught the Faith at every opportunity. In a short while he had confirmed Alice, his new mother-in-law, and she, as a club woman and social leader often reported on in the press, opened many doors. Alice, Florence and Khan working together established the first Bahá'í community in Boston. They were also able to spread word of Bahá'u'lláh's Teachings in other New England cities, helped greatly by Khan's summer classes at Green Acre.

One of Khan's friends at this time was Nathan Haskell Dole, author of the book *Persian Poets*. Another, a Mr French from Davenport, Iowa, a student at Harvard, studied Persian with him.

At the height of these activities, the young couple found it necessary to leave Boston and go away for a rest. Florence had fallen ill. Khan was frightened by this development but need not have been, for it turned out to be her first pregnancy – 'nothing', he wrote, 'except what nature decrees as a result of married life'.

They had gone to Portsmouth, New Hampshire, about two hours from Boston, and found rooms in the house of a Mrs Toner, the wife of a railway conductor. Khan knew Mrs Toner from his two previous summers at Green Acre, just across the river in Maine.

The publicity from his marriage and lectures had followed him, and the Ministers Association of New England, with offices in the town, invited him to address them on the Bahá'í Faith. Other lecture invitations also came, and were remunerative. He continued to have a heavy Bahá'í correspondence.

A French observer has said, 'Marriage is a long conversation, constantly interrupted.' The two of them talked: especially about 'Abdu'l-Bahá and Khan's struggles to reach Him, and all that he had learned while living beside Him.

A captive Himself, harried by enemies without and within, working with few qualified helpers and they temporary, fallible, often more trouble than they were worth, 'Abdu'l-Bahá had sent Bahá'ís to far away places, had continually followed up their work and established the Faith worldwide. No wonder the years bowed Him down.

No wonder there were tear lines on His beautiful face. He had been like an artist who takes up charcoal, brush or crayon, only to have it, after a few strokes, break in his hand. He had seen many of His own workers fail or betray Him. He had been like a deer with the hounds after Him.

Florence and Khan also discussed ideas which came as he read Carlyle, Emerson, Goethe, Swedenborg. To Khan, such as these reflected the light slowly dawning over the world from the promised advent of Bahá'u'lláh.

Even for New Hampshire, that year was exceptionally cold. Stories are legion about New Hampshire cold, both as to natives and weather. Telling about the climate and the silence and the reserve of local people, Richard Merrifield says in *Monadnock Journal* that during four years in a New Hampshire village, almost every morning he had gone to a cafe and drunk a cup of coffee alongside one of the Selectmen, but they had never spoken. At last the situation changed. There came a winter when for a week the thermometer stood at thirty degrees below zero. Finally one day it registered only minus twenty-nine.

'Getting warmer, I see,' said Merrifield to the Selectman.

'It's moderatin',' the latter agreed.[123]

Every day, Florence and Khan took long walks in the snow. As spring came and the sunlit ice diamonds dripped off the bare trees, and the earth began to show through again, they extended their walks to the beach. And one day, close by the Hotel Wentworth, at the shore, Khan had an awakening. A great mystery that had bothered him during all his years with Mírzá was suddenly cleared up.

Khan had often asked Mírzá about the afterlife and whether it was on a plane entirely beyond man's experience in this world. Each time, Mírzá would smile and evade the issue. Then, late one afternoon in New York when they were out for their daily walk in the dreaming old cemetery of Trinity Church, uptown near the Hudson, Khan decided to back Mírzá into a corner and force an answer. He began a first sentence on the subject and as usual Mírzá shied away. But this time Khan took hold of him and said he insisted on an answer and would keep on trying until he received one. It was something like Jacob wrestling with the angel in the Bible: 'I will not let thee go, except thou bless me.'[124]

'It would be best for your own good', Mírzá said, 'not to force me. For I would have to give you an answer that would hurt your pride.'

'Never mind that,' Khan pleaded. 'No matter how I would feel, you tell me.'

'Well, here is my answer. You would not be able to grasp it.'

'What makes you think so? I read Kant. I read the Greeks.'

'Yes,' said Mírzá, 'but I know you could not understand about immortality. How do I know? The reason is, because you ask. This is a mystery that will not pass into words. It can only be felt in the soul.'

Khan, quick to anger, was indignant. After all his studies, he was being called an ignoramus. You may call a Persian many things and perhaps get by with it, but you should never, never impugn his intelligence.

Gently, consolingly, Mírzá continued, 'You keep on serving our beloved Faith. I shall pray that you, in due time, will find your answer.'

That morning on the beach at Portsmouth, enjoying the sunlight on the rippling blue water, Khan noticed some men going into a boathouse nearby. He watched idly as they dragged out a heavy rowboat, launched it, climbed aboard and rowed away. Deep in his thoughts, he kept an eye on the boat, and he saw that the farther it moved on, the smaller it got, until, to his surprise, it vanished completely and nothing remained of it but empty blue water and the bow of the horizon.

Khan said to himself, 'What happened to the boat? Where are the rowers gone? Did they melt away into another world, and onto a different sea? Or are they still out there rowing in our world, on this very same sea? And because they are moving and I am sitting on the beach, the limitations of my physical body and the curve of the earth have thrust us apart.'

With these thoughts, Khan felt he had his answer that could not be put into words, and he thanked Bahá'u'lláh for it and blessed Mírzá Abu'l-Faḍl (who had gone back to the Middle East the previous year). Florence wrote that it was not yet fully realized how much Mírzá's books, lectures and Biblical interpretations had done to demonstrate 'this great Truth', the Faith, adding that 'forever the history of the Bahá'í Faith in America will be interwoven with the labors of this saintly soul . . .'

One day their landlady told them of a big event in the town. The newly-completed YMCA on Main Street was being dedicated. Why not go?

They went. A long flight of stairs led from the sidewalk to the entrance. With the ceremonies over, the two of them left and started back down. The steps were newly polished. Florence slipped and fell all the way from the top to the pavement.

Khan called a carriage, got her home and sent for a doctor. He assured them there was no immediate danger of a miscarriage, but it probably would hasten the birth. Frightened, they called the family in Cambridge (who lived at 45 Dana Street by then), hurriedly packed, and left for Boston, where the family met them at the train. On the advice of friends, they sent for a Dr Crocker, considered a good obstetrician, and prepared for the confinement.

About then a Tablet came to them from 'Abdu'l-Bahá. In it the Master quoted lines about a birth in the long ago from Persia's great epic, *The Book of Kings*, of Firdawsí. He referred specifically to a prince in the story, born of a Persian King and a daughter of the King of Túrán: 'the sign of two personages bears this auspicious one – of Afrásíyáb (King of Túrán) and of Kávús (King of Persia).'

The couple rejoiced; there would, they felt sure, be a boy, safely born, and with an auspicious future before him. Florence used to tell of this Tablet wherever she went.

The terrible birth, when it came, went on for long hours of agony and fear, and Khan held the ether cone over Florence's face when the baby had to be taken by instruments.

When news of the birth of Rahim reached the Master He revealed another Tablet calling the child 'the first fruits of the spiritual union between East and West'.

FORTY

Khan – Come – Abbas

Life for the Khans was about to make a sudden turn, but for a time its course was predictable. Delighted with her healthy baby boy, Florence had the usual Victorian motherhood photograph taken, in a white floating negligee, hair loose on her shoulders, the infant at her breast. As for Khan, he kept on with his teaching and translating work, his paid public lectures on Persian literature and art.

Then, increasingly, he began to get letters from his friends in Persia. They were playing active roles by now in the new movement to establish a constitutional regime. There had been revolts in several places – in Tehran, in Ádhirbáyján – and the people, or at least a small group of intellectuals, wanted a change.

Muẓaffari'd-Dín Sháh was ailing and Russia had provided him with funds to go to Europe for a cure. Now the Russian loan was used up, the Shah was back and still ailing. The incipient revolution was growing but still in an early stage. What the leaders wanted badly was Persians with experience of the Western world. Khan was the only young Persian who had spent several years in America and made a name for himself, and introduced his country to the United States. Also important was his marriage to an American, a young woman of distinction, for, among other considerations, it had been widely publicized in America, noted in the European press, and word of it spread in Persia. Friends and relatives at home, who had lamented his abandoning them to teach the Bahá'í Faith, were now ready to forget and forgive if he would take on a new role and work to promote a constitutional government. They wrote, cabled, urged him to come back, and to bring Florence too, since she could aid in educational reform (not incidentally, she could help raise the status of women, but, being men, his correspondents were not much concerned with that).

Several problems held Khan back. He had antagonized important connections at home, among them highly-placed relatives, by not only joining but also promoting what was to them a false and rightly proscribed sect, its members in large numbers chained, jailed and put to death by the country's spiritual leaders, who certainly knew best, its Head in a desolate prison town on the Mediterranean Sea. As to this, Khan had written his brother about these Shiah Muslim attitudes and acts, saying that the future would show who was the gainer, who the loser.

A second problem – receiving permission from the Master to leave his work in America and return to Persia – seemed less large, for 'Abdu'l-Bahá had promised him that he would surely see Him again in 'Akká, and also go back to his family and home.

But there was, in any case, the matter of expense. Khan had no resources for such a costly journey. It was Florence who, having every confidence in her husband's future, was able to borrow the travel funds from a former schoolmate. With these in hand, the two of them with their toddler prepared to leave for 'Akká.

A short while before they sailed, May Bolles Maxwell invited them to Montreal to visit and teach in her home. That must have been the time when the infant was put to sleep in the safest place for him to be, a bureau drawer. Many years later, inviting Rahim to visit, she wrote him to the effect that she could put him up better than in the 'old bureau drawer days'.

It was while the family were here in Montreal that they received this cable: 'KHAN COME ABBAS.' They sailed from Boston April 28, 1906.

FORTY-ONE

To the Land of All Desiring

The steamer at Port Said was blowing her whistle for departure half an hour ahead of schedule, but Florence and Khan with the baby made it up the big ship's ladder as the engines began to turn. Ahmad Yazdi, the Persian Consul, who had come out to the steamer with them in the small boat along with their luggage, including five trunks, waved them goodby. Slowly, the ship turned about, and they were heading for their goal. When Florence woke up the next morning they were anchored off Jaffa. Through the porthole of their stateroom she saw blue sky and light green waters, and swinging along the sea beach like a page of history, a camel caravan. She dressed and went up on deck to join Khan, already pacing there.

'When do we see 'Akká?' she asked him.

'I think this afternoon.'

About three, Khan took Rahim to the railing on the starboard side of the upper deck and stood with Florence, watching and waiting for the first longed-for glimpse of the prison-city. Soon they were sailing past a green hill.

'We have reached Mount Carmel,' Khan said.

'The Holy Mountain of God!' Florence thought to herself.

'Watch now,' Khan told her, 'and you will see 'Akká, on the opposite shore. Then we turn into the Bay, to Haifa, at the foot of the Mountain, and go ashore.' Breathless, she waited.

'There! There is 'Akká!' cried her husband.

Across the sparkling waters, peaceful in the afternoon light, lay the white town that was the heart of the Faith, and the Master's prison home. 'At last', exulted Florence to herself, 'I am looking at the actual spot on earth where 'Abdu'l-Bahá is, where He breathes, and walks, and lives His life.'

When the ship dropped anchor in the harbor at Haifa and small boats crowded around her to row the passengers ashore, they chose Cook's boat, 'an enormous deep dory, high at the ends', the largest and safest, manned by eleven rowers, to get themselves and their luggage ashore. One of the rowers, Khan hurriedly whispered to her, was a Bahá'í, and this one tenderly carried the baby down to the boat, he and Khan exchanging silent greetings. Once on land, Khan handed over his keys and passport to Cook's agent. Their trunks would follow later.

Unable to obtain a Persian hat, Khan had on a red fez. A Turkish official was scanning the passengers one by one as they walked by, and Florence saw the official secretly pointing out Khan as a person to watch. She, used to American freedom, walked past the man, indignant but trembling. Here and there as they drove through Haifa's winding streets, a Bahá'í face smiled a greeting. Their room at the 'neat German hotel' looked out on gardens planted with Lombardy poplars and on a white road leading up from the deep blue bay.

That afternoon, pushing Rahim in his small carriage, Florence and Khan walked up the slopes through orchards to the Tomb of the Báb. Bordering the road were 'the thrifty little homes and gardens of the German farmers', whose now-dead fathers had established the colony to wait here for the coming of the Lord. Florence wrote of the Tomb as 'an imposing structure . . . two stories high . . . and which will, when finished, I understand, have an added story'. She could not, of course, have visualized its future golden dome, which would make this Shrine 'the Queen of Carmel'. But she wrote of 'Abdu'l-Bahá's achievement in building this Tomb though Himself a captive – He the 'humblest and mightiest of the servants of Bahá'u'lláh'. She told how one day, the Bahá'í prophecy said, ships of all nations were to ride down there in the blue Gulf of 'Akká,[125] and how, up gleaming flights of white marble stairs, pilgrim kings, gifts in their hands, would be climbing to this Shrine.

The mountain was scented with wild flowers and 'in that singular rich peace' she could hear the music of the waves breaking on the shore.

That evening Mírzá Jalál, husband of the Master's daughter Rúhá Khánum and son of Iṣfáhán's 'King of Martyrs', came visiting. The next morning came a relative of the Báb, Mírzá Muḥsin Effendi, husband of the Master's daughter, Ṭúbá Khánum. He had on flowing robes and a red fez and, being a Siyyid, wore a green band around the fez and a green girdle about his waist. His dignity and 'cultivated voice so frequently met with amongst the Eastern Bahá'ís' pleased Florence. He said that Khánum, the Master's daughters and their children were awaiting her in Haifa and wished to see her either at the hotel or where they resided. Going to them, Florence walked a little apart from the men, as was the custom. Their pace was leisurely, unhurried, contrasting with the brisk American walk to which she was accustomed.

The villa, on the lower slopes of Carmel, through an unfinished garden, had a high, cool hall of three pillared aisles, vestibule to a great inner hall running the whole width of the house. Hádí Effendi, 'Abdu'l-Bahá's son-in-law and father of Shoghi Effendi, who welcomed them at the door, had a delicate face and frame which reminded her of an Eastern Robert Louis Stevenson.

Mírzá Jalál was there and young Badí' Effendi. In the four corners of the inner hall were closed doors, opening out, and in the pillared aisles across the horizontal ends, high windows gave on garden views and Mount Carmel to the east, and gardens and the blue Gulf of 'Akká to the west, and the bright Mediterranean Sea beyond all. Florence and Rahim were led into a large drawing room, and the men left to allow the ladies to cross the hall from their rooms, unseen. First came Khánum, the Lady, sister of the Master, 'the silent half to 'Abdu'l-Bahá'.

In her letters Florence gives the meanings of certain Persian names here, such as Raḥím, a name of God, 'the Compassionate'; 'Azíz, another of His names, 'the Mighty One'; Ḍíyá Khánum (Shoghi Effendi's mother), 'Light'; Ṭúbá, the blessed tree that grows in Paradise.

Although the garments they wore, and plain white head scarfs, were extremely simple, the dignity of these ladies 'amounted to majesty'. Some (Florence especially mentions Rúḥá Khánum and Munavvar Khánum) could speak English, and Florence gave them messages from American Bahá'ís. After a time most of them rose to go, to proceed with their many household tasks; but Munavvar Khánum stayed on, and she and Florence sat by a high open window looking out at the blue water while Rahim slept. When luncheon was announced the daughters told Florence, 'You are to eat with the men.' Florence asked them to come too, and they laughed. 'We cannot do these things yet, in these countries.' 'Oh dear, I wish you were coming!' Florence said to Rúḥá Khánum, and through a tiny opening in the door Rúḥá laughed and said, 'I envy you!'

Afterward, back to the hotel for a siesta, 'indispensable in the East', and late in the afternoon a drive up the mountain to pray at the Shrine.

That evening a Tablet came from the Master in 'Akká, saying that they were to leave for 'Akká in the morning and stay at His house. They had now reached the last stage of the journey to His presence.

The next morning they drove over in Cook's three-seated covered wagon with three horses abreast. It took an hour or so along the shore, 'Akká lustrous as a pearl to their loving eyes, ever nearer and nearer. Waves surged about the wheel hubs and sometimes the spray was high as the cover over their heads. Then through the gates of the tiny prison-town with its winding lanes, then the doorway and believers and attendants hurrying out and Khan's whisper: 'This is the Master's house – we are here!'

FORTY-TWO

The Welcome

It was the afternoon of Saturday, June 9, 1906. The Household had had their midday meal, but lunch was brought to the new pilgrims in their room. And soon afterward they were called into the room at the side of theirs, to the Master's presence.

He embraced Khan and kissed him on both cheeks. 'Oh Khan,' the Master said, 'this is increase and blessing. You went to America one and came back three.' To Florence He said, 'Welcome! Welcome! Marḥabá! Well done!' After asking about their health and if they had a good journey, He seated Himself on the sofa and she sat nearby with the baby in her arms. 'I see that you love Rahim Khan very much,' He said. He asked the baby's age – a year and four days. (Rahim was the youngest pilgrim to have come from America.) And again to Florence, 'Praise be to God that as a result of the Revelation of al-Abhá, the East and the West have embraced like unto two beloved ones. You are the first American bride to be united to a Bahá'í from Persia. Praise God for this great favor.' And now He said, as He would say more than once, 'Because Rahim is the first fruit of the union between East and West, whoever looks upon his face loves him.'

The baby was restless and began to give his mother trouble. 'Abdu'l-Bahá called to him in Persian, 'Bíyá ínjá, Rahim Khan' – come here. The baby toddled over. The Master lifted him to His knee and offered him His rosary to play with – a precious rosary of black beads of scented wood with a purple silken tassel, and the child quieted down. Florence thought of how natural the Master was, noted the 'utter absence of cant or pose'.

She found 'Abdu'l-Bahá 'dazzlingly spotless and shining, from snowy turban-cloth, to white, snowy hair falling upon His shoulders, to white, snowy beard'. Over a long white garment, He wore the Eastern 'abá, and very faintly, there seemed to emanate from Him the prized odor of the East, attar of roses. She stole glances, when she could, at the lofty arch of His forehead, noted the play of expressions in His eyes and their changing colors, His smiling, kingly glance. She knew she could 'never get her fill of the divine beauty of His lower face, the finely-molded nose, the sculpted lips'. His attire was so crisp and fresh that you would never guess He had been toiling since early morning in the summer heat, visiting the sick and helping all who besieged His doors. 'There is ever His own spiritual radiance and fragrance coming from Him, which one perceives spiritually and which uplifts one's inner being into a heavenly atmosphere of harmony, delight and content, and brings one into the garden of the All-Glorious. His face is astounding, selfless, the stamp of suffering upon it. Alas for humanity, that crucifies God's Holy Ones!'

He inquired after May Maxwell. Khan spoke of the recent visit to her home in Montreal where he had taught the Faith to large gatherings every night. 'Abdu'l-Bahá asked if the visit had lasted nine days and Khan said yes. He told of Mrs Maxwell's great devotion and said she had purposely taken a house with a large parlor for meetings. The Master asked about her health and Khan said she seemed much better since becoming a believer. The Master said, 'Some years ago when Mrs Maxwell came to 'Akká, she was very weak and ill, so ill that no one could believe she would ever get well. But God healed her.'

Concerning the Faith in Montreal, Khan also spoke of Mr Woodcock and his work, and the Master was much pleased to hear of it.

Later that day 'Abdu'l-Bahá showed him a letter which had come from Persia, and told him to read it and see how the Cause was growing there, and with what ardor the believers were bringing in new souls.

Khan and Florence had been given a large corner room with four double windows, two on the sea and two on the garden. The next morning they heard a gentle rapping on their door. Khan opened it and there was 'Abdu'l-Bahá with a large handkerchief full of flowers. 'Give these flowers to Florence Khánum', He said, 'and bring me back the handkerchief.' Khan instantly obeyed. To his and Florence's delight, the flowers were a bridal bouquet of white roses. Within the bouquet was another, tiny one. The meaning of it was clear. Florence shed tears. 'This answers a long-time prayer of mine', she told Khan, 'that I would receive a rose from the hand of 'Abdu'l-Bahá.'

Khan would speak of various believers, for example of Mrs Cole, and her deep devotion. Later, of Madame de Lagnel, the Master said, 'She came here with Mrs Jackson and remained for some time. Though she was poor, she was always happy. I had her stay with us in the Household. Here she worked very hard to cook certain dishes. She said she wished to learn how to cook Persian dishes for the Bahá'ís in America. Her great, continuous sorrow had been the dying of her only son, but once she became a believer she found true happiness. If she had not become a believer in this Manifestation, her grief would have destroyed her, because the son was all she had of love or hope in the whole world.'

The Master spoke at length of 'repose of the heart' or 'peace in the

THE WELCOME

soul'. 'This', He said, 'is a state of true faith, which gives one such confidence, such assurance of God's bounty that the trials and tribulations of all the earth cannot affect him.'

On June 11 the Master was walking alone in His garden within the walls of the house. He summoned Khan to Him. Since the time seemed right, Khan spoke of his distress at seeing 'Abdu'l-Bahá closely confined within the walls of 'Akká, and of the very long time the Master had lived as a captive.

To comfort him, 'Abdu'l-Bahá said: 'We have wished it so. For many reasons, this incarceration is useful to me. One reason is that this protects me, for our enemies, finding us imprisoned, will not think of taking other steps to harm us. Besides, after the Blessed Perfection (Who was a prisoner forty years), we must delight in being a prisoner, and no other state can do us good and no freedom can give us rest. Our purpose is to serve at the Threshold of the Almighty, whether we be imprisoned or free. If we lived in a King's pleasure dome, surrounded by beatific gardens and meadows, with every means for tranquillity and peace at hand, but news should come that the believers were not on fire with the Faith and were not acting in accord with the laws and the urgent appeals of God – what comfort could all the gilded luxury of such a palace have to offer? No, news of that kind would make our palace as dark as the pit. But now that I am in prison and you have come here from America and bring me word that since his return from 'Akká Mr MacNutt regularly speaks at the Bahá'í meetings with great enthusiasm and love, and has attracted the hearts of the believers – this good news turns my prison into Paradise. Imprisonment, then, can inflict no pain upon us, for our purpose is to act in accordance with the commandments and urgings of God.'

Áqá Mihdí, the gardener of Bahjí, came in with a bunch of white jasmine. 'Abdu'l-Bahá gave Khan half the flowers to share with Florence and they walked back to the courtyard. A basket of apricots was presented to Him. He took the fruit and distributed it to the believers. He gave several to Khan and several others 'to take to Florence Khánum'. He also gave Khan an extra one which He said was 'for Rahim Khan'.

On the afternoon of Tuesday, June 12, 'Abdu'l-Bahá sent the couple and Rahim to the Holy Shrine at Bahjí. Florence wore her Persian veil, the chádur (tent), in accord with the Master's command, and wore it all during their ensuing visit to Persia. She being a Persian's wife, this was a necessary thing at the time.

It was not easy for Khan, after bowing down at the Sacred Threshold and presenting his wife and child, to go back in memory to many days when he had entered the inner garden under the glass roof with the Master and crowds of pilgrims. Had stood outside the small, embellished corner room under which the Manifestation rests, and faced the Threshold beyond which you do not pass – on it the bouquets of tuberoses and other scented flowers.

Back again in 'Akká he found the Master in a tent pitched in his little garden outside the house. He asked about Khan's visit to the Tomb. Khan said he was broken-hearted, remembering the old days, when the Master had led large gatherings of pilgrims from faraway places to that Holy Threshold.

Consoling him again, 'Abdu'l-Bahá quoted a verse from Ḥáfiẓ:

> These poison-bitter days will pass on by,
> And once again will life be sugar-sweet.

'All will be well,' He said. 'A time is coming when pilgrims from every land will extend from the 'Akká Gate all the way to the Shrine in one unbroken stream. People from every region of the world will come to visit this consecrated Spot.'

'Oh, Khan!' He continued, harking back to the time about six years before, when Khan had served Him as amanuensis and crowds of men and women of once hostile creeds and nationalities had come to Him in peace – 'Oh, Khan! Do you remember the old days in Haifa? Those happy times! Do you remember that night in Haifa when people of so many countries were present at dinner – Americans, Persians, Europeans; Persian Turks in their huge sheep-skin hats and those American ladies in their own amazing hats and the Turkish judge in his turban, and the Governor of Haifa, the Qá'im-Maqám, who came too. How the words flowed, and the explanations! How great was the radiance and joy! Even the Governor and the judge rejoiced and were radiant. What a night that was!'

FORTY-THREE

The Uses of Adversity

To Florence every act of 'Abdu'l-Bahá's was full of divine mysteries, and 'the material is but the shell containing the pearl of some spiritual teaching'. At luncheon once, He asked if she were pleased with the food and if not to ask for some other dish. She said it was delicious. The Master said, 'It is your love that makes it so – the dishes really are not that much.' And then, glancing across at Ḥájí Khurásání, a Bahá'í indigo merchant from Cairo, He added, 'Delicious food is what one eats at Ḥájí's table,' and Ḥájí smiled at the compliment.

At first Florence had not really cared for the characteristic snow-white rice, the pulaw (often listed on Western menus as pilaf), until one evening at table the Master heaped spoonful after spoonful on her plate and told her, 'Eat plentifully of this, because rice makes good milk.'

Florence, a nursing mother, felt at a later meal that she must apologize for her large appetite. In reply He referred to her maternal duties and the labors of being a mother and the nursing mother's need for more nourishment: if she neglected herself, she neglected the child. 'Virtue, excellence,' He continued, 'consist in having true faith in God, not in one's appetite or lack of it for food, or such-like matters. Jináb-i-Ṭáhirih had a robust appetite. When asked about it she would answer, "The Holy Traditions tell us that one of the attributes of the denizens of Heaven is that they 'continually partake of food'."' (According to Khan's gloss on this ḥadíth, its spiritual sense is this: when a man, through faith, is brought into the Paradise of the presence of God, he continually partakes of divine bounties and favors.)

The Master added that Persians eat frequently throughout the day, Ṭáhirih being an example. 'Yet she,' He said, 'delicately bred, highly learned, had the spiritual power to sit in a rough, jolting cart, and thus to be drawn through the streets of the city, and cursed and stoned.'

'When a man partakes of food', the Master said, 'it reinforces whatever mood or state of mind or condition he happens to be in at the time. If, for example, he is filled with love, eating increases his love. And on the contrary, if he is angry, the food intensifies his anger. Thus it is necessary that man should dwell only on the love of God. Then if he eats a little more food than may seem customary, no harm is done. But if he lacks the love of God, whether he eats little or much is all the same.'

Then 'Abdu'l-Bahá turned to Ḥájí Khurásání, who had been through a long period of mental and physical indisposition, and told him, 'The best cure for your illness is joy. Joy does more good to the sick than a thousand medicines. If you wish to heal a person who is ailing, bring joy to his heart.'

Honoring Ḥájí Khurásání, one night dinner was served in the large dining room at a long table covered with a snow-white cloth over which white petals of Indian jasmine were profusely scattered. In one corner of the room tall potted plants and flowering vines were banked, making the effect of a conservatory. Florence had been placed at the head of the table, the Master sat at her right, Khan across from Him at her left.

Of joy, the Master said on another occasion, 'If a man lives his life without joy, then death would be better. True happiness and joy come from composure of the heart, and this comes from faith. Praise be to God for giving us this repose of the heart. It is because of this that we are always happy. I beg of the Abhá Beauty that He will bless every one of his servants and handmaids with the joy that comes from certitude and composure of the heart (iṭmínán-i-qalb).'

He mentioned a believer of whom He said, 'She is very brave, very firm. She writes that, on a teaching trip, a band of children ran after her in the street, and called out insults and mocked and made fun of her. She said this gave her joy, because it befell her on the pathway of God.' Regarding this, 'Abdu'l-Bahá continued, 'In America, certain men will appear, wielding the power of religion, and they will rise up against the Cause and will try to keep the people from approaching this Truth. When this comes to pass, the Cause will advance, and among the believers there will be an increase of radiance and joy.'

Concerning the fact that blows, sufferings, afflictions endured by true believers make the Cause of God advance, He said in part: 'Paul and Peter, the Apostles, once entered a Greek city and began to teach the Truth. In that city was a temple which bore the inscription, "To the name of the Unknown God". Paul stood up and addressing the multitude, said, "We bring you tidings from this same Unknown God," and thus preached the message of Christ. A great number of Greeks who were present became interested in the Cause, and this aroused jealousy in the Jews, who began to make mischief. Stirred up by the agitators, the crowd charged the Apostles and beat them until they fell unconscious, then dragged their bodies along the road and threw them outside the city. Paul and Peter remained in a death-like coma all night. Early in the morning Paul came to himself and said to Peter, "There is going to be a fair in this neighborhood today, and it will attract many people. Let us step along and preach the Gospel there." Peter indicated their bruised and lacerated bodies. The two of them were at first too weak to move, but finally they rose and got themselves to the fair and preached. To sum it up, their afflictions had spread the Cause of Christ still further afield, removing them to a different place where they preached to new multitudes.'

Luncheon was usually served in the small room giving on the sea, a room next to the Master's reception room, and one which meant much to Khan because it was here he had toiled and lived so long.

The second day at luncheon Khan told of grieving over the death of Helen Ellis Cole (a cousin of May Maxwell's) and of how he had been remembering her and praying for her since arriving in 'Akká. The Master said, 'I was very much saddened by her death. She was very pure in spirit, very devoted and firm. She never fell short in serving the Cause. She did her utmost to help the friends. Therefore she was an honored handmaid of God and a child of the Kingdom.'

They were still at table when Rahim, the toddler, came in. 'Abdu'l-Bahá welcomed him most lovingly, and then gave him a piece of bread, with His blessing. Florence thanked the Master for the restful sleep she had been enjoying in the Holy Household. He said she had not yet rested enough but would experience real rest during her visit.

That afternoon He sent for Khan and asked for news of the Faith in various leading cities of America, including San Francisco. Khan spoke of the untiring labors of Mrs Goodall and her daughter, across the Bay in Oakland, and this rejoiced Him greatly. (The daughter, Ella Goodall Cooper, is the same who, in after years, provided for San Francisco's imposing Bahá'í Center in her mother's memory.)

The Bahá'í Publishing Society of Chicago had sent the Master a message, delivered by Khan, and regarding this He said, 'The Assemblies of Chicago, Washington and New York must be in agreement with each other as to their publications. When one of these Assemblies plans to publish, it should see to it that the Publishing Societies of the other cities are first notified, so as to forestall any occasion for inharmony.'

Of Hooper Harris's projected journey to India, the Master said: 'If Harris and [Howard] MacNutt travel to India together, this will be most useful for the Cause.'

FORTY-FOUR

Questions and Answers

On Wednesday, June 13, at luncheon, Florence asked 'Abdu'l-Bahá for the meaning of Christ's words, 'For he that hath, to him shall be given: and he that hath not, from him shall be taken even that which he hath.'[126]

'Abdu'l-Bahá answered in part, 'In a short and simple utterance, Christ has unraveled one of the great mysteries of God's wisdom. The meaning is this: in the world of existence, any pause or discontinuation of progress marks the beginning of a fall, a decline. For example, a bird thrusts upward into the air, it soars, it progresses, but no sooner does it arrest its flight than it begins to descend. Or take a merchant: as long as he lives on the income his capital provides, his business goes forward, but no sooner does he begin to use up his capital than a downward trend sets in and bankruptcy confronts him. That is why men of the business world often say of one who is living on his capital, "It is all over with him!"

'Very briefly, the words of Christ, "for he that hath, to him shall be given", signify this: to him that has a capital of truth and faith, and using this capital, lives up to the obedience which his faith requires, and communicates his faith to others by word and deed – to him an increase of truth and faith shall be given. Thus too, he who has any ability or capacity must continually strive to increase it, for otherwise his gift will deteriorate. Bahá'u'lláh has remarked that whenever a person has some art or craft, it is his duty to try and develop it to the point of perfection, even if that art be as humble as weaving a mat of coarse straw. For the Báb has said that the perfection of a thing is its paradise: that is, when a thing is developed to its highest possible point, it has reached its paradise, while failure to reach that point is its hell. One's failure to develop his ability would be like consuming his capital, and degenerating to the point where he fulfills in himself the words, "from him shall be taken even that which he hath".' This theme, that the responsibility to develop his talents rests on the individual, was a favorite of the Master's.

Florence mentioned a certain Christian denomination which seeks to heal physical ills and whose members feel that they live a better life than do other Christian communions. 'Do they have a special excellence,' she wanted to know, 'claiming as they do to surpass the rest in charity and good deeds – or are they simply like the many other new sects of Christianity?'

'Abdu'l-Bahá replied to this effect: 'Whatever good deeds are done by man in this world were originally taught him by the Prophets and Manifestations of God. Were it not for the teachings of the Prophets, man would have remained as heedless and neglectful as the brute beasts. If, for example, out of a thousand sheep, nine hundred and ninety-nine were butchered before the very eyes of the diminishing flock, the last sheep, quite unconcerned, would busily graze on.

'Materialistic philosophers tell us that they would perform good deeds in any case and therefore are in no need of a religion. They do not know that the very "good deeds" they claim to perform were originally taught by the Prophets of God. True excellence, then, consists in acknowledging the Holy Manifestations and living up to Their teachings. (For it is They Who set the standard of a truly good life and Who enable men to do good deeds.)[127]

'As to healing ills of the body and caring for the sick and poor: this is very good, but the result of it is not permanent. A man may be cured of one physical ailment, but will sooner or later be afflicted by another, and in the end he will be overtaken by death. The healing performed by the Holy Manifestations, however, is of the soul, and it is permanent: the life that They confer is a spiritual one and it keeps man alive forever.'

Florence asked, 'If we are associated with a group of people, or a family, who need help, and we try to assist them, but with no encouragement or cooperation from them, and we feel helpless to do more, should we keep on trying, or simply leave them and go about our business?'

The Master replied with a verse from the Qur'án: ' "God will not burden any soul beyond its power." '[128]

Again He was asked, 'If one feels grieved at one's failure to help others enough, while one has the desire and intention to help them more, what should one do?' 'Abdu'l-Bahá said in part: 'In this case, the fact that one had the will and the intention to help them is enough, for "God judgeth the deeds of men according to the intention behind them". An authentic tradition has come down from the Prophet Muḥammad which states: "A man's intent is better than his deed." That is, when a man, in his heart, desires to perform a righteous act, that intention cannot be anything but unalloyed, although selfish reasons may intrude in doing the deed. A man may perform a good deed in his own personal interest, and such a deed is not untinged by insincerity and deceit – but his intention, by itself, cannot be anything but good.

'Again, a man may have the desire to perform a righteous act, but not have the means to carry it out. He may wish, for example, to help the poor and succor the orphan. Such an intention will have its effect in the world of existence, and will be accepted in the Kingdom of God. And if he is enabled to carry out his intention, that will be "light upon light"[129] [i.e., doubly blessed].'

They asked the difference between sagacity and intelligence. The Master replied, 'Sagacity is a power which enables one to become cognizant of the existence of something by means of the outward senses, or to feel the presence of something by outward signs. For instance, a slight motion felt in a room can make one conscious that someone is on the roof, without, however, one's knowing who it may be. This is the limit of the knowing power of sagacity (dhakávat). Most animals have it, while human beings have it to a much lesser degree. If, during the night, someone enters your house by stealth, the man of the house may remain unconscious of it, while his dog will know it at once. Thus where instinct is concerned, the dog is more sagacious than his master, but the dog has no intellect, this being a gift peculiar to humankind. The intellect ('aql) is a power whereby man ponders a matter and from this derives tangible results.' (Elsewhere the Master has said that the intellect is a power by which man reasons from the part to the whole, or is consciously led from premise to conclusion.)

Of child training, He said, 'Among children, some grasp a thing quickly, while others take their time to arrive at a conclusion. The former are called intelligent and praised by some as being superior to the latter, who are laughed at and considered stupid. Often, however, a child of the second group, who seems slow, is gifted with a superior intellect, and therefore needs to ponder a thing before pronouncing judgment. He has less sagacity, less quickness of parts, than the other, but in real intellect, he is superior.'

They asked 'Abdu'l-Bahá about what is called the sixth sense, intuition or inner perception. 'Intuition', He said, 'is a power, or a light, by which a human being perceives the realities of things without the medium of the outward senses. To illustrate: there are four kinds of light: (1) the outward, phenomenal light, which makes things manifest or visible but does not discover them; (2) the light of the eye – eye-sight – which makes things visible and also discovers them, but does not comprehend them; (3) the light of the intellect or reason. This light makes things manifest, discovers them, comprehends them – but phenomena pre-exist it (that is, its own existence is subsequent to the creation of things); (4) the Light of God. This is the revealer of things, the discoverer of things, and the comprehender of things, and it both precedes the creation of all things and follows the creation of all things. As the Qur'án says, "God is the Light of the Heavens and of the Earth."[130]

'Briefly, that light which is the manifestor of things makes things visible; that light which is the discoverer of things discovers them; that light which is the comprehender of things grasps them. Furthermore, a human being's outward faculties and senses discover and perceive the appearance of things. But the light of intuition (or inner perception) is a light which comprehends the reality of things, the core of things. Intuition means the Divine Universal Reason, it comprehends supernatural phenomena and conditions which cannot be grasped by the outward senses.

'The Prophets and Divine Manifestations have taught that this sense of intuition, inner perception, or innate reason exists in man. Philosophers are also in accord with the Prophets in this – that is, to the degree of believing it possible that such a power may exist in man; for philosophers do not deny the existence of powers which are supernatural. But Prophets demonstrate the existence of this inner perception and intuition of humankind in a practical way. (That is, the Prophets prove the existence of inner perception by showing forth a comprehension beyond the powers of man. They also inspire Their disciples with, and develop in them, the same power.)'

Florence thanked Him for all His kindness and for the rest she was enjoying in His Household. He answered with great tenderness, 'We have done nothing for you. We have been able to do nothing worthy of mention. But we have love in our hearts and this is the main thing, and this is the important thing.'

FORTY-FIVE

Consider the Candle

In 'Akká, when Florence was seated at the Master's table in the small room which led from her living quarters, she could not see the military guard pacing up and down in front of some barrack-like buildings a little way from His house. Only when she stood and watched from either of the two windows could she see the guard. She would look from the heavily-barred windows and see the man pacing up and down and this would remind her that the Master – unbelievable for one of His demeanor – was a prisoner.

One day after lunch, when all had departed and only Florence, Khan and Manshádí were left, Manshádí said, standing by one of the open windows and breaking off a fragment of rust, 'Look at these bars! This family has to live in a climate which even eats into iron!' From the Writings then, he quoted, ' "Consider the candle, how it weeps its life away, drop by drop, that it may shed its light." '[131] And all three were deeply moved.

Another time, in one of the little vaulted hallways, Florence met the Master's wife and saw that she was pale and ill. Munírih Khánum had not had an easy life in the prison-city, and five of her children had died. Now she wept and said, 'Yes, they send us here to perish, like the flame in the lamp. Our lives go down, down – and all is over.' That evening the Master arranged for His wife to visit a relative in Tiberias, for a change and rest.

Together, the two had lived through those five deaths. We read in *Maḥmúd's Diary* that one day the Master said: 'I had a little son. When he was three or four, and I would be asleep, he would come and very gently, very softly, slip into bed beside me. It was an indescribable joy.'[132] A year or so later, the little boy was gone.

Once in the depths of the night, Florence was awakened by abysmal groaning. She listened. The sound was as if it came from one freely abandoning himself to a supposedly unheard sorrow.

'Never had I listened to such suffering, such grief. What should I do? Should I awaken Khan? Should I send for help?'

Then to her astonishment she recognized the voice of 'Abdu'l-Bahá.

She asked herself: 'What superhuman, not-to-be-borne grief was afflicting His radiant spirit? Who had hurt Him? Who had failed Him? What were the always-active enemies of the Faith conspiring still further to do?'

He went on sorrowing and grieving, and the wall between their room and His seemed very thin.

'It came to me, that awed as I was by such massive grief, perhaps I could understand it even so: 'Abdu'l-Bahá's tender heart, lacerated and bowed under, was bearing all the sufferings and sorrows, the sins and disobediences of all humankind.'

After a while the sounds quieted, and she slept.

One remembers an anecdote from a lecture by Rúḥíyyih Khánum, about a Christian woman named Lydia who came time and again complaining about her husband to 'Abdu'l-Bahá. One day He said to her, 'Lydia, Lydia, you cannot put up with this one man, and I have to put up with the whole human race.'

Each day of her thirty-three day pilgrimage, with one exception, Florence was invited by 'Abdu'l-Bahá to sit at the head of His table for lunch. This lunching with Him was not the rule. Most visiting ladies would have their midday meal with the ladies of the House.

'Bifarmáyíd!' He would tell her, bidding her be pleased to sit down, then taking the seat at her right and placing Khan at His right. Khan would translate for her, in a low voice, throughout the meal. (All were silent at table and only 'Abdu'l-Bahá would initiate the talk.)

One thing Florence especially mentioned in her copious notes was that 'Abdu'l-Bahá did not say grace, that is, never offered a vocal blessing, although sometimes at table she saw Him raise His eyes heavenward, His lips moving, as if in prayer.

She was also invited to join the others who gathered in the Master's presence at the late evening meal, served around nine or even ten.

Although she did not attend the men's evening meetings, she heard from Khan that the Master sometimes asked an aged, blind Muslim to chant on these occasions.

Florence did not know why she was placed at the head of the table. 'One reason may be', said Khan, 'that the Master wishes to teach Eastern men that a woman can be a lady even if she does not veil and is accustomed to the society of men. Another reason may be that He wishes them to observe the table manners of the West.'

At table, she sat by 'Abdu'l-Bahá with an ecstatic heart. 'Here I am,' she told herself in wonderment, 'seated as an honored guest at the table of Him Who is the King of all the Kings of this world, but is also a loving father and an exemplary host.' She studied Him, she wrote afterward, like someone dying of thirst in the desert – and, like a starving soul, gazed day after day, night after night, at that beautiful, worn and selfless face.

When all were seated, Bashír, the steward, would bring in a platter of food, offer it to 'Abdu'l-Bahá for His inspection, receive a nod of approval and wait for the Master to serve Himself. To Bashír's invariable disappointment, the Master would gesture toward Florence, meaning she was to be served first.

'How can I?' she would murmur to Khan, and he would say quietly, 'Obey!'

Sometimes, as if to please Bashír, the Master would serve Himself next, but mostly He would gesture toward the others and serve Himself last.

One hot mid-summer day, the centerpiece was passed around for dessert – a platter of fresh mulberries, over which fresh white jasmine blossoms had been scattered.

All the kindnesses and bounties 'Abdu'l-Bahá showered upon Florence were not, she was sure, due to any merit on her part; rather they came from His overflowing generosity, and because of His joy in this first Bahá'í marriage of East and West.

Bahá'ís who were present confirmed later what the Khans had already heard: that when the cable announcing the marriage reached the Master He clapped His hands and sent for sweets to be brought in, to celebrate.

Further evidence of this pleasure were the fourteen to sixteen Tablets from 'Abdu'l-Bahá, all connected with their Persian–American marriage, that he sent them in their early years together. He wrote that there would be many such marriages in future – but 'ye are the first!'

It is clear that what rejoiced Him, rather than the individuals concerned, was the symbol – the early beginnings of unity between East and West. If it had not been these two, it would have been two others.

In a Tablet He bestowed a Bahá'í name on their infant: 'Abdu'l-Husayn, the servant of Husayn (Bahá'u'lláh). The name of the little son of the Master's who died was Husayn.

Florence Khánum asked 'Abdu'l-Bahá about the training of children. 'Should the parents', she asked, 'train their children according to their own wishes and their own judgment, or should children be trained along lines for which they show a natural ability?'

'Abdu'l-Bahá replied: 'Parents must discover that calling or profession for which their children show the most aptitude and inclination, and then they must train them in the same, by engaging their attention in that direction – for sooner or later, a child will make known his natural abilities and gifts. To train his natural abilities in a manner conflicting with them is not right. It has often been seen that parents have forced their child to study in some field desired by them, for which the child himself had no natural aptitude. Then the child squandered years of his life in that field, making no progress whatever, showing that his abilities lay elsewhere.'

Asked as to the training of young children and whether it was allowable to punish them, 'Abdu'l-Bahá said, 'If by punishing is meant striking, no, this is very bad for the child. Children must be trained through love. If, however, the parents show them the utmost love without requiring good behavior of them in exchange, and thus make them feel that their parents will love them anyhow, no matter what they do – this will lead to disobedience and rebellion on the part of the child. For he will see that whether he behaves well or badly, his parents will still love him. A child must be treated in such a way that, even though he is sure of his parents' great love for him, he will be surer still that his parents love high human qualities and perfections even more than they love him. That is, they love him because of such qualities as godliness, faithfulness, truthfulness, devotion – qualities which he must show forth to justify their loving him. When the child sees that his parents love him more for his good qualities than simply for his own self, then he will try to obey his parents by developing those good qualities. For he will understand that by such means, his parents' love for him will grow, and that by neglecting such means, he will forfeit their increasing affection and love.

'If such a training method be neglected, the child will grow up discourteous, disobedient, untrained. [Some] do not train their children well, for when their children show no regard for desirable human traits and persist in disobeying, not only do the parents fail to reprimand or correct them, but they even feel displeased and resentful if other people remark on their children's undesirable behavior. Thus [these] children grow up disobedient and untrained. In brief, parents should so conduct themselves that the child will know they love his good character and his excellent qualities even more than they love him.

'But by no manner of means should the child be beaten. If the beating is meant to frighten the child, he really has no greater fear than that of offending his parents and losing their love through his bad conduct and disobedience. This feeling should be developed in children.'

The Master was then asked, 'How should little children such as ours – a year old – be trained?' 'Abdu'l-Bahá said: 'Children are of two kinds, those capable of distinguishing (tashkhís) and those incapable of distinguishing [right from wrong]. [Khan's explanatory note adds here: "Some are dull by nature, some not yet of an age to understand, and some are geniuses and discern a thing immediately."] Now this child is too young to have that power of discernment and his sense or feeling is not yet developed. He should therefore be allowed to remain as he is until he grows older and develops the capability for and adaptability to training.

'In training their children it is essential that parents should never tell them anything but the truth, and never try to cheat or soothe a child by some untrue statement or promise. For instance, if the parents wish to visit a garden and wish their child to stay at home, they should not try to deceive him by saying they are not going to a garden, but to the bath or some other place which he does not care about. No, if it is not advisable to take him along, they should tell him the truth: that they are on their way to a garden but that, because of this or the other justifiable reason, it is not permitted for him to go with them. For if the parents set out to visit a garden, and tell the child they are on the way to some other place – then when they come home with, by chance, roses or other flowers in their hands, the child will see this and understand he has been cheated and will thus learn not to believe what they say.

'In the same way, a child should not be frightened into good behavior by any talk of a wolf or other improbable terror, for once he observes that no wolf has showed up after all, he will know that his parents have not told him the truth. This will make him discount what they have to say, lessen his respect for them, and finally lead to his being ill-trained and exhibiting undesirable behavior.

'To sum it up, parents must so conduct themselves in front of their children that, both in words and acts, they will be a noble pattern for the children to follow.'

FORTY-SIX

Munavvar's Dream

Munavvar Khánum once told her, when Florence asked if she had ever had a revealing dream, that yes, she had. And she recounted a special dream which came when they were deep in mourning for Bahá'u'lláh, and the family was harassed from within by the Covenant-breakers, questioning the station of 'Abdu'l-Bahá, her father. One night in her dream she looked from outside into a garden and saw the Master walking there, with light all about Him, streaming from His heart. He approached, and in the center of His heart was the face of the Báb, shedding the unearthly light. He drew nearer still, and she saw the Báb's face replaced there in His heart by the face of the Ancient

Beauty. Then this, too, vanished and was replaced by the Master's. He smiled lovingly at her and she wakened and was at peace.

Writing of 'Abdu'l-Bahá's station – He not a Prophet but called by Bahá'u'lláh the 'Mystery of God', He the 'occupant of an office without peer or equal in the entire field of religious history'[133] – Shoghi Effendi says of the Master that He forms with the Báb and Bahá'u'lláh the 'Three Central Figures' of the Bahá'í Faith, 'towers, in conjunction with them, above the destinies of this infant Faith of God from a level to which no individual or body ministering to its needs after Him, for no less a period than a full thousand years, can ever hope to rise.'[134]

Looking back, now that almost a century had passed since 'Abdu'l-Bahá was appointed to head the Faith, one asks who else could have been the Head? How ever could the Faith have flourished under those schemers and plotters whose only aim in life was to annihilate 'Abdu'l-Bahá? As the Persians say, even if there were no gazelle, who would follow after the wolf? But in those awful days after Bahá'u'lláh left the world, hastened away to His 'other dominions whereon the eyes of the people of names have never fallen'[135] – time had not shed its light on the truth, and a 'crisis, misconceived as a schism', 'for no less than four years . . . fiercely agitated the minds and hearts of a vast proportion of the faithful . . .' and temporarily eclipsed 'the Orb of the Covenant . . .'[136]

So far as the world could see, 'Abdu'l-Bahá was cut off, bereft of power, virtually alone in 'Akká, with only His sister, wife, an aged uncle, and four daughters to keep Him company. The Covenant-breakers took over the mansion of Bahjí, and they would not even let the Master pray at His Father's Shrine, so that at times He could be seen standing out in the fields and performing His visitation from far away.[137]

The Covenant 'on which not only His own authority but the integrity of the Faith itself depended'[138] had been violated, but it held firm. This was the background of Munavvar Khánum's dream. 'Abdu'l-Bahá triumphed. Not long after the ascension of Bahá'u'lláh, He established the Cause in America, the 'Great Republic of the West', trained the American community over the years, and gave it the specific responsibility of carrying the Faith of Bahá'u'lláh around the globe. Through tests and trials, the American believers stayed fast. America, the Guardian told pilgrims, was 'the strong right arm', and a few years before the close of his supremely difficult life, Shoghi Effendi wrote: 'But for America's multitudinous services and unparalleled record of achievements my burden of cares both past and present would be unbearable.'[139]

Florence said that the questions asked of the Master, even by intellectuals, were 'as spoonfuls of water of that great ocean revealed by

Him – His wisdom that flowed as the eternal seas'. Having been so often among such people, and – especially in New York – among the creative, she had wondered why the humbler people, of no general culture, seemed to be of better character and more spiritually awakened, than a famous artist, perhaps, or a great actor. One day she ventured to ask 'Abdu'l-Bahá why this was. He told her, 'Consider the mole beneath the ground. He constructs galleries and tunnels there, he builds with faultless art, yet he is a creature who lives in darkness, under the earth, not able to bear the sunlight, not able to work in the sweet air.' 'Again,' He continued, 'look at the spider. What artist could create anything better made than a spider's web? Even so those artists whose creations are perfect, and who themselves are ignorant of the life of the spirit, are like the mole and the spider, far below the level of the man of faith.'

He told Florence that the turning toward God in thought, and a prayer-like appeal from the heart, is prayer, and is heard of God. Words are not necessary, the heart is enough. He was not referring here to the obligatory daily prayers, one of which is chosen by the believer to recite, nor other prayers revealed for special times – He meant that a prayer-like attitude of the heart is essential. (It is worth noting that a single prayer of Christ's has nourished Christianity for two thousand years, while in this Dispensation we have received hundreds, maybe thousands, of revealed prayers.)

One day 'Abdu'l-Bahá asked Rahim to run about the room, and gave him a piece of bread, telling him not to eat it. Rahim toddled over to Him, leaned one hand against Him, and looked up at Him in a long gaze, as though realizing the Master's beauty. 'How he looks at me!' 'Abdu'l-Bahá said. Rahim started to eat the bread, the Master scraped a piece for him and gave him the crust to chew.

Florence often thought of the petty as well as the great persecutions in 'Abdu'l-Bahá's prison life, of the countless fleas that infested 'Akká, which untiring cleanliness could not control. (A holy Muslim tradition says, 'I announce unto you a city, on the shores of the sea, white, whose whiteness is pleasing unto God – exalted be He! It is called 'Akká. He that hath been bitten by one of its fleas is better, in the estimation of God, than he who hath received a grievous blow in the path of God.'[140]) She thought of the climate that harassed Him and, from His enemies, of the ceaseless danger of death He was in, at no moment's notice.

At least with this renewal of His strict imprisonment inside the walls of 'Akká, reimposed August 20, 1901, He could no longer be exposed to the dangers of Haifa by night. Dr Yúnis Khán, who served the Master from 1900 to 1909 before he was sent to study medicine in Beirut, tells of how lawless were the night hours of Haifa. The Master would insist on making His rounds to the poor through those dark streets where shots so often rang out and no murderer was ever arrested. Sometimes, alone, He would not even take a lantern-bearer with Him, and believers would secretly watch over Him from a distance and finally see Him home.

One evening when Khan and other pilgrims were in the Master's holy presence, 'Abdu'l-Bahá said: 'Certain officials in this city have asked me to write out a petition for them to offer higher authorities to obtain my release from this captivity. I told them, "God forbid that I should write such a thing! This is far from what I would care to do." This imprisonment', He continued, 'is a rest for me. There is no hardship in it. God willing, by the grace of the Blessed Perfection, I must suffer great hardships and persecutions.'

He then proceeded to quote some verses from Bahá'u'lláh's beautiful poem 'Varqá'íyyih' (Nightingale Song), where He says: 'The mark of the irons is still to be seen on My throat, the scar of the fetters is plain to be seen on My limbs.'[141] The Master continued, 'When Bahá'u'lláh had such persecutions to bear, God forbid that we should look for anything but suffering, hardship and pain.'

Speaking of what He called 'the rest' given Him by His renewed captivity, and the many heavy responsibilities He had to shoulder before He was confined within 'Akká's walls, He said, 'When we were in Haifa, we had to endure many troubles. That is, much of our time was taken up with responsibilities that could not be avoided, such as the encounters with people from outside. But now I rest, and my outside occupations are not even one half what they were. How can I call this a prison? There are roses here, trees, plants, a view of the sea. Besides, it is necessary for a human being to bear hardships, because they train him for higher effectiveness. Ease and pleasure are fit for the lowest of the people. No one who has the smallest particle of faith in God looks for the least degree of ease and idleness. Were pleasure and ease and freedom from hardship to be accounted the highest goals of human life, no man could equal the cattle; for the richest, most honored man in the world is far surpassed, when it comes to peace and contentment, by a cow grazing on the side of a hill. The cow enjoys the whole pasture as her very own, while a man of means must wrestle with problems and overcome obstacles only to benefit others. A small bird, perched on the highest branch of a tree on a hilltop, enjoys a height and a sweeping view that kings might envy. It has no trials, no griefs. But its high-placed freedom is of no importance, while as for a man who gives up his ease and comfort to win great goals – such a one is free indeed.'

'Great is your blessing', the Master told Florence one day, 'that you live on earth at such a time as this, and that you have attained to 'Akká.

You are seeing what the Holy Prophets and saints have prayed down the ages to behold.' Sometimes at table He would break bread and give a portion to Khan, a portion to Florence. Sometimes He would take rice from His plate before eating and put it on their plates. And Florence would think to herself, 'Who is fed by the Master will never lack either spiritual or material food, in this world or the next.'

One day as she, veiled, hurried through the courtyard to join the ladies, already waiting for her in the carriage, she heard a voice calling, 'Khánum!' Through her veil she saw no one. Finally she raised the veil and saw Him standing at the head of the long flight of steps that led to His reception room. Since 'Abdu'l-Bahá obviously was calling for something, she decided to summon Khan, but the Master laughed and waved her on her way. Later, Khan told her that he had found 'Abdu'l-Bahá leaning against the wall at the top of the stairs and laughing heartily. To a man from the East, an American woman, ungainly in her chádur, can be as comical as a Westerner in drag. When the ladies were outside the city gates they put back their veils and enjoyed the countryside, the rolling plains and distant mountains, the fertile fields in the care of Arab farmers, fine agriculturists, getting rich yields. Once back in the 'Akká bazaar and market place, Florence noticed how delicately Khánum drew the veil across her face. 'The gesture was so patrician, recalling, as one forgets in the spiritual character and manner of these ladies, that there is no higher blood in Persia than flows through their veins. I wished all who erroneously think the women of the East are subservient, or inferior creatures, had been there to note the gesture's unconscious majesty.'

Eastern women pilgrims often sought to kiss the Greatest Holy Leaf, or others of the ladies, on the hand or the shoulder, offering homage, but were gently forbidden. The Aqdas forbids the kissing of hands, and apparently deep bowing was not favored by the Master. While each individual may rise through prayer and effort to great heights, and the Almighty will judge each one on his own merits, still all are not equal, and the American 'I am as good as you are' is hardly a Bahá'í concept – 'I am less than you are' is the Master's teaching. At the same time God does not desire the humiliation of His creatures (such as before priests), and obsequiousness is not called for.

It was on one of her outings with the ladies of the Household that Florence noticed how the poor and sorrowful would apply for help not only to 'Abdu'l-Bahá but to any member of His close family. One day in the Riḍván garden a Syrian Muslim girl, twelve years old, came weeping to Munavvar Khánum. She was an orphan and they had married her to a boy of seventeen who did not love her and who mistreated her. 'I must see what I can do,' Munavvar said. 'Perhaps I can find work for her in the Household.'

Usually, Florence's days were spent like this: first, morning prayers with the Family, later on luncheon with the Master, then her siesta, then, after tea, a drive to one of the Master's gardens outside the city in a four-seated covered wagon with three horses abreast and Isfandíyár cracking his long whip in the air and shouting the Arabic word 'Balak!' (give way) through the tortuous streets. Sometimes she and the ladies would walk about the Riḍván garden along the little winding river, have tea beneath the two giant mulberry trees, watch the small white marble fountain, its waters taking on a lily shape, and a flame burning at its heart, amid the flowers. There were peacocks, hens and pigeons at one end of the garden, and sometimes the visitors would sit in the little room there where Bahá'u'lláh Himself used to sit not many years before. Jasmine filled the air. Across the meadow was another garden, the Firdaws or Paradise, with many varieties of vegetables and fruits and the finest date palms, brought from Egypt. Then back to 'Akká, with lights in the bazaar and market place, and crowds of men at little tables in the open square drinking their tea and smoking their waterpipes. As the lights gleamed on their carriage, the ladies covered their faces again. Then home to the Master's house, where Florence would put Rahim to bed. Then the nine o'clock dinner in the presence of 'Abdu'l-Bahá, 'the Rose of all the world, the beating heart of all mankind'. And penetrating the days and nights were living memories, vivid reminders of what humanity had done with God's greatest bestowal, His Manifestation and proof. Once, returning from the drive, as they entered the winding way by the barracks where the Family were imprisoned two years (August 1868 – October 1870), the Master's wife touched Florence's arm and said, 'Up those stairs Bahá'u'lláh toiled in chains, bound like a common criminal.' Each time they passed the place, the ladies called Florence's attention to it, and she too would shudder at the thought of its inner horrors, its squalor, gloom and filth.

One morning when Khan was in the Master's presence with the other pilgrims, a believer came in from a neighboring town. 'Abdu'l-Bahá asked him about a certain Turkish official. He said that this official was now in prison and closely guarded by four soldiers; that he was not allowed to see or converse with anyone. Turning to the pilgrims, 'Abdu'l-Bahá said: 'See how, for the sake of a trifling gain, people will subject themselves to terrible difficulties and afflictions, though it brings them no result or benefit whatever. This is what comes of exerting oneself to gain the things of this world. But such is not the case with the Cause of God – for whoever takes even one step, or bears the least hardship for the sake of God, that step, that hardship, will never be lost or prove fruitless. Consider how many people in this world have sacrificed life and property and sacrificed their families to bondage and captivity! But as they did not endure these things on the path of God, they profited in no way, nor were their names praised or even mentioned among men. Then consider Ḥusayn who suffered martyrdom for the sake of God. His enemies even refused him water to drink. His family were taken prisoner. But his very cry for water as he died reached out so far that even now it rings in the ears of millions, all because he met his death for God. On the other hand, look at the war between Japan and Russia: about one million people died during that war, either in actual battle or from disease or from exhaustion on the mountain slopes and in desert wastes. There were many men of fame and glory among them, but no word of them is ever heard. Yet when one single individual is martyred for the Cause of God, and gives up his family and his possessions, the memory of him will continue for all time, because he suffered for a Cause that cannot die, he bore his pain for a purpose that was of God.'

On the same theme, 'Abdu'l-Bahá continued: 'When we were in Tehran, Mírzá Áqá Khán of Núr was the Prime Minister, and the Núrí family held high positions and enjoyed official honors and were distinguished among men. A little while passed, and that court of glory was shut down, and it became the turn of Amínu'd-Dawlih of Káshán to be named Prime Minister. His carpet was also folded up and his time ended. The reins of affairs were then given into the hands of Mírzá Ḥusayn Khán, "The Commander in Chief". He too passed on and was no more. Then Mustawfíyu'l-Mamálik became the Premier. He went on by and his times changed. Then the Premier was Amínu's-Sulṭán [the Atábak]. He too passed by, his glory was as a carpet folded away. [Khan adds here that when these prophetic words were spoken, Amínu's-Sulṭán was in Europe, virtually certain of reappointment. A year from then, in 1907, he was recalled to Tehran and reappointed Prime Minister, but he was assassinated in the same year. Hence these words of 'Abdu'l-Bahá described an event that had not yet taken place.]

'Briefly, all these things transpired. Men came and men went by. But during all these many transformations and changes in Persia, we have continued here, always in the same condition, occupied with our own affairs, suffering no change in our position. And this, because our whole interest is confined to the Cause of God, and we have no attachment to the things of this world.'

Then reverting to the Turkish official, He said: 'This official suffered imprisonment and all these other hardships for the sole reason that he had a salary of one thousand piastres and he wished to raise it to fifteen hundred.'

In the evening at dinner, 'Abdu'l-Bahá asked about Hooper Harris.

Khan spoke highly of him, his eloquence, his services to the Cause. 'Abdu'l-Bahá was very pleased and said in part: 'Observe that Mírzá Muḥammad-'Alí has claimed that Áqá [the Master] put an end to the Cause of God and wiped it out! Judge for yourself whether I – who have made the Cause of the Blessed Perfection to reach both East and West until many devoted and eloquent souls such as Mr Harris have appeared therein – have obliterated the Cause, or whether Mírzá Muḥammad-'Alí has, he having done so much harm by rising against me!'

Again He said, 'That Bahá'u'lláh appointed me to be the Center of His Covenant was not because I was His son. No, I swear by His Holy Spirit, had He found a native of Zanzibar more capable than I, He would have appointed him in preference to me! Mírzá Muḥammad-'Alí did his utmost to have me exiled from 'Akká, in the vain hope that with me being absent the believers would follow him, or that he would be safe. He is too heedless to understand that if my life is put an end to, a terrible calamity would then come upon him.'

When this conversation took place, in 1906, 'Abdu'l-Bahá would soon be facing a time so dark that, as the Guardian writes in *God Passes By*, 'even some of the poor . . . forsook Him . . .'[142]. A Commission would arrive in 'Akká, early in 1907, sent by the Sulṭán to determine 'Abdu'l-Bahá's fate.

The renewal of His strict incarceration was brought on by the plottings of the Covenant-breakers and began in August, 1901, that same summer when Mírzá Abu'l-Faḍl and Khan arrived in America. The Master was interrogated for days by the Turkish authorities, and one of the his 'first acts was to intercede on behalf of His brothers'[143] who were also strictly confined within 'Akká's walls. His enemy kindred were not appeased however. They could never forgive the difference between His enchanting qualities and their own hideous selves. They continued their plottings, lying reports, bribery of officials, affirmations that Bahá'u'lláh's Covenant concerned not humanity but the family's own 'private interests'.[144] Their hatred of His perfections was unslakable. To a paranoid Sultan they sent word that 'Abdu'l-Bahá was constructing a fortress and vast ammunition depot on Mount Carmel, had raised an army of 30,000 men, and, with English and American help, was planning to seize power from the Sultan himself.[145] It was this that prompted the Sultan to send his Commission to 'Akká.

'Abdu'l-Bahá continued that evening: 'Mírzá Muḥammad-'Alí went so far as to plan an attempt on my life. Directly from here, he sent Jamál to Tehran. He called on the Turkish Ambassador there, and told him: "I have lived for years in Turkish countries and enjoyed the blessings of peace and freedom under the Ottoman Government. As a result, I have become a well-wisher of Turkey, and to express my gratitude to your authorities, I feel it my duty to inform you of something which is a threat to the security of your nation." And so on.

'Then he told the Ambassador: "Abbás Effendi has brought the British into 'Akká, and he has it in mind to turn Syria over to Great Britain, and he is collaborating with the Sultan's foes, the Party of the Young Turks." And so on, and so forth.

'Briefly, by these falsehoods, Jamál stirred up such sedition and made such misrepresentations that it seemed very difficult either to explain or counter them. Finally, to prove their utter falsity, Jináb-i-'Ádilih [one of the venerable Bahá'í teachers in Tehran] gave a copy of the Book of Aqdas to the Turkish Ambassador to see the truth for himself. We too sent directly to the confidants of the Sultan two hundred and fifty petitions, letters received by us from the American Bahá'ís, for his consideration. Thus it was made clear to him that our work is wholly of a spiritual nature and our mission spiritual, and the charges bore no relation to the facts; that by the commandment of Bahá'u'lláh we are obedient to government and have nothing to do with revolutionary acts.'

Referring to Mírzá Muhammad-'Alí's two trips to India for hostile purposes during the lifetime of Bahá'u'lláh, when even at that time he tried to form a party with Názir's help (Názir being a breaker of the Covenant) to work against the Covenant, the Master said, 'I swear by His Holy Spirit that one day Bahá'u'lláh called me to Him and said, "Áqá! Áqá! [Master! Master!] See how limited is the intelligence of your brother, when a man like this Názir has managed to lead him twice to India and then bring him back."'

FORTY-SEVEN

The Lure of Leadership

The plottings of Muhammad-'Alí and Názir, referred to here, were aimed at preparing the way for leadership of the Faith after the departure of Bahá'u'lláh. The Manifestation knew of all this only too well, as is proved by numerous Tablets, and especially by His revealing the 'Book of My Covenant', in which He clearly appoints 'Abdu'l-Bahá as the One to Whom, following His own passing, all without exception should turn.

Another morning, among various topics, the Master spoke of Bahá'í consultation and said: 'Taking a vote is a practical means for settling a matter under consideration, especially because those consulting together may naturally advance opinions that differ.' He then dwelt at length upon the subject of the House of Justice, and spoke to this effect: 'The House of Justice is so mighty an institution that no one shall have the right to resist or oppose it. By this is meant the Universal House of Justice . . . for such a House of Justice shall be under the protection and infallibility of the Blessed Perfection, and favored by His confirmations.'

Khan's note here refers to Bahá'u'lláh's Tablet of Infallibility, where He speaks of the infallibility of the Manifestations of God and Their authority to do as They will, They being Manifestations of the Almighty, Who is the possessor of omnipotence and unquestioned authority. He adds that Bahá'u'lláh has conferred this absolute authority on the Universal House of Justice, for it is an institution which safeguards the order and unity of the world and the peace of society, and it would fall short of this vital function were its authority to be called into question. Khan now asked about the infallibility, and whether this referred to the power of the Universal House.

The Master said, 'Infallibility is of two kinds: (1) intrinsic [belonging to the essential nature of a thing] or immediate infallibility; (2) conferred, extrinsic [not inherent] or mediate infallibility. Intrinsic or immediate infallibility means that of God, exalted is His glory, and none else save Him has any portion thereof. He is the doer of that which He willeth. And His infallibility is confined to His universal Manifestations Who appear at the head of each great cycle.

'The conferred, extrinsic or mediate infallibility is that of those holy souls who are under the protection of the divine Manifestations, for preservation from error is conferred upon souls as a pure bestowal of God. God's infallibility is intrinsic, whereas that of the holy souls under the protection of His Manifestations is extrinsic, for it is acquired as a gift or quality from Them. For instance, the light of the sun is intrinsic or immediate, but the light of the planets is acquired from the sun, and is therefore extrinsic. The light of the sun is independent of the planet, whereas that of the planet is dependent upon the light of the sun. To put it briefly, God will raise up pure, righteous and sincere beings for the House of Justice, who will be under His protection, and the decrees of the House of Justice shall be effective in all matters not specifically "provided for in the Book".'

Asked as to the sex of the membership of the Universal House, 'Abdu'l-Bahá answered, 'The members of the Universal House shall be all men.' Asked if they will be nine in number, He said, 'The membership is not limited to nine. No, nine is the minimum number and it will gradually be increased nine by nine. For instance, it will be raised to numbers which are multiples of the number nine, such as eighty-one which is equal to nine times nine, and so forth.'

One day the Master, speaking of the early stages of the Cause in

America, told them: 'That which always brings about inharmony and slows the progress of the Faith is self-interest, the love of leadership. Those who have such tendencies imagine that they can be concealed from the others. They do not understand that, sooner or later, whatever your qualities may be, praiseworthy or objectionable, they cannot possibly not become known to the rest. If hidden today, the quality will be exposed tomorrow. And if an individual does not possess a certain good quality, he cannot persuade others that he has it, simply by dint of proclaiming that he has.

'What favors the progress of a soul is humility, meekness, selflessness. Every individual must suppose every other to be gifted in a way which he himself is not, to have some gift of which he is deprived. This will put each one in a position of lowliness relative to the others. One must not think of becoming a leader of men. If one imagines that he has this or that excellent quality, and has superior powers not possessed by the others, this will fill him with pride. But when each regards the next person as having excellent gifts, and therefore defers to him, by this means each and all will be humble, and the love of leadership will vanish away. This will conduce to the progress of each individual and of the Cause of God. But the one who lives to lead will suffer deprivation in the end, and will never succeed in serving the Cause.

'For example, every one in Persia, writing to us, praises Mírzá Ḥaydar-'Alí, but all the letters used to complain of Jamál. The reason was that Ḥaydar-'Alí was always deferential and humble. He has been very successful as a servant of the Faith and all the believers love him. But Jamál was disliked because of his arrogance, and you see what happened to him in the end.

'Briefly, every one of the believers, when mentioning another, must speak highly of him. On a certain occasion the believers asked Siyyid Yaḥyá of Dáráb [the great Vaḥíd, chosen envoy from Muḥammad Sháh to the Báb] as to the character of the Bábu'l-Báb [Mullá Ḥusayn, the first to believe in the Báb]. His answer was, "Oh, would that I were worth one hair of his head!" This was the degree of Vaḥíd's humility, although his rank in the world was so high that whenever he was to arrive in Tehran, over thirty thousand mullás, grandees and others would go out of the city to meet him and respectfully escort him in.

'On another occasion, Mullá Ḥusayn was asked about Vaḥíd and he replied, "I am of less worth than the dust he treads on." Briefly, this is what is meant by humility, and it is the noblest attribute of the people of faith.

'One evening Quddús [eighteenth Letter of the Living, who led the Bábís at Fort Ṭabarsí] went to the house of Mullá Ḥusayn. Ḥaḍrat-i-

Quddús was not known then as a man of rank and authority, being regarded only as a student of religion. Mullá Husayn was occupying the highest seat in the room, and Quddús sat down near the door. During that night the two had a long conversation, and the high degree of knowledge possessed by Quddús became known to the host. On the following morning, when guests of the day before again sought the presence of Mullá Husayn, they found that a great change had taken place: there in the seat of honor was the young student, while before him in all humility stood Mullá Husayn.

'To sum it up: the basic thing in the Cause of God is humility, meekness, service, not leadership. I remember that once when I was a small child, Jináb-i-Táhirih was holding me in her arms, while Siyyid Yahyá, Vahíd, was outside the door. He was a man of high endowments and vast erudition. He knew thirty thousand holy Traditions by heart, and would demonstrate the Báb's Advent by quoting from the Qur'án. To him Táhirih said, "Oh, Jináb-i-Siyyid, if you are a man of high deeds, perform a deed!" This statement of hers so influenced the Siyyid that he immediately turned humble. It dawned on him that the matter at hand was another matter altogether, that one had not only to demonstrate the truth of the Báb's claim, but to offer up one's life to spread His teachings. He set out, traveled and taught from city to city, and in the end suffered martyrdom.'

FORTY-EIGHT
Bibliomancy

One day in 'Abdu'l-Bahá's holy presence, Khan spoke of various American Bahá'ís like Marie Watson – who, in spite of being physically handicapped and almost without funds, rendered services that astonished the rest.

The Master said, 'This is one of the conditions for a teacher of the truth: he must be severed from the world, so that his words will influence his hearers to such a degree that even if they do not become believers and accept the truth, they will be moved by his sincerity and devotion, and acknowledge the fact that he has no attachment whatsoever to the world, and that his one and only goal is truth.'

To illustrate, 'Abdu'l-Bahá continued: 'During the years at Baghdad, word came that Mírzá Yahyá Khán, Governor of Mázindarán, nephew of the Prime Minister [Mírzá Áqá Khán of Núr] had come on pilgrimage to the Shrines of Karbilá and Najaf, and was now at Kázimayn [a city about three miles from Baghdad, where two of the holy Imáms are buried]. Because of a former acquaintance with him, the Blessed Perfection bade me go and call upon him.

'When I arrived at his house, I found that Siyyid Ibráhím of Iṣfáhán, a Muslim mujtahid, was with him, and they were conversing together on various subjects. Among other things, the mujtahid asked the Khán where he was going. He answered, "Najaf" [the tomb of 'Alí]. "Oh, no!" said the mujtahid. "Now that you have come this far, you should go on to Mecca as well, and take me along on your pilgrimage to that sacred Spot."

' "I have to be back in Persia soon," the Khán told him. "Much work awaits me there, I have to be back within three or four months. However," he said, "once I return and see to my affairs, God willing I will set out on the Mecca pilgrimage the following year." The mujtahid persisted, and said that many a would-be Mecca pilgrim had come this far, and gone home in the hope of making his pilgrimage at some future date, and died, or other circumstances had prevented his ever visiting the House of God.

'Briefly, the mujtahid finally succeeded in persuading the Khán to consult the Qur'án. [Called bibliomancy, this means opening a page of Scripture at random and taking guidance from the verse your eye falls upon.]

'The Khán sent for a Qur'án. The mujtahid, first performing the requisite ablution of face and hands before touching the holy Book, took it and opened it. To his utter amazement, the verse at the top of the page, on which the decision depended, seriously advised against the proposed undertaking.

'For a quarter of an hour, the mujtahid sat silent, lost in thought. He did not know what to say or do. Finally he said the verse was subject to a different interpretation, and he explained it in such a way as to constitute an absolute command.

'The Khán protested, astonished at the liberty the mujtahid was taking with the sacred verse. The mujtahid, intent on proving his point, offered an example, and began: "When Siyyid 'Alí-Muḥammad the Báb . . ." No sooner did he say "the Báb" than the Khán realized the mujtahid did not know me, and might offend me if he were allowed to go on, and might speak against the Cause. To avoid any awkwardness, the Khán kept trying to gesture to the mujtahid so as to stop him. But I fastened my eyes on the Khán, thus preventing him from making his gesture without my noticing it, because I wanted to hear what the mujtahid was going to say about the Báb.

'Therefore the host sat motionless, and the mujtahid went on: "When the Báb appeared and his followers were on their way to the fortress of Shaykh Ṭabarsí, there was a man in Karbilá called Ḥájí Muḥammad-Taqí of Kirmán who was also one of the Báb's followers, but he was a man of noble character, and had all the high attributes of the people of Faith. That is, he was well known for his loyalty, rectitude, trustworthiness, sincerity, generosity, charity, and obedience to the Laws of God. He was also a man of wealth and unstintingly provided funds to poor students of religion. In short, he led a perfect life, and no one could find a flaw in him. But alas! Such an excellent soul was a Bábí, and was determined to go and join his co-religionists at Fort Ṭabarsí.

' "The Muslim doctors and mullás in Karbilá did their utmost to save him from the error of following the Cause of the Báb and returning to Persia. He responded with many a proof of the Báb's claim and held to his purpose of going back home and helping the others. The mullás, attempting to save his soul, tried in vain to show him how ignorant he was, and how mistaken. Finally they prevailed upon him to accompany them to the Shrine of Imám Ḥusayn, stand with all humility before the Imám's tomb, and after earnest prayer, to open the sacred Book and ask for guidance.

' "They all agreed that if the verse included a command, the believer could be sure of the rightfulness of his Cause and depart on his journey, without any more interference from them.

' "Well, to make a long story short, at dawn a body of mullás, along with the believer, proceeded to the holy Shrine. After chanting the Visitation Tablet and performing the morning prayer, they expressed this wish: 'O holy Imám, we pray thee to make clear to us, through the verse in this sacred Volume which we are about to consult, whether this Báb is in error, or whether his claim is true, and sanctioned by God.'

' "Then they reverently took up the Qur'án and they opened it, and this was the verse they found: 'And whoso turneth away from My remembrance [Dhikr, a title of the Báb], truly his shall be a life of misery.'[146]

' "The mullás were astounded, for they all knew that the Báb had declared Himself to be the Dhikr, the Remembrance of God.[147] [Furthermore, many commentators of the Qur'án had taken this verse as a clear reference to the Manifestation of the Qá'im, He Who ariseth, the Promised One of Islam.]

' "There was an uproar. Terribly agitated, they wondered what to do next. Finally they attempted an interpretation. They said, 'Verses of the Qur'án are of two kinds: Perspicuous Verses and Ambiguous Verses. Now this verse is not to be taken in its literal sense. Rather, we should interpret the word Dhikr to mean the holy Faith of Muḥammad, and not as a reference to the Báb.' "

'The mujtahid resumed: "In short, the verse only reinforced the Bábí's conviction, he would not hear of any other interpretation, and set out for Persia to join the rest at Ṭabarsí. But he never got there. He no sooner arrived in Tehran than they arrested him and put him to death for being a Bábí."

'I turned to the mujtahid and said, "Oh eminent Sir! What is your authority for considering this verse Ambiguous, and to require interpretation? Do you not know that the authoritative commentators of both the Shiah and Sunní Schools have named it Perspicuous?"

'He replied, haughtily, "We have the authority and the right to interpret the verse as Ambiguous, and we also have the right to interpret as such this present verse referring to the Khán's pilgrimage to Mecca."

'I told him: "You are clearly wrong in your interpretation of both these verses. For by Ambiguous verses is meant those whose literal meaning is not in accordance with the fundamental principles of the Law, and which therefore are liable to symbolic interpretation. By Perspicuous verses is meant those whose literal sense is plainly in accord with the general laws and basic rules of the Faith. And these are to be taken literally."

'Sometime later this same mujtahid, Siyyid Ibráhím, attained to the presence of the Blessed Perfection. In later years I heard Siyyid Muḥammad of Iṣfáhán say that this Siyyid Ibráhím, in Karbilá, finally became devoted to the Faith. For Siyyid Muḥammad called upon him, and the mujtahid had returned the call and expressed to him the love he cherished for this Truth.

'This illustrates the fact that even though the mujtahid considered Muḥammad-Taqí a man in error as to his religion, still he bore witness to the latter's noble character and way of life. Thus must the Bahá'ís live such a perfect life amongst men, that even those who refuse to see or accept this Truth will be impressed by how they live.'

FORTY-NINE

Always the Cause Goes Forward

One night at dinner 'Abdu'l-Bahá spoke of Florence with joy, saying she was blessed with great faith. In emphatic tones, He testified to her faithfulness and certitude, and concluded His remarks by saying, 'This is what faith means! This is nothing but true faith! She is indeed possessed of perfect certitude! She shall indeed rest, she shall indeed enjoy perfect peace.'

In after years, this statement of the Master's would remind one of Florence's daughters of the Qur'án verses: 'O thou soul which art at rest. Return unto thy Lord, pleased, and pleasing Him.'[148] 'This day shall their truth advantage the truthful. Gardens shall they have 'neath which the rivers flow, and remain therein for ever: God is well pleased with them and they with him.'[149]

Speaking at length of true faith, 'Abdu'l-Bahá said, 'When a man has faith, all the mountains of the world cannot turn him back. No, he will endure any trial, any disaster, and nothing will weaken him. But one who is not a true believer, one who lacks real faith, will lament over the least disappointment, and cry out against the slightest thing which mars his peace and pleasure.

'When, in company with the Blessed Beauty, we arrived as exiles in Constantinople, we were filled with joy, our minds were completely at peace. Then, removed to Adrianople, we continued on with that same spirit in our new place of exile. None of us had any complaints, except for three persons: Mírzá Yaḥyá, extremely depressed and confused; Siyyid Muḥammad of Iṣfáhán; and Ḥájí Mírzá Aḥmad of Káshán. [All three later denied Bahá'u'lláh. Mírzá Yaḥyá, the Manifestation's half-brother, became the creature of Siyyid Muḥammad, who was 'the Antichrist of the Bahá'í Revelation.'[150]] These three complained of the hardships the whole time and bothered the believers. At least Mírzá Yaḥyá and Siyyid Muḥammad did not openly complain to the others – they simply went about looking sullen and miserable, their faces showed dissatisfaction, they were lost in their gloom. But Mírzá Aḥmad, even though he was a brother of Jináb-i-Dhabíḥ [one of the great Bahá'í martyrs], continually troubled the believers with his ill temper. He complained of how violently cold the winter was, how harsh the frost and snow, and would bitterly and often repeat: "I said many a time in Baghdad that Shaykh 'Abdu'l-Ḥusayn the mujtahid was busy making trouble for us, in company with the Persian Consul, and I warned that they were working to get us exiled, but nobody would listen. Now as you all see, they succeeded in having us banished to this wretched place, and inflicted these terrible calamities on us in this cold country. And now we, God's faithful servants, are subjected to all these trials!" And so on, and so on.

'Briefly, he continually found fault with everything, and showed such irritability, that several times the believers were so provoked that they wanted to give him a good thrashing in the hope that he would go away. Each time I stopped them. But the rest of us, over fifteen in number and all living in the same one room, were perfectly at peace and happy. To pass the time, each day one of us would cook a dish for the others to enjoy. And so the harsh winter with all its snow and cold passed by and that well-known enchanting springtime of Rumelia came on. The weather was now so delectable that even Mírzá Aḥmad began to praise the region for its glorious air.

'In short, he had no faith, and that is why he found the winter unbearable and could not control his lamentations and wait until fine weather should take over from the cold.

'Now this is the difference between one with faith and one without. A man of faith bears every trial, every hardship, with self-control and patience. One without faith is always wailing, lamenting, carrying on. He cannot endure hardship, he never thinks of better times coming that will take the place of present ills.'

At this point in his pilgrim notes Khan added that he and Florence often remembered these, to them, prophetic words during her long, life-and-death illness in Tehran, soon to come.

During their pilgrimage they met a Zoroastrian Bahá'í from India named Mihrabán, a powerful, athletic young man. One day on his way to the Garden of Riḍván with other pilgrims, he and a Bahá'í Siyyid from Persia started to wrestle with each other. The Zoroastrian underestimated the other and the match, begun as a joke, ended up with the Zoroastrian suffering a broken leg. As a result he was obliged to stay on a number of weeks in 'Akká till the bone healed. When Khan and Florence arrived he was just beginning to get around on crutches, and every day he and the other pilgrims would come to the house of 'Abdu'l-Bahá. He was very happy over his broken leg, because it allowed him to stay so long in 'Akká. Besides, 'Abdu'l-Bahá Himself would often visit him at the traveler's hospice and ask about his health.

One evening, with others including the young Zoroastrian, Khan was in the holy presence of the Master. 'Abdu'l-Bahá spoke of Mihrabán and how much severe physical suffering he had been through, and yet what great happiness his broken leg had brought him, letting him stay in the holy city so long.

'Many a time', 'Abdu'l-Bahá continued, 'a calamity leads to a bounty. Not until a man has endured hardship on account of a thing will he appreciate the full value of that thing. The more one suffers because of something or other, the better will one understand the worth of it. As the Qur'án says: "Never will they attain (unto Divine bounty), except through severe trials." The more you search down in the earth, the deeper you dig into its breast with the plough, the more fruitful will it become. For the people of faith, trials and disasters and tribulations lead to spiritual progress, that is, if one bears them with patience and detachment from all save God. It is said in the Qur'án: "Think ye to enter Paradise, when no such things have come upon you, as on those who flourish before you? Ills and troubles tried them . . ."[151] Man can never be intoxicated, unless he drink of these. Never can he feel the bliss of those who are drunk with the wine of loving God, unless he too has a draught from calamity's cup. The more you beat upon the steel, the sharper is your sword. The longer you leave the gold in red-hot fire, the purer will it be.

'Even among the people of the world, busy with their material pursuits, tests and trials play the same part. The more a man struggles, the more trials he bears in learning a profession or craft, the more skillful and adept he becomes. One whose days are leisurely and inactive never becomes proficient in anything.

'A great general told us this story: "When I was still a youth, unversed in the arts of war, I, in company with other young officers, led an army corps to battle. We had no sooner met the enemy when we lost our wits, and knowing nothing of combat, turned tail and fled. Running for our lives, we met a band of veterans, scarred by many wars. 'Oh our officers,' they cried. 'Where are you off to? You, our generals and our leaders? Go back! Command us to charge the enemy, and we will obey you, and the day will be ours!' We took heart, went back, led our troops into battle, and won." See how tried and experienced soldiers put new life into their generals. This is the wisdom of tests and trials, the advantage of having borne hardships and afflictions. Calamities, griefs, advance a true believer to high stations. We must value afflictions and wish for whatever may befall us on the pathway of God. In one of His supplications, His Holiness the Exalted One, the Báb, has written [addressing Him Whom God would make manifest], "Were it not to bear afflictions on the pathway of love, I would never have consented to be born into this world." This is how precious are trials on the Divine path.'

One evening 'Abdu'l-Bahá was in the little garden outside the house. A number of pilgrims were present. He called attention to the trees and flowers He had planted. 'This was a hateful place,' He said, 'nothing but refuse and dirt.' Referring to the previous year, He continued, 'When 'Akká was in turmoil and there was a whirlwind of tests, and the persistent rumor was that we were to be exiled to a distant country, we kept busy laying out this garden and planting these trees and flowers. See how delightful it is now! How surprising is the claim of some, that life requires no trainer or educator! Were it not for the direct results of care and training, this place would still be a heap of rubbish.' Followed by them all, He walked toward the house.

In the sitting-room downstairs He continued: 'When obstacles stopped us on all sides and calamities hemmed us in, we started building the Báb's holy Tomb on Mount Carmel. We also saw to the much-needed repair and restoration of other places. The sacred House of the Báb in Shíráz was in urgent need of repairs, but the people of that city were so violently opposed to the Cause and made trouble to such a degree that the believers could not even walk down the street where the House is situated – much less go to work on repairing it. So aggressively did the populace rise up against the Bahá'ís that even the Governor was unable to control them. He finally declared that nothing could be done and that in order to save themselves the Bahá'ís should leave the city. Such was the news that reached us at the time from S͟híráz. We notified them to ignore the statement and repair the sacred House at once. "Go and build it up", we wrote, "and let them come right back and tear it down again."

'Well, they started work on the repairs, and by God's providence no one interfered or said a word against what they were doing, whereas the believers had thought, naturally enough, that no sooner would they lay a single brick than the people would carry it off. All the repairs were made.

'Furthermore, during the confusion and agitation in 'Akká, we arranged the weddings of some of the Bahá'ís in the city, and held feasts to celebrate them. Those involved shed tears, and protested. They said, "This is no time for weddings." But we insisted that a period of turmoil and trouble made those wedding festivities essential. And indeed God worked wonders and poured out grace. For those times were very hard to bear. What an astonishing tempest that was! What gigantic waves! God does His work of protection when we need it most. Events of this kind are the means whereby He carries out His plans. Sometimes a stupendous calamity, unforeseen, comes from means intended to produce calm and peace – sometimes calamity brings on tranquillity and repose. Confusion precedes composure, destruction leads to rebuilding.

'When 'Alí-Áqá was about to sail from Haifa, the Governor ordered his effects returned to the city and forbade him to leave. This was very strange. The Governor then had them go through and minutely examine all his belongings. The only thing they found to object to was a sheet of paper bearing the words "Yá Bahá'u'l-Abhá". They confiscated this, as if he should not be allowed to have it in his possession. The Consul lodged a protest with the Governor for this kind of treatment of a foreign subject, stating that the Bahá'ís were Persian nationals and entitled to the same good treatment as other foreigners. The Governor replied that the Bahá'ís were not to be classed with other foreign subjects, that they were hated by the Persian Government, and it was not advisable for him, the Persian Consul, to make a protest on their behalf.

'But see the power of God! Some time afterward, this very Governor fell upon evil days and had none to assist him. Overlooking what he had done to the Bahá'ís, I showed him kindness and also gave him an 'abá for a present. I treated him with such affection that he decided that I had been completely unaware of what he did to the Bahá'ís during his days in office. He imagined that he had used such skillful diplomacy in making mischief against us that all had remained concealed. How, otherwise, could he account for my treating him as a friend, showing him kindness during his days of trouble?

'To be brief, when he was arrested for personal reasons, and jailed by order of the Government, and no one dared go near him, I expressed sympathy by sending him word that I would have called on him in person, had I not thought that his enemies would use my visit to do him further harm.

'The truth is, nothing is sweeter for a man than doing good to someone who has done evil to him. Whenever he remembers having been kind to his enemies, his heart will rejoice. In brief, I showed kindness to every one of the officials who, during those days of trouble, had treated the friends badly. This was such a surprise to them that they imagined me to be ignorant of what they had done. I never showed the slightest sign that I was well aware of it, so as not to embarrass them and make them feel ashamed.

'If men had a sense of justice, when they observe that even during such periods of awful turmoil and with so many obstacles raised against it, still the Cause of God continues on its steady forward course – they would acknowledge its truth. God be praised, in Persia, in the very midst of agonizing persecutions, still the Cause of God continued to advance. But I did not mention this fact, lest it create an uproar. It is obvious that, were this Cause not the truth, such turmoil, such hindrances would already have put out its light. Since, however, this is God's Cause, it goes forward in spite of every obstacle, and torrents of hatred only feed its flame. If they had sent us away, exiled us to some far-off place, this would have created a still bigger fire of enthusiasm, and the Cause would suddenly have made much more progress everywhere.'

FIFTY

Give Her Her Money

Florence waited every day for the little knocking at her door which invited her to morning prayers with the Holy Household.

Reaching their long reception room with its latticed blinds, she would remove her shoes and enter in stocking feet. A gentle breeze blew through the blinds, and beyond them she could see the green vineyards of Mount Carmel, spread out in the morning sun. Alone, at the head of the room on a divan, sat the Greatest Holy Leaf. Regal and yet at the same time self-effacing, she wore the graceful flowing headscarf and garments of the East. Another divan ran the length of the room under the many windows, and at its head, at the right hand upper corner and near His sister, sat 'Abdu'l-Bahá. Halfway down from the Master was His consort, Munírih Khánum. Beside her, one of her daughters was chanting prayers of Bahá'u'lláh and verses from the Qur'án. At the further, the 'lower', end of the room were little boys and girls of the Household, and from time to time one or another child would sweetly chant.

Here too were the tall samovars, and quietly moving about, women in Eastern dress were serving hot tea in small glasses placed on saucers. The tea was being unobtrusively served and drunk simultaneously with the prayers. The meeting was not cold and formal – it was natural and easy, more like people gathered as a family to listen to music.

Florence especially remembered one grandchild, Shoghi Effendi, chanting in a slightly sleepy voice that reminded her of the dawn chirpings of awakening birds.

Invited to sit by Khánum, Florence said she regretted that she knew so little Persian. Khánum's translated response was: 'Your spiritual eyes see, your spiritual ears hear, and that is much better than knowing Persian.'

From time to time the Master, sitting quietly on the divan, would look over toward Mount Carmel and the Shrine and watch the birds wheeling under the bright blue sky.

A woman attendant expressed the wish that He would soon be released after His by now four years within the walls of 'Akká. (In the event, there would be another three years before the gates would at last fly open to release Him.)

He answered patiently but concluded with, 'Let us speak of other things.'

Florence followed Him from the room, and gave Him Khan's request: to be permitted to translate The Most Holy Book, the Aqdas.

'Khan is my best English translator,' the Master replied. 'Tell him that later on the Aqdas will be translated by a group of universal scholars.'

As she remembered it, He also said He hoped that at that time Khan's assistance would be of value. Who knows, Marzieh's work on the Aqdas in Tehran with Jináb-i-Faḍil, at the Guardian's direction, may possibly have fulfilled this.

Florence regained their cool bedroom, with its two windows looking over the Bay to Mount Carmel, and two others to the sea. There in the small dining room next door, her breakfast was waiting: a large cup of fragrant coffee (as a special favor, they had at first added rosewater to it, but she induced them to change), marmalade, a piece of toast on a plate, on this a mammoth poached egg. 'What could this be?' she asked herself. 'Duck egg? Turkey egg?' Cautiously tasting it, she found it delicious. Later they identified it – a peacock's, or rather a peahen's, egg.

Tea was most people's morning drink. Florence learned later that in Persia, rose-scented coffee in a small cup was served on two occasions: as a signal that the party is over, the long parade of tea, sherbet, cakes, fruits, nuts, sweets, has ended. And at funerals.

Florence was in Heaven during her whole pilgrimage. She was treated with nothing but love. 'Those serving here', she wrote, 'bring me at all hours whatever I wish.'

It was 'Abdu'l-Bahá's custom to go the rounds of the house and garden, have a word with those concerned with the household affairs of the day, and often even order the meals. He showed little interest in His own food but was very thoughtful of the guests', people from many parts of the world, especially those from the West with their tastes so different.

'There are no servants,' Florence wrote, 'or rather all are servants.' Of the attendants she said that Ba<u>sh</u>ír was from a province of India bordering on China, and he had been in 'Akká fourteen years, arriving in the days of Bahá'u'lláh. Another from the same province was <u>Kh</u>usraw and another, Isfandíyár the driver.

Out in the sun it was hot, but the house of stone was cool and there were many rooms, halls, passageways, vaulted or open to the sky. This house, close to the sea, had belonged to the Pá<u>sh</u>á who governed 'Akká at the time when Napoleon laid siege to it. Had Napoleon won 'Akká he would have held the key to the East. When driving out to the Bahjí Shrine, Florence would pass by a great mound called 'Napoleon's Hill', under which lay many of his soldiers, young men who were never to see their homeland again; they, like the Bahá'í great ones, also forced to this place, they by a general, the Bahá'ís by two kings.

One morning in a hallway Florence was speaking with the Greatest Holy Leaf, Muníríh <u>Kh</u>ánum and Munavvar <u>Kh</u>ánum, when 'Abdu'l-Bahá passed by, saw them together, smiled and said heartily in English, 'Sisters!' as He went on His way. Muníríh <u>Kh</u>ánum would lovingly lament, 'What is this thick cloud between us! When you learn to speak Persian we shall converse clearly and freely.'

Although 'Abdu'l-Bahá gave to the poor each day and all the time, Friday – the Middle Eastern Sunday – was His special day for them. The sick, the distressed, the needy would pour in to see Him this day from all the countryside. Normally He would minister to them Himself, but on one particular day He had sent His attendant, Ba<u>sh</u>ír, to distribute the silver coins. Florence, wearing her <u>ch</u>ádur, walking out alone and looking for Ba<u>sh</u>ír, came upon groups of men and women waiting at the great portal. She saw a father with a sick boy, saw the well leading or holding up the ailing, people of all the local nationalities and races, patiently waiting. She walked through the portal to the outer courtyard and came upon an astonishing number of people sitting along the walls. Dozens and dozens of people. There she was, alone among strange beings, terrified that her veil would blow off and disclose her foreign face. She crossed the wide courtyard, all those eyes upon her, reached the outer gate under the tower, and at last saw Bashír with a few men believers to help. He was busy handing out a silver piece to each of the poor. The crowd surged noisily around him and he could not hear Florence's muffled cry, 'Oh, Bashír, there you are!' As she pushed toward him the believers who were with him took her for an importunate beggar and someone said, 'Oh, Bashír, give her her money and let her pass by.' She almost lifted her veil to protest, but remembered in time, and called out a muffled, 'I am Florence Khánum!' The believers, taking a second look, burst out laughing and led her safely out of the mob. She stood aside and, terrified, hypnotized, watched the crowd going by. She had been to many parts of the world – to Lapland, Italy, Greece, Turkey, the American Wild West – but had never seen faces like these. To her they were half humans in their soiled turbans and rags; men, women, children, frowning harshly from their afflictions, all diseased, showing sores, and some, she was certain, were lepers. They were loathsome, like ill-kept animals, and the eyes of the desert women especially were wild, untamed. An earlier witness to these very scenes, the Countess M. A. de S. Canavarro, sister in Buddhism of Myron Phelps, saw that 'Abdu'l-Bahá's hands were injured by the crowd He served, the backs were scratched and torn.[152]

FIFTY-ONE

The Splendoring Dawn

Now came the first of the two commemorations of the Declaration of the Báb that Florence was privileged to celebrate in 'Abdu'l-Bahá's presence, the other one being years later at her mother's home in Cambridge, Massachusetts.

He had once commented on how a meal reinforces the initial mood of the partaker, and had said, 'That is one reason why the Bahá'í Feasts make all so happy. United in love, this love is strengthened within us when Bahá'ís eat together.'

In 'Akká that day, alone most of the time, staying in her room with

Rahim, Florence had been in a low frame of mind. She had thought the Master would rest on His birthday (for He was born not only on the very day, but in the same year the Báb declared His mission), but Khan reported that He had worked since dawn helping with the preparations – even kneading dough to be baked, Persian-fashion, on the sides of the ovens where lambs were being roasted. She felt separated from His presence by all the bustle, all the guests.

This morning she had visited the Ladies' part of the house and found that they too were busy receiving guests. As each guest greeted Khánum, the Greatest Holy Leaf, one after the other attempted humbly to kiss Khánum's hand or her arm or the hem of her robe, and Khánum gently forbade it.

The little boy, made much of by the ladies, grew restless and, reluctantly, Florence took him away, back to her room. She wished afterward she had gone to the window in the corridor and looked down on the historic scene: 'Abdu'l-Bahá moving among and greeting and addressing some two hundred men guests. Khan came in, radiant, and told how the Master had Himself helped to pass the platters of delicate Persian food, the mounds of saffron rice, every grain separate, and the young lamb cooked with vegetables, and the fruits of such fragrance and bright colors.

That morning the Master had taken tea with the believers and the Tablet for this Feast, revealed by Bahá'u'lláh, was chanted. 'Abdu'l-Bahá had a copy of this Tablet given to Khan, to translate and send to the West, and this he did with great joy.

At morning tea, the essence of what the Master said was: 'In the East, these Bahá'í Feasts are celebrated according to the lunar calendar. We also celebrate them here by the lunar reckoning, for this was the custom during the days of the Blessed Perfection. Some wish to convert these into solar dates, but such matters are entrusted to the House of Justice to deal with according to the requirements of the times and varying circumstances.'

Recalling the celebration of this Feast in the previous year, He said, 'A year ago, on this day, there were great difficulties and great turmoil in 'Akká. However, those times were better than these, for those hardships produced good results for the Cause. Last year this Feast Day could not be celebrated here on account of the troubles, but still, it was better than now, for the very obstacles which stopped the celebration helped to spread the Cause of God. By and by there will be freedom for the believers in Tehran. Even now, they celebrate these Feast Days.'

The food served to about a hundred Bahá'ís at noon was simple and plain, but with 'Abdu'l-Bahá waiting on each one it was a festival unlike any on earth. As He served the guests, the Master walked around the tables and with great seriousness and eloquence addressed the believers to this effect:

'This is a plain meal, uniform and the same to all. Simplicity and plainness are good, not only in food, but even in dress, in heart, in temperament. This day is a blessed day. Many Tablets have been revealed for this day by Bahá'u'lláh. The Blessed Beauty celebrated this day every year, for this day of the Báb's Declaration is the dawning of the advent of this Cause. The daybreak is a blessed time. Although at dawn the sun is not revealed in its full splendor, still, as the dawn brings glad-tidings of the sunrise, it comes up with great purity and a brightness of the sky, and the air is then at its most fresh and sweet.

'Therefore the beloved of God must think of this day as very blessed, and applaud it and acclaim it. They must bring it to a close in utter happiness, and gather together in a spirit of boundless love. If there has been estrangement between two individuals, they should cancel it out as this day dawns, for bliss should be the bond of all who come together at this Feast.

'By chance, on this day my birth took place as well, but all must celebrate the day as the Anniversary of the Declaration of the Báb, and although my birth also happened to come on this day, they must not consider this of any import. Let the meaning of this day be the Declaration of the Báb, and not my birth.

'In America the believers have celebrated this day as my birthday – but this day marks the beginning of the upraised cry, the beginning of the spirit, the beginning of the splendor, of the advent of Bahá'u'lláh. For these must it be celebrated, and for the dawn of unity, which happened on this day, and also because it was celebrated by Bahá'u'lláh, and because He revealed many Tablets in its honor. With exceeding joy must the believers commemorate this day, and to mark it for any other reason whatever is against the Law of God. No Feast Days can be set aside or introduced except those relating to the Blessed Beauty and His Highness the Exalted Báb.'

Then, very earnest, very emphatic, addressing all of them, He said, 'Do you understand what I am saying? For if anything contrary to this be done, the Faith would become similar to those sects which have so many holidays and feasts that out of three hundred and sixty-five days in the year, some one hundred and eighty are feast days.

'To sum it up, the meaning is that this day is the Anniversary of the Báb's Declaration and must be celebrated as such. Not only my birth, but the birth of hundreds of thousands of people took place on this day – so that it was only a coincidence and must not be celebrated as a feast for my birth.'

On into the afternoon Florence continued to feel depressed, and also worried that even though absent, 'even from afar', 'Abdu'l-Bahá would know it. She was not proud to be in such a discordant condition. She had not seen Him at morning prayers as usual, nor sat beside Him as usual during lunch. She somehow felt 'bereft, even neglected', chided herself but could not throw the feeling off.

Alone with the boy and still in gloom, about four o'clock that afternoon she was surprised to find 'Abdu'l-Bahá suddenly appearing with Khan. She was called into the dining room. The Master sat down, and told her to be seated, while Khan stood to translate.

'I have been very busy today', 'Abdu'l-Bahá said, 'and unable to greet you until now.'

Much abashed at this special visit on such a day – the fact that, undoubtedly in response to her mood, He had come to cheer her – she humbly thanked Him, and He rose and went away with Khan, leaving her at the same time both comforted and chagrined.

The expression for 'going on pilgrimage' in those days was 'attaining to 'Akká'. Florence ventured to tell the Master, 'I wish all the Bahá'ís in America might attain to 'Akká.'

He paused before answering and then replied, 'I am always with those who love me.'

She understood this to mean the 'spiritual attainment' was greater than the physical.

'I wish particularly', she added, 'that my parents and family might come here and attain to your presence.'

Slowly and gravely, He replied, 'Inshá'lláh. If not here, then hereafter.'

Khan said the Master's meaning was, He had accepted her family into the Kingdom.

It was as they were rising from His luncheon table that the Master looked down at the floor and she, following His gaze, saw a strange insect hurrying toward her chair. The Master rose and firmly stamped out its life.

'This kind', He said, 'is poisonous.'

The early believers taught that, besides the literal, visible sense, untold spiritual meanings were wrapped up in whatever He said and did. His every act and word were lessons and examples.

'In voice,' she wrote, 'in every gesture, I saw in 'Abdu'l-Bahá perfect manhood, and a divinely-inspired intelligence which enabled Him, whether present or absent, and with unerring accuracy, to read the human heart.'

She noted the majesty of Him, His enchanting ways, His wit, His living sympathy for every human being – and thought in after years of the Guardian's words, when he wrote of 'the mysterious power of so magnetic a personality'[153] and of the Master's 'magic name'.[154]

'In studying 'Abdu'l-Bahá', Florence said, 'in the first day or two (for after I had discovered His perfection there was no more attempt to "study" Him), I could only gaze at Him in shyness and awe.

'I said to myself, "in this angelic Being I see One from a higher sphere." ' She was especially glad, she wrote, to find that one of His qualities was humor.

'Now I know that laughter is a gift of the gods – and joy and merriment will surely be there in Heaven, and we shall not have to remain solemn throughout all eternity.'

The early believers were certain they would be received into the Kingdom of God. In fact, they were there already. This was an undoubted blessing of those days of the three Central Figures. But as time went by, Marzieh, for one, felt that being received into the Kingdom was something you had to struggle and hope against hope for. (When a certain New York bachelor confided in her that the Guardian had written him his place in the next world was assured, she could not resist saying, 'Better take along a Palm Beach suit.')

On Friday, June 29, in the evening, the Master, addressing the pilgrims, pointed to the stars and said, 'Were all on earth to join forces and try to keep these stars from emitting rays, they still would fail. Now observe how mistaken are the enemies of the Cause, trying as they do to withstand this Truth and put out this light. How foolish they are! They do not even see the power of Bahá'u'lláh, Who demonstrates the truth of Christ to unbelievers after nineteen centuries, the truth of Islam after thirteen centuries, the truth of Abraham after four thousand years! They do not recognize the bounty of this Manifestation, upholding the reality of all religions, unifying all humankind on the basis of faith in one God.

'When Sulṭán Muḥammad II had laid siege to Constantinople, was bombarding the city walls and was about to break through at the head of his victorious troops, a minister of State hurried to the residence of the Christian Patriarch to report on the terrible crisis and ask for advice. He found the Patriarch seated at his desk and calmly writing.

'The minister asked, "What is Your Eminence writing?"

'The Patriarch replied, "A book disproving the mission of Muḥammad."

'The minister, shaking with emotion, told him: "Now is hardly the time to write against a Prophet Whose followers' troops have already entered the city and will soon be controlling the whole of it."

'Today those who oppress the Cause exhibit this same unawareness. While this Cause is spreading with the speed of lightning, and its radiance is already blessing all nations, still its enemies attempt to resist its might and block its life-giving influence.

'When Christ was crucified He left only eleven disciples, but see how Christianity has encompassed the whole world. Bahá'u'lláh, when He departed, had between one and two hundred thousand followers. Since they have already filled up the world with His light, see how marvelous will be the effect of it in times to come.

'When, from Baghdad, we were exiled to Constantinople, the Persian Ambassador did his utmost to bring about our ruin. Suppose he had managed to destroy us – could he destroy the Cause of God? They said they would utterly annihilate the Cause by destroying the Báb. Did they succeed in that? No, the very martyrdom of the Báb reinforced His Cause a thousandfold.

'Now there are some who imagine that the Cause of God is dependent upon my being alive, and that in doing away with me, they will do away with the Cause. How wide of the mark! Not at all! The Cause will make great progress after I am gone. Remember this! You can destroy me, you can put an end to me, but you can never destroy, never put an end to the Cause of God.'

In saying goodby to some departing pilgrims 'Abdu'l-Bahá told them, 'You came, you visited the Consecrated Spot, you associated with God's loved ones. The hope is that you will carry away with you the effects of this visit as a gift to your countrymen. The fruits of such an encounter are good deeds, devotion, enthusiasm, love for humankind, rectitude, honesty, harmony, gentleness, benevolence, and glad-tidings of the love of God. Do not look upon the world, or the doings and sayings of its peoples, or their hostility, or lack of kindness. Look upon the Blessed Perfection, and show you love to every human being for His sake.

'If any harm you with his tongue or hands, do not be grieved, but smile and be rejoiced, and deal with him in your turn with unfeigned love. If in your hearing anyone reviles you and expresses hate, pay it no mind. Say to him that the Blessed Perfection has ordered you to wish good things for those who hate you, to love all those who wish you harm, to look upon the stranger as a friend, to cleanse your eyes from what men do, and turn them unto God Whose grace embraces all that is. Say you are bidden to speak not a single evil word against man or government.

'The truth is, Muẓaffari'd-Dín S͟háh is very gentle in his acts, and indeed it is not possible for him to show you more consideration than he does. And further, God has now brought it about that the nation's affairs should be in the hands of both the people and the government. [This was a reference by the Master to Persia's new Constitutional Regime.]

'To sum up, God willing, the confirmations of the Blessed

Perfection will come to your aid. You will be favored by His protection, you will win His good pleasure.'

FIFTY-TWO

The Food of Love

On Friday, July 6, in the evening, 'Abdu'l-Bahá was seated in His reception room downstairs with the believers gathered around Him. The room gave on a corner of the courtyard, in the center of which was a palm tree and a flower garden.

When all were seated, He spoke of always continuing firm and steadfast in the Faith, no matter what should come to pass. He said: 'The believers must not be affected by conditions in 'Akká, whether 'Akká be in turmoil or quiet calm. Whatever may take place in 'Akká, the believers of all lands should fix their gaze on the Cause of God, which is ever stronger, ever undisturbed, no matter what the turmoil in 'Akká.

'Last year when 'Akká was in chaos the believers became agitated everywhere. The only place where they remained calm was Tehran – there, they attended to their teaching and other Bahá'í duties as usual. 'Akká is the Most Great Prison of the Blessed Perfection, therefore it is bound to experience sudden changes, ups and downs, to be calm and serene for a time, again to go through troubles, now to be at peace, again to be in turmoil. But the beloved of God must look to the Cause of God which, considered as a whole, is not subject to such changes: that is, they must always hold to their fervor and their devotion, and obey the laws and the urgent appeals of Bahá'u'lláh.

'The meaning is that all must be firmly attached to the Cause of God itself. They should not suppose that the Cause is in need of great numbers to carry out its mission. No, I swear by God beside Whom there is no other God, that if five should rise up and act entirely and literally in accord with the laws and exhortations of the Blessed Perfection, they would be the equivalent of five million. Thus, the believers must choose good deeds and pure acts for their adorning and follow the Law.'

Pointing to the oil lamp in the room, He said: 'Just as this lamp is effective through its light, men's light is their deeds.

'Briefly, whatever may be taking place in 'Akká, the believers throughout the world must not become lax in their duties – no, they must keep on serving the Cause, for this is paramount. When His Holiness the Spirit [Christ] was martyred, the only one who remained unperturbed was Mary Magdalen – all the others were bewildered and lost heart. When Mary became a believer, she had fallen upon the feet of Christ, and although she was a village woman of ill repute, He did not draw back His feet, and this made many among His followers as well as many among the Jews to turn away from Him. But Christ, not heeding them, said to Mary, "Arise. Thy sins are forgiven." And she rose, and repented, and from that moment on, she devoted herself to the service of the Cause.

'Mary had a friend among the Roman officers, they being masters of the Holy Land then. He was the one who guarded her from enemies after the death of Christ. When, following the crucifixion, she had gathered the disciples together and confirmed them in service and put courage into them, she herself set out for Rome and entered the presence of the Emperor. How marvelous were the words she spoke to him! She said to him: "I have come on behalf of the Christians to bring to your notice the fact that Herod and Pilate martyred the Christ at the instigation of the Jews. But now the two of them have repented of what they did. To them, Roman governors, Jews and Christians were all alike. Indeed it was not the Romans, but the Jews who were the chief antagonists of Christ. And now that the two have repented, they are punishing the Jews and suppressing them, because they led the two of them to commit this act. I have come here to appeal to the Emperor, to prevent Herod and Pilate from punishing the Jews. For neither Christ nor we Christians are pleased to see the Romans punishing the Jews because they condemned Christ."

'The Emperor was much moved by her words, and praised Mary highly, and that was why, in those days, the Christians did not suffer persecution in those regions, and went about spreading the Gospel.

'Later on, the Roman officer who had protected Mary asked her to become his wife. Mary's answer was that, as a follower of Christ, she would not marry him unless he too became a believer. Thus he was converted and united to Mary according to the ceremonies of Christian marriage.

'The reason for relating this is to show the steadfastness and firmness manifested by Mary after the crucifixion of Christ. Now the beloved of God must carry out their duties, and serve the Cause, and remain firm and steadfast no matter what may come to pass in 'Akká. Let them fix their gaze on the paradise of the Cause and obey the laws of Bahá'u'lláh.'

One evening the Master said: 'Both Peter and Paul suffered martyrdom with all steadfastness, by order of Nero. This is a clear and indisputable fact.' Khan found the statement a great help to him because he had not yet seen any text in the revealed word of the Manifestation regarding the martyrdom of St Paul.

Again on the subject of struggles and sufferings, 'Abdu'l-Bahá said: 'Men are trained and developed through these: through poverty and vicissitudes and want. Otherwise God would have ordained that His friends and holy ones should be opulent, and possessed of all material means. All must beg God to grant them true severance and detachment from the world, for this is of the utmost importance.' (Explaining the symbolism of the Adam and Eve story to Laura Barney a year or so earlier, 'Abdu'l-Bahá told her, 'The meaning of the serpent is attachment to the human world.'[155])

Another evening the Master addressed the pilgrims, saying: 'Those who first arose to persecute us, and plotted against us, are now seeking a way to reconciliation. We have no quarrel with anyone. We never have had. Praise be to God, the Blessed Perfection set us free. He blessed us with peace. He forbade conflict and strife and commanded us to show forth loving kindness to everyone on earth. Strife is to be shunned. It is the worst of all things, for it diminishes man's spiritual powers, it destroys his soul, it keeps him subjected to continual torment.'

They spoke of the feasts they were enjoying, and the delicious foods. He said: 'Food that is prepared with love and eaten with love gives great delight. When we were in Baghdad there was a poor man who lived off in the desert, and he eked out a living by gathering thorns and selling them in the city. He was a very devoted believer, and many a time he had invited me to eat a meal with him in his home. Finally we agreed to come to him, with some of the believers. He lived about twenty miles out of Baghdad. It was a hot day and we walked the whole distance and at last reached his house – a small, humble dwelling made of reeds put together in the form of a triangle with a little entrance to it. He lived there all alone with his wife, a very old woman, out on the lonely wastes. He invited us into the hut. We found it very confined, and so hot that we all went outside again. But then there was nothing to shield us from the blazing sun, so we had to go back in and make the best of it.

'Then the man dug a little hole in the ground, set fire to a bundle of thorns, and, fashioning some lumps of dough as we looked on, and without yeast, he threw them on the fire and covered them over with ashes: this was his bread. A few minutes later he pulled the lumps out of the fire. The outside was burnt black, and the inside was plain dough. Then he brought us some dates and served them with the bread. And we all enjoyed that primitive food, because he was a true believer and had great love in his heart. He had strong faith, and he was blissful because we had come to his home. The meal we ate in that poor dwelling tasted so good that I still relish it in memory.

'To sum it up, the world is full of delicate foods and rich things to eat, but whatever is served with love and eaten with love, tastes the best. We spent the night with him, and went back to Baghdad the next morning. He rejoiced to have us, and we rejoiced to be with him, because he loved much.'

One day Bashír told them of the Master's tender goodby to some departing pilgrims who had just sat with Him at His luncheon table for a final meal.

'Abdu'l-Bahá came back into the room. The table had not been cleared yet. Some bits of dessert remained on the plates. The Master went around the table, taking a morsel from each plate, stopping at each, tasting a bit from what the guest had left, as though the crumbs were food from Heaven. And at each place, He breathed 'Ah!' as if savoring the love of each departed guest.

FIFTY-THREE

No Fear Can Come upon Me

'Abdu'l-Bahá spoke of the troubles in 'Akká the year before, and how Bahá'u'lláh protected Him and the friends from terrible mischief set afoot by His enemies.

'Our shelter is strong,' He said. 'Our Protector is powerful. He watched over us last year when enemies bore such false witness against us as might well have led to our ruin. They accused us to the Government of acts, which, had anyone committed them, he would deservedly have been condemned to death. For example, they said we had founded a new dynasty and established a new religion. They even produced a flag on which were the holy words "Yá Bahá'u'l-Abhá" and sent it to the Sublime Porte [the seat of the Ottoman Government in Constantinople], saying we had hoisted that flag and carried it about the city and among the Arab tribes and called upon the Arabs to rally to us and raise a revolt. They even said that the Arabs had responded to our cry, had all become Bahá'ís and were poised for action against the Government. They even sent in the absurd report that we had created a new Mecca, that is, the holy Tomb of Bahá'u'lláh, and a new Medina, the holy Tomb of the Báb on Mount Carmel. They reported that we were revolutionaries, mischief-makers, foes of law and order. This while the whole world knows that we seek only unity and peace. When Bahá'u'lláh has commanded us to love all mankind and work to establish universal peace, and has forbidden us to be corrupt and seditious, how could we ever have done such evil things? God forbid the very thought of them! We wish only for the well-being of all humanity. The Blessed Perfection has forbidden all humankind to bear rancor or hatred toward anyone. He has cleansed our hearts from hate. He has blessed us with love for each one.'

Then in gentle tones, addressing Himself to His Father, He proceeded to chant a few lines from a poem, one or two of them to this effect:

> O Lord, I beg of Thee
> Between us let there friendship be.
> With every hand against me,
> And the whole earth my foe,
> No fear can come upon me
> If by Thy side I go.

Far from thundering at an individual or excoriating him, if the Master wished to address someone's failing, He might tell a story showing the way for the individual to overcome it: a general story, addressed to a group – often an amusing story, and all would laugh – and the one for whom the hidden point was intended would understand, learn and not be hurt.

Florence was careful to keep her little son immaculate. For contrast another pilgrim had come, a 'beautiful soul', but bringing with her a dirty baby, of about the same age as Rahim. Rúḥá Khánum said, 'Try as we may, we cannot bring ourselves to kiss and hug that child. The mother is completely indifferent to its needs. When it sleeps, she lets the fleas crawl over its dirty little face. Our mother called your baby to her attention, and said how clean and sweet you keep him. We finally bathed her infant ourselves and provided a netting for him, to keep the fleas out.'

The end of the story as Florence told it was that when the pilgrim left, the Master lovingly held and kissed the dirty baby.

When the family's trunks had been left in Haifa and Florence needed another dress, one with long sleeves that would protect her arms from insect bites, Muním̄rih Khánum and Rúḥá Khánum assisted a Baháʼí seamstress to design it. The dress still exists, small-waisted and delicate, even coquettish, not the no-nonsense, utilitarian garment one might have expected. It has a fetching 'sailor' collar trimmed with narrow lace, and the skirt dips in the back. Of a light cotton weave, it is cream-colored now, but when they made it for her it was pink. They would not let her pay for it. It came to her with a message from 'Abdu'l-Bahá that the dress was a present, and if she wished another one made, to say so, it would be a pleasure to fulfill her wish. She felt it was yet one more symbol of the Master's fatherly care.

One afternoon Florence found herself taking tea with her husband and a number of other Eastern Bahá'í men, they in all forms of native headgear, some with the brimless, black, Persian kuláh, some Turks with red fez and black tassel, another in a voluminous turban showing many wrapped folds of white cloth, one – a Siyyid – in a green turban and sash. To her, they were noble-looking, saint-like, gentle and courteous. 'Many of them,' Khan told her quietly, 'great Bahá'í teachers, have been made to languish in prison solely because they are Bahá'ís. Some have been imprisoned as many as thirty times.'

Another day Florence asked him, 'By the way, who were those two strangers among the guests at table today?'

'Which ones do you mean?'

'Well, one of them made me think of a hissing serpent – standing on his tail and hissing. And the other made me think of one of those slugs we have at home in America that leave a slimy, glistening trail behind them wherever they go.'

'But this is amazing!' Khan told her. 'How clearly you read them!'

'Who can they be?' she persisted.

'They are two of the Master's half-brothers. As you know, all those half-brothers became the Master's jealous enemies.'

'Then what are they doing at His table?'

'They are in a phase of being forgiven. They have both expressed repentance, and begged to return to Him. He has given them another chance, and been most merciful to them. But they have remained exactly as you see them. They are the same as ever, and none of us knows what will come of it.'

A few years later she learned that they had turned enemy again.

A prophecy 'Abdu'l-Bahá made about one of them was that in future this one would become a porter (ḥammál) at the docks and would be seen begging Bahá'í travelers to let him carry their trunks on his back, and they would ignore him and pass on by – a prophecy then almost unimaginable to be made of the son of that princely House.

At the Family's door, Florence chanced to encounter, one afternoon a strange woman, obviously not an attendant or outside guest.

'Who are you?' she asked Florence in Persian, barring the way. 'Where are you going?'

Florence, etiquette-minded, resented the brusque questions.

'I am seeking Khánum,' she answered, meaning, of course, the Greatest Holy Leaf.

'Khánum?' the woman inquired with an unpleasant smile. 'What Khánum?'

'I want to see Khánum,' Florence said firmly. 'The sister of 'Abdu'l-Bahá.'

'Oh, very well,' the other replied. She went her way and Florence never saw her again.

Later on, Khan explained to Florence that she must have encountered the third wife of Bahá'u'lláh. 'She is eaten up by her ill-will for the Household,' he told her. 'She probably wanted you to believe that in reality it is she who is the Khánum of the House.'

Such meetings inevitably reminded Florence of the words of Christ: 'And a man's foes shall be they of his own household.'[156]

By contrast, she noted the loving servitude of the Master's daughters in seeing to His needs. They took turns in serving Him. One of them told Florence that He liked to go up on the flat roof of the house under the stars and moon and pace up and down and chant prayers. A daughter would sit at the head of the stairs, within call, then aid Him to retire for the night.

(Once in Tehran, Munírih Khánum Ayádí, mother of the Bahá'í youth who later became famous as Shah Mohammed Reza Pahlavi's physician, told the writer that the Master had said girls must be trained to be hard-working and industrious. This statement would also apply to boys, since the Master says, 'There must be no difference in their education.'[157] 'Education' being the English word for which there are three components in Persian: training, imparting knowledge, nurturing.)

Florence wrote that a Bahá'í, turning to God in prayer, encounters continual instances of the protection of the Holy Spirit. Such experiences, however, are for the individual only, except for close friends. Because even those witnessing the miracles of the Prophets often do not believe their eyes.

'Did others see this?' the skeptics ask. 'Is anyone living who was there?'

She then proceeded to relate what she considered a miracle that she witnessed at the table of 'Abdu'l-Bahá.

One day Bashír came in with a platter of food, a favorite dish of hers and, she noted, also popular with the others. Bashír offered it to her and she was disappointed to see the platter was smaller than usual. About enough for four, was her estimate, and there were eight or nine present. 'Go slow,' she admonished herself, although she had her usual keen appetite. 'Take only half a portion!' Reluctantly, she returned the serving spoon to the platter but 'something pushed my elbow' and back came the spoon and she was giving herself a double helping. 'Now what?' she chided herself. 'How will these men get fed?'

When presented to the man at her left, who with no concern served himself generously, the platter still looked about half full. Holding her breath, she watched as the third man took a lavish portion.

'That platter ought to be empty by now,' she said to herself, 'yet it looks almost full. I'll keep my eye on it.'

The food was offered all around the table and each guest served himself plentifully, yet when Bashír retired with it the platter was still seven-eighths full.

Florence, an experienced hostess, could not believe what she had seen. Humanly, it could not have taken place. Afterward she told Khan, 'I have witnessed the miracle of the loaves and fishes.'

FIFTY-FOUR

Episodes

When bidding farewell to a body of pilgrims 'Abdu'l-Bahá said, 'Although I lacked the time to answer all the letters you brought me from your cities, you yourselves are the real letters that I am sending in reply. For letters are of two kinds: ordinary, written ones, and living ones. The living letters are the beloved of God, for they are the Luminous Book in which the mysteries of creation can be read. Those who act in accord with the urgings of the Blessed Perfection are as eloquent volumes which no amount of reading can ever exhaust.'

Of the fact that Bahá'ís must live a holy life, He said, 'Today the eyes of the world are fixed on the lives of the Bahá'ís. When they see a believer committing an evil deed, they may imagine this to be something done by all Bahá'ís, or something permitted by the Founder of the Faith. Thus they may judge the whole community by the misdeeds of one member. He whose deeds do not accord with his words is not a true Bahá'í. That is, a non-Bahá'í who lives a good life does less harm to the Cause than a Bahá'í whose life is not righteous.'

Condemning the use of alcohol, He said: 'Man should make himself drunk on the wine of knowledge, and slake his thirst out of the chalice of wisdom, for this will afford good cheer that will continue beyond life to eternity. A human being should inebriate himself by increasing his intelligence, not by that which diminishes consciousness and puts out the light of the mind.'

One day when she was invited to drive with the ladies to Haifa, Florence asked them about the nine cypress trees on the slope of Mount Carmel, where Bahá'u'lláh had walked. (Of His four visits to Haifa, one lasted three whole months.)

Khánum pointed out the path to her and pressed some jasmine blossoms into her hands. Florence climbed up to the 'sacred circle' and counted the trees, and listened to the stillness. Way below her was the little town of Haifa, the curving Bay of 'Akká and the wide sea.

She prayed and meditated in the gentle, fresh breeze and looked at the vineyards below the Báb's Shrine and thought of the Holy Ones, all the way back to the Prophet Elijah (his cave not far away), who had trodden the paths of 'the Mountain of God'.

She thought how 'Abdu'l-Bahá, Himself a prisoner, slandered by the Covenant-breakers, therefore suspected by the aroused authorities who were His captors, had against all odds raised up the Shrine of the Báb (the location of His sacred remains, near as they were by then, still a secret to her). Under the turquoise sky the fruit trees, their emerald branches glowing with golden oranges and red pomegranates, begemmed the terrace of the Shrine.

Another time in 'Akká, late one afternoon, she and Khan walked together along the beach and watched the fishermen with their bronzed faces and bodies, their rough hair and coarse voices, dragging in their nets, heavy with leaping fish.

'Peter and Andrew, James the son of Zebedee, and John,' said Florence.[158]

'Yes,' said Khan, 'but after nineteen hundred more years of civilization.'

One night the full moon turned all the world to molten silver. Florence looked down from her window and saw in the Master's garden by the sea a huge, Eastern tent, illuminated from within by many lamps and shining white in the moonlight.

Khan came in and said, 'Tonight, the Master is entertaining official guests at dinner.'

It gave Florence pleasure to see Him, even in confinement and exile, 'receiving as a princely host, and dispensing hospitality to the outside world'.

Suddenly at a luncheon 'Abdu'l-Bahá said to Khan, 'Your wife must veil in Persia.'

'Oh!' cried Khan, astonished. 'But my wife is American! Did Miss Barney veil in Persia?'

'No,' the Master said, 'but that was different. Your wife is the wife of a Persian.'

To Florence, veiling in the prison was understandable, but she had not known that she must veil in Persia as well. Naturally, they accepted His command at once, no matter how unexpected it was.

Paradoxically, Bahá'í women, by unveiling then, would have greatly retarded the liberation of Persian women in general, for the fanatical mullás would have told the faithful that their unveiling was a Bahá'í teaching, and against Islam.

The actual decree for doing away with the <u>ch</u>ádur would not come until 1935. As we write, the <u>ch</u>ádur has been re-instated, but not the veiling of the face.

When Rúḥá <u>Kh</u>ánum, the Master's daughter, walking with her Father, asked Florence what to call her, the answer was, 'Florence <u>Kh</u>ánum'.

'But you are an American!'

Then the Master, joining in, said, 'She is <u>Kh</u>ánum, for she is the wife of <u>Kh</u>án.'

With Khan and her little son, Florence walked past an open door and caught sight of 'Abdu'l-Bahá resting on a couch. His daughter Munavvar <u>Kh</u>ánum was with Him. Rahim ran into the room, Khan went in to bring him back, the Master invited the three of them in.

His daughter handed 'Abdu'l-Bahá a comb, which He drew through his shining white hair. Then she gave Him a basin and held up a pitcher of water and poured. Dipping His fingers in the water, smiling gently, He sprinkled Rahim's head and forehead, then shook off water drops from His fingers and sprinkled the infant from head to foot.

'Rahim has been baptized,' Florence whispered to Khan, 'and by 'Abdu'l-Bahá!'

Some years later when they were entering their son in a private school in Virginia, the Episcopalian spinster in charge of the school inquired, 'Has your child been baptized?'

'Yes,' replied Florence, 'in the Holy Land.'

After about an hour with the hyperactive infant Rahim, a grown-up would be exhausted and dripping with sweat. Sometimes Ba<u>sh</u>ír relieved Florence and Khan of his care, and one day Ba<u>sh</u>ír took him for a walk in 'Abdu'l-Bahá's garden. Eastern fashion, they both hunkered down on their heels and examined the ants, which to Florence seemed larger here than in America. Ba<u>sh</u>ír kept repeating to the toddler, 'Múr<u>ch</u>ih! Bugú múr<u>ch</u>ih! (Ant! say "ant"!).' Up till then Rahim's vocabulary had consisted of only three words, the usual Mama, Papa, and da-da. Ba<u>sh</u>ír kept on and suddenly the child, in a voice surprisingly deep for a one-year-old, said, 'Múr<u>ch</u>ih.'

The next day Ba<u>sh</u>ír took him to the garden again and they watched the peacock. 'Bugú ṭávús!' And after several tries by Ba<u>sh</u>ír, Rahim burst out with the second real word of his life, 'Ṭávús'.

From then on, from Constantinople up the Bosporus and across the Black Sea to Bátúm, and then by rail to Bákú, and again by boat across the Caspian, and then by horse-drawn carriage over rocky plains and past bare mountains to Tehran, Rahim learned Persian. He understood his parents when they talked to him in English but would answer them in Persian. Even for some little time after they returned to America, Persian was his language.

One day Bashír, who had been watching Rahim, came in laughing. 'Two Bahá'ís have arrived from Shíráz,' he said. 'When they heard the baby was your son, they gave him two gold pieces. As soon as he found out the gold pieces were not good to eat, Rahim threw them away as far as he could. Then they offered him an orange from the Báb's tree in Shíráz and he started right in on the orange, and is now fast friends with them.'

Freed by Bashír one afternoon, who, as he often did, took off with the baby, Florence was walking in 'Abdu'l-Bahá's garden and came upon Asadu'lláh kneeling beside the flower bed at the center, putting in new flowering plants with all his might. He laughed and said in Persian, 'See, Khánum, how hard this ground is! It is like the hard hearts of the people of this world. We Bahá'ís toil and toil to soften up the ground and plant in the seeds of truth – until out of the waste land, a garden blooms.'

Florence was walking alone one late afternoon near the Master's house when, across the road at an open window, she saw looking down at her a tall, angular lady wearing European dress, in her eyes a terrible, concentrated hate. Florence was shocked to learn that she was a Christian missionary, who would become enraged whenever she saw Western women walking there in the garden of 'Abdu'l-Bahá. There she was, supposedly fed and clothed by funds from the West, at work in Christ's name, and scarcely twenty miles from where He had lived out His days in love.

Another time, at the tea hour, hearing music, Florence glanced into the ladies' sitting room. They were entertaining a number of guests and an Arab girl was dancing for them, with dignity and grace.

Sometimes she would glimpse the Greatest Holy Leaf sitting regally yet in sweet humility amongst the ladies, in her white head scarf and flowing garments of the East. Florence heard the Master say, 'I do not know what I should do without the Greatest Holy Leaf and Munírih Khánum' – so greatly did He love them and so faithfully did they love and serve Him.

When an inexplicable tragedy or calamity occurred, members of the Household would always say, 'There is a wisdom in it.' Florence wrote that 'the lives of these consecrated souls accept the will of God'.

One day a gaunt, wild desert woman in soiled rags paused in the doorway, saw Rahim and made as if to kiss him. Florence, terrified, drew him away. The woman laughed teasingly, advancing toward the baby a few steps and saying, 'She does not want me to kiss her beautiful boy!'

Then the wild woman approached the Master. Hoarsely, she spoke to Him, and He replied in gentle tones. He left, returned, touched her hand, and she emitted a loud cry of joy and began a ritual dance. Later, Florence asked Rúḥá Khánum about her.

'What did that strange woman say? Why did she dance?'

'She is a tragic case,' Rúḥá Khánum told her. 'Her father was killed. Now she is an orphan, and very poor. The Master gave her a piece of silver and she thanked God, according to her custom. What she said was, "I will pray for you."'

'And what was His answer?'

'He thanked her.'

How did such a woman dare to tell Him *she* would pray for *Him*? Florence wondered to herself. And how humble and divinely courteous was His reply.

FIFTY-FIVE

The Path of Jewels

One morning Florence found Rahim, whom she had just bathed and put in a clean white dress, out in a corridor, with the Greatest Holy Leaf. Khánum was half-kneeling by the child and speaking softly to him. Tears were still on his cheek. It was, Florence wrote, perhaps his first disillusionment: a little bird had flown in through one of the open arches and was tame enough to peck at a piece of bread in the boy's hand. Rahim had reached out for the bird, frightened it, and it pecked his hand and flew away. The pain and the sudden loss of the bird had brought on tears, and Khánum was comforting him.

'She is so gentle,' one of the old Bahá'ís said to Khan, 'Khánum is so gentle, she would not even say písh-písh to a cat.' (Písh-písh is what you say to a cat in Persia to chase it away – like 'scat' to an American cat.)

In the Household, Florence met daughters of devoted believers or relatives of martyrs. Like daughters in a family, they took part in the duties of the house. Two lovely young girls, one of them Zeenat Khánum, who later married Zia Bagdadi, took care of Florence's room. Over a ten-year period, the Master would summon her when He was about to chant prayers, and in this way she learned His own musical patterns for the different prayers. (In Persian music, the individual improvises within the given pattern.) It was a singular blessing for the American believers in after years to hear her rich mezzo-soprano voice, raised up in the House of Worship at Wilmette, chanting the actual melodies she had learned from 'Abdu'l-Bahá.

Zeenat would tell Florence how much they all revered Khánum. One day, she said, three of the girls had to clean out a room. It was very hot, the task was not easy and they were exhausted when it was done. Khánum sent for them. She had herself prepared a cooling fruit-drink for the three and served it to them with her own hands.

Such a service from 'the Lady' was not like a service from even the kindest one of us, Florence wrote. It was a gift from a being divinely angelic.

Florence was very pleased, one day, when Khánum and all four daughters of the Master paid her a visit in the quarters she shared with Khan, and where the baby slept by them in a small crib covered with mosquito netting. Each one kissed her, lovingly welcoming her, upon entering. Of the daughters, all were married by 1906 except one, and her suitors were legion; for the Holy Household was besieged by believers wishing to join the family, just as one prominent family after another had offered their crowning beauty to 'Abdu'l-Bahá.

In 1906 the Bahjí Shrine could be visited, but not the Mansion close by – for the Manifestation's hostile relatives were living in the Mansion then. Devoted believers kept up the garden that the Master and the Bahá'ís had wrested from the sand. The great old pines of Bahá'u'lláh's day were still there and would be for some decades to come. And beyond them lay the turquoise sea, which would be there always.

When Florence went to Bahjí she was asked to veil, but outside the Master's house, in His garden, she simply wore her Western dress and threw a scarf over her hair – since others could see her from adjacent buildings, and would take her for a Jewish or Armenian lady who did not veil.

Now she rode out with the ladies to visit the Shrine. Older believers had told Khan at the century's end, that after the ascension of Bahá'u'lláh they had seen 'Abdu'l-Bahá kneel and kiss the ground, footstep by footstep, on this path where His Father had walked. Entering the lofty Shrine, where living vines and plants reached to the glass roof, Florence listened as 'Abdu'l-Bahá's consort at the doorway of the inner Shrine room, hauntingly, touchingly, chanted a prayer. But she broke off before its conclusion and wept, while the others kept silent. Then Khánum arose, steady, calm, triumphant, and continued the prayer to the end. There was a white embroidered linen cloth on the threshold to the small inner room beneath which the Manifestation is buried. Set on the cloth were silver vases holding flowers, and there were also small heaps of fragrant petals. Munírih Khánum sat down by the threshold to rest. She smiled, picked up a handful of blossoms, and like a benediction showered them over Rahim. Suddenly the toddler climbed the threshold and entered the inner Shrine. In consternation, Florence called after him. Munírih Khánum smiled and said, 'Let him stay. You too may enter and take charge of him.' With awe, Florence entered the holy peace of the inner Shrine room with its great costly central rug, and outlining this, votive lamps, some of purest hand-wrought silver, and other magnificent tokens of love and wealth poured out in gratitude. Meanwhile Khánum and the daughters carried on with their task – which was to measure the various windows for a gift from Alice Barney: green velvet hangings that she was going to order in Paris for the Shrine. The first of the rich curtains had already arrived and had been hung at the entrance to the larger room. Afterward, Khan was dumbfounded when he learned that his wife and child had been in the inner Shrine. He said the ladies must surely have had 'Abdu'l-Bahá's permission to allow them in. He himself had never entered there, nor heard of a similar case.

Then the ladies had finished, and Florence and her little son followed them out. Riding homeward in the 'beach-wagon' driven by Isfandíyár, they stopped at a garden which a believer had presented to 'Abdu'l-Bahá, and the ladies went in to call on the custodian's wife. Florence speaks of two gardens here, Ridván and Firdaws, gifts to the Manifestation and the Master.

Meanwhile Florence, with Munírih Khánum and the baby, sat down on the edge of a large pool of clear water. The three of them were still faintly scented with attar from their anointing at the Shrine.

Because of her miraculous birth, Munírih Khánum was called 'the Morsel of the Báb'. As Nabíl relates in *The Dawn-Breakers*, her parents, an infertile couple, longed for a child. Apprised of this, the Báb took a portion of food from His plate and sent it to them. 'Let them both partake of this,' He said; 'their wish will be fulfilled.'[159] Munírih Khánum had wide brows, a slightly arched and aristocratic nose, and a delicate small mouth.

The evening sky was turning to gold leaf and pale, rose-petal pink, as they waited there in the hushed garden, in the stillness and peace, and watched the sunset drifting across the pool. Florence went back in memory to her spiritual mother, Mary Hanford Ford, who used to tell her: 'Rose-pink is the love color. Green is the color for music. The singing angels are put in green by the Renaissance painters.'

Florence was one of those people who begin to speak a foreign language almost at once, any which way. They do not pore over grammar or memorize paradigms, but they communicate. She could, somehow, understand Munírih Khánum, and even answer a little. Besides, there were young women of the Household to translate and further explain.

As they drove homeward, Munírih Khánum began to speak of how beautiful her husband, the Master, had been in His youth. His black hair fell to His shoulders. His face was like a light, a glowing rose shining through an alabaster lamp. His eyes were soft and bright, sometimes blue, sometimes hazel or brown. Whoever looked at Him was drawn close to Him, and with her in her young girlhood, it was love at first sight. But now His hair and beard were white from much suffering. His youthfulness was gone.

'He still is the most beautiful being I ever set eyes on,' said Florence.

Munírih Khánum smiled. 'Ah,' she said, 'but if you had seen Him then.'

Of the Riḍván and Firdaws gardens, Florence said that both were walled, the gates being locked and opened by the resident caretaker. The Master loved to have the believers enjoy them.

'All that I have is for the believers,' He said.

Once when Florence visited there with Khan, a young girl picked a spray of white jasmine, stripping the blossoms off the stems, and filling Florence's cupped palms with them, telling her to bury her face in the flowers and inhale the fragrance.

Together they passed a creaking water wheel, a patient, elderly mule hitched to it, going round and round to bring up the water. They came to the two ancient mulberry trees, beneath which the Manifestation used to sit on a white throne-like garden bench. It was hard to believe that only fourteen brief years before, Florence might even have seen Him in the body as He rested under these trees – here in this place He called His 'Verdant Isle',[160] where He breathed in the identical sweet scents, as she did now, and listened to the same music of the running streams.

As Khan and the elderly gardener approached, the young girl veiled her face and slipped away. The gardener welcomed Florence and began to speak of the days of Bahá'u'lláh.

'One day He called me to Him', the gardener said, 'as He rested under the mulberry trees. He asked me, "Do you see these Persian tiles of clay which cover this pathway before Me?"

'"Yes, Lord."

'"The time is coming when the Bahá'ís will greatly increase in numbers, and they will visit here after I am gone. They will tear out these clay tiles, and replace them with tiles of pure silver. More time will pass and still greater numbers will come. They will take away the silver tiles and replace them with tiles of pure gold. And still more time will go by, and other Bahá'ís will visit here. They will take out the golden tiles and lay this path with precious gems."'

FIFTY-SIX

The Leave-Taking

One of Florence's much sought-after glimpses of the Master was this: watching Him from her window she saw Him as He walked in His little garden by the sea. He had on a long black 'abá over a long white under-tunic, and a gleaming white turban on His whitening hair. He paced swingingly to and fro, His hands clasped behind Him, He deep in thought. She noted 'the rhythmic planetary swing of His motion, the unconscious harmony of His movements with the universal rhythm of all creation . . . Of all natural people, 'Abdu'l-Bahá is certainly the most natural.'

She especially liked to see Him in a cafe-au-lait or similar light-colored 'abá, with a few pink roses carelessly thrust into His white cummerbund. He wore this at their last luncheon, and although it was high noon and He had been at work for many hours, He appeared as fresh and shining as the dawn sky.

Near the end of their stay He sat with them in the little dining room and listened to the messages they had brought from the United States. Florence had written down several pages of them and to each He spoke an answer. It was this day that He said of Florence, 'I testify thou art a true believer.'

His parting gift to Florence was a black agate, perfectly engraved with the Greatest Name, which they were to have mounted in Tehran. He gave it to her because He wished her to have this particular stone which the Greatest Holy Leaf considered above rubies. Somewhere in their continual travels it vanished and its fate is unknown.

Their last evening came. The next morning they were to drive to Haifa and later board a steamer of the Messagerie Maritime Line for Constantinople, via Beirut and Smyrna, and then on to Persia. That night, Khan came to Florence and said that the Master was walking up and down, dictating Tablets, among them answers to the friends' messages. This they must see. They went through the little dining room, out onto the stone parapet, under dark heavens gleaming with stars, and looked through a door to the lighted chamber beyond. He was pacing there, His white turban slightly pushed back on His forehead, and rapidly, earnestly, unhesitatingly dictating to Mírzá Munír Zayn (the latter unseen by them). These were spontaneous messages addressed to the hearts of persons whom the Master had never met. (Earlier on, in a Tablet, He had given Florence the name Rúháníyyih [spiritual].) She was wishing the Master would pause in the lighted room so that she could see Him better, and He did pause in His doorway, looking out into the night, and they drew backward.

As she gazed in awe 'upon that sweet embodiment of all God-like attributes, suddenly a dazzling radiance began to burn about Him, growing rapidly so luminous that I was frightened and shrank back.' When she looked again, He had resumed His dictating and pacing. Again she wished He would pause so that she could see His face better, on this last night. Again, He paused in the doorway and the light from Him, unlike any she had ever seen, the dazzling radiance, emanated from His entire body in blinding glory. She was terrified, and then it vanished and He resumed His pacing. To her it was what the Transfiguration on the Mount could have meant. They withdrew into the silence of their own room.

On the last 'Akká morning 'Abdu'l-Bahá seemed somehow to warn Florence of the future. He said, among other things, that whatever trials or hardships came, or whenever they came, to bear them patiently as they were for a great end, a great purpose. And to be like Him – whether surrounded by friends or enemies, to keep right on. 'Now you have entered on the path of God', He told her, 'and this is a matter of supreme importance.'

That day a huge crowd came to tell them goodby. It was then that Florence met 'the oldest living Bahá'í', Mírzá Haydar-'Alí, who wrote *The Delight of Hearts* – very old indeed now, but 'marvelously sweet and winning'. At the very last there was Bashír, who climbed up on the carriage, his tears streaming down, kissed Rahim on both cheeks and fled.

Khánum had a luncheon prepared for them to eat on their way to Haifa, since they would not be able to stay for the midday meal. As they were about to leave, a water jar was brought to them from the tent of 'Abdu'l-Bahá. And so, Florence wrote, 'we drove back to the world again'.

The Master's daughters received them in Haifa until sailing time. On the night before they left, Florence stood with Rúhá Khánum, looking out the window at a lighted steamer in the bay below. Rúhá Khánum was expecting her first child.

'That is the steamer that will carry you away from us tomorrow evening,' she said affectionately.

'Yes,' answered Florence with sadness.

'We envy you,' Rúḥá Khánum said. 'The American women are free to travel, to see the world. You do not have to veil and live such secluded lives as we women of the East must live.'

'Would you like to travel and see the world?' Florence asked.

'Of course,' she answered simply. 'But we must continue to wear the veil until the Muslim women of Persia discard it, such is the command.'

Earlier, along toward evening, they had driven up Mount Carmel for their last visit to the Tomb of the Báb. They were on their way back down the mountain when suddenly out of the shadows there appeared Shoghi Effendi, oldest grandson of 'Abdu'l-Bahá. The child had prevailed on his tutor to let him ride down the mountain on his donkey from their summer home and meet the Khans' carriage for a last goodby.

'God bless the dear little fellow!' wrote Florence, all unknowing that one day this little boy would, as Guardian of the Faith, carry the Bahá'í world on his shoulders for thirty-six years, and during the days of those years redirect the fortunes of the planet forever.

Their steamer pushed out under heavy gray clouds the evening of the next day. Florence, on the deck, strained her eyes for a glimpse of 'Akká.

'Like a little fortress,' she wrote afterward, 'I saw 'Abdu'l-Bahá's house standing steadfast and undaunted, facing seaward amid all the grayness. And reverently I thought of Him, toiling in poverty, exile, hardship – of Him the gentle object of countless bitter enemies – working patiently through many sorrows and nearly insurmountable difficulties for the uplift of humanity towards the light of the new Day.'

And the steamer carried the three of them on through the darkening clouds, away from the Land of all Desiring, out into the unguessed-at future, the precarious times to come.

Appendix

A letter dated March 15, 1955, and signed by Khan, has fortunately turned up in his papers. During his later years, because of a tremor in his hand (which he felt was due to all the dictated Tablets and his translations and his enormous correspondence with the believers) he would dictate his letters, and the friends would take them down.

This letter was addressed to Mrs Alfred M. Raubitschek of West Englewood, New Jersey. It says:

> Dear Baha'i Friend
>
> I received your letter of March 9th and was happy to learn of your recent pilgrimage and your visit with our beloved Guardian. With regard to your reference to my mention of the Blessed Remains of the Bab, at the time of my stay in Acca and Haifa in 1900, as the Master's amanuensis, and translator for our beloved Master, I hasten to correct a misunderstanding before it spreads any further.
>
> I never stated at any time that 'I had sat' on a box containing the Sacred Remains. What I did say was that in the Master's house at Haifa, the room next to the Master's reception room, which He assigned to me for work, contained a number of objects, and household appliances. But there was also the large sarcophagus ordered by the believers at Rangoon, Burma and sent to the Master to be used for the interment of the Remains of the Bab, when the time for that event would arrive. This sarcophagus was stored in that room pending the completion of the building of the Holy Shrine of which the foundation was being excavated.
>
> Later I heard, I believe from Mohammad Ali, the Master's servant, that the box containing the Sacred Remains, which had been brought from Persia in the previous months, had been put in that empty sarcophagus. But I knew nothing of this while for many months I sat at the table near the window in that room and did my translations.
>
> You now realize how wise is the command that we, in this day should not give any full credit to hearsay or stories related by visitors or as personal experiences.
>
> The other story referred to in your letter is what took place when I first entered the Master's presence. After welcoming me, and saying that my coming was in fulfillment of Baha-u-llah's Words, that many would be raised up who would assist the Master in spreading the Faith in the Day of the Covenant, and that, as one who knew English, I was

led into His Presence, to translate His Writings and the Holy Tablets into English etc., He then bade me remain and assist Him etc.

He then took from the table several folded Tablets, written on the usual glossy cream colored paper and handed them to me, saying: 'These are answers I have written to letters received from the American Baha'is. Go and translate these.' As I unfolded and looked at them I told him (sic) that they were in Arabic which I had not studied as my work at college was the study of European learning and languages, etc.

Looking at me with His eyes shining with a burning light He said, 'Hold your hands together,' and He reached (for) a plate on the table which was filled with rock candy. And filling both his (sic) hands with the same, He poured it into my hands; and then patting my cheeks with both His hands He said, 'Go and partake of this and in the Name of Bahaullah be assured that you will have the power which would enable you to translate not only from the Arabic into English, but that it will become easier for you to translate into Arabic than into Persian . . . [Probably should read: from Arabic than from Persian.]

From that time on I worked as He said and his (sic) words were literally fulfilled – I also have found a miraculous healing power in the Blessed Candy whenever I gave a taste of it to ill persons over the years.

Now one word about the location of that house: About 3 to 400 steps from the center of the then business quarter near the sea the street ran parallel within a block from the sea and then to the left, a brick stairway led to the courtyard surrounded on 3 sides by rooms. This is the best I can remember. Then in Nov.–Dec. 1924, when on my way back to the U.S. my family and I were guests of the Guardian for 33 days at Haifa I asked one of the believers to walk with me, in search of that house. The city had so changed with so many large buildings, that I only found the stairway courtyard at the top. The rest was absorbed by new big buildings all around.

I hope you will forgive this brief account. I am preparing my memoirs in which all these matters will, I hope be dealt with. But I personally am suffering from writer's cramp and have no facilities for properly writing my memoirs and my good friend, Mrs Frances Fales is the only person who is kind and generous in helping me whenever possible, as she does this letter.

In writing the Hand of the Cause Dr Giachery kindly remember me to him and his wife. He may recall that when he was about to leave N.Y. for Italy I prayed and told him that he would render great services to our beloved Cause, in Europe.

With best wishes and sincere regards to you and your family I am Faithfully yours, (signed) Ali-Kuli Khan

Bibliography

'Abdu'l-Bahá. *The Promulgation of Universal Peace*. Compiled by Howard MacNutt. Wilmette, Illinois: Bahá'í Publishing Trust, 1982.
— *The Secret of Divine Civilization*. Translated by Marzieh Gail. Wilmette, Illinois: Bahá'í Publishing Trust, 1957.
— *Selections from the Writings of 'Abdu'l-Bahá*. Translated by a Committee at the Bahá'í World Centre and by Marzieh Gail. Haifa: Bahá'í World Centre, 1978.
— *Some Answered Questions*. Collected and translated by Laura Clifford Barney. Wilmette, Illinois: Bahá'í Publishing Trust, 1964.
— *Tablets of 'Abdu'l-Bahá Abbas*. New York: Bahá'í Publishing Committee, 1930.
— *Will and Testament of 'Abdu'l-Bahá*. Wilmette, Illinois: Bahá'í Publishing Committee, 1944.
Abul-Fazl, Mirza. *The Baháï Proofs*. Chicago: The Grier Press, 1914.
Appreciations of the Bahá'í Faith. Wilmette, Illinois: Bahá'í Publishing Committee, 1947.
Bahá'í Prayers. A selection of prayers revealed by Bahá'u'lláh, The Báb, and 'Abdu'l-Bahá. Wilmette, Illinois: Bahá'í Publishing Trust, 1982.
Bahá'u'lláh. *Epistle to the Son of the Wolf*. Translated by Shoghi Effendi. Wilmette, Illinois: Bahá'í Publishing Trust, 1962.
— *Gleanings from the Writings of Bahá'u'lláh*. Translated by Shoghi Effendi. Wilmette, Illinois: Bahá'í Publishing Trust, rev. edn 1963.
— *The Hidden Words*. Translated by Shoghi Effendi. Wilmette, Illinois: Bahá'í Publishing Committee, rev. edn 1954.
— *The Kitáb-i-Íqán*. Translated by Shoghi Effendi. Wilmette, Illinois: Bahá'í Publishing Trust, 1950.
— *Prayers and Meditations*. Translated by Shoghi Effendi. Wilmette, Illinois: Bahá'í Publishing Trust, 1962.
— *Tablets of Bahá'u'lláh*. Compiled by the Research Department of the Universal House of Justice and translated by Habib Taherzadeh with the assistance of a Committee at the Bahá'í World Centre. Haifa: Bahá'í World Centre, 1978.
Balyuzi, H. M. *'Abdu'l-Bahá*. London: George Ronald, 1971.
Benjamin, S. G. W. *Persia and the Persians*. Boston: Tichenor, 1887.
Browne, E. G. *A Literary History of Persia*. In four volumes. Vols. I and II. Cambridge University Press, 1924.
— (ed.) *A Traveller's Narrative written to illustrate the Episode of the Bab*. Edited in the original Persian, and translated into English, with an Introduction and Explanatory Notes. Vol. I, Persian Text. Vol. II, English Translation and Notes. Cambridge University Press, 1891.
— *A Year Amongst the Persians*: Impressions as to the Life, Character and

Thought of the People of Persia, received during twelve months' residence in that country in the years 1887–8. London: A. & C. Black, 1959.
Dorys, Georges. *The Private Life of the Sultan.* New York: Appleton, 1901.
Gail, Marzieh. *Dawn over Mount Hira and Other Essays.* Oxford: George Ronald, 1976.
Gibbon, Edward. *The Decline and Fall of the Roman Empire.* New York: Random House, The Modern Library Series.
Glover, T. R. *The Conflict of Religions in the Early Roman Empire.* Boston: Beacon Press, 1961.
Gobineau, M. Le Comte de. *Les Religions et les Philosophies dans l'Asie Centrale.* Paris, 1865, 1866, 1900.
Haggard, Howard W. *Mystery, Magic, and Medicine.* Garden City, New York: Doubleday, Doran, 1933.
Herbert, George. *The Temple.* London: Pickering, 1850.
The Holy Bible. Containing the Old and New Testaments. Translated under King James. Cambridge University Press, 1911.
Jackson, A. V. Williams. *Persia Past and Present.* London: Macmillan, 1906.
Jones, Sir William. *A Grammar of the Persian Language.* London: W. Nicol, 1828.
The Koran. Translated from the Arabic by J. M. Rodwell. London: Dent, 1963.
Landor, A. Henry Savage. *Across Coveted Lands.* London: Macmillan, 1902.
Lawrence, A. W. (ed.) *The Travel Letters.* London: Jonathan Cape, 1930.
Longford, Elizabeth. *Eminent Victorian Women.* New York: Knopf, 1981.
Merrifield, Richard F. *Monadnock Journal.* Taftsville, Vermont: The Countryman Press, 1975.
Nabíl-i-A'zam. *The Dawn-Breakers.* Nabíl's Narrative of the Early Days of the Bahá'í Revelation. Translated by Shoghi Effendi. Wilmette, Illinois: Bahá'í Publishing Trust, 1962.
Nicholas, A.-L.-M. *Seyyèd Ali Mohammed dit le Bâb.* Paris: Dujarric & Cie., 1905.
Phelps, Myron H. *Abbas Effendi, His Life and Teachings.* New York: The Knickerbocker Press, 1903.
Savage, Philip Henry. *Poems.* Boston: Copeland and Day, 1898.
Shoghi Effendi. *Bahá'í Administration.* Wilmette, Illinois: Bahá'í Publishing Trust, 1968.
— *Citadel of Faith.* Wilmette, Illinois: Bahá'í Publishing Trust, 1965.
— *God Passes By.* Wilmette, Illinois: Bahá'í Publishing Trust, 1970.
— *The World Order of Bahá'u'lláh.* Wilmette, Illinois: Bahá'í Publishing Trust, 1955.
Shuster, W. Morgan. *The Strangling of Persia.* New York: The Century Co., 1912.
Star of the West. The Bahá'í Magazine. Vol. 3. Chicago: Bahá'í News Service.
al Suhrawardy, Sir Abdullah al-Mamun. *The Sayings of Muhammad.* New York: Dutton, 1941.
Sykes, E. C. *Persia and its People.* London: Methuen, 1910.
Sykes, Sir Percy. *Persia.* Oxford University Press, 1922.

BIBLIOGRAPHY

Thatcher, G. W. *Arabic Grammar*. Heidelberg: Julius Groos, 1927.
Vámbéry, Arminius. *His Life and Adventures*. Philadelphia: J. B. Lippincott, 1886.
Zarqání, Mírzá Maḥmúd-i-. *Kitáb-i-Badáyi'u'l-Áthár*. Diary of 'Abdu'l-Bahá's travels in Europe and America, written by His secretary. Bombay: Vol. I, 1914; Vol. II, 1921. (*Maḥmud's Diary*)

Newspapers

New York *American and Journal*, January 31, 1904.
New York *Evening Post*, January 30, 1904.
New York *Herald*, January 1904.
New York Times, January 31, 1904.
San Francisco *Call*, February 6, 1904.

Notes

1. A. H. Savage Landor, *Across Coveted Lands*, vol. 1, p. 263.
2. ibid. pp. 268–9.
3. Quoted in Jackson, *Persia*, p. 403.
4. Jackson, *Persia*, pp. 412–13.
5. Nabíl, *The Dawn-Breakers*, p. 500.
6. Gobineau, *Religions*, pp. 231–2.
7. Nabíl, *The Dawn-Breakers*, pp. 512–15; 522.
8. Qur'án 6:12.
9. Bahá'u'lláh, *Hidden Words*, no. 32 (Arabic).
10. ibid. no. 14 (Arabic).
11. Qur'án 9:28.
12. Jackson, *Persia*, p. 419.
13. ibid.
14. 'Abdu'l-Bahá, *Secret of Divine Civilization*, p. 8.
15. Bahá'u'lláh, *Hidden Words*, no. 2 (Arabic).
16. Bahá'u'lláh, *Tablets*, p. 157.
17. Bahá'u'lláh, *Kitáb-i-Íqán*, pp. 50–51.
18. Nabíl, *The Dawn-Breakers*, pp. 231–2n.
19. Longford, *Eminent*, p. 8.
20. Bahá'u'lláh, *Hidden Words*, no. 55 (Arabic).
21. Qur'án 2:216.
22. Qur'án 5:92.
23. Qur'án 22:42.
24. al-Suhrawardy, *Sayings*, p. 103.
25. Quoted in Nabíl, *The Dawn-Breakers*, p. xxvii.
26. Nabíl, *The Dawn-Breakers*, p. 6.
27. *Holy Bible*, p. xi.
28. One could pause to lament the fact that this Shah, in an excess of nationalism, not only tried to sift Arabic out of the language but also made the world that had over the centuries grown to love the word 'Persia' because of flying carpets, the genii in bottles, the princesses with pearls in their hair — replace that word with Iran. A proud sound to Persians, but as meaningless to the rest of the world as 'Kansas City' to a Persian.
29. Jones, *Grammar*, p. 146.
30. Bahá'u'lláh, *Hidden Words*, no. 52 (Persian).
31. Nicholas, *Seyyed Ali Mohammed*, pp. 200–205.
32. E. C. Sykes, *Persia and Its People*, p. 216.
33. Browne, *Literary History*, vol. I, p. 110.
34. Bahá'u'lláh, *Kitáb-i-Íqán*, p. 171.
35. Benjamin, *Persia and the Persians*, p. 278.
36. ibid. p. 76.
37. Browne, *Literary History*, vol. II, pp. 201ff.

38 Browne, *Year Amongst the Persians*, p. 544.
39 'Abdu'l-Bahá, *Selections*, p. 149.
40 Gibbon, *Decline and Fall*, vol. III, p. 127.
41 Glover, *Conflict of Religions*, p. 243.
42 Nabíl, *The Dawn-Breakers*, p. 41.
43 Benjamin, *Persia and the Persians*, p. 74.
44 Vámbéry, *His Life*, p. 101.
45 Vámbéry, quoted in *Appreciations*, pp. 19–20.
46 Shoghi Effendi, *God Passes By*, p. 66.
47 Qur'án 14:26, 27.
48 'Abdu'l-Bahá, *Some Answered Questions*, p. 141.
49 Gail, *Dawn*, pp. 39ff.
50 Shoghi Effendi, *God Passes By*, p. 120.
51 ibid. p. 138.
52 ibid. p. 201.
53 ibid. p. 75.
54 E. C. Sykes, *Persia and Its People*, p. 9.
55 ibid. p. 41.
56 Dorys, *Private Life*, pp. 78, 183.
57 Balyuzi, *'Abdu'l-Bahá*, p. 92.
58 Herbert, *The Temple*, p. 200.
59 Browne, *Traveller's Narrative*, pp. xxxi, xxxiv, xliii.
60 See, for example, Bahá'u'lláh, *Kitáb-i-Íqán*, pp. 24–5.
61 Laura Dreyfus Barney told this to an audience at the House of Worship in Wilmette in 1944, an occasion on which the author was present.
62 'Abdu'l-Bahá, *Tablets*, vol. I, p. 152.
63 Balyuzi, *'Abdu'l-Bahá*, p. 87.
64 Bahá'u'lláh, *Hidden Words*, no. 63 (Persian).
65 Shoghi Effendi, *God Passes By*, p. 139.
66 As with so many other valuable things considered Occidental, the Muslims had had the equivalent long before. Back in 1717, writing from Adrianople, Lady Mary Wortley Montagu reported: '. . . I am going to tell you a thing that will make you wish yourself here. The small-pox, so fatal, and so general amongst us, is here entirely harmless by the invention of *ingrafting* . . . There is a set of old women who make it their business to perform the operation every autumn . . . People send to one another to know if any of their family has a mind to have the small-pox: they make parties for this purpose . . . The old woman comes with a nut shell full of the matter of the best sort of small-pox, and asks you what vein you please to have opened . . . and puts into the vein as much matter as can lie upon the head of her needle' then binds the wound with a hollow piece of shell. Lady Mary adds that thousands undergo the operation every year and nobody dies of it, and she would gladly write to English doctors about it 'if I knew any one of them that I thought had virtue enough to destroy such a considerable branch of their revenue for the good of mankind.' (Lawrence, *The Travel Letters*, p. 163.) Meanwhile Cotton Mather of witchcraft fame (d. 1728) had already introduced inoculation into America. (Haggard, *Mystery*, p. 83).

67 Told to the author by Dr Hermann Grossman.
68 Mrs Olive Rose found a taped copy of the Smythe recording among the effects of her former husband, Edward Schlesinger, and had copies made. She kindly gave one of the tapes to the author, who also possesses one of the 78 RPM records originally made of 'Abdu'l-Bahá's chant.
69 *Star of the West*, vol. III, no. 7, p. 5.
70 Shoghi Effendi, *God Passes By*, p. 248.
71 ibid. p. 247.
72 Bahá'u'lláh, *Prayers and Meditations*, no. LIV, p. 77.
73 Shoghi Effendi, *God Passes By*, pp. 273–4.
74 Qur'án 69:17.
75 ibid.
76 Qur'án 33:12.
77 Qur'án 22:4.
78 Qur'án 14:27.
79 Shoghi Effendi, *God Passes By*, p. 115.
80 ibid. pp. 237–8.
81 Quoted in Thatcher, *Arabic Grammar*, p. 337.
82 Matt. 4:3.
83 Matt. 4:5–6.
84 Mark 8:33.
85 Translation by author.
86 'Abdu'l-Bahá, *Promulgation*, p. 253.
87 Bahá'u'lláh, *Gleanings*, no. CXXV, p. 266.
88 Qur'án 46:8.
89 John 14:6.
90 'Abdu'l-Bahá, *Promulgation*, p. 109.
91 Matt. 12:32.
92 Shoghi Effendi, *World Order of Bahá'u'lláh*, p. 131.
93 Shoghi Effendi has stated that 'the eating of pork is not forbidden in the Bahá'í Teachings.' (Shoghi Effendi. *Dawn of a New Day*. New Delhi: Bahá'í Publishing Trust, 1970, p. 201.
94 *Bahá'í Prayers*, p. 45.
95 Shoghi Effendi, *God Passes By*, p. 260.
96 Related to author by Juliet Thompson in an interview in 1951.
97 Shoghi Effendi, *World Order of Bahá'u'lláh*, p. 144.
98 'Abdu'l-Bahá, *Will and Testament*, p. 25.
99 Shoghi Effendi, *God Passes By*, p. 259.
100 It is seldom mentioned that Mírzá liked a joke. Once when a sumptuous Church hierarch was brought to see him, he punned untranslatably on the word 'bishop': ' 'Ajab píshábíyih,' he said.
101 Shoghi Effendi, *Bahá'í Administration*, p. 21.
102 Shoghi Effendi, *God Passes By*, p. 326.
103 'Abdu'l-Bahá, *Will and Testament*, pp. 14, 20.
104 'Abdu'l-Bahá, *Selections*, pp. 146–50.
105 'Abdu'l-Bahá, *Promulgation*, p. xx.
106 Translated by the Research Department of the Universal House of Justice at the Bahá'í World Centre in March 1987. It was originally

NOTES

translated by Khan on June 18, 1902, in New York City.

The short postscript added by the Master was also translated by the Research Department.

107 Shoghi Effendi, *Bahá'í Administration*, p. 43.
108 Stated in Abul-Fazl, *The Baháï Proofs* (1914), pp. 5–6.
109 At the request of Laura Barney, Khan kept among his papers the copyright issued by the Library of Congress to her mother.
110 The sailing date was January 30, 1904. The author's family was very good about keeping press clippings, from which the following accounts are taken. However, they did not always remember to include the newspaper's name and date of publication. In other cases, these were torn off from many handlings through the years.

The New York *Evening Post* on the day of sailing carried a very long and colorful story of the event. An even longer account – 22 column inches – is found in another New York paper, the name of which is missing. On the following day the *New York Times* carried the story, while the New York *American and Journal* devoted 25 column inches to a large photograph of Ellen Goin and the accompanying text.

The San Francisco *Call* of February 6 reported Jules Clerfayt's experiences with the Atábak whilst escorting him from San Francisco to New York. A condensed version of this appeared in the New York *Herald* on the 7th.

The most colorful account, and the one to which the author is most indebted, appeared in the newspaper whose name is missing. Internal evidence shows that it was an evening paper, printed in New York on January 30. It was also venerable, for it boasted – next to the missing masthead – of being in its 107th year.

111 People wonder why names are often mangled in the press. This may be due to the misinformation given to reporters by the featured people themselves. For example, the name Bahá'í, which even today is sometimes misspelled, was written differently by the Western believers themselves at different times. Amusingly enough, a dispute arose between Khan and Helen Ellis Cole, who did not know Persian, as to the spelling of Bahá. The amusing part is that Helen Cole was right and Khan wrong. On March 16, 1904, Mrs Cole wrote from St Augustine to say that she had the name spelled 'Baha' all though the *Iqan*, 'as I have been convinced for some time that the nearest approach to the Persian sound was (thus) attained . . .' It was now too late to change the spelling to 'Beha' as Khan apparently preferred, even if this spelling appeared only on the title-page. 'It seems to me', Mrs Cole went on, 'that it would be a great defect not to have it homogeneous throughout. Do you agree? . . . but if you wish it so, I am quite willing.'

A Tablet from the Master addressed to His 'spiritual friends' settled the matter '. . . Baha is correct; Beha is incorrect . . . Should ye attribute a mistake to a person, it will be the cause of offense and grief to him . . . All will eventually follow the correct spelling.' ('Abdu'l-Bahá, *Tablets*, vol. I, p. 20).

112 Shuster, *Strangling of Persia*, p. xxiii.

113 ibid., p. xxvi.
114 P. Sykes, *Persia*, p. 145.
115 P. H. Savage, *Poems*, p. xxx.
116 ibid. p. 89.
117 'Abdu'l-Bahá, *Some Answered Questions*, p. v.
118 ibid. p. vi.
119 Shoghi Effendi, *God Passes By*, p. 260.
120 'Abdu'l-Bahá, *Some Answered Questions*, p. v.
121 Bahá'u'lláh, *Gleanings*, no. CXIV, pp. 234–5.
122 ibid. no. C, p. 202.
123 Merrifield, *Monadnock Journal*, p. 7.
124 Gen. 32:26.
125 Since Florence recorded these notes, Haifa has grown in importance and in size; hence this body of water is now called the Bay of Haifa.
126 Mark 4:25.
127 The words in parentheses here and on the following pages are Khan's. When Khan translated the words of 'Abdu'l-Bahá he tried to be very exact; and if there was a place where he, as translator, had not made the meaning clear, Khan would put an explanatory word or phrase within parenthetical marks to show they were his and not the originals. Notice the same practice in his early translations such as the *Íqán* (1904), p. 61 and elsewhere. At the time it was always understood that the parenthetical material was Khan's. Such material was really an extension or repetition of 'Abdu'l-Bahá's thought. Khan was always a teacher, always explaining.
128 Qur'án 2:286.
129 Qur'án 24:35.
130 ibid.
131 Translated by the author.
132 *Mahmud's Diary*, p. 149.
133 Shoghi Effendi, *God Passes By*, p. 245.
134 Shoghi Effendi, *World Order of Bahá'u'lláh*, pp. 131–2.
135 Shoghi Effendi, *God Passes By*, p. 221.
136 ibid. p. 246.
137 Balyuzi, *'Abdu'l-Bahá*, p. 58.
138 Shoghi Effendi, *God Passes By*, p. 251.
139 Shoghi Effendi, *Citadel of Faith*, p. 88.
140 Bahá'u'lláh, *Epistle*, p. 179.
141 Translated by the author.
142 Shoghi Effendi, *God Passes By*, p. 270.
143 ibid. p. 265.
144 ibid. p. 248.
145 ibid. p. 266.
146 Qur'án 20:124. Rodwell translated dhikr as monition, while some other translations give reminder. Obviously the weight of authority goes with Shoghi Effendi's use of remembrance (as in *God Passes By*, p. 57), and it is for this reason that the author departs in this instance from Rodwell.
147 Shoghi Effendi, *God Passes By*, p. 57.

148 Qur'án 89:27.
149 Qur'án 5:119.
150 Shoghi Effendi, *God Passes By*, p. 164.
151 Qur'án 2:210.
152 Phelps, *Abbas Effendi*, p. 105.
153 Shoghi Effendi, *World Order of Bahá'u'lláh*, p. 131.
154 ibid. p. 134.
155 'Abdu'l-Bahá, *Some Answered Questions*, p. 141.
156 Matt. 10:36.
157 'Abdu'l-Bahá, *Promulgation*, p. 76.
158 Matt. 4:18, 21.
159 Nabíl, *The Dawn-Breakers*, p. 208.
160 Shoghi Effendi, *God Passes By*, p. 193.

www.ingramcontent.com/pod-product-compliance
Lightning Source LLC
Chambersburg PA
CBHW020745160426
43192CB00006B/246